THE YEAR'S WORK IN *SHOWGIRLS* STUDIES

The Year's Work:
Studies in Fan Culture and Cultural Theory

Edward P. Dallis-Comentale and Aaron Jaffe, editors

THE YEAR'S WORK IN *SHOWGIRLS* STUDIES

EDITED BY
MELISSA HARDIE,
MEAGHAN MORRIS,
AND KANE RACE

INDIANA UNIVERSITY PRESS

This book is a publication of

Indiana University Press
Office of Scholarly Publishing
Herman B Wells Library 350
1320 East 10th Street
Bloomington, Indiana 47405 USA

iupress.org

Manufactured in the
United States of America

First printing 2024

Cataloging information is available
from the Library of Congress.

ISBN 978-0-253-06815-6 (hardback)
ISBN 978-0-253-06816-3 (paperback)
ISBN 978-0-253-06817-0 (ebook)

CONTENTS

ACKNOWLEDGMENTS

Many years in the making, this book has required a lot of love to bring it to completion from its beginnings in a small conference organized by Melissa Hardie for the intellectual pleasure of *Showgirls* fans in 2015. We must therefore first thank our contributors for their patient commitment to the project, and we thank Kate Lilley, André Frankovits, and Stephan Omeros for living through the process with us. We also express our gratitude for the meticulously caring work of Gareth Richards, Helena Dodge-Wan, and Eryn Tan of Impress Creative and Editorial in consolidating our manuscript for presentation to Indiana University Press.

Given that *The Year's Work in* Showgirls *Studies* is critically concerned with labor in visual and performance culture, we are deeply indebted to the generosity of people who have gone out of their way to provide us with artwork and images that articulate this concern to broader social contexts. We say thank-you to Exotic Cancer, Glitta Supernova, Katia Schwartz, Bella Green, Queenie Bon Bon, Frankie Valentine, and Despo Debby for using their artistic mediums and creative platforms to build stripper culture, and to Carol Burman-Jahn, Sylvia Cowen, and Lynne Hutton-Williams for helping us document some historical links between circus and showgirl life in the mid-twentieth century. Grateful thanks go to Shlomo Adam Roth and family for their time and generosity in facilitating permission to reproduce a precious photograph of a 1995 *Showgirls* billboard.

Another key concern of this book is the community-building power of small or local cultural events and the productive longevity and spread of the conversations these enable. Kane Race is indebted to Sydney's long-running film festival Queer Screen for the unique experience of watching *Showgirls* with a gay and lesbian Mardi Gras crowd in Double Bay's Village Twin Cinema in the late 1990s.[1] While Melissa Hardie and Meaghan Morris first saw the film in the more mundane context of its 1995 Sydney commercial release in downtown Sydney's Village Cinema City, a shared conversation about it began with BOLD, a Philosophy and Women's Studies conference convened in Canberra at the Australian National University's Humanities Research Centre by Elizabeth A. Wilson and Helen Keane in July 1996. On the invitation of Efi Hatzimanolis and Brigitta Olubas, this event led to the publication of Melissa's pathbreaking paper "Loose Slots" (here, chap. 11) in an early feminist refereed journal, *Xtext*, based in the School of English at the University of New South Wales.

The editors wish to thank Derek Covington Smith for allowing us to reproduce a portion of his artwork "Neon Nomi" for the cover of this book.

Apparently long gone now, these and other experimental cultural initiatives created on the boundary between community activism and academic work in and around the time of *Showgirls* unleashed energies that continue to shape our lives and our work today. Without them, this book would not have come into being.

Note

1. "Queer Screen History," Queer Screen, https://queerscreen.org.au/aboutus/history/#_ga=2.9686256.496548770.1666848795–1796401238.1666848795.

THE YEAR'S WORK IN *SHOWGIRLS* STUDIES

INTRODUCTION

MELISSA HARDIE, MEAGHAN MORRIS, AND KANE RACE

The twentieth anniversary of the release and catastrophic box office failure of Paul Verhoeven's film *Showgirls* in 2015 prompted celebrations, interviews, reappraisals, and reflections as diverse—and divergent—as the responses elaborated over the preceding two decades. Proliferating online with a galvanizing force not available to fan communities in 1995, when *Showgirls* recouped less than half of its $45 million budget and scored a record number of Razzie nominations for "worst of the year" awards, the flow of passionately thoughtful public engagement with this much-derided film did not subside with the anniversary year. In 2017, for example, the Film Society of Lincoln Center for the Performing Arts in New York hosted a screening and a discussion with Verhoeven and actor Gina Gershon; Adam Nayman's short monograph *It Doesn't Suck: Showgirls,* first published in 2014, had a special new edition in 2018; and an archive of critical essays together with *Showgirls*-related clips and interviews has expanded online.[1] Then, in 2019, Jeffrey McHale released *You Don't Nomi,* a feature-length documentary about the reception and significance of *Showgirls* today.[2]

The form of this reputational controversy is not unique in film history. In the 1950s, Douglas Sirk's sumptuous and torrid Hollywood melodramas were widely dismissed as soapy trash. A general consensus around their brilliance formed only after some key interventions, led in the first instance by Jean-Luc Godard and Rainer Werner Fassbinder, whose essays from 1959 and 1971 respectively were translated into English around the same time as *Sirk on Sirk: Interviews with Jon Halliday* was published by the British Film Institute, while Halliday coedited *Douglas Sirk* with Laura Mulvey for the Edinburgh Film Festival.[3] Perhaps no European auteur since Sirk, however, has been more misrecognized and rehabilitated than Verhoeven, whose 1990s Hollywood films *Basic Instinct* (1992), *Showgirls* (1995), and *Starship Troopers* (1997) were almost parodically misread and consigned to the trash heap.[4] The impulse to "rescue" *Showgirls*, Verhoeven's most infamous work, from the ignominy of dismissal has followed two tracks, both neatly reproduced in *You Don't Nomi*. One track rehabilitates *Showgirls* by asserting the vision of an auteur, tracing its debt to and interaction with Verhoeven's pre-Hollywood oeuvre and finding complexity in his adaptation of genre conventions within that auteurist vision. This is the Sirkian mode of revision. The other track prosecutes an argument about the varieties of encounter the film elicits: camp and cult consumers whose wit and close-reading verve demonstrate the depths of what can be known about the film. This track of rehabilitation urges revival rather than revision: not inclusion in a canon but seclusion as a unique instance whose various parts make an inimitable whole.

It's not an accident that scenes of vomiting from a series of Verhoeven films are spliced together in *You Don't Nomi* to make these points. A montage of vomiting, typically into a toilet bowl, metaphorizes elements of *Showgirls'* narrative that McHale's film deftly goes on to narrate: the intrusion of an unpleasant phenomenon or experience into the everyday, the return of the unexpected, and a revisiting of earlier pleasures in a distinctly unwelcome form. It also captures the critical disgust of many early reviewers of *Showgirls* as viscerally as they often expressed it at the time, but then it negotiates this disgust by making its very representation, in its repetitions, a sign of an auteurist project. Disgust is often aligned with cult and camp spectatorship and with the witting deployment of tropes of off-center consumption in camp and cult cinema.[5] Led by Nomi's vomit scene early in *Showgirls*, this physical embodiment of disgust or fear is aligned with other ways in which Nomi's body is laden with meaning.

David Schmader, a promoter of camp reception events, comments in *You Don't Nomi* that on first viewing *Showgirls* he was struck by "Nomi having bizarre responses to people who are just trying to give her a hand," a comment illustrated by scenes of Nomi responding aggressively to either physical or verbal approaches from strangers or, in a couple of cases, her boss. Schmader's comment feels awkward both in the context of the film's diegesis, which abundantly demonstrates why Nomi fears for her own safety, and in the context of watching the film today, post #MeToo. It strains credulity on any watching of the film to understand these strangers as merely "giving a hand," as the gentle Good Samaritans they sometimes purport to be. And that makes it all the more surprising that Schmader uses Nomi's physical domination in these scenes as an index of the bizarre rather than as an assertion of her bodily strength and autonomy. But it reminds us that a certain strain of "cult" reading reproduces the reductive logic by which *Showgirls* (and Elizabeth Berkley's performance as Nomi) was minimized as a feminist icon and fable when the film was released.

For students of fan cultural phenomena, however, a different dimension for thought is opened up by perhaps the most poignant of the 2015 anniversary celebrations, the Cinespia screening of *Showgirls* in the Hollywood Forever Cemetery, Los Angeles, on June 28, with Elizabeth Berkley present for her first viewing in twenty years of the film that derailed her career. Accessible endlessly for now on YouTube, the *love* exchanged between the four thousand fans who turned up for the screening and Berkley as she blurred into Nomi onstage manifests itself with an intensity echoing Berkley's performance in the film itself.[6] In thanking those fans for keeping faith with the film over the years and giving her the "sweet" moment she expected but was painfully denied in 1995, Berkley bears witness not only to the capacity of fan formations over time to affect critical judgment but to the power of shared popular cultural pleasures, passions, and sensibilities to transcend a myriad of personal traumas in communal moments of joy.

This volume, too, had its genesis in the anniversary year, with a one-day symposium at the University of Sydney organized by Melissa Hardie in September 2015, precisely with the communal aim of sharing intellectual joy. Small-scale and informal, the "Showgirls 1995–2015" event brought some of our contributors together for the first time and confirmed at the outset our interest not only in the mutable pleasures the film has provided over the years but also in its capacity to activate responses connecting with wider social worlds of sexuality, spectacle, and labor, then and now. This collection leans toward the view of *Showgirls* as offering the realistic vision of life that Verhoeven's first auteurist champion, Jacques Rivette, memorably described in 1998 as "surviving in a world populated by assholes."[7] This is not a simple orientation to adopt, however, since the filmmaking process itself folded into the "real" of that vision by putting intimate survival pressure on some of the performers. If all "backstage" stories reflect in some way on the cultural industries enabling their creation, *Showgirls* in 1995 was embedded in a gendered production economy of intense exploitation, with novice female stars Berkley, Gershon, and Gina Ravera playing roles devised by the then Hollywood alpha male team of Verhoeven and writer Joe Eszterhas, flush with the box office success of *Basic Instinct* and testing the power of the NC-17 rating to put "in-your-face sexuality, copious nudity and over-the-top melodrama" into a mainstream cinema release.[8]

The subsequent critical trashing of Berkley's acting is well known, but Gina Ravera has only recently described the "ordeal" of filming the gang rape scene in her role as Nomi's friend, Molly Abrams. Unprepared for what it would it be like ("you've got two men holding you down; my wrists were bruised, and my body was just covered in bruises after it because of what was asked for the camera"), she was traumatized physically as well as emotionally by the "exuberance" of Verhoeven's pursuit of realism: "The [punch] you see in the film made contact. My jaw was not right for years."[9]

In spite of this, for Ravera the experience of making *Showgirls* was "mixed; there's some good stuff," and she credits Verhoeven with understanding that she was playing the Hollywood stereotype of "Black best friend" and giving her freedom to develop the role. In this collection, we emphasize the labor and the perspectives of performers, whose "ways of knowing" (as Anna Breckon puts it in her chapter) have been occluded by the prominence in much *Showgirls* appreciation of the figure of the camp spectator. Accordingly, the problematic "realism" of *Showgirls* is explored here not only in critical essays but through documentary, ethnographic, and archival approaches to those "mixed" experiences that inform and continue to relay the significance of the film to fans.

In particular, the "Conversations" section provides a thick documentary context of three dialogues dealing with life experiences and ideas that may enrich our understanding of the serious social import of *Showgirls*. This section situates the showgirl historically and socially in a series of skilled professions and takes up issues of race as well as gender and sexuality that were not always well addressed in the earlier reception life of the film. In the first of these conversations, Jane Park and Shawna Tang interview Lynne Hutton-Williams about Lynne's life as a trapeze artist "accidentally" turned Las Vegas showgirl some decades before the time in which the film is set, situating that performance culture in relation to the circus world familiar to Lynne and tracing her trajectory through to adventures in British and Australian feminist institution building in the 1970s. This is followed by a chapter by Zahra Stardust drawing on her use of autoethnography among strippers, pole dancers, burlesque artists, queer performers, and sex workers in Sydney today to document the literature, arts, and storytelling produced by strippers themselves as they organize and advocate from within the industry. The third conversation piece takes the form of a dialogue on race, gender, aesthetics, and the moment of *Showgirls* in US social history and popular culture between Meaghan Morris, speaking from an "outside" as an Australian film critic, and the American cinema scholar Kara Keeling, whose book *Queer Times, Black Futures* provides concepts that enable their cross-cultural dialogue.[10]

These conversations are complemented by an archival section that serves to complicate our sense of the history of *Showgirls'* reception. We introduce this section with Melissa Jane Hardie's essay "Loose Slots" from 1996.[11] The essay was originally published in an Australian small press journal, *XText*, which was devoted to theoretically and politically informed cultural criticism across academic and institutional boundaries (the "X" or "cross" of the journal's name). We assume from experience that the popularity of *Showgirls* among feminist academics in Australia was not exceptional, although it is rarely represented in traditional histories of the film's reception. Hardie presented her essay as a paper at a feminist conference, BOLD, at the Australian National University in Canberra. Convened at the Humanities Research Centre by Elizabeth A. Wilson and Helen Keane in July 1996, under the auspices of the Australian National University's Women's Studies and Philosophy programs, BOLD proposed that compelling feminist cultural analysis arose when diverse disciplinary practices were brought together (coeditor Meaghan Morris also presented on martial arts studies at BOLD).

"Loose Slots" here represents tangible evidence of a feminist, antihomophobic, theoretically informed fandom for the film from its release.

A critical moment in the history of *Showgirls*' reappraisal was the 2003 publication of a set of short responses to *Showgirls* in *Film Quarterly,* which we reprint. Rather than argue a simple revision of the film as a lost classic, the round table identified evaluation itself as a critical vulnerability exposed by the reception of the film. Across this group of responses, the film complicates popular and academic versions of film criticism because of its capacity to complicate or blur distinctions vested in taste culture. For example, Akira Mizuta Lippit's contribution (pp. 349–353) dissects the film through an evaluative apparatus supplied by *Leonard Maltin's Movie & Video Guide 2002*. Before IMDb, Rotten Tomatoes, and other online resources made evaluative descriptions of films easily available, Maltin's guides were exercises in epigrammatic description and assessment of value. Lippit's intricate deconstruction of the apparatus of evaluation—star ratings and Maltin's version of the "thumbs down," the BOMB rating—demonstrates how all varieties of judgment are encapsulated in this system and its application to *Showgirls*. Lippit's hypothesis that *Showgirls* concatenates pornography and melodrama as "pornodrama" signals some of the work the film does to play with genre; he describes these generic medleys as "immersions" of styles that never settle into a blend as such but that sit together in a state of suspense.

Reflecting on one such style, a mode of satire ("the blood that we do not see") that does not signpost itself as such and allows only fleeting glimpses of an underlying moral of redemption, Chon Noriega sketches a complex critique of its racial foundation in the subservient roles of the Black characters and of the crushing by a celebrity production team of the "rank and file actress who did what she was paid to do" (p. 361). In a different approach to evaluation, Jeffrey Sconce's "I Have

Grown Weary of Your Tiresome Cinema" introduces the principle of rewatching as transformative, noting that it takes precisely "four screenings of the film to transform it from one of Hollywood's most notorious flops to absolute transcendence" (p. 377). This account of sublimity achieved through repetition introduces a common trope in *Showgirls* critical history: a narrative of conversion, one already centered elsewhere by Adrian Martin in his famous 2000 essay, "The Offended Critic."[12] Appropriately, given Sconce's emphasis on the critic whose viewing experiences calibrate the film's value, his piece concludes with a call for a wry version of Barthesian bliss and the liberation of the critic from the dreary role of "cultural custodian" in favor of the pleasure of being smart about film.

These and other essays in the archival *Film Quarterly* round table offer precedents for the critical chapters of this collection as they identify key historical and formal contexts for understanding the reception of *Showgirls* and its endurance as an object of fascination, repulsion, and celebration over more than twenty years. These chapters complicate both auteurist traditions whose efforts to revalue the film place the director in complete control of the meanings that can be made of it and camp and cult reading practices whose pleasures depend on a reassertion of its categorization as bad. Instead, these essays explore the capacity of *Showgirls* to generate new pleasures and insights into the workings of gender, sexuality, labor, performance, taste, genre, popular culture, mediation, and media ecologies.

In "Getting It Just Right: Elizabeth Berkley's Ways of Knowing in *Showgirls*," Anna Breckon opens the essay section by developing a reoriented epistemology for the film grounded in the figure of the actor and her identification with the ambitions of her character. This alignment gives Berkley's performance an erotic and expressive agency that defies conventions of taste, objectification, and directorial intention. Next, in

"Self-Shattering in *Showgirls* and *Black Swan,*" Kane Race investigates how women who dance for a living navigate the demand to deliver authentic performances of heterosexual desire and stay "classy" in cultural institutions where investments in class are used to exploit them. Where the protagonist of *Black Swan* takes the "suicidal ecstasy" of masochistic desire literally, Nomi plots a different course that mobilizes another more situated sense of self-shattering.[13]

Kieryn McKay's "'Ain't anyone ever been nice to you?': Discharging the ~~Guilty~~ Pleasure of *Showgirls*" tracks the mechanisms by which MGM/United Artists strategically repurposed their box office flop as a camp midnight movie and then as a DVD boxed set for cult home viewing. Repackaging *Showgirls* for commercial advantage mobilizes a politics of taste that for McKay precludes the film's sincere appreciation. In "Badness," Adrian Martin suspends the question of the badness of films in favor of an exploration of the staging of badness *in* films. His wide-ranging tour of the mechanism of the "show within the show" queries feelings of security in matters of taste and showcases some diverse ways in which the varied tastes of spectators can be represented, reworked, redefined, and reclaimed.

Billy Stevenson's "*Showgirls, Showgirls 2,* and the Fate of the Erotic Thriller" situates *Showgirls* in relation to the changing media ecologies, historical genres, and visual aesthetics of late millennial screen culture. If *Showgirls* makes a case for the cinematic spectacle as a category of pleasure, it also allegorizes its own displacement by the postcinematic technologies used to cobble together its unlikely sequel. For Melissa Hardie in "Fifty Shades of *Showgirls*: Better Living through Mediation," bringing together *Showgirls* and a more recent flop, *Fifty Shades of Grey,* helps to historicize the films' interest in plots of female rivalry and their embedding of that generic mainstay in scenarios of libidinal complicity and contracted labor. *Showgirls* orients its ingenue through a representation of her capacity for calculation but more through her "thinkiness," where intellectual action joins other kinds of activity in her negotiation of genre and medium. Finally, in "The Instability of Evil: Double Trouble and the Working Girl," Meaghan Morris connects *Showgirls* to Pitof's *Catwoman* (2004) through the twinning of ethically imperfect female characters around the issues of women's labor in creative industries that structure both films in different ways. Exploring the use these films make of the motifs of the double and the orphan to model practices of self-invention for women outside the bonds of family life, Morris draws on the autobiographies of the singer, actor, and dancer Eartha Kitt (for whom duality was a key to survival in the performance worlds she knew) to propose a queer historiography capable of tracing in temporal depth the diverse experiences and life struggles of women who labor in cultural industries that then claim to "represent" them.

The essays that make up this volume are addressed in diverse ways to the disciplines from which they emerge—film studies, cultural studies, gender and queer theory, and others. They are also consciously engaged with the practices and professional identities that the film investigates and celebrates, finding an amplified account of the "showgirl" as complex professional identity and physical and intellectual praxis assists academic engagement with the film's dense account of a historic moment in its history. The collection therefore folds into its fandom and appreciation of the film the wisdom afforded by a renewed interest in workplace sexual dynamics, race and ethnic presence, and the insights of antihomophobic theory alongside the documentation of experiential and historical presence in the showgirl zone. But they all share one thing: they are written from outside the zone of equivocation that has characterized writing on *Showgirls* in the past. Instead, they perform the kinds of fandom they explore, putting in plain view intellectual, affective, and libidinal investments in this extraordinary film.

MELISSA HARDIE is Associate Professor of English at the University of Sydney. Her recent work appears in *Australian Humanities Review, Textual Practice, Film Quarterly,* and *Angelaki*. Her most recent book chapter (with Amy Villarejo) is on the 1978 Briggs Initiative and the television drama *Family,* in *Television Studies in Queer Times*. She is editor of the Oxford University Press series Approaches to the Novel.

MEAGHAN MORRIS is Professor of Gender and Cultural Studies at the University of Sydney. She is author of *The Pirate's Fiancée: Feminism, Reading, Postmodernism*; *Too Soon Too Late: History in Popular Culture*; and *Identity Anecdotes: Translation and Media Culture*.

KANE RACE is Professor of Gender and Cultural Studies at the University of Sydney. He is author of *Pleasure Consuming Medicine: The Queer Politics of Drugs*; *The Gay Science: Intimate Experiments with the Problem of HIV*; and (with Gay Hawkins and Emily Potter) *Plastic Water: The Social and Material Life of Bottled Water.*

References

Alter, Ethan. "'Showgirls' at 25: Gina Ravera Discusses the Cult Movie's Most Controversial Scene." Yahoo!Entertainment, September 23, 2020. https://www.yahoo.com/entertainment/showgirls-gina-ravera-controversial-scene-paul-verhoeven-220338697.html.

Bersani, Leo. "Is the Rectum a Grave?" *October* 43 (1987): 197–222.

Bonnaud, Frédéric. "The Captive Lover—An Interview with Jacques Rivette." Translated by Kent Jones. *Senses of Cinema* 79 (September 2001). First published in French, 1998. http://sensesofcinema.com/2001/jacques-rivette/rivette-2/.

Breckon, Anna. "The Erotic Politics of Disgust: *Pink Flamingos* as Queer Political Cinema." *Screen* 54, no. 4 (2013): 514–33.

Fassbinder, Rainer Werner. "Six Films by Douglas Sirk." In *Douglas Sirk,* edited by Laura Mulvey and Jon Halliday, 95–106. Edinburgh: Edinburgh Film Festival, 1972.

Film at Lincoln Center. "'Showgirls' Q&A: Paul Verhoeven & Gina Gershon." YouTube, March 1, 2017. https://youtu.be/vj7JB_Otn3A.

Godard, Jean-Luc. "Tears and Speed." Translated by Susan Bennett. *Screen* 12, no. 2 (1971): 95–98. First published in French, 1959.

Hardie, Melissa Jane. "Loose Slots: Figuring the Strip in *Showgirls*." *XText* 1 (1996): 24–35.

Keeling, Kara. *Queer Times, Black Futures*. New York: New York University Press, 2019.

Maltin, Leonard. *Leonard Maltin's Movie & Video Guide 2002*. New York: Signet, 2002.

Marsh, Calum. "*Starship Troopers*: One of the Most Misunderstood Movies Ever." *The Atlantic*, November 7, 2013. https://www.theatlantic.com/entertainment/archive/2013/11/-em-starship-troopers-em-one-of-the-most-misunderstood-movies-ever/281236/.

Martin, Adrian. *Mysteries of Cinema: Reflections on Film Theory, History and Culture 1982–2016*. Perth: University of Western Australia Publishing, 2020.

———. "The Offended Critic: Film Reviewing and Social Commentary." *Australian Quarterly* 27, no. 2 (2000): 10–16.

McHale, Jeffrey, dir. *You Don't Nomi*. XYZ Films, Grade Five Films, 2019.

Nayman, Adam. *It Doesn't Suck: Showgirls*. 2nd ed. Toronto: ECW, 2018.

Sandler, Kevin S. "The Naked Truth: *Showgirls* and the Fate of the X/NC-17 Rating." *Cinema Journal* 40, no. 3 (2007): 69–93.

Sirk, Douglas, and Jon Halliday. *Sirk on Sirk: Interviews with Jon Halliday*. London: Secker and Warburg for the British Film Institute, 1971.

toofab. "Elizabeth Berkley Embraces 'Showgirls' 20 Years Later." YouTube, June 29, 2015. https://youtu.be/tk8XR3U71D0.

Notes

1. See Film at Lincoln Center, "'Showgirls' Q&A: Paul Verhoeven & Gina Gershon," YouTube, March 1, 2017, https://youtu.be/vj7JB_Otn3A; and Adam Nayman, *It Doesn't Suck: Showgirls*, 2nd ed. (Toronto: ECW, 2018).

2. Jeffrey McHale, dir., *You Don't Nomi* (XYZ Films, Grade Five Films, 2019).

3. Jean-Luc Godard, "Tears and Speed," trans. Susan Bennett, *Screen* 12, no. 2 (1971): 95–98; Rainer Werner Fassbinder, "Six Films by Douglas Sirk," in *Douglas Sirk*, ed. Laura Mulvey and Jon Halliday (Edinburgh: Edinburgh Film Festival, 1972), 95–106; Douglas Sirk and Jon Halliday, *Sirk on Sirk: Interviews with Jon Halliday* (London: Secker and Warburg for the British Film Institute, 1971).

4. See, for example, Calum Marsh, "*Starship Troopers*: One of the Most Misunderstood Movies Ever," *The Atlantic*, November 8, 2013, https://www.theatlantic.com/entertainment/archive/2013/11/-em-starship-troopers-em-one-of-the-most-misunderstood-movies-ever/281236/. Another case in point would be feminist auteur Chantal Ackerman, whose European oeuvre has generated veneration and approval within critical circles but whose extraordinary *Un divan à New York* (1996) is relatively unremarked.

5. See, for example, Anna Breckon, "The Erotic Politics of Disgust: *Pink Flamingos* as Queer Political Cinema," *Screen* 54, no. 4 (2013): 514–33.

6. toofab, "Elizabeth Berkley Embraces 'Showgirls' 20 Years Later," YouTube, June 29, 2015, https://youtu.be/tk8XR3U71D0.

7. Frédéric Bonnaud, "The Captive Lover—An Interview with Jacques Rivette," trans. Kent Jones, *Senses of Cinema* 79 (September 2001), http://sensesofcinema.com/2001/jacques-rivette/rivette-2/.

8. Ethan Alter, "'Showgirls' at 25: Gina Ravera Discusses the Cult Movie's Most Controversial Scene," *Yahoo!Entertainment*, September 23, 2020, https://www.yahoo.com/entertainment/showgirls-gina-ravera-controversial-scene-paul-verhoeven-220338697.html.

9. Ibid.

10. Kara Keeling, *Queer Times, Black Futures* (New York: New York University Press, 2019).

11. Melissa Jane Hardie, "Loose Slots: Figuring the Strip in Showgirls," *XText* 1 (1996): 24–35.

12. Adrian Martin, "The Offended Critic: Film Reviewing and Social Commentary," *Australian Quarterly* 27, no. 2 (2000): 10–16. Republished in Adrian Martin, *Mysteries of Cinema: Reflections on Film Theory, History and Culture 1982–2016* (Perth: University of Western Australia Publishing, 2020), 353–70.

13. Leo Bersani, "Is the Rectum a Grave?" *October* 43 (1987): 197–222.

PART I
ESSAYS

GETTING IT JUST RIGHT 1

ELIZABETH BERKLEY'S WAYS OF KNOWING IN SHOWGIRLS

ANNA BRECKON

The significance of Elizabeth Berkley's performance in *Showgirls* has not been overlooked. However, unlike the performance of Berkley's costar Gina Gershon, which was available to be read through self-aware styles of performance and hence register as agential, Berkley's performance has almost consistently been read as a product of Joe Eszterhas's script and Paul Verhoeven's direction. While it is established that Verhoeven directed Berkley to exaggerate her expressions, this is only one aspect of a performance that comes about as the combined result of the process, style, approach, personality, attitude, feeling, and fantasy as well as ways of being, seeing, and knowing that Berkley brings to her performance in *Showgirls*. In this chapter, I consider Berkley's ways of knowing that have largely been disregarded due to the reframing of the film through self-conscious writing and reading practices such as camp, auteurism, cult, and satire. I argue not only that Berkley, through her performance, writes her perspective into *Showgirls* but also that the particularities of her ways of knowing are central to the meaning of the film itself. In this sense, I argue for Berkley's recognition as a coauthor of the film.

This chapter understands authorship as a productive approach that continues to serve an important function for revisionist literary and film work, and for supporting and upholding spaces for minority voices. I follow feminist film theorists who engage poststructuralist theories of authorship while privileging its political and cultural valences over epistemological certainty.[1] Authorship brings to light questions of agency and causality, who is speaking, and what is being said. Examinations of authorship have the capacity to bring to light alternative ways of knowing a text. Emphasizing the importance of notions of authorship for minority subjects, Janet Staiger closes her introduction to *Authorship and Film* with a way of theorizing authorship that can underscore authorial agency while avoiding essentialism: "The message produced should not be considered a direct expression of a wholly constituted origin with presence or personality or preoccupations. Yet the message is produced from circumstances in which the individual conceives a self as able to act. The individual believes in the author-function, and this works because the discursive structure (our culture) in which the individual acts also believes in it."[2]

Staiger's theory enables me to address the erasure of Berkley's subjectivity and agency in the ongoing reception of *Showgirls* and to consider her performance, as well as the theories, methods, and processes that Berkley articulates as being central to it, as meaningful acts of authorship.

The fields of star studies and performance studies have demonstrated the range of ways in which performers can warrant recognition as authors. This scholarly work has outlined the historical deficit of research in this area caused in part by the popularity of the discourse of auteurism, which privileges the director as author and, with that, has concentrated on the modes of selection and the mechanisms of control at the director's disposal.[3] Focusing on performance opens up possibilities for new readings of films that have been interpreted in relation to the director as the central maker of meaning. Building on this body of work, this chapter considers Berkley as a creative agent of *Showgirls*. Following an exploration of the sexist and classist assumptions underlying much of the criticism directed at Berkley, I argue that the actress's interpretation of the script and her method and process of performance bring into being a radically de-hierarchizing feminist erotic politics.

On its release, many critics went to lengths to distance themselves from the desire displayed in the film, emphasizing *Showgirls'* lack of eroticism and excoriating the film's star for her performance's failure to arouse. *Showgirls* was described as "a bare-butted bore"; "disentertainment"; not "sexy," merely "X-ie"; drearily conventional and contrived; and about "as genuinely arousing as intricately-choreographed nude livestock."[4] Verhoeven, Eszterhas, and Berkley were denounced for their presumed attempt and failure to create erotic spectacles. However, the difference in rationale behind the vitriol directed at Berkley and that directed at Verhoeven and Eszterhas evinces a number of gendered and auteurist assumptions. *Showgirls* was frequently framed as either a representation of the writer's and director's heterosexual male fantasies or the two men's fantasy of what they imagine heterosexual men want. "*Showgirls*," one review states, "offers a slumming party inside the moviemakers' libidos."[5] In her initial response to *Showgirls*, Linda Ruth Williams writes: "'Adult' pretensions notwithstanding, it is written in the spirit of lascivious amazement which accompanies a schoolboy's first erection, and directed with a smug assurance that the images are arousing enough to sweep the viewer past the manifold absurdities of plot and characterisation."[6]

While Verhoeven and Eszterhas were criticized for the nature of their fantasies, Berkley was criticized less for the artistic choices she made than for those that she apparently did not. One critic writes: "In the shooting script to *Showgirls*, director Paul Verhoeven and screenwriter Joe Eszterhas detailed exactly how they wanted the lap dance between Nomi (Elizabeth Berkley) and Zack (Kyle MacLachlan) to proceed: on what beat she should bury her blond head in his lap, when she should crawl naked across the floor in front of him. . . . It is an elaborately choreographed bit of manipulation, on many levels. The two male creators, Verhoeven and Eszterhas, are contriving a degrading experience for their female character."[7]

Janet Maslin for the *New York Times* also interprets the actress as an agentless erotic prop, describing Berkley as a sex toy. Maslin writes, "With the open-mouthed, vacant-eyed look of an inflatable party doll, Ms. Berkley should have been well suited to a film that treats its heroine like a shiny new toy."[8] Berkley is represented here as Verhoeven's and Eszterhas's cinematic material; for these viewers, the only sexuality at stake belongs to the film's writer and director. Williams's review supports this idea in her statement that "female sexuality is not at issue here; in *Showgirls* sexual women are always at work, never in play or in love. . . . Female sexuality for *Showgirls* is only a function of commercial ambition."[9] Putting aside Williams's elision of the lesbianism and lesbian eroticism saturating nearly every scene of the film, she also leaves no space to imagine Berkley—or any of the female cast for that matter—as having the capacity to affect the terms of the desire represented. For Williams, Verhoeven's and Eszterhas's erotic desires and fantasies are endlessly detectable in *Showgirls*. Those belonging to either Nomi or Berkley are absent.

When Berkley's agency is conceptually reduced to that of an "inflatable party doll," a particular familiar erotic economy emerges—that is, *Showgirls* begins to look like an instantiation of what it claims to critique. The hypocrisy of a blockbuster that condemns Vegas (and Hollywood as its allegorical correlate) as an industry based on the buying and selling of sexualized images of women by selling sexualized images of women was rarely missed by critics. For example, Rita Kempley in the *Washington Post* writes: "When it comes to acting, there's very little to complain about. Luckily, Berkley's lines could be written on a G-string. Like the bimbo she plays, Berkley's minimal acting talent limits her choice of roles. That makes the filmmakers little better than the club owners who prostitute their employees. They're selling women's bodies, and *Showgirls* is an overcoat movie for men who don't want to be seen going into a porno theater."[10]

Maslin, in the *New York Times*, goes even further to directly describe Berkley as a whore: "[Berkley] has trouble repeatedly insisting, 'I am not a whore.' As declarations of integrity go, that one appears to rank with 'I am not a crook.'"[11]

Some might argue that bad acting was the main reason Berkley copped so much flak. Yet poor acting does not explain the deeply personal nature of many of the comments directed at the actress. Berkley was panned not only for her appearance, her dancing, and her acting but also for being overly ambitious, naive, and talentless. She was also criticized for wanting to become a star too quickly and for allowing herself to be sexually exploited. One reporter even asked her what it felt like to be a failure.[12] One explanation for the personal nature of the comments directed at Berkley is that Berkley's desires as well as her means for achieving them closely aligned with those of the character she played in a way that was abhorrent to middle-class tastes. Berkley was a teen sitcom actress with the aspiration to become a film star. Paid only $100,000 for her role, she was not in it for the money. Remuneration was to come in the form of increased star status. In a culture where class is determined as much by celebrity as by economics, Berkley saw *Showgirls* as her means to upward mobility. In this sense, Berkley, like Nomi, pursued ambitions to become a star through erotic representation. The idea that one could acquire class status through vulgar sexual exhibitionism may have been too much for critics to handle. Yet, while Berkley's fantasy of upward mobility was never realized, it remains central to her performance of working-class female sexuality in *Showgirls*.

Adam Nayman's 2014 book *It Doesn't Suck: Showgirls* attempts to offer a sustained revision of the film's initial critical reception by attributing intentionality to Eszterhas and Verhoeven through an auteur-based close reading.[13] In doing so, he extends the chauvinism of the film's original reception. His interpretation of the film proceeds from the notion that Eszterhas's and Verhoeven's bodies of work both consistently demonstrate sophisticated mastery of medium. Nayman follows the redemptive logics of interpretation deployed by I. Q. Hunter in his auteurist article "Beaver Las Vegas! A Fanboy's Defence of *Showgirls,*" which, with Verhoeven's oeuvre as the framework for semiotic analysis, makes a case for reading *Showgirls* as satire.[14] Berkley marks the limitations of Nayman's rehabilitation project. Nayman claims that attempts to redeem the film through intentional camp or satire come at the expense of Berkley. In an effort to avoid contributing to the vitriol directed at the actress and her performance, Nayman asks, "If it's possible to discern a satirical perspective in Verhoeven and Eszterhas's contributions to *Showgirls,* then mightn't we wonder if Berkley is actually in on the joke too?"[15] Although he points to the potential of feminist camp as a frame for considering Berkley's performance—a frame more suitably applied to the performance of Gershon—Nayman is unable to substantiate this possibility with textual or extratextual evidence.[16] Instead, all material directs him to the contrary. With knowingness as his only tool for redemption, he cannot find a viable alternative to the idea of Berkley as a victim of a "very mean" manipulation.[17] Verhoeven, he speculates, may have "deliberately encouraged Berkley to do maladroit work" to make a critical point about American ambition and the Hollywood system.[18] In this scenario, the "seriously failed seriousness" of Berkley's performance is interpreted as a marker of the director's rather than the actress's intention, and Verhoeven's exploitation of Berkley as an actualization of the film's "cautionary tale about inexperienced women becoming the grist for the showbiz mill."[19] In this account, Verhoeven, not Berkley, is credited as the primary author of her performance.

Nayman wants to be the one to rescue Berkley, but his professed impartial scholarly position cannot allow it. In compensation, he credits her performance as the reason people continue to screen *Showgirls*, the reason "any idiot [referring to himself] would write a book about it," and as "key to this movie being amazing."[20] This is, however, not because of but despite her ability and intention. His use of the word *amazing* seems to refer to a kind of ecstatic affective experience, generated by Berkley, that points to the limit of his discourse; it indicates a state of suspension, a conceptual blockage, a kind of stupor. The description of the film as "amazing" also harks back to filmmaker Jacques Rivette's 1998 commentary on *Showgirls* as, in what appears to be a burst of emotion, he brings into being one of the only positive reviews Berkley received at the time: "And that actress is amazing!"[21] Berkley's performance appears to be at the center of both Rivette's and Nayman's experience; however, in Rivette's earlier reading, this operates as an index of Berkley's ability as a performer. While it is commonly understood that Berkley's performance is central to the film's continued cult following and critical revision, this has not led to a consideration of Berkley's performance as a product of her own making.[22]

Berkley's ambitions and dreams were crushed by the critical reception. However, they continue to exist, captured in real time in the making of the film. Berkley not only recognized the parallel between herself and Nomi but also used her situational identification with the character as the imaginary and emotional material for her scenes. As the lead performer, Berkley writes her fantasies into the film, infusing her sexual spectacles with her desire and ambition to make it in Hollywood. Across multiple interviews prior to the official release of the film, Berkley actively promoted her identification with the character she plays and spoke of the way in which this identification was central to her performance. On reading the script, Berkley claims to have recognized her own ambition and passion in the character: "I thought, 'I have to do this.' I mean, this role, I would kill for. It's very rare you read a script where the whole focus of the film is on a woman. Also, I'm so passionate about what I go after and I really felt a lot of connection with the character right away. I just knew I had to get in the room with Paul and show him what I can do so that he could see because I really felt this strong connection."[23]

The way in which Berkley infused her performance with her narcissistic fantasy of her star rising is expressed in an account of herself misidentifying one of the posters on the set reading "Cristal Connors Is a Goddess" as "Elizabeth Berkley Starring in *Showgirls*," claiming the experience to be "so emotional."[24] In a post on Instagram, the actress offers another account of her situational identification during a moment in which she watches Gershon's character, Cristal Connors, perform onstage. She writes: "This was a rare moment during the filming of #showgirls where the director let the camera run and captured my authentic longing for my own dream to be a performer. . . . In turn he captured #nomi's longing, while watching the star of the show, Crystal [*sic*]."[25]

In conjunction with a lesbian eroticism in which the desire to be and the desire to have are blurred, this moment also depicts a masturbatory fantasy of upward mobility; Nomi looks at the spectacle, imagines herself as a star, and begins to touch herself. Berkley's comments point not only to the way she drew significantly on her personal desires in her performance but also to the way in which Nomi's sexuality is inseparable from her dreams of success. Berkley's comments offer an alternative to Williams's claim that "female sexuality for *Showgirls* is only a function of commercial ambition." For Berkley, Nomi's sexuality is primarily oriented around commercial ambition.

Berkley makes Nomi's (and her own) professional desires central to the sexually objectified body by incorporating them into the physicality of her performance. This is made clear in an interview during the production of the show in which Berkley explains her approach to the dance sequences, including the strip routines at the Cheetah's club:

> Marguerite Derricks and I, the choreographer and I, really have worked on just bringing a sense of artistry to the dance, and even when I am stripping in the Cheetah club, it's not just [*moves shoulders back*] moving, you know, simple moves as a stripper. It's still that same style that Nomi has, she choreographs herself, she . . . doesn't just get out there and . . . just move a little bit. She wants to be the best at everything she does, so nothing is halfway, so everything, all the dancing is, throughout the film, is the basic feeling that Nomi has, that comes through her dance. It's interesting because a lot . . . of the time when I was preparing for the role through the dance rehearsals I found out so much about the character just through the movement of the dance, which is usually, you'll see through . . . Nomi, is thrashing and hard . . . a lot of her anger is through her dance, a lot of her sexuality is through her dance. So, I can only tell you, I mean when you see the film, you'll see what I am saying, but I can only tell you, as being the one that's up there: it feels pretty hot up there.[26]

Berkley's comments point to her process of performance as an earnest identification with her character. She interprets the dance sequences as a way to physically and emotionally connect with Nomi. She understands the stripteases as existing, for Nomi, beyond the function of exhibiting the body for money, as an expression of desire, rage, passion, and sexuality. By taking the pole dance as a site for the expression of her character's desires, Berkley transforms a scene conventionally understood to exemplify the exchange of female sexuality for money at the expense of her subjectivity into an expression of a woman's erotic fantasy of exceeding her given bounds.

Berkley's comments once again indicate the degree to which her desires and fantasies are central to her performance. Toward the end of this interview passage, Nomi's and Berkley's desires and pleasures are blurred, character experience and situation and actor experience and situation become indistinguishable, and Nomi's and Berkley's sexuality become one and the same. Berkley's claims that "it feels pretty hot up there" and that "when you see the film, you'll see what I am saying" indicate the way in which she imagines the film to be capturing her, rather than Nomi's, erotic experience as a performer. By Berkley's account, *Showgirls* is a record of her erotic fantasy of becoming a film star. Berkley interprets her strip numbers, which include finger flicking, pole licking, breast touching, nipple licking, lesbian pole riding, and acrobatic dry-humping, as the gestural material that will make her and her character a star. Berkley sees the strip sequences not only as the mode through which Nomi can express her artistry but also as that through which she can express her own. Berkley's capacity to engage the striptease as a means of fulfilling self-expression exemplifies what Martha P. Nochimson calls the "creative power of a woman artist," which has the capacity to transcend "the seeming limits of a violent world predicated on commodities and empty signs" by making them "instrumental to the evolution of an organic form of victory and pleasure."[27] Berkley's capacity to transform sites of objectification and commodification into sites of artistic self-expression becomes, through her performance, key to the gender and class politics of the film itself.

At the core of Berkley's performance is a lack of discernment between historically determined hierarchies of sexual display. Berkley's lack of discernment in her engagement with low forms of sexual representation presents a political relation to taste-based hierarchies that is distinct from those commonly understood to structure subcultural filmmaking and viewing practices that engage with taste and its cultural functions. Self-conscious discernment is core to definitions of subcultural objects and viewing practices such as trash cinema, camp, cult, and paracinema. These subcultural taste systems are frequently pitted against, and framed as superior to, dominant culture's conceptualization of the good and engage with denigrated cultural product in ways that bring into question dominant taste hierarchies. This is outlined by trash filmmaker John Waters in his much-quoted account of the distinction between "good bad taste" and "bad bad taste": "There is such a thing as good bad taste and bad bad taste. It's easy to disgust someone; I could make a ninety-minute film of people getting their limbs hacked off, but this would only be bad bad taste and not very stylish or original. To understand bad taste one must have very good taste. Good bad taste can be creatively nauseating but must, at the same time, appeal to the especially twisted sense of humor, which is anything but universal."[28]

Waters distinguishes "good bad taste" from "bad bad taste" on the basis that the former demonstrates a high level of discernment, specialist knowledge, and a self-conscious and sophisticated understanding of taste and its cultural functions. Within Waters's framework, Berkley's performance would fall into the category of "bad bad taste," lacking the critical distance and comprehension of taste hierarchies required to be described as being in "good bad taste." However, moving beyond Waters's quote to his films, specifically to Divine's performances, brings to light, through comparison, a more nuanced portrait of the erotic politics of taste made available through Berkley's performance. Waters's films starring Divine work well as a point of comparison for theorizing Berkley's performance, not only because Waters's films exemplify the qualities of "good bad taste" but also because in the performances of both Divine and Berkley, the politics of taste is inextricable from the politics of sexuality.

Michael Moon and Eve Kosofsky Sedgwick describe Divine's performances as embodying a feeling they call "divinity," the divine feeling of "abjection and defiance."[29] In its display of narcissism in abjection, Divine's performance makes available an affective experience of belonging to a world in which all norms, ideals, and dominant social hierarchies are inverted: the more outcast, perverse, degenerate, obscene, and rotten you are, the higher your social standing. Berkley's narcissistic exhibitionist pleasure in abject sexual performance affectively and stylistically resonates with the trash performances of Divine. However, while Divine offers her audience a model of refusal by demonstrating pleasure in occupying the space of the socially repudiated, Berkley, as I will demonstrate, offers an affective experience of being in a world in which norms of sexual display do not apply. The Divine role from Waters's oeuvre that most closely resembles Berkley's Nomi is Dawn Davenport in *Female Trouble*. Although *Female Trouble* does not overtly appear to be a reference for *Showgirls,* both films draw on a similar archive of lowbrow genres such as the 1950s women's melodrama and the 1960s sexploitation movie and follow the storyline of a young woman who pursues celebrity status in a corrupt and exploitative industry. *Female Trouble* follows the journey of Dawn Davenport from adolescent delinquency through childbirth, the joy and cruelty of motherhood, a career in sex work and petty crime, marriage, divorce, and a career in modeling and criminality to her death by electric chair. Like Nomi, Dawn succeeds in becoming famous. However, Dawn's launch into major celebrity status comes after she stars in a one-woman show in which she performs tricks on a trampoline, tears a phone book in half, simulates sex acts with dead fish, and then wraps it up by firing bullets at random into the crowd. Dawn's journey is from disobedient teenager to mass murderer. In the montage sequence titled "Dawn Davenport: Career Girl, 1961–1967," we see Divine working a number of low-status service jobs. The first scene expresses her dissatisfaction as a waitress, the second her exhibitionistic pleasure as a go-go dancer, the third her low-level boredom from soliciting on the sidewalk. Dawn's go-go dancing represents the first in a series of choices—based on the imagined minimization of labor and maximization of reward—that will lead her into a life of violent crime. It also expresses the narcissism and exhibitionism that will continue to drive her desire to be famous. Dawn's pleasure in the go-go dancing sequence is expressed through masturbatory gestures that are designed to visually arouse. She touches her breasts, shakes her flesh, and simulates oral sex with a range of penetrative and circular tongue gestures. Divine's taking up of perverse erotic content as the material for sexual display is distinct from Berkley in that Divine exhibits a knowing relation to the social norms and erotic ideals that would register her display as abject. In this sense, Divine's performance must be understood in terms of "good bad taste"—as distinct from "bad bad taste"—as it relies on a sophisticated understanding of taste cultures and how they work to produce and sustain cultural hierarchies.

Berkley's performance does not possess an ironic or defiant relation to erotic norms, nor does it demonstrate a sophisticated engagement with taste and its cultural function to naturalize and justify social inequality. Berkley is not knowingly reveling in debased sexual representation. Instead, she does not register modes of sexual expression through the set of cultural norms that determine the value of erotic display. Demonstrating a lack of regard for hierarchies of sexual representation, Berkley's performance expresses a fantasy and emotional experience of being in a world in which stratifications of sexualized female performance do not apply. In his essay "Beaver Las Vegas!" Hunter argues that "*Showgirls* mocks distinctions between good/bad, art/trash, authentic/inauthentic, the aesthetic and ethical ideals trashed by the logic of consumption. . . . In *Showgirls* trash is indistinguishable from art; stripping from dancing; self-expression from pretentiousness; low-budget filth from expensive porn; Vegas from Hollywood; Hollywood from America. It's all grist for the mill of exploitation, the closed unbeatable system of consumer capitalism."[30]

Berkley's performance, however, does not appear to mock the "aesthetic and ethical ideals trashed by the logic of consumption." Instead, she registers these commercial erotic practices—Vegas and the Hollywood production—as a space for artistic expression. The distinction here is affective and evaluative—while Hunter suggests that for *Showgirls* it's all trash, Berkley sees it all as art. My point is not to pit Hunter's reading against Berkley's but rather to illuminate, through his argument, the radical de-hierarchizing effect of Berkley's investment in the choreography of the striptease as the material for self-expression. Berkley's unwavering commitment to deploying the content of the striptease to express the emotions of her character and her proficiency as a dancer presents a de-hierarchizing relation to modes of sexual display and their associated female bodies.

Berkley's performance does not evidence a naive reading of *Showgirls*. Her performance results from the fact that she does not perceive Nomi's desires, sexuality, and fantasies as deficient. Berkley's investment in and alignment with Nomi's way of knowing allows the film to offer an alternative to knowingness as a means through which to express female sexual agency. Refusing to see herself as anything but a dancer, Nomi fails to recognize the way in which genre and context determine class categorizations. Gershon's Cristal Connors regularly attempts to explain to Nomi the ways in which social stratifications work, detailing the difference between dancing and stripping, between being a "whore" and not being a "whore." For Cristal, whoredom is using your body to sexually arouse a person for money—"We take the cash, we cash the check, we show them what they want to see." Nomi refuses to accept

Cristal's lesson that receiving payment for sexual display equates with a loss of status—signified by the term *whore*. For Nomi, stripping at the Cheetah's club is not just a matter of showing her body with the intent to arouse but a demonstration of her craft. Nomi sees stripping as a medium for artistic self-expression. Likewise, Berkley takes *Showgirls* as material for serious dramatic performance. Berkley could not tell the difference between a classy sexual spectacle and a crude one. She imagined *Showgirls* was going to do for her what *Basic Instinct* did for Sharon Stone. She did not register the difference between *Basic Instinct*'s "shadowy and fleeting" crotch-flashing and *Showgirls*' no-holds-barred explicit displays.[31] She interpreted the most vulgar conventions of erotic performance as the means to her upward mobility. Critics, however, took their lead from Cristal and, through the characterization of Eszterhas and Verhoeven as pimps, branded Berkley a whore. However, instead of humiliating the actress for making a foolish sexual spectacle out of herself, these critics could have learned a thing or two from Berkley. By taking the pole dance as a serious site for the expression of her character's desires, Berkley transforms a scene classically deployed to represent female objectification and commodification into an expression of a woman's erotic fantasy of upward mobility. Further, by not registering culturally debased forms of sexual display as antithetical to cultural conceptualizations of art, Berkley offers a nonhierarchical perspective on female sexual performance and the women associated with its culturally despised forms. It is Berkley's embodiment of Nomi's passionate commitment to move beyond her allocated class through vulgar sexual exhibitionism that allows *Showgirls* to offer spectators access to an affective and imaginary experience of being in a world in which the class-based hierarchies that determine aesthetic norms of sexual display do not exist. This fantasy is—even if available only for a moment—something worth investing in.

ANNA BRECKON earned her PhD in queer and feminist film theory from the University of Sydney. She is an independent theatermaker, artist, filmmaker, and film studies scholar. Her recent work appears in *Screen*, and she has presented at major institutions, galleries, and festivals, including the Brooklyn Academy of Music, the Australian Centre for Contemporary Art, the Harbourfront Centre, and Weiwuying: National Kaohsiung Center for the Arts.

References

Berkley, Elizabeth. *Ask Elizabeth: Real Answers to Everything You Secretly Wanted to Ask about Love, Friends, Your Body—And Life in General*. New York: G. P. Putnam's Sons, 2011.

———. "This Was a Rare Moment." Instagram, April 22, 2015. https://www.instagram.com/p/1vn9EsSwLh/?utm_source=ig_embed&ig_rid=a365f0ac-38ed-48be-812b-d7f1a78ff54f.

Bonnaud, Frédéric. "The Captive Lover—An Interview with Jacques Rivette." Translated by Kent Jones. *Senses of Cinema* 79 (September 2001). First published in French, 1998. http://sensesofcinema.com/2001/jacques-rivette/rivette-2/.

Burgos, Ryan. "*Showgirls* (1995) Behind the Scenes Interviews: Elizabeth Berkley." YouTube, 1:48, April 18, 2018. https://www.youtube.com/watch?v=184Vb03xv4k.

Butler, Jeremy G., ed. *Star Texts: Image and Performance in Film and Television*. Detroit: Wayne State University Press, 1991.

Corliss, Richard. "Valley of the Dulls: A Rancid Show-biz Tale with Lots of Nudity, *Showgirls* Gets an NC-17 Rating and Finds a New Four-Letter Word for Sex: Yawn." *Time*, October 2, 1995.

Grant, Catherine. "Secret Agents: Feminist Theories of Women's Film Authorship." *Feminist Theory* 2, no. 1 (2001): 113–30.

Hunter, I. Q. *Cult Film as a Guide to Life: Fandom, Adaptation, and Identity*. London: Bloomsbury, 2016.

Kempley, Rita. "*Showgirls* (NC-17)." *Washington Post*, September 22, 1995.

Lovell, Alan, and Peter Krämer, eds. *Screen Acting*. London: Routledge, 1999.

MacFarquhar, Larissa. "Start the Lava!" *Premiere*, October 1995.

Maslin, Janet. "$40 Million Worth of Voyeurism." *New York Times*, September 22, 1995, C1.

McHale, Jeffrey, dir. *You Don't Nomi*. XYZ Films, Grade Five Films, 2019.
Moon, Michael, and Eve Kosofsky Sedgwick. "Divinity: A Dossier, a Performance Piece, a Little-Understood Emotion." *Discourse* 13, no. 1 (1991): 12–39.
Nayman, Adam. *It Doesn't Suck: Showgirls*. Toronto: ECW, 2014.
Newsweek Staff. "Base Instinct." *Newsweek*, January 24, 1995. https://www.newsweek.com/base-instinct-182848.
Nochimson, Martha P. "*Inland Empire*." *Film Quarterly* 60, no. 4 (2007): 10–14.
Setoodeh, Ramin. "Gina Gershon on *Killer Joe*, Tom Cruise, *Showgirls*, *Bound*." *The Daily Beast*, July 18, 2012. https://www.thedailybeast.com/gina-gershon-on-killer-joe-tom-cruise-showgirls-bound.
Staiger, Janet. "Authorship Approaches." In *Authorship and Film*, edited by David A. Gerstner and Janet Staiger, 27–55. New York: Routledge, 2002.
Taylor, Aaron, ed. *Theorizing Film Acting*. London: Routledge, 2012.
Thomas, William. "*Showgirls* Review." *Empire*, January 12, 1996.
TIFF Originals. "Adam Nayman on *Showgirls*." YouTube, 24:38, March 29, 2014. https://www.youtube.com/watch?v=sSsXR-8sdgY.
Verhoeven, Paul. *Paul Verhoeven: Interviews*. Edited by Margaret Barton-Fumo. Jackson: University Press of Mississippi, 2016.
Waters, John. *Shock Value: A Tasteful Book about Bad Taste*. New York: Thunder's Mouth, 2005.
Williams, Linda Ruth. *The Erotic Thriller in Contemporary Cinema*. Bloomington: Indiana University Press, 2005.
———. "Nothing to Find." *Sight and Sound* 6, no. 1 (1996): 28–30.

Notes

1. Catherine Grant, "Secret Agents: Feminist Theories of Women's Film Authorship," *Feminist Theory* 2, no. 1 (2001): 113–30; Janet Staiger, "Authorship Approaches," in *Authorship and Film*, ed. David A. Gerstner and Janet Staiger (New York: Routledge, 2002), 27–55.

2. Staiger, "Authorship Approaches," 50.

3. For early examples of this field, see Jeremy G. Butler, ed., *Star Texts: Image and Performance in Film and Television* (Detroit: Wayne State University Press, 1991); Alan Lovell and Peter Krämer, eds., *Screen Acting* (London: Routledge, 1999); Aaron Taylor, ed., *Theorizing Film Acting* (London: Routledge, 2012).

4. Janet Maslin, "$40 Million Worth of Voyeurism," *New York Times*, September 22, 1995, C1; Richard Corliss, "Valley of the Dulls: A Rancid Show-biz Tale with Lots

of Nudity, *Showgirls* Gets an NC-17 Rating and Finds a New Four-Letter Word for Sex: Yawn," *Time*, October 2, 1995; William Thomas, "*Showgirls* Review," *Empire*, January 12, 1996.

5. Corliss, "Valley of the Dulls."

6. Linda Ruth Williams, "Nothing to Find," *Sight and Sound* 6, no. 1 (1996): 29.

7. Newsweek Staff, "Base Instinct," *Newsweek*, January 24, 1995, https://www.newsweek.com/base-instinct-182848.

8. Maslin, "$40 Million Worth of Voyeurism," C1.

9. Linda Ruth Williams, *The Erotic Thriller in Contemporary Cinema* (Bloomington: Indiana University Press, 2005), 173.

10. Rita Kempley, "*Showgirls* (NC-17)," *Washington Post*, September 22, 1995.

11. Maslin, "$40 Million Worth of Voyeurism," C1.

12. Elizabeth Berkley, *Ask Elizabeth: Real Answers to Everything You Secretly Wanted to Ask about Love, Friends, Your Body—And Life in General* (New York: G. P. Putnam's Sons, 2011), 118.

13. Adam Nayman, *It Doesn't Suck: Showgirls* (Toronto: ECW, 2014).

14. I. Q. Hunter, *Cult Film as a Guide to Life: Fandom, Adaptation and Identity* (London: Bloomsbury, 2016), 23–40.

15. Nayman, *It Doesn't Suck*, 88–89.

16. Gina Gershon's performance speaks to the feminist camp style of Mae West and the gold diggers of early Hollywood musicals, the satirical performances of 1950s Hollywood bombshells such as Marilyn Monroe, Jayne Mansfield, and Jane Russell, and the self-assured aggressive sexuality of the femme fatales of 1990s noir. In an interview, Gershon claims not only that she intentionally camped it up but also that *Showgirls* was a radical departure from her training in the classics. Ramin Setoodeh, "Gina Gershon on *Killer Joe*, Tom Cruise, *Showgirls*, *Bound*," *The Daily Beast*, July 18, 2012, https://www.thedailybeast.com/gina-gershon-on-killer-joe-tom-cruise-showgirls-bound.

17. TIFF Originals, "Adam Nayman on *Showgirls*," YouTube, 24:38, March 29, 2014, https://www.youtube.com/watch?v=sSsXR-8sdgY.

18. Nayman, *It Doesn't Suck*, 92.

19. Ibid., 92, 93.

20. TIFF Originals, "Adam Nayman on *Showgirls*," 21:52.

21. Frédéric Bonnaud, "The Captive Lover—An Interview with Jacques Rivette," trans. Kent Jones, *Senses of Cinema* 79 (September 2001), first published in French, 1998, http://sensesofcinema.com/2001/jacques-rivette/rivette-2/.

22. Berkley as a key point of continued interest and attachment is demonstrated in the recent documentary *You Don't Nomi*, which spends its largest section describing a

range of attachments to Berkley and her performance. It does not, however, grant her authorial credit for generating these feelings, experiences, and attachments. She is still largely framed as a victim of manipulation. Jeffrey McHale, dir., *You Don't Nomi* (XYZ Films, Grade Five Films, 2019).

23. Paul Verhoeven, *Paul Verhoeven: Interviews*, ed. Margaret Barton-Fumo (Jackson: University Press of Mississippi, 2016), 105–106.

24. Larissa MacFarquhar, "Start the Lava!," *Premiere*, October 1995, 84.

25. Elizabeth Berkley, "This Was a Rare Moment," Instagram, April 22, 2015, https://www.instagram.com/p/1vn9EsSwLh/?utm_source=ig_embed&ig_rid=a365f0ac-38ed-48be-812b-d7f1a78ff54f.

26. Ryan Burgos, "*Showgirls* (1995) Behind the Scenes Interviews: Elizabeth Berkley," YouTube, 1:48, April 18, 2018, https://www.youtube.com/watch?v=184Vb03xv4k.

27. Martha P. Nochimson, "*Inland Empire*," *Film Quarterly* 60, no. 4 (2007): 14.

28. John Waters, *Shock Value: A Tasteful Book about Bad Taste* (New York: Thunder's Mouth, 2005), 2.

29. Michael Moon and Eve Kosofsky Sedgwick, "Divinity: A Dossier, a Performance Piece, a Little-Understood Emotion," *Discourse* 13, no. 1 (1991): 15.

30. Hunter, *Cult Film*, 29.

31. Williams, *Erotic Thriller*, 171.

2 SELF-SHATTERING IN *SHOWGIRLS* AND *BLACK SWAN*

KANE RACE

Self-shattering has become something of a keyword in queer theory over the past few decades. Generally mobilized as a way of invoking the radically destabilizing power of sex, the term envisages a link between the ecstatic disorganization of the self that is said to be a feature of (some kinds of) erotic activity and the disruptive shattering of the social/political/sexual order that queer theory prizes. "The self which the sexual shatters provides the basis on which sexuality is associated with power," Leo Bersani claims in the dynamite essay that is generally credited with occasioning many of the key proposals of that strand of queer theory known today as the antisocial thesis or queer negativity.[1] But this is a broad and suggestive claim that demands further qualification, for the precise mechanism of this shattering is subject to different interpretations and conceptual commitments. How should the self be theorized here? Through what mechanisms is it articulated with power? How will its shattering impact power relations precisely? And what aspect of "the sexual" is capable of inducing such shattering?

Most proponents of the term can be assumed to agree that power produces selves that become available for sexual shattering. Bersani is especially concerned with "the fantasies engendered by [the body's] sexual anatomy and the specific moves it makes in taking sexual pleasure"—the dynamics of mastery and subordination, domination and submission, control and relinquishment that particular sexual roles and activities are taken to express or condense as re-presentations of social power.[2] He mobilizes a Freudian framework to promote the disruptive potential of "the *jouissance* of exploded limits"—a form of "ecstatic suffering" or masochistic desire that shatters and disaggregates the psychic organization of the self by pushing the body "beyond a certain threshold of endurance."[3] The dramatization of power relations that are taken here to be self-evident in practices of penetrative sex should be acknowledged rather than apologized for, Bersani argues, in the interest of refusing what he calls the "*redemptive reinvention of sex*."[4] For example, he applauds the "indictment of sex" that anti-porn feminists were propounding at the time and "their refusal to prettify it, to romanticize it, to maintain that fucking has anything to do with community or love," which he sees as having the "immensely desirable effect of publicizing" the "ineradicable" negativity of sex—its unsettling, disruptive, disturbing qualities that should be cherished rather than buried, Bersani contends rather perversely.[5] In the shuddering final moments of the essay, he makes the notorious claim that gay sex should be celebrated, not because of any of the usual redemptive, socially acceptable explanations but because "it never stops re-presenting the internalized phallic male as an infinitely loved object of sacrifice. Male homosexuality advertises the risk of the sexual itself as the risk of self-dismissal, of *losing sight* of the self and in so doing proposes and dangerously represents *jouissance* as a mode of ascesis."[6]

This dazzling passage has a habit of infiltrating and perturbing any attempt to think with or through the politics of self-shattering, and since it condenses and connects a number of technical terms, it deserves some unpacking.

Bersani's tethering of self-shattering to the "kinds of sex" people practice means the concept tends to get swapped out variously for orgasm, being penetrated, sadomasochist (S/M) sex, or masochistic desire.[7] Other key proponents of the term are less concerned with the drama of penetration, the physiology of sex acts themselves, or the apparently irresistible appeal of "copping it." Lee Edelman, for example, adopts a Lacanian definition of *jouissance,* affiliating self-shattering with the death drive itself—the violent irruption of the Real into the Imaginary-Symbolic order.[8] Dispensing with the biologism and positivism of Freudian psychoanalysis in favor of the (post)structural linguistics that informs Lacanian accounts, Edelman casts queerness as the historically variable, deliberately unspecified figure of negativity itself—a structural location whose critical capacity to disrupt the sociopolitical order hinges on its refusal of programs of reproductive futurity and redemptive sociality by embracing the radical negativity of jouissance.

The theoretical sleight of hand that would render the "*jouissance* of exploded limits" synonymous with orgasm might give us pause considering the disdain with which the latter has been regarded by a range of prominent leftist thinkers whose work is considered critically enabling for queer and cultural theory.[9] As Annamarie Jagose has discussed, philosophers who disagree on a range of theoretical questions such as Michel Foucault, Gilles Deleuze, and Jean Baudrillard converge on this point, generally conceiving orgasm as a normalizing measure that arrests the radical potential of pleasure, seduction, or desire.[10] In the first volume of *History of Sexuality,* Foucault cautions against investing in the "lyricism of orgasm and the good feelings of bio-energy," remarking that "these are but aspects of [power's] normalizing operation."[11] In the work of Deleuze, "pleasure, orgasm, *jouissance* are defined as veritable suspensions or interruptions" of flows of desire that presumably frustrate the transformative potential of the latter and their immanent productivity.[12] Even Baudrillard gives the experience of orgasm short shrift since it brings the destabilizing force of seduction and play he promotes to a "quick and banal end."[13] If erotic experience does harbor some potential to shatter the social and political order, these thinkers would have us search for this sweet spot almost anywhere other than orgasm.

In the same volume that Foucault denounces the lyricism of orgasm, he proposes that "the rallying point for the counterattack against the deployment of sexuality ought not to be sex-desire, but bodies and pleasures."[14] Against the disciplinary force of the "sexual sciences" (*scientia sexualis*), Foucault installs the "erotic arts" (*ars erotica*) as an alternative way of elaborating sexual knowledge and invests the latter with counterpolitical potential.[15] These corporeal experiments with bodies and pleasures are recalled in the opening pages of *The Use of Pleasure*, in which Foucault discusses how certain "arts of existence" can effect a "straying afield of [one]self"—by which he means *losing sight of* the proper subject of disciplinary knowledge.[16] Foucault frames his thinking on these matters in terms of "'ascesis,' *askēsis*, an exercise of oneself in the activity of thought"—a term that denotes corporeal experiments driven by the need to think, to feel, to perceive, to know, to become otherwise.[17] Importantly for Foucault, the *self* that such exercises enable "one to get free of" is a product of disciplinary and normalizing practices, consistent with earlier work.[18] That is to say, it is shaped, constrained, materially *situated*, and held in place by historically specific power operations and concretizing relations.[19]

Foucault can be read here as proposing a form of self-shattering that enlists the erotic but is hardly reducible to the psychology of orgasm. Rather, it relies on devising modes of "*ascesis* that would make us work on ourselves and invent (I don't say discover) a manner of being that is still improbable"—a manner of being wrought from relations of "differentiation, of creation, of innovation" rather than selfsame identity.[20] There are distinct traces of Foucault's vocabulary here in Bersani's conception of "the risk of the sexual itself as the risk of self-dismissal, of *losing sight* of the self," and especially in his proposal of "*jouissance* as a mode of ascesis"—the essay's climactic political claim.[21] But hang on: isn't Bersani attempting to have it both ways here? By invoking jouissance as a *mode of ascesis,* he forcibly conjoins what might otherwise be seen as wildly incongruous, countervailing theoretical projects. It is not simply that a psychoanalytic concept is being prescribed here as a solution to a historical situation in which the hold of psychoanalytic truths is at stake. In advancing a psychoanalytic definition of self-shattering "to get at the 'essence' of sexual pleasure," Bersani effectively evacuates modes of ascesis of their political traction by extracting them from the historical situations they are designed to rework and which constitute their primary domain of intervention.[22]

Part of the problem here may be the rather stripped-down version of power relations Bersani is concerned with. His analysis of power is "polarized into relations of mastery and subordination" that are just as likely to be found in sex (whether consensual or not) as they are in any other social relation.[23] There are significant differences here between Foucault's problematization of power and how it is exercised. For Foucault, domination always describes a historical situation because of what he calls the *strategic reversibility* of power relations. As Colin Gordon explains on this basis, power "is never a fixed and closed regime but rather an endless and open strategic game."[24] But for Bersani, the strategic reversibility of power relations is beside the point. He is troubled by the master–slave relation he finds as a zero-sum game in every expression of power.[25] Indeed, Bersani's preoccupation with the "indissociable nature of sexual pleasure and the exercise or loss of power" is what allows him, finally, to disregard the historical coordinates of ascetic interventions and turn to psychoanalysis to find his answers.[26]

And then there is the question of gender and its significance for these counterpolitical exercises in self-shattering. Certainly, whatever men's "sexual equipment appears to invite by analogy . . . neither sex has exclusive rights to the practice of sex as self-hyperbole," Bersani maintains.[27] But his closing remarks about the possibility of "*jouissance* as a mode of ascesis" are conspicuous in their specification of *male homosexuality* as its agent.[28] Indeed, the essay is famous for invoking the "seductive and intolerable image of a grown man, legs high in the air, unable to refuse the suicidal ecstasy of being a woman."[29] This is what the figure of male homosexuality "advertises" and "dangerously re-presents" and also, one might well assume, where its political significance lies.[30] Do women stand to benefit from this particular mode of ascesis when the jouissance is theirs and the "internalized phallic male," however loved, is typically (mis)taken to be either beyond their reach or else already ceded?[31] In short, could the image of a *woman*, "legs high in the air, unable to refuse the suicidal ecstasy of being a woman," ever hope to be just as intolerable or disruptive?[32]

This essay pursues these questions by comparing the figuration of self-shattering in *Showgirls* (directed by Paul Verhoeven, 1995) and *Black Swan* (directed by Darren Aronofsky, 2010)—two films that have sparked a string of popular comparisons but model what I take to be radically different versions of the practice. In his review of *Black Swan*, critic David Edelstein compares the character of the director of ballet to a "method-acting guru" who "lectures [Nina] on letting go, losing herself, surrendering completely to her sexuality. *Black Swan* dramatizes that surrender and its overpowering side effects, and it plays like a Roman Polanski remake of *Showgirls*."[33] This comparison is pertinent for my argument. Both films chart the rise of ambitious young women in the heterosexualized dance and entertainment industries of late millennial commodity culture; both explore the sexual politics of female rivalry in these contexts. Both cite *All about Eve* as a principle narrative precedent, and both serve equally generous lashings of the "bitchy and overheated backstage melodrama" that made the former a camp classic.[34] But while critics panned *Showgirls* on its release, *Black Swan* enjoyed significant critical acclaim, scoring an Academy Award for its lead, Natalie Portman, among several other nominations. Not that Elizabeth Berkley's performance in *Showgirls* went entirely without record: she won Worst Actress at the Raspberry Awards, where the film notched up a record number of nominations. Despite these divergent critical fates, the thematic similarities between the two films were a source of voluble critical commentary. Rob Kirkpatrick compared *Black Swan* to *Showgirls* and *Burlesque,* concluding "*Black Swan* is simply higher-priced cheese, Aronofsky's camembert to [the other films'] cheddar."[35] Ed Gonzalez described *Black Swan* as "*Showgirls* stripped bare of its camp affectations" (apparently a good thing) but argued that *Showgirls*' empathy for the plight of female dancers runs deeper—a claim I will agree with.[36]

When comparing the critical reception of these films, we can see how the degree of cultural capital each film lays claim to effectively mediates the respectability of the subject positions they make available for critics and viewers. The situation of the critic here is reminiscent of *Showgirls*' character James, who claims for himself the capacity to adjudicate between artistry and eroticism and pimps himself out to aspiring dancers on this basis. As Melissa Hardie has observed, the success of James's claim ultimately turns on his ability to conceal his "erotic investment in 'pussy'"—and this would be no less true of the cultural authority of critics, viewers, and performers of sexualized material.[37] In the case of *Showgirls,* critics rigorously disavowed any such investment, usually by ridiculing or trashing the film. Compare the critical reception of *Black Swan,* summarized by Stephanie Bunbury as follows: "Some found its theatricality maddening, but most declared themselves 'swept away.'"[38] The higher cultural status of the ballet film would seem to provide a license for less guarded, more explicit expressions of pleasure—the kind of self-surrender that runs no risk of undermining one's hold on cultural sovereignty. Here, cultural status helps to redeem experiences of jouissance and turn them into legitimate declarations. This brings cultural capital into focus as a resource of potential utility for redemptive projects: a social reserve that can be instrumentalized and put to work in pastoral efforts to "prettify sex."

The similarity between *Showgirls* and *Black Swan* might be thought to extend even more intricately into the narrative predicaments faced by each of the films' protagonists. Christine Griffin et al. have described postfeminist cultures and contexts as "profoundly dilemmatic [spaces]" since "hyper-sexual femininity calls on young women to look and act as agentically sexy within a pornified night-time economy . . . but to somehow distance themselves from the troubling figure of the 'drunken slut.'"[39] Nomi and Nina are forced to navigate precisely such dilemmatic spaces and might be taken on this basis as postfeminist figures par excellence. The problematic that each of these films depicts is a power situation in which a premium is placed on the authentic expression of sexual excitement as a measure of feminine performance. What is demanded from their rising stars, in other words, is not simply that they make erotic spectacles of themselves for the benefit of the male gaze, but also that they demonstrate their erotic investment in the entire apparatus of production that subjects them—that is, the truth of their desire. This demand is most obviously embodied in the figure of the chauvinistic artistic director of the dance company in each film—the menacing patriarch who calls the shots, taunts the workers, scrutinizes their bodies, humiliates them, assesses and adjudicates their performances. This figure is at his most sleazy and coercive in the demand he makes of his dancers to demonstrate *passion on command*, as Edelstein's review of *Black Swan*, cited above, suggests. The subjection of *Showgirls*' Nomi to such pressures is even more explicit. Demanding the dancers show him their breasts in an audition lineup, Tony Moss, the artistic director, says regarding Nomi's nipples, "I'm erect, why aren't you erect?" before suggesting she "play with them a little" to remedy the situation.[40]

Such demands dramatize more or less precisely the disciplinary bind that Foucault characterized as the regime of sexuality: *tell me your desire, and I will tell you what you are*. Everyone knows by now that power works by disciplining the body. But it also develops technologies for ascertaining the true worth of subjects through their "voluntary" articulations or expressions of desire. Since Nina and Nomi develop quite different ways of contending with this situation, *Black Swan* and *Showgirls* can be read as allegorical tales about different kinds of investments in self-shattering. Since sexual self-surrender tends to feature in both these texts less as an escape from regulatory power than as a basic precondition of contemporary "hetero-sexy" performances, it makes a difference how one situates the *self* that such exercises are said to obliterate, or what version of "*losing sight* of the self" is taken to constitute a mode of ascesis. "People will say, perhaps, that these games with oneself would better be left backstage," Foucault remarks when explaining his interest in transformative modes of ascesis.[41] What better place to test the mettle of these "preliminary exercises" than two films that place these exercises and their dramatic implications for their respective lead characters front and center?

Dancers and Hookers

I have suggested that the drama of both *Black Swan* and *Showgirls* hinges on the challenge their respective protagonists face of having to manage the disreputable aspects of sex in performative contexts that demand from them signs of its authentic expression. In *Black Swan*, Nina is exhorted to embrace her dark side and struggles to find a way of doing so that doesn't completely destabilize her. Nina has spent her life working very hard to become something her mother has trained her to want to be to acquire recognition. Nina's problem is that the extensive discipline it takes to make her body into that of a ballerina inhibits her from doing what is said to be required to give an outstanding performance—"letting go." *Letting go* entails losing sight of herself and unleashing her sexual energy in the presence of others, something she is afraid to do in public. Nina's body cannot seem to sustain what it takes to effect this desubjectification because she has become attached to the identity of the "sweet girl" under her mother's watchful eye. Producing the carefully controlled and culturally valorized posture of a ballerina requires hard drills and rigorous work, not to mention signing up for a whole lot of *class*. Nina's intensive self-formation through this process means she has a hard time acknowledging the aggressive and destabilizing force of her desire or finding an acceptable mode of expression for it. For sweet girls, sexual energy is disruptive and disgusting and violent and unseemly.

Showgirls' Nomi, by contrast, has no problem embodying the negativity of sexual aggression: it is how she has learned to fend for herself in a hostile world. From the first scene onward, we are struck by her body's explosive and ejaculatory expressivity; "she burns when she dances," "she's all pelvic thrust," "she prowls," "she's got heat," "she's got it." At first, these qualities are mistaken by James and other characters for raw sexual energy or "natural talent"—"she certainly didn't learn it" quips Marty, the assistant director of *Goddess*. But his boss, Tony Moss, offers a better appraisal of Nomi's talent: "She learned it alright, but it's not the sort of thing they teach in any class." In this moment, whatever work Nomi has done to form herself into an expressive subject is analytically distinguished from formal training, with its disciplinary structures and class associations. But *Showgirls* leaves open the possibility of appreciating other forms of learning. The self-stylization this involves is best encapsulated in Nomi's nails—a form of artistry involving careful attention that Nomi apparently has a knack for. In *Showgirls,* doing nails is depicted as a creative practice of self-shaping, while Nomi's capacity to finesse and singularize these key tools of the trade is recognized as a gift—one that might be shared with other workers in moments of potential solidarity and bonding. The elaborate artifice of nails in *Showgirls* stands in marked contrast with the nails of *Black Swan,* which emerge as self-mutilating figures of discipline turned inward that scar Nina's body. In later sequences they are also made to evoke a brutal and monstrous nature that threatens to protrude at any moment and for this reason must at all costs be hidden and covered over.

While Nomi's embodiment is not the outcome of classes, then, she is certainly engaged in her own redemptive project. She is desperate to shake off the abject associations of what she has learned on the street—she's not a stripper, she's a *dancer*—and she reacts explosively to any suggestion she is a hooker or a sex worker. Cristal tries to goad Nomi into identifying with such figures at numerous points throughout the film and almost gets there when the two connect over their shared enjoyment of doggy chow. Nomi's admission in this scene that she doesn't have the taste for "brown rice and vegetables" allows her to drop any class pretensions she might espouse in a moment of solidarity and bonding. But she beats a hasty retreat when Cristal admires her breasts and asks if Nomi likes nice tits too. "I like having nice tits," Nomi responds carefully. "How do you like having them?" Cristal snaps back. Nomi says she likes having them "in a nice dress"—revealing her attachment to prettifying sex—but adds that showing them off at Cheetah's made her feel like a hooker.

In the exchange that follows, Cristal unflinchingly assumes the identity of a whore in a pedagogical gesture that seems designed to bring the realities of the industry into focus. Nomi's refusal of this gesture is followed by an express disidentification with Cristal—"I'll never be like you!"—though subsequent events suggest that Cristal's claim of similitude is not exactly unfounded. Later in the film, Nomi's violent aversion to this proposed identity is given a backstory. We learn her real name is Polly and her criminal record reveals a background of petty crime and soliciting. In her persistent disavowal of the erotic economy of the industry and her adamant refusal of the whore as a crystallization of her identity, Nomi initially emerges as a figure of what Bersani calls "redemptive pastoralism." Indeed, on more than one occasion she is referred to as "Pollyanna" in the film—a name that suggests and reflects Nomi's investment in hegemonic optimism.[42]

Cristal's readiness to embrace the identity of the whore appears to offer certain strategic advantages: it gives her a realistic perspective on Vegas—its politics, the exploitative nature of its workplaces, its conditions of labor, and the possibilities they afford her. We learn that Cristal, lying in the hospital after Nomi pushes her down the stairs, has stayed hush on Nomi's perpetration of the assault on her. The reasons Cristal gives for this not only furnish further evidence to support Cristal's earlier assertion that she and Nomi are "exactly alike" ("How do you think I got my first lead?") but also demonstrate the payoffs of her realpolitik approach. She "needed a rest," she says—and besides, her lawyers got her "a real nice settlement." It turns out Cristal has hit the jackpot she deserves: she cashes out and quits while she is ahead—a judgment call that demonstrates her nous as a Vegas player.

As much as one might love Cristal for rejecting "redemptive pastoralism" and the benefits this affords her—embracing her abject identity in the industrial order—my point is not to vindicate any one way of inhabiting sexual identities or the position of the sex worker. I am just as interested in what might be learned when one attends to the shifting identifications that the Stardust's industrial triangle makes available to its female performers. Much of the dramatic intrigue and tension in *Showgirls,* and indeed in *Black Swan,* consists in these films' depiction of rivalry between women. The machinations of the various female characters and the counterpolitical potential of the bonds they form are treacherously patrolled and brought into line by the identities of the whore, the lesbian, and the diva/goddess (the successful recipient of collective adulation).

Whores and Lesbians

"In any erotic rivalry, the bond that links the two rivals is as intense and potent as the bond that links either of the rivals to the beloved," Eve Kosofsky Sedgwick famously argued in *Between Men.*[43] Sedgwick drew on the work of René Girard to support this claim but was critical of his failure to consider the ways in which "gender and sexuality were always pertinent to the calculus of power through which the erotic triangle functioned," as Robyn Wiegman has underlined more recently.[44] In the case of men, homosocial desire runs the risk of being derogated as homosexuality when its erotic intensity becomes too explicit. But in contemporary heterosexual economies, rivalry between women is governed by a different calculus since lesbianism, while discrediting, may be entertained to the extent that it can be framed as an erotic spectacle put on for men's benefit. In *Showgirls,* lesbianism sometimes also works as a way of redirecting the erotic energy of female rivalry into a form of alliance—a potential form of solidarity.

Subtending the identity of the lesbian, the figure of the whore serves as the principal means through which the gendered power relations of these heterosexual economies are reproduced and regulated. The whore *makes a career of* (or derives an income from) women's sexualized status within an economy that substantially relies on both women's unpaid labor and their sexualization.[45] Heterosexual economies could be said to stipulate the repeated, on-demand performance of self-surrender as a precondition of membership for women. By claiming the surplus value of gendered and sexualized labor for herself, the whore threatens to reveal the economic dimensions of heterosexuality and for this reason is ruthlessly degraded. Refusing to "lose sight of herself" except on her own terms, the whore comes in for some particularly intense scorn and punishment on this basis. This is achieved by assuming the right to adjudicate which performances of self-loss are authentic and which (like the whore's) are not genuine. In *Showgirls* and *Black Swan*, this figure of social abjection is deployed accordingly. Leaving aside for a moment the question of what might count as an effective feminist counterstrategy in this context, we can observe for the time being that the women who stand to benefit most from this (particularly mean and exploitative) system are those who play by the rules or learn to rehearse its conventions to get what they want while dodging the scouring rays of whore-attribution.

In the triangular economy of *Black Swan*, Nina is made to navigate the risks of becoming both a whore and a lesbian to realize her ambitions. The film presents this challenge as a trial of feminine performance but remains invested in the drama of authenticity that emerges from its equation of self-shattering with idealized performance. "Watch the way she moves," the director of ballet tells Nina as they watch her rival, Lily, dance, "she's not faking it"—and Nina takes his power of adjudication to heart. "Every time you dance I see you obsessed with getting each and every move perfectly right," he later tells her, "but I never see you lose yourself. Ever." But Nina is deeply disturbed by the uncontrollability of the force that she struggles to unleash to give an exemplary performance and become worthy of critical acclaim and what might happen to her identity in the process. Paradoxically, getting the lead role seems to demand from Nina a particularly selfish form of self-loss that she finds deeply disturbing and unbecoming of a ballerina, especially in its propensity to manifest as perversity, disconcerting self-abandonment, and destructiveness.

Nina is made to confront the perils of whore-attribution at several points in the film: once in an encounter with the embittered former principal dancer (played by Winona Ryder) and once in an unidentified attack we presume to have been perpetrated by a rival dancer, when she discovers the word WHORE smeared in lipstick on the mirror of her dressing room. In line with Sedgwick's argument about homosocial desire, Nina's passage to the top is routed through erotic fantasies about Lily, her principal rival, who exudes "black swan" but manifests as Nina her*self* in Nina's more paranoid, fantasized encounters with her. In one of these encounters, Lily pokes her head up from between Nina's post-coital legs, vampirically calls her a "sweet girl" (an appellation usually deployed by Nina's mother), and then proceeds to smother her with a pillow. It is as though the moment Nina drops her guard and gives in to her desire, her eroticized capitulation to homosocial desire comes up against the specter of the smothering mother. Nina's discomfort with her "lezzie wet dream" (as Lily later refers to it) and her apparent inability to "own" her queer feelings are cleverly dramatized when she convinces herself that the episode must have been the result of having had her drink spiked in an act of sabotage by Lily. We can recognize this claim as a defensive maneuver on Nina's part that desperately attempts to disown her desiring intentions: *we* know that Nina *knew* the drink was spiked but decided to drink it anyway. This episode can be read as an instance of what I have described elsewhere as "exceptional sex"—that is, sex that appeals to the purportedly disinhibiting effects of drugs to mobilize the structure of the exception.[46] Caught between intense desire and fear of its social consequences, the subject will try anything to avoid being identified as the author of their sexual actions.

The only way of escaping this bind in the world of *Black Swan* is for Nina to embrace her displaced desire, in all its destructiveness, in a phantasmatic battle with her rival self in which she staggers between assuming and vanquishing the figure of her rival, Lily, in front of a broken mirror. This culminates in her stabbing the "sweet girl" she once felt herself to be—or the monster she has become, it's unclear—and the wound, it turns out, is fatal. "It's my turn!" she declares triumphantly before realizing what she has done, and when she *does* realize she somehow manages to give the performance of a lifetime but dies in the process. What a situation to be in!

The rules of the game are similar in *Showgirls,* but the players adopt different strategies, less burdened by the demands of authenticity. When Tony, the self-described "all-knowing prick," asks Nomi to pinch her nipples to give the appearance of genuine arousal, Nomi rightly experiences it as the ultimate indignity. Cristal, for her part, seems genuinely turned on by Nomi, but who can say? Her attempts at seduction are almost always territorial and seem designed to make Nomi confront the sense in which her backstage tactics enact the discrediting identity of the whore. Nomi first assents to Cristal's overtures when Cristal offers to help her with her turns, only to have Cristal strip her top off and vindictively announce, "You see darling? You *are* a whore." Cristal appears to get her kicks from assuming a proprietorial relation over Nomi and pulls the strings accordingly. A question remains, though, about whether these overtures are merely a case of one-upmanship or whether they might not be considered pedagogical on the model of queer negativity.

Following another such humiliation (the boat scene), Nomi sets out to seduce Zack ("It's showtime!") and secures an audition to be Cristal's understudy. The seduction comes on the heels of a touching interlude in which Al and Mama from the Cheetah's club visit Nomi at the Stardust and Al remarks, "It must be weird not having anybody come on you." Moments later, Nomi is seducing Zack by telling him she "liked it when he came," producing an equivalence between Nomi's modus operandi at the Cheetah's club and her modus operandi at the Stardust. Does Nomi fake her orgasm in the pool scene with Zack that follows? We cannot know for sure.[47] But at least *Showgirls* has the decency to depict the expectation of female jouissance as something that is built into the infrastructure of Vegas *by design*, part of its obscene architecture, its gushing fountains surrounded by outstretched neon palms that make a glaringly artificial and thus fitting backdrop for Nomi's athleticism.

"It's Showtime!"

Following Wiegman, I have been reading the erotic triangles that motivate the drama in *Black Swan* and *Showgirls* as "a means of engaging the relational," of attending to the "various ways that identity can be disrupted, confirmed, congealed, doubted, rebuked, and celebrated."[48] By approaching identities as situational and uncrystallized, we can begin to explore the techniques through which women are made to "doubt the authority of [their] own self-definition as a woman."[49] This may give us a better analysis of power, how it is exercised in concrete situations, and how it is disrupted rather than the celebration of any one crystallized identity or position. I pursue this line of inquiry to explore the critical effectivity of different elaborations of self-shattering in these films and consider their implications for postfeminist self-production. Eve's triangles become all the more treacherous, I would suggest, when jouissance gets linked ontologically to sex (as it is in *Black Swan*) to constitute a measure of personal authenticity or critical efficacy. Why not take the performative infrastructure that constitutes the experience of the self *itself* as the mechanism and target of destructive shattering?

In *Showgirls,* real pleasure is to be found in this, I think: the look on Nomi's face, for instance, when she "kicks the shit out of" Andrew Carver as payback for the brutal rape of her friend Molly. In "watching [the director of *Goddess*] be a prick" she has developed a very precise sense of the enemy—the Stardust's capacity to *cover up* its exploitative violence, its whoring, its traffic in women—and she does not fail to hit her target. She carefully prepares for this scene, repurposing her tools of the trade to achieve her mission. Nomi has learned how to mime the conventions of desirable femininity to best direct her body's explosivity: "It's showtime," as she says in the setup of this sequence. But this is not simply a case of unleashing her brute or hidden inner nature: it involves a radical stylization of her body, as it is historically given, into a series of gestures with counterstrategic potential. Her nails, painted a deliberate black, find their logical extension in her switchblade, and she decorates her breasts with red lipstick so they can no longer be taken as the measure of authentic arousal but still entice her target. Unlike *Black Swan*'s Nina, who finds herself trapped in a man-made drama of authenticity she cannot survive, Nomi is now prepared to let herself go—it is just a matter of finding the most effective register for it (and, refreshingly, she doesn't have to kill herself in the process).

At the beginning of *Showgirls,* Nomi states she is not going to gamble; she is going to Vegas to *dance,* and she is going to win. Over the course of the film, she comes to accept that she has been gambling all along and that the line that separates dancers from whores is always poised ready to be drawn against her. When the situation comes to a head, she draws on the careful exercises in self-stylization she has engaged in throughout the film, but in the end she doesn't become a dancer, a whore, or even a goddess—though she manages to play each of these roles winningly. In her brave decision to stick up for a friend, she finally manages to get free of each of these selves and becomes something "improbable" in the process: a kickboxer.

Coda: The Joy of Mash-Ups

Soon after the release of Aronofsky's *Black Swan* in 2010, a mash-up appeared that spliced sound from *Black Swan* onto footage from *Showgirls* to create a hypertheatrical mock trailer.[50] The intense and apprehensive tones of *Black Swan*'s audio gave *Showgirls*' depiction of Vegas entertainers a seriously psychotic intensity. The mash-up had the further comic effect of launching *Showgirls*' socially and sexually degraded characters into the orbit of Aronofsky's reputedly much classier piece of dance-flickery.

Soon enough another mash-up appeared, this time setting *Black Swan*'s visuals to a high-energy soundtrack mixed with dialogue from *Showgirls*.[51] This second mash-up gave Aronofsky's film a brutal dressing down by pimping it out to a tacky Vegas soundscape. The hilarity and laughter these artifacts provoke consist in the proximity they create between two films and worlds of wildly different cultural status and critical standing. If the world of *Showgirls* is fit for dancers, as its protagonist Nomi defensively insists, the world of *Black Swan* might involve whoring and stripping—or so these mash-ups would suggest. "You and me, we're exactly alike," they propose, just as Cristal goads Nomi in *Showgirls*.

But where the second mash-up took aim at the high cultural pretensions of *Black Swan*, the original mash-up entertained the more tender possibility of treating *Showgirls* with the kind of respect, gravitas, and discernment usually reserved for art house and "Oscar-worthy" productions—an identity *Showgirls* never came close to attaining.

Jeffrey McHale, the creator of the original mash-up, went on to produce *You Don't Nomi* (2019)—a documentary made a full quarter century after *Showgirls*' release that explored the film's surprising ongoing popular-critical trajectory. "I think we're still talking about *Showgirls* because we're not done with it," the documentary suggests in its opening moments, framing *Showgirls* as something more than a passing fad or titillating spectacle. Indeed, *Showgirls* emerges here as nothing less than a dynamic event whose critical impacts and disconcerting affects keep on reverberating—a point that speaks, perhaps, to its ongoing shattering of modes of social ordering.

KANE RACE is Professor of Gender and Cultural Studies at the University of Sydney. He is author of *Pleasure Consuming Medicine: The Queer Politics of Drugs*; *The Gay Science: Intimate Experiments with the Problem of HIV*; and (with Gay Hawkins and Emily Potter) *Plastic Water: The Social and Material Life of Bottled Water.*

References

Aronofsky, Darren, dir. *Black Swan*. Fox Searchlight Pictures, 2010.

Baudrillard, Jean. *Seduction*. Translated by Brian Singer. New York: St. Martin's, 1990.

Berlant, Lauren, and Lee Edelman. *Sex, or the Unbearable*. Durham, NC: Duke University Press, 2013.

Bersani, Leo. *Homos*. Cambridge, MA: Harvard University Press, 1995.

———. "Is the Rectum a Grave?" *October* 43 (Winter 1987): 197–222.

Bunbury, Stephanie. "Venice's Red Carpet Fades but Movie Magic Shines Bright." *Sydney Morning Herald*, September 5, 2010. https://www.smh.com.au/entertainment/movies/venices-red-carpet-fades-but-movie-magic-shines-bright-20100904-14vds.html.

Deleuze, Gilles. "Dualism, Monism and Multiplicities (Desire-Pleasure-Jouissance)." *Contretemps: An Online Journal of Philosophy* 2 (2001): 92–108.

Edelman, Lee. *No Future: Queer Theory and the Death Drive*. Durham, NC: Duke University Press, 2004.

Edelstein, David. "Tortured Swans and Sugarplum Fairies." *New York Magazine*, November 24, 2010. https://nymag.com/movies/reviews/69780.

Foucault, Michel. *The History of Sexuality*. Vol. 1: *The Will to Knowledge*. Translated by Robert Hurley. London: Penguin, 1978.

———. *The History of Sexuality*. Vol. 2: *The Use of Pleasure*. Translated by Robert Hurley. London: Penguin, 1992.

———. "Sex, Power and the Politics of Identity." In *Ethics: Subjectivity and Truth*, edited by Paul Rabinow, 163–74. London: Penguin, 1997.

Gonzalez, Ed. "Review: *Black Swan*." *Slant*, November 23, 2010. https://www.slantmagazine.com/film/black-swan.

Gordon, Colin. "Governmental Rationality: An Introduction." In *The Foucault Effect: Studies in Governmentality*, edited by Graham Burchell, Colin Gordon, and Peter Miller, 1–52. Chicago: University of Chicago Press, 1991.

Griffin, Christine, Isabelle Szmigin, Andrew Bengry-Howell, Chris Hackley, and Willm Mistral. "Inhabiting the Contradictions: Hypersexual Femininity and the Culture of Intoxication among Young Women in the UK." *Feminism and Psychology* 23, no. 2 (2013): 184–206.

Halperin, David. *Saint Foucault: Towards a Gay Hagiography*. New York: Oxford University Press, 1995.

Hardie, Melissa Jane. "Loose Slots: Figuring the Strip in *Showgirls*." *Xtext* 1 (1996): 24–35.

Jagose, Annamarie. *Orgasmology*. Durham, NC: Duke University Press, 2013.

Kirkpatrick, Rob. "*Burlesque* and *Black Swan*: The *Showgirls* of Burlesque vs. the *Showgirls* of Ballet?" HuffPost, January 9, 2011. https://www.huffpost.com/entry/burlesque-and-black-swan_b_806378.

McHale, Jeffrey. "Showgirls | Black Swan Trailer Mashup." December 10, 2010. https://vimeo.com/17679018.

———, dir. *You Don't Nomi*. XYZ Films, Grade Five Films, 2019.

Niveux, Thana. "Swangirls (*Showgirls* vs *Black Swan*)." November 12, 2013. https://www.youtube.com/watch?v=GEJg69tXKtY.

Race, Kane. *Pleasure Consuming Medicine: The Queer Politics of Drugs*. Durham, NC: Duke University Press, 2009.

Rubin, Gayle. "The Traffic in Women: Notes on the 'Political Economy' of Sex." In *Toward an Anthropology of Women*, edited by Rayna Reiter, 157–210. New York: Monthly Review, 1975.

Sedgwick, Eve Kosofsky. *Between Men: English Literature and Male Homosocial Desire*. New York: Columbia University Press, 1985.

Shaviro, Steven. "Black Swan." The Pinocchio Theory, January 5, 2011. http://www.shaviro.com/Blog/?p=975.
Verhoeven, Paul, dir. *Showgirls*. Carolco Pictures, Chargeurs, United Artists, 1995.
Wiegman, Robyn. "Eve's Triangles, or Queer Studies beside Itself." *Differences* 26, no. 1 (2015): 48–73.

Notes

1. Leo Bersani, "Is the Rectum a Grave?" *October* 43 (1987): 197–222.
2. Ibid., 216.
3. Ibid., 217.
4. Ibid., 215.
5. Ibid.
6. Ibid., 222.
7. Ibid., 210.
8. Lee Edelman, *No Future: Queer Theory and the Death Drive* (Durham, NC: Duke University Press, 2004).
9. Bersani, "Is the Rectum a Grave?" 217.
10. Annamarie Jagose, *Orgasmology* (Durham, NC: Duke University Press, 2013), 1–9.
11. Michel Foucault, *The History of Sexuality*, Vol. 1: *The Will to Knowledge*, trans. Robert Hurley (London: Penguin, 1978), 71.
12. Gilles Deleuze, "Dualism, Monism and Multiplicities (Desire-Pleasure-Jouissance)," *Contretemps: An Online Journal of Philosophy* 2 (2001): 98.
13. Jean Baudrillard, *Seduction*, trans. Brian Singer (New York: St. Martin's, 1990), 22.
14. Foucault, *Will to Knowledge*, 157.
15. Ibid., 57–58.
16. Michel Foucault, *The History of Sexuality*, Vol. 2: *The Use of Pleasure*, trans. Robert Hurley (London: Penguin, 1992), 11, 8.
17. Ibid., 9.
18. Ibid., 8.
19. See Jagose, *Orgasmology*, 197.
20. Foucault, cited in David Halperin, *Saint Foucault: Towards a Gay Hagiography* (New York: Oxford University Press, 1995), 78; Michel Foucault, "Sex, Power and the Politics of Identity," in *Ethics: Subjectivity and Truth*, ed. Paul Rabinow (London: Penguin, 1997), 166.
21. Bersani, "Is the Rectum a Grave?" 222.
22. Ibid., 217.

23. Ibid., 216.

24. Colin Gordon, "Governmental Rationality: An Introduction," in *The Foucault Effect: Studies in Governmentality*, ed. Graham Burchell, Colin Gordon, and Peter Miller (Chicago: University of Chicago Press, 1991), 5.

25. See, for example, Leo Bersani, *Homos* (Cambridge, MA: Harvard University Press, 1995), 77–97.

26. Bersani, "Is the Rectum a Grave?" 216.

27. Ibid., 218.

28. Ibid., 222.

29. Ibid., 212. As Jagose remarks, "This image might now be regarded as one of queer theory's primal scenes." Jagose, *Orgasmology*, 12.

30. Bersani, "Is the Rectum a Grave?" 222.

31. Ibid.

32. Ibid., 212.

33. David Edelstein, "Tortured Swans and Sugarplum Fairies," *New York Magazine*, November 24, 2010, https://nymag.com/movies/reviews/69780.

34. Steven Shaviro, "Black Swan," The Pinocchio Theory, January 5, 2011, http://www.shaviro.com/Blog/?p=975.

35. Rob Kirkpatrick, "*Burlesque* and *Black Swan*: The *Showgirls* of Burlesque vs. the *Showgirls* of Ballet?" HuffPost, January 9, 2011, https://www.huffpost.com/entry/burlesque-and-black-swan_b_806378.

36. Ed Gonzalez, "Review: *Black Swan*," *Slant*, November 23, 2010, https://www.slantmagazine.com/film/black-swan.

37. Melissa Jane Hardie, "Loose Slots: Figuring the Strip in *Showgirls*," *Xtext* 1 (1996): 24–35.

38. Stephanie Bunbury, "Venice's Red Carpet Fades but Movie Magic Shines Bright," *Sydney Morning Herald*, September 5, 2010, https://www.smh.com.au/entertainment/movies/venices-red-carpet-fades-but-movie-magic-shines-bright-20100904-14vds.html.

39. Christine Griffin, Isabelle Szmigin, Andrew Bengry-Howell, Chris Hackley, and Willm Mistral, "Inhabiting the Contradictions: Hypersexual Femininity and the Culture of Intoxication among Young Women in the UK," *Feminism and Psychology* 23, no. 2 (2013): 187.

40. In both these films the dancers under their direction aptly refer to each of these characters as a "prick." When Tony Moss asks the auditioning dancers what they are doing there, for example, Nomi cuts to the point defiantly and retorts she is *watching him be a prick*.

41. Foucault, *Use of Pleasure*, 8.

42. Here I mean to reference the debates in queer theory around the political value of negativity and optimism. See Edelman, *No Future*; Lauren Berlant and Lee Edelman, *Sex, or the Unbearable* (Durham, NC: Duke University Press, 2013).

43. Eve Kosofsky Sedgwick, *Between Men: English Literature and Male Homosocial Desire* (New York: Columbia University Press, 1985), 21.

44. Robyn Wiegman, "Eve's Triangles, or Queer Studies beside Itself," *Differences* 26, no. 1 (2015): 59.

45. See Gayle Rubin's classic essay, "The Traffic in Women: Notes on the 'Political Economy' of Sex," in *Toward an Anthropology of Women*, ed. Rayna R. Reiter (New York: Monthly Review, 1975), 157–210.

46. Kane Race, *Pleasure Consuming Medicine: The Queer Politics of Drugs* (Durham, NC: Duke University Press, 2009), 164–79.

47. Here I have in mind Annamarie Jagose's Foucauldian conception of fake orgasm as an "inventive bodily technique that differently addresses itself to the regulatory apparatus of sexuality." Jagose, *Orgasmology*, 195.

48. Wiegman, "Eve's Triangles," 62.

49. Sedgwick, quoted in Wiegman, "Eve's Triangles," 61.

50. Jeffrey McHale, "Showgirls Black Swan Trailer Mashup," December 10, 2010, https://vimeo.com/17679018.

51. Thana Niveux, "Swangirls (*Showgirls* vs *Black Swan*)," November 12, 2013, https://www.youtube.com/watch?v=GEJg69tXKtY.

3 "AIN'T ANYONE EVER BEEN NICE TO YOU?"

DISCHARGING THE ~~GUILTY~~ PLEASURE OF SHOWGIRLS

KIERYN MCKAY

Paul Verhoeven's *Showgirls* (1995) is a film whose reputation tends to precede it. Famously decried on its release as the worst film of an already lackluster year, *Showgirls* was quickly reread and revived as a camp extravaganza. In certain circles, the film is now reified as a prime example of the camp cult object, backed by decades of viewers "reading against the grain."[1] Since the film's camp reception has led (as it often does) to the eventual recuperation of the film's heavy financial loss at the box office, the film's production studio and distributors (MGM/United Artists, hereafter "the studio") are often framed as the lucky beneficiaries of a chance cultural and commercial windfall.

Much has been made of the film's camp reclamation, which is often cast in redemptive terms: *Showgirls* was declared dead on arrival at cinematic release, camp gifted its afterlife. Subsequently endorsed by alternative tastemaker John Waters as "great trash forever" and still a feature midnight movie across the United States, *Showgirls*' status as a cult camp film seems assured.[2] Such is the force of its camp revival that a quarter century after its release, *Showgirls* is reemerging in the mainstream, with critics increasingly citing the film on ever-proliferating lists of "guilty pleasures." But if *Showgirls* camp is so redeeming, then why do these critics feel so guilty?

A closer review of *Showgirls*' reception history unearths a curious discovery: first by accident and then on purpose, the studio engineered both the film's critical demise and its recuperation by the secondary market. Seen through this lens, it is the studio and not the film's camp reader that emerges as the custodian of the film's lasting cultural and economic capital, such that today's camp audiences are reading less *against* and more *with* the grain of the studio's promotional strategies—a view that deflates at least some of the film's countercultural power. It also goes some way toward explaining why, when *Showgirls* has been a camp hit for decades longer than it was a flop, the film remains a site of acute cultural contestation.

Campaign One: How Hot Is *Showgirls*?

On its release in 1995, *Showgirls* was a critical failure of legendary scale. Dubbed "everything you feared it might be and less" and "one of the worst movies in Hollywood history," *Showgirls* received near-unanimous critical condemnation.[3] For many commentators, the film's critical failure was a fait accompli: "Make an extreme movie and get an extreme response."[4] But the film's initial negative reception was to a significant extent influenced by the spectacular misjudgment of its prerelease promotional campaign.

Launching its promotion for the highest-budget, widest-release NC-17 film in Hollywood history just months after presidential candidate Bob Dole renewed public debate around the "mainstreaming of deviancy" by entertainment products that feature "mindless violence and loveless sex," the studio chose perhaps the obvious path: to flaunt, rather than apologize for, its explicit rating.[5] Eager to build anticipation, the studio aired its first teaser trailer (of several) months ahead of *Showgirls*' cinematic launch. The teaser opens to black and a synthesized, accelerated beat, overlaid with heavy breathing and amorous (female) moans. Text flashes and slides across the screen:

3.1 Still from *Showgirls* teaser trailer, 1995.

How Far / (MONEY) / Would You Go / (BODY) / For Your Dreams? (SOUL)

A succession of three still images breaks the otherwise uniformly black background, simulating motion (fig. 3.1). Elizabeth Berkley, dressed in black lingerie and shrouded in shadow, starts in a crouched position, gliding her tongue progressively upward, tracing the shaft of a silver dance pole:

From the writer of / From the director of / *Basic Instinct* /
Comes a motion picture event
SO EROTIC /
SO DANGEROUS /

SO CONTROVERSIAL /
That we can't show you a thing.
(FANTASIZE)
(INDULGE)
(SURRENDER)
Not even the title.[6]

A purposefully rough cut that plays on the allure of the unseen and unedited, the teaser locates this film's star as the focal point of a cinematic seduction in the making. Patently pitched to heterosexual male audiences, this and the studio's subsequent teasers proceed as a striptease. The second reveals one more item: "Except the title / *Showgirls*."[7] The third issues an extra promise: "The hottest film of the year / or any year." Released in both green-band (censored) and red-band (explicit) versions, the film's official trailer sets up *Showgirls* as the natural extension of Paul Verhoeven and Joe Eszterhas's wildly successful erotic thriller *Basic Instinct*: "Last time they took you to the edge. This time they're taking you all the way."[8]

The extended publicity pitch promised risqué, raw sexuality, and it penetrated far and wide. Times Square and Sunset Strip billboards laid out Berkley in a provocative horizontal, an adaptation of Tono Stano's "Sense" that became the signature artwork of the studio's campaign series (fig. 3.2).[9] The billboards and their small-scale duplicates (mostly printed in newspaper sports sections) debuted the campaign's most resonant tagline, a proposition to prospective audiences that recalls the teaser's final instructional statement (SURRENDER): "Leave your inhibitions at the door."[10] Berkley herself was put to work as interviews, features, and flirtatious, sometimes explicit multipage spreads appeared in *Playboy, Detour,* and *Esquire,* honing in on their target audience.

3.2 *Showgirls* billboard in the Times Square area, September 1995. © Bedrich Grunzweig Photo Archive (GrunzweigPhoto.com).

As the film's premiere neared, the campaign gathered momentum. In early September, three weeks ahead of cinematic release, the studio partnered with web developer rVision to pioneer an interactive *Showgirls* website, directly linked to *Playboy Web,* comprising mainly nude stills of Berkley and her female screen mates. According to rVision's president, the site excited the "prurient interest" of more than 150,000 users and clocked one million hits per day (exceedingly high traffic for its era).[11] A week prior to launch, around three million households sampled the studio's final teaser—a free-to-rent eight-minute "advance sneak preview" boasting "6 minutes of the most erotic footage you'll ever see" (and two, presumably, less so).[12] In the last days before release, another three million viewers watched Berkley get physical on the *Late Show with David Letterman*, taunting the host in the "basic position" of a lap dance as a handsy Letterman hammed up his arousal to a catcalling live audience.[13]

This network of paratexts—teasers, trailers, billboards, news advertisements, magazine features, websites, television appearances—bears influence on our eventual encounter with the feature film. In a commercial sense they are, of course, geared to motivate that encounter. As Gérard Genette describes of paratexts more generally, "They surround [the text] and extend it, precisely in order to *present* it, in the usual sense of this verb but also in the strongest sense: to *make present*, to ensure the text's presence in the world, its 'reception' and consumption."[14] But, as Genette also theorizes, paratextual encounters are not cleanly divisible from textual ones. Rather, they are interstitial artifacts "without any hard and fast boundary on either the inward side (turned toward the text) or the outward side (turned toward the world's discourse about the text)."[15] In this sense, the studio's promotional paratexts are not merely adjuncts to the film experience but rather form part of a cinematic articulation; they don't just prefigure but also "begin" the textual experience. As Jonathan Gray renders, "They tell us what to expect, direct our excitement and/or apprehension, and begin to tell us what a text is all about, calling for our identification with and interpretation of that text before we have even seemingly arrived at it."[16]

As *Newsweek* reflected at the time, *Showgirls* arrived "with heavy promotional foreplay and two burning questions: how hot is it and how bad is it?"[17] The first of these questions (how "hot" is *Showgirls*?) was promptly taken up by the critics: the film was *too* sexy—"a sleaze-fest," "shameless," and a "dirty-old-man fantasy"—or, indefensibly, not sexy enough—a "big tease."[18] If critics were ambivalent about the precise nature of *Showgirls'* impotence, they were unanimous on one assessment: hot or not? Not. Read through the studio's hypersexualized campaign, *Showgirls* was seen by conventional standards of taste, style, and quality to transgress the normative codes of respectability. The film was dismissed as a mélange of empty signifiers, with Berkley (the focus of the campaign's undelivered promises) chief among them. Savaged with perverse, often misogynistic attacks, Berkley was frequently cited for a failure to animate her designated role as an object of sexual display: Janet Maslin of the *New York Times* remarked on Berkley's "open-mouthed, vacant-eyed look of an inflatable party doll"; Rita Kempley of the *Washington Post* compared her "minimal acting talents" to "the bimbo she plays"; and Sean P. Means of the *Salt Lake Tribune* observed, "Berkley . . . couldn't act her way out of a wet paper bag. She knows how to wear lingerie and how to take it off, but that's all."[19]

Would-be cinemagoing audiences took heed of the damning critical response, and lackluster box office takings saw a significant early financial loss.[20] In a final effort to salvage the film's credibility, screenwriter Eszterhas went rogue, remonstrating via a full-page plea in *Daily Variety* against MGM's "misguided, fast-buck advertising." [21] Eszterhas asseverated the film's moral virtues, urging prospective audiences, especially women and teenagers, to view the film. But Eszterhas had little impact, and within four months of *Showgirls'* release director Verhoeven diagnosed "a perception problem." "The trouble was," he reflected, "audiences went looking for thrills and emerged unaroused. . . . That made them hate the film."[22] And hate it they did.

Entry to the VHS Market: A Spontaneous Second Wave

Despite having shaped their own failure with an off-the-mark prelaunch publicity campaign, the studio barely adjusted course on entry to the video rental market. Its prerelease video screener (geared at persuading retailers to stock the film) refused to cede its straight male target audience, pledging "a national pre-street television campaign . . . with key buys at the times men watch television the most."[23] Stano's stylized billboard imagery continued to dominate in-store promos, posters, and collateral, with the teaser trailer's inflammatory three-word descriptors artfully sublimated for all-ages aisle-browsing consumers: "EROTIC" withers to the more benign "SENSUAL" and "DANGEROUS" de-escalates to the plainly descriptive yet readily suggestive "AVAILABLE," while the mild but prophetic "CONTROVERSIAL" is truthfully retained.[24] The campaign's original tagline ("Leave your inhibitions at the door") disappeared in quiet capitulation, but without any meaningful transfiguration of messaging.

Nevertheless, *Showgirls* quickly surfaced in the top twenty VHS rentals, and it nestled there for several months as sporadic, often bewildered news reports confirmed an unpredicted emerging audience. The *New York Times* documented a Manhattan nightclub director regularly "getting drunk and watching *Showgirls*" with friends in a Hell's Kitchen apartment.[25] *Entertainment Weekly* reported the film had headlined Betty Buckley's *Sunset Boulevard* cast party, where "everyone yelled at the screen. . . . Screaming the lines, doing the routines with the girls"—a response that became, according to Buckley, rapidly entrenched: "Since then we've all imitated the choreography *ad nauseam*."[26] Naomi Klein, then writing for the *Toronto Star*, recounted a more widespread phenomenon: "Trendy twenty-somethings are throwing *Showgirls* irony parties, laughing sardonically at the implausibly poor screenplay and shrieking with horror at the aerobic sexual encounters."[27]

Emboldened by the privacy of the home video environment, these informal *Showgirls* viewing parties are akin to Doreen Massey's "constellations of temporary coherence," spaces that, though marginal and transitory, nonetheless produce meaning through interaction.[28] Here, endorsing *Showgirls* as high camp delivered ritualistic possibilities for collective celebration and a joyous revelry in the film's aesthetic excesses, contesting the critics' deflated response. In sharing a fondness for *Showgirls,* these new enthusiasts repossessed the marginal artifact, refashioning it into something personal and aesthetic, remaking *Showgirls* as "the 'in' taste of a minority elite."[29]

The theatricality of *Showgirls* is ripe for this kind of participatory play. It has a tantalizingly chintzy script that solicits citation.[30] It is full of spectacle, melodrama, and excess. Its setting is Las Vegas, the most excessive of American cities. *Showgirls* is a veritable "cinema of attractions" that has, to call on Susan Sontag's key camp ingredient, "the spirit of extravagance."[31]

Sontag's contentious but highly influential 1964 essay "Notes on 'Camp'" offers various access points for understanding the camp qualities of *Showgirls.* She writes, "Camp sees everything in quotation marks. It's not a lamp, but a 'lamp'; not a woman, but a 'woman.' To perceive Camp in objects and persons is to understand Being-as-Playing-a-Role."[32] For *Showgirls,* Sontag's duplicitous quotation marks might be repurposed as (among others) "fries" not fries; "tits" not tits; and "dance" not dance—each a site of humor and a synecdoche for the film's larger thematic interests around the female body, its curation, its dexterities, and its commodification by the male gaze. "Being-as-Playing-a-Role" also synopsizes various textual and extratextual elements of *Showgirls.* Las Vegas: "being-as-playing-a-role" urbanized. Berkley's swift maturation from teenage sitcom star to serious cinema actress by way of an overtly sexualized starring role (a familiar trajectory): "being-as-playing-a-role" personified. Nomi's insistence on the distinction between dancer and hooker: "being-as-playing-a-role" idealized.

The "self-conscious flamboyance" with which *Showgirls* approaches its thematic interests is typified by Berkley's Nomi, for whom "being-as-playing-a-role" is also an apt description.[33] Nomi is self-possessed and determined, and Berkley plays her histrionic, such that her sporadic gestural excess, often reactive to or through "fries," "tits," and "dance," marks her erratic and unpredictable. She is also changeable—variously deliberate, obdurate, fierce, then artless, tender, and wounded to the extremes, not infrequently in a single scene.[34] Her vacillations are embellished by Berkley's full-tilt performance, which is marked against the steady dependability of Gina Ravera's Molly, the straight dramatic stylings of Kyle MacLachlan's Zack, and the steely-eyed consistency of Gina Gershon's wry and sensual Cristal. Nomi's volatility and Berkley's exaggerated performance style intensified critics' hostility toward the film's star, but they also render the inherent performativity of the ambitious female in an exploitative patriarchal economy. Through this lens, Berkley's rendition might emerge as "the proper mixture of the exaggerated, the fantastic, the passionate and the naïve," a representation that works to undermine the "presumed naturalness" of Nomi's positional femininity.[35]

Locking onto the film's hyperbolic aesthetic, *Showgirls'* fringe audience championed the film and Berkley along with it, reappraising it and her by "a different—a supplementary—set of standards" that privileges artifice and spectacle.[36] As the Manhattan-based party host playfully reimagined, "Rather than thinking Elizabeth Berkley is a horrendous actress, we think . . . everyone was acting out the film as a drag queen."[37] Betty Buckley projected the excesses of the text onto the film's producers: “The movie’s so over the top I thought the filmmakers had to know what they were doing. Finally, I concluded it was drug damage and they had no idea.”[38] Here, drag and drugs provide the necessary distantiation to activate a camp sensibility, but it is Buckley’s comment “they had no idea” that submits *Showgirls* to Sontag’s “pure” or “naïve” camp, a film of failed serious intent.[39] Her statement, though one among many, was thought to typify this second wave’s counterposition to the mass critical response, reclaiming *Showgirls* by way of celebratory reversal: *Showgirls* is so bad, it’s good.

Campaign Two: How Bad Is *Showgirls*?

Of course, camp is not a fixed or singular category, and the film offers up a wider variety of sustained camp attachments than that described by Buckley or attributed by the narrow application of Sontag’s theories here. But Buckley’s attendant ironic subjectivity has come to define accounts of *Showgirls*’ second-wave reception, eliding other camp apprehensions of the film.[40] One reason is that hers was among the first documented recastings of the film’s value; another is that *Showgirls*’ release dovetailed with deepening paracinematic appreciations among broader alternative film audiences. Published in the same year as *Showgirls*’ release, Jeffrey Sconce’s seminal article “‘Trashing’ the Academy” describes paracinema as an emerging “reading protocol,” distinct from camp, but with which camp—especially naive camp—has much in common. As “a counter-aesthetic turned subcultural sensibility devoted to all manner of cultural detritus,” the primary paracinematic reflex to “valorize all forms of cinematic ‘trash’” neatly aligns with the ironic subject position signaled by Buckley and others.[41] Klein’s early reporting immediately diagnosed the consumptive practices of *Showgirls*’ new audiences as symptomatic of this broader cultural trend, complaining,

“Everybody knows that kids these days have a way of taking something lousy and tacky . . . and making it ironic and cool.”[42] Apparently, the studio was both prepared and equipped to exploit this development in the secondary market.

The studio recognized early the opportunity to reshape their message in line with the film’s emerging audience and seized it quickly. Within a month, they relaunched *Showgirls* as a high camp midnight movie at both Village East in New York and Laemmle Sunset 5 in West Los Angeles—both specialist independent film theaters, the selection of which anticipated, off the back of Buckley and her younger counterparts, a cinephilic “knowing” audience. Openings were custom-made for the kind of participatory viewing prefigured by Buckley’s fete but realized so far only at private screenings and home theater dress-up events. Putting the most readily identifiable agents of camp to work, the studio hired sequined drag performers to distribute interactive scripts, complete with dialogue prompts and other staging instructions for viewer involvement in the film’s most outlandish and unexpected moments.[43]

With the rerelease of the film came revamped promotional material, saturated with camp stylistics. Maintaining the general format of the original but shifting Berkley upright and cloaking her in nostalgic leopard print, the studio’s redesigned publicity poster structured the midnight screening as an aesthetic event.[44] Into this context, the poster masterfully co-opts the film’s dissenting reviewers into a revisionist discourse around the film.

Published on September 22, 1995 (the date of *Showgirls*’ cinematic release), Janet Maslin’s original *New York Times* review neither sincerely prophesizes *Showgirls* as “an instant camp classic!” nor celebrates the adoption of a camp sensibility. Indeed, in her review we find none of the enthusiasm forged by the poster’s intruding exclamation point. Instead,

Maslin's review is a lament. Her full sentence reads: "Unfortunately, the strain of trying to make America's dirtiest big-studio movie has led Mr. Verhoeven and Mr. Eszterhas to create an instant camp classic." Not two sentences later, Maslin delivers her oft-quoted condemnation: "The absence of both drama and eroticism turns *Showgirls* into a bare-butted bore." For Maslin, "camp" is shorthand for "failure."[45]

Bereft of irony and far from animated (as signified by his appended exclamation "It is 'All About Eve' in a G-String!"), Sean P. Means's *Salt Lake Tribune* article declares in its title that *Showgirls* is a "No-Pulse Peep Show." For Means, the film is "clumsy," "idiotic," and "shallow," its *All about Eve* storyline "sketchy," and Nomi's ambitious trajectory "excruciating." The film displays its G-stringed flesh "with as much imagination and appeal as the meat at a deli counter."[46]

While Gary Thompson does predict the eventual coming of a subcultural audience, the ellipsis that collapses his "Cult trash . . . on a spectacular scale!" renders invisible the damning nature of his expanded forecast: "*Showgirls* will be remembered as one of the most expensively indulgent horrible movies ever made—cult trash certain to be treasured by connoisseurs of bad dialogue, lousy performances and crap on a spectacular scale."[47] Here, MGM's preservation of "cult" and "trash" but omission of "crap" in the contracted "quote" deliberately plays on the specificities of subcultural capital. Trash is redeemed by cult; crap may be irredeemable. Keeping just enough key words to make logical sense and repurposing the "right" words to interpellate the "right" audience, the poster performs a kind of mercenary *détournement*, a capitalist spin that appropriates subcultural rereading practices for its own ends.

Affixed to the end of every extracted quote, the forged exclamation marks recast the original dissenting texts as hyperbolic revelries. The exclamatory appendages also figure a collective camp subjectivity; they are affixed as virtual graphemes for the squeals of Buckley's Planet

Hollywood guests and the glee-filled shrieks of Klein's "trendy twenty-somethings." The exclamations activate a reversal and take their place as appurtenances of the camp sensibility. The studio, the maker of the marks, is now in on the joke.

These strategic interventions both cannibalize *Showgirls'* camp enthusiasm and contain the critics' damning reviews, actively intervening in the film's rereading to shape it toward commercial ends. The revisionist discourse is a paracinematic maneuver, its multiplying campish allusions ("trash," "kitsch," "sleaze," "tackiness") working to amplify an "aesthetic of vocal confrontation" that elevates *Showgirls* to the status of "counter-cinema," which the cinemasochistic midnight movie market is ready-made to consume.[48] The revamp met its purpose, drawing disparate onlookers into cinemas and back again, quickly forming a collectivized "taste public" of unified perspective. Said one New York University student (of several spotted) at a midnight screening, "It represents everything that's terrible in the world of film, and we love it."[49] And another: "I have never seen a movie this poorly written or directed in my entire life, and it's just a riot to watch. Movies like this shouldn't even be out, but it's just hilarious."[50] Paul Verhoeven, for his part, reluctantly conceded: "Maybe this kind of ritualistic cult popularity isn't what I intended, but it's like a resurrection after the crucifixion."[51]

Soon after its first round of successful midnight screenings, the studio released a second and more confident iteration of its camp marketing campaign. This revised poster exchanges "girls" for the campier "babes," brags of its "unprecedented" Razzie Award wins, and retains the bastardized critical reviews. But it also appropriates public statements made by the film's makers, with Eszterhas's earnest plea to *Showgirls'* scandalized first wave audience ("morality tale") and Verhoeven's eventual concession to its second ("resurrection") drafted into the studio's calculated camp rebranding. This assertive ploy avows *Showgirls'* artless camp naivete while securing the studio's place as a "knowing" participant in the mockery of its own product. Its annexation of the camp revival is well underway: the studio is now an affirmed insider, a cognoscente; the film and its players are the joke's "bare butt."

Campaign Three: Prepackaged Cult Experience

In the intervening years since the studio relaunched *Showgirls* into midnight screenings, it has continued to mold and commodify *Showgirls*' paracinematic status. The limited edition 2004 DVD box set makes a direct appeal to the commodity-completist tendencies of the cultist and embeds insider credibility in its title: *Showgirls: V.I.P. Edition*. Purpose-built for interactivity (party games, playing cards, shot glasses, trivia quiz, lap dance tutorial), the set transports the midnight mass experience back to the private setting where it began with Buckley and her compatriot "trendy twenty-somethings," this time prepackaged as a cult experience.

Rather than a director's commentary, expected fare for cult merchandizing of this type, the box set features a satirical audio commentary by David Schmader, a key player in the studio's third campaign. Schmader, a playwright and then columnist for Seattle's alt-newsweekly the *Stranger*, gained minor celebrity touring live annotated *Showgirls* screenings from 1999. With the *V.I.P. Edition*, he is installed as *the* authorized fan. He is all too happy to maintain the party line: "The best I've ever been able to think about it is that *Showgirls* triumphs in that every single person involved in the making of the film . . . is making the worst possible decision at every possible time, and it's this incredible density of failure that makes *Showgirls* sublime."[52]

By extolling the negative pleasures of *Showgirls*, first live and now on record, Schmader seeks to distinguish himself from the usual mechanisms that circumscribe the parameters of "good taste." At live performances, he is a tour guide for trash. Hidden among the audience with a microphone and remote control, Schmader literally stages a so-bad-it's-good reversal: rolling out commentary, signposting kitsch landmarks, rewinding occasionally to revisit a particularly satisfying line of dialogue, skipping past the film's infamous rape scene.[53] In interviews, he positions himself as a knowing preacher. His prime target is not the *Showgirls* faithful but its skeptic—"someone who is too snooty to [have seen] *Showgirls* [before]."[54] His is an "ironic form of reverse elitism," a subcultural superiority satiated by the conquest of bringing new believers into the fold.[55] His task is to proselytize, to convert the uninitiated to the cause. He expects little resistance.

As his "snooty" verdict on the virgin viewer suggests, Schmader is aware of the sociocultural position he occupies. His recurrent fan chronotope (trotted out in various interviews, in Jeffrey McHale's recent film, on his personal website, and elsewhere) is almost obsessively authenticating: that he was a latecomer to *Showgirls* who first avoided the film on the presumption it was "misogynistic crap" yet intuited its *badfilm* diversions on first viewing dissociates him from the film's earliest receptions and exceptionalizes his own reading. His supposition that "maybe this . . . hit my g-spot and not everyone's" and surprise that "other people saw what I saw" disavow knowledge of the studio's strategic second campaign and antecedent audiences; his recounted anticipation of a "cease and desist" instruction (rather than an invitation) from the studio positions himself counter to its commercial interests.[56] These kinds of attestations to singular legitimacy are a familiar gambit among fans of cult films, and Schmader deploys them here to distract from his patent complicity in the studio's commercial enterprise. Despite Schmader's posturing, it is his willful evangelism that the studio procures and he freely supplies. By lending his ministry to the *V.I.P. Edition* (and all reissues thereafter), Schmader furnishes the most enduring mechanism for the studio's commodification of *Showgirls* camp. The drag queens who hawked *Showgirls'* camp cachet at midnight screenings were contracted to the studio on hire, Schmader now permanently sermonizes on its behalf.

Showgirls Camp, Boxed In and Boxed Up

When Buckley and her compatriots, having been instructed otherwise, ascribed a camp sensibility to the text, they undertook what Andrew Ross calls the "(hard) *work* of a producer of taste," and Matthew Tinkcom designates the "work-as-play" of camp expression.[57] Valuing *Showgirls* (and not for its nudity) constituted an act of sociocultural resistance to a uniform bloc—an alliance formed by the studio's earliest promotional paratexts, the film's critic detractors, and would(n't)-be audiences who abandoned the film at critics' advice. Since, as Ross continues, "'taste' is only possible through exclusion *and* depreciation," camp pleasure is generated at least in part by that resistance, by its affective differentiation from the mainstream.[58] In this sense, the camp affect relies for its expression on the culture that oppresses it. As Barbara Klinger narrates, "Camp represents a gleeful alternative to repressive cultural canons circumscribed by respectability, a way in which certain individuals can 'drop out' of society and flex their aesthetic muscles in unconventional ways."[59] But a camp sensibility is tied to its parent culture at a deeper root, as Pamela Robertson further explains: "Rather than an avant-garde oppositional stance, camp represents a subculture's negotiated means of access to the dominant culture; it operates as much by taking alternative pleasures in mass-cultural objects as it does by creating its own objects. In this sense, it registers a subculture's recognition of failed access to and not simply refusal of the cultural industry."[60]

Always already positioned by and subject to its dominant culture, camp reading as a brokering of subcultural identity offers its subjects limited vitality. Adopting an expressly ironic stance toward *Showgirls* only submits it to the same conditions since, as Robertson (drawing on Linda Hutcheon) asserts, "As a form of ironic representation and reading, camp . . . 'is doubly coded in political terms; it both legitimates and subverts that which it parodies.'"[61] Hence, for all their revelry, *Showgirls'* constellating second-wavers could only ever go so far to "rescue" the text.

In another way, an ironic camp subjectivity narrows the relational degrees of freedom within the textual field. As Melissa Hardie cautioned in the very first academic treatment of *Showgirls*, to "subscribe to a reading of the text as bad, impos[es] another form of aesthetic segregation, one which can only open the question of the relationship between this text, a camp reader, and a lesbian camp aesthetic."[62] While this "aesthetic segregation" is part of the subcultural allure of camp, since it supports notions of exclusivity and "insider" prestige, it has real consequences for the interpretive possibilities of the text, especially where the studio's publicity campaigns appropriate these insider significations for its own ends.

By the time Schmader is formalized as a *Showgirls* V.I.P., the text is held captive within a logic of ironic camp discernment, a logic that still services the originating context that condemned it. The so-bad-it's-good reversal staged by Schmader (and his remote control) and enacted by the studio's earlier recasting of damning reviews as celebratory exclamations *compel* an ironic appreciation for the film. Far from liberating the text from its original critics, these paratexts foreclose on it, delimiting its relational field and confining it to the politics of taste. *Showgirls* is bad, and it's so bad it's good; pleasure is available, but *only* with tongue in cheek. (Recall Waters on *Showgirls*: "great trash forever.")

Foreclosure on the text is, of course, the driving purpose of the studio's strategy of containment for profit. By integrating Schmader's commentary into its cultish repackaging of *Showgirls*, especially at the expense of Verhoeven's voice, it narrows the potential readings to create a readily digestible product. With the release of the *V.I.P. Edition*, *Showgirls* camp is, finally, boxed in and boxed up.

Worrying about Camp

The studio's exploitation of camp's use value in the formation of subcultural counterpublics is a leading cause of its success in recouping its early financial loss at the box office, a capital accumulation made possible only by expanding its field of camp subjects. In this the studio establishes itself, and not the film's camp reader, as the custodian of *Showgirls*' lasting subcultural and economic capital. Published in 2003, roughly simultaneous to the release of *Showgirls: V.I.P. Edition*, Ara Osterweil takes the marketization of camp as her subject in *Film Quarterly*'s "*Showgirls* Round Table."

In her brief introduction, Round Table editor Ann Martin expresses hope that lending voice to some of *Showgirls*' "secret and not-so-secret devotees" might support *Showgirls* to "stand a chance" of revaluation.[63] Osterweil's contribution, "A Fan's Notes on Camp, or How to Stop Worrying and Learn to Love *Showgirls*," is a playful recounting of her tussle to "make Stardust-worshipping converts out of [her] students" who "found it utterly loathsome that *Showgirls* was on the [Trash Cinema] syllabus," believing on spec that "*Showgirls* somehow didn't 'deserve' the subversive status [she] was attempting to bestow upon it."[64] Yet the article betrays its title's stated intent. Despite her declared *un*fannish detachment (her first infidelity), Osterweil assures she is "prepared to defend it as a misunderstood camp extravaganza" and goes on, to some extent, to do so. But Osterweil's efforts are hampered by her own "intrinsic ambivalence" and a series of curious readings of the film: it promises but fails to generate pathos within its melodrama; it promises but fails to generate genuine excitement from its "soft-core" bodily spectacles; as a *badfilm* specialist, she finds it more complex than she is used to; its tone "connotes a type of mainstream directness and sincerity" rather than (as she would prefer) "an already marginalized audience of underground artists and homosexuals."[65] Osterweil takes each of these assessments as prima facie evidence of *Showgirls*' failure to satisfy as a camp object, hence her incapacity to "stop worrying" that it is one.

Leaving aside our own appraisals of Osterweil's readings that produce her frustrations with the text (several of which are contested in this volume), Osterweil's main discomfort arises from a generalized suspicion that *Showgirls* portends a tipping point in the mass popularization of camp: "If every blockbuster teen horror film, sitcom, and advertising campaign threatens to steal the signs of 'being-as-playing-a-role' from the community of outcasts who first exalted it, then the political significance of camp begins to recede. The anxiety *Showgirls* created, and continues to create, among leftist intellectuals stems from the fear that camp, like everything else remotely subversive, is in danger of being co-opted by 'the Man.'"[66]

Though she does not specify, we can assume that if Osterweil were conscious of the studio's camp-commodifying strategy (still progressing as she writes), she might take particular issue with its treatment of *Showgirls*. She may also resist the rarefied progenitors of *Showgirls* camp—a Manhattan club director, "trendy" youth, and a Broadway star.

As Osterweil figures it, camp is at a precipice, perched at a precarious ledge and at risk of being thrust into commercialized oblivion. (Re)signifying *Showgirls* as camp threatens to depoliticize, refamiliarize, and otherwise dilute the assertive subcultural capital that camp produces in more marginal circumstances. But Osterweil's counsel is rather late to the game. It is an old script about the mainstreaming of trash aesthetics—rehearsed since the "big bang" of Andy Warhol, Susan Sontag, and Robert Venturi "outed" and "heterosexualized" camp for the masses in the 1960s and 1970s—that extends Sconce's familiar profile of a paracinematic audience to its natural conclusion, presenting not only "a dispute over *how* to approach the cinema as much as a conflict over *what* cinema to approach" but also a contest over *who* gets to make those determinations.[67] Osterweil's sentiments echo Paul Rudnick and Kurt Andersen's moniker "Camp Lite" twenty years prior, used to describe an emerging "irony epidemic" diagnosed by the authors in *Spy* magazine in the early 1980s. The epithet "Camp Lite" itself implies a dilution of substance or seriousness, and the authors further cautioned: "When a minority form is coopted, there is always a loss of dynamic, of nuance. Camp Lite at its mass-marketed worst . . . has no edge, no gilded layers. . . . After a million and then 10 million repetitions, the once ironic gesture begins to lose the perversity that made it interesting in the first place."[68]

Osterweil, Rudnick, and Andersen express nostalgia for a *purer* form of camp founded for and by the "already marginalized audience" of Osterweil's imaginings. On this, Osterweil goes furthest: "For me the desire to steal camp back, wherever it may be located, has become a kind of categorical imperative."[69] But who are the rightful owners of camp? By the authors' own logics, the desire to contain camp at its marginalized origins would prohibit at least two among them—Andersen, a straight man; Osterweil, a woman—from properly accessing the maximal political force for which they yearn since, as Pamela Robertson maintains, essentializing its historical record "presumes that camp's aestheticism is exclusively the province of gay men"—a contention Robertson herself successfully extinguishes with her own "feminist camp" treatise.[70] More importantly, as Matthew Tinkcom reminds us, the emergence of queer male camp in the post-Second World War era was "like any instance of cultural production, particular to its own historical moment."[71] If culture and subculture are, by definition, coextensive, and if camp's political charge has been in decline since (and because of) the 1960s/1970s "big bang," is a return to camp's full potency really desirable? Was the pre-Stonewall era of camp's maximal power really so halcyon? If the expression (the "perversity") of the camp affect relies on the culture that oppresses it, then what, precisely, are we fetishizing here?

Given the studio's near-total annexation of *Showgirls'* second-wave camp revival, it would be absurd to hold up the text as a wholly transgressive camp object in its current era. But—as more recent collective camp celebrations of *Showgirls* attest—there also seems little point in excluding *Showgirls* from any camp canon on the basis of its co-optation by "the Man."[72] Rather, *Showgirls'* popular success as a camp object reminds us that camp texts are intrinsically both cultural and commercial products. Osterweil's own claim that *Showgirls* "boasts of being . . . intensely erotic" lays bare the obvious fact of cinema's inherently capitalist (and not just artistic or cultural) objectives, given it was the studio's promotional paratexts, rather than the film or its makers, who did the boasting. And as Ross prompts us, "If camp can be seen as a cultural economy which challenged and, in some cases, helped to overturn legitimate definitions of taste and sexuality, it must also be remembered to what extent this cultural economy was tied to the capitalist logic of development which governed the culture industries."[73]

Illuminating camp's links to capital does not diminish its strategic aptitude for instigating subcultural formations in consequential ways. Indeed, identifying camp's embedment within the structures of capitalist modernity is at the heart of Tinkcom's quest to "take camp seriously."[74] His extended study of camp labor, *Working Like a Homosexual* (roughly contemporary with Osterweil's article), urges that comprehending camp as an engaged intellectual and critical response *to the conditions of capital* is an essential means for regarding camp as "something more than the seemingly lightweight pleasures of consumption."[75] For Tinkcom, camp is occupied with the contradictions and incoherent logics of capital, especially the "ruptures and fluctuations of monetary and cultural value," which camp subjects (queer men or otherwise) examine, exploit, tamper with, and upend through the "work-as-play" of camp expression.[76] By reordering cinema's "value codings," camp reception shapes an alternate "way of knowing capital in its lived dimensions," giving rise to a consciousness that allows its subjects "to recognize themselves in exteriority" to capital's social regulations.[77] But camp is not an escape hatch out of capitalism. Rather, as Tinkcom attests, camp reading is one way "some subjects of capital forge their own compelling understanding of themselves *within* it."[78]

Where camp seeks to salvage any derided cultural object, it does so within the conditions of capital. Yet, like all appeals to "bad taste" that define themselves against mass commodification in favor of the minor text, Osterweil's anti-commercial impulse is confronted by a necessary participation in the market. Much of Osterweil's performative "worry" stems from a conflict between her distaste for commercialism and the inexorable truth that camp texts, themselves commodities, are exposed to market manipulations, including corporate appropriation. As the studio's canny, sustained, even aggressive promotion of *Showgirls* as camp makes manifest, Osterweil's anxiety is futile—the market will have its way. We recall Andrew Calcutt and Richard Shephard, who, writing of cult fictions a few years prior, lamented, "In one respect, we are already too late . . . transgression is no longer as transgressive as it was. . . . What was the counterculture is now over-the-counter culture, the deviant behavior at the core of cult fiction has reached the middle of the marketplace, and there is nothing anyone can do about it."[79]

Osterweil, who situates her academic distinction by adhering to the minor text, is alarmed that its resignification has become "the sign of hipness among cinephiles" while "the text itself . . . becomes quite unimportant," a development that (she believes) might have been prevented had camp been kept out of the mainstream.[80] But any notion of camp as a marker of transgressive identity (the source of its political power) activates the transcendent properties of camp taste (symbolic meaning and status value) over the material properties of the text. As Ross details at length, the political potentiality of camp rests in its "transitional function . . . as an *operation of taste*," where camp taste is mobilized by its subjects to, however slowly, gain traction and visibility in contemporary culture.[81] Camp reading, then, as a mechanism of commodity renewal only propels the capitalist logic of development. Thus, while camp's new status as "hip" deflates its countercultural power, it is also a marker of its success, the desired result of camp's transitional trajectory. Unpalatable though it may be for the camp subject wishing to maintain their hold on the degraded object, the studio predictably marshals the *Showgirls* text back into the mainstream, where it is destined to be signified and resignified by the mass culture to which it is now more visible. "Camp Lite" may be an inevitable result. But it is ironic camp itself that leaves the text unredeemed and undefended as it reenters the mass market. Since ironic camp taste both "legitimates and subverts" the object, its fate is tied to that of its subject in inverse relation—the increased visibility and status for the camp subject *always* comes at the expense of the text. The foundational principles of ironic camp limit its redemptive capacity; hence *Showgirls* reemerges in the mainstream not as a restored object of incontestable value but as one part "cult classic," one part "bomb."[82]

Showgirls and Guilty Pleasure

For three months in 2014, the *Guardian* featured a "My Guilty Pleasure" series, for which various staff writers outlined "the films they're ashamed to confess they like."[83] As the subheading suggests, the making of such a list is usually peddled as a subversive act, a breaking of taste taboos that mark its writers as "edgy" and lend publications like the *Guardian* some degree of cultural cachet for supporting the transgression. If camp is a means for the marginalized subject to negotiate access to the mainstream, the guilty pleasure signals the critic's desired admission to the margins. But unlike the proliferating catalogs of obscure cult films that permeate mass culture, "guilty pleasure" curricula tend to be decidedly unobscure and inoffensive. This one is tenanted by comedies, romantic dramas, actions, commercial horror, and a series of "star-value" films, most of which were either critically or commercially successful in their day. The *Guardian*'s list corroborates Jennifer Szalai's observation that "these so-called 'guilty pleasures' never involve actual transgression: the bland escapades of Bridget Jones are a guilty pleasure; the depraved orgies of the Marquis de Sade are not."[84] The guilty pleasure, then, is not concerned with rehabilitating forgotten texts or even those derided by mass culture. Instead, it serves to expose the historic bifurcation of the mass-cultural artifact and critical esteem. Third on the *Guardian*'s list is *Showgirls,* selected by music editor Harriet Gibsone, a nomination that understands *Showgirls*' transposition out of the cultural margins and into "the middle of the marketplace," here snugged between Disney's *Tangled* and *Dude, Where's My Car?*

If the apparent logic of the *Guardian*'s list is to be believed, we might expect this final site of contestation to open new redemptive possibilities for *Showgirls* as a critical subject via a revaluation of the film's original critical assessment. But while Gibsone's brief article contends *Showgirls* is "startling to watch" and "more inspiring than . . . other big budget Hollywood movies," and shows interest in the same ingredients that sparked the film's spontaneous second wave (Nomi's feminist ferocity, ambition, and self-possession), Gibsone also attributes the merciless critical savaging of *Showgirls* to the film's "gaudy ridiculousness," a view she supports rather than resists. *Showgirls,* she writes, "is unquestionably vulgar."[85] Gibsone's conflict—that she is impressed by the feminist credentials of the film's central character and yet maintains its "vulgarity" (a loaded class judgment)—constitutes her "guilty pleasure," a state that finds her simultaneously "more inspired" than usual yet also "ashamed." Gibsone's guilty pleasure, then, is an irresolution of the critic's competing claims on the world, an unresolved affect attenuation induced by the critic's desire to have it both ways.

As Gibsone's review bears out, the core ingredient of the guilty pleasure is not a radical potentiality, as the *Guardian* and others would have it, but rather a very *un*radical ambivalence. And as a cultural negotiation it does less to break with taste conventions than to affirm them. In his introduction to *Sleaze Artists,* Sconce construes the "guilty pleasure" as delivering passing relief from the strictures of dominant taste: "'Guilty pleasures' remain a staple of popular film writing, allowing otherwise tasteful critics to temporarily escape the crushing responsibility of a more artistically ambitious cinema to champion their own personal love of down-and-dirty genre pictures."[86] Sconce's configuration seems to support the "guilty pleasure" as a kind of transitory paracinematic subjectivity, a radical assertion of the self momentarily held in opposition to externalized hegemonic framework. But, as Sconce is well aware, such frameworks are not extrinsic for the critic but rather the organizing principle of their very function. The critic is an intellectual tastemaker, and interpretive expertise is their cultural currency; defining and enforcing regimes of taste is precisely their work.

Far from mobilizing the possibility of attachment to mainstream texts (unpopular, neglected, or otherwise) to challenge or elsewise expand the taste frameworks that supervise the critic's engagement, the critic's appeal to a "guilty pleasure" all but ensures those structures survive intact as hegemonic common sense. Labeling the pleasure as "guilty" is a performative utterance, an illocutionary act that both admits transgression and upholds the logics that would determine it as such. Attachment to the nominated text is a lapse in judgment, a blip on an otherwise unblemished cultural scorecard. Sconce's list-maker, then, isn't a subversive who (however temporarily) undermines the field of cultural arbitration so much as they are highbrow proponents joyously slumming it in lowbrow culture (Gibsone's "vulgar"), a segregation to which they subscribe. Thus, Gibsone's nomination of *Showgirls* as a guilty pleasure, like ironic camp, holds *Showgirls* at a distance, firmly at the margins of dominant taste.

How to Stop Worrying about *Showgirls* (or, *Showgirls* and ~~Guilty~~ Pleasure)

In conversation at a *Showgirls* screening for the Film Society at Lincoln Center in 2016, Gina Gershon reflected on the predominance of the film's early critical reception: "It was the groovy thing to go against it. . . . It almost became this chic thing." Hardly news, if not for Gershon's follow-on: "But [some people] would say to me in hushed tones, 'Y'know, I really like the movie.' And I'm like: 'It's okay that you like the movie. Why are we whispering that we like the movie?'"[87] Gershon's mid-1990s whisperers (a silent minority?) may well have been the first to mark *Showgirls* as a guilty pleasure: registering tension between the privately felt and publicly acceptable, acquiescing (through murmured sublimation) to the prevailing orders of taste.

Twenty-one years later, Gershon was indignant: "Have your own opinion!"

In her rationalizing of the state of camp politics, Osterweil passingly describes *Showgirls* as "the last guilty pleasure this side of postmodernism," a claim that rests on the presumption that the kind of aesthetic ambivalence a guilty pleasure necessitates cannot typically be upheld within the newly diversified marketplace of post-postmodern culture.[88] Yet *Showgirls,* like a cockroach, is somehow resistant—the one guilty pleasure to survive the cultural fallout of the postmodern nuclear bomb. If Osterweil is right, it would be easy to lay blame with critics like Gibsone who continue to locate *Showgirls* outside the realms of acceptable taste. But if Osterweil is right, it is also because *Showgirls* was never fully redeemed by camp, which offers little incentive for the critic to revise their judgment.

Besides, if we are to impugn Gibsone for clinging to the hegemonic ideals that underwrite her taste, we should also impugn Osterweil, whose own (purposive) performative posture boxes herself (and her students) in by constraining *Showgirls* within a *badfilm* curriculum—a decisive evaluation that regulates her ways of seeing the text despite her persistent, even "inherent" ambivalence observing more in *Showgirls* than her camp taxonomy allows. In this, Osterweil's worrying about camp is equivalent to Gibsone's guilty pleasure. Encountering *Showgirls,* neither reviewer's logic is singularly supportable (if they are supportable at all), yet both refuse to concede.

If a sincere revaluation of *Showgirls* is to be inspired (if the film is to "stand a chance," as Martin hopes), both Osterweil's and Gibsone's encounters with the text should put us on notice. We must work to remove the ambivalences that attenuate our pleasure in the text by first divesting *Showgirls* of the forces that produce them: our overreliance on *Showgirls* (or any text) to service our cultural and political intentions. We must discharge both Gibsone's guilt and Osterweil's worry. We must liberate Gershon's sublimating whisperers. We should affect a new orientation, one that accommodates all the pleasures *Showgirls* has to offer. And if we are to open *Showgirls* to expanding audiences and new interpretations, we must cleave it from the promotional paratexts that so forcibly instruct how to read and reread the text. We should cast off the prompts first arrived at by *Newsweek* ("how hot?" / "how bad?") to begin again with the most radical proposition of all: how great is *Showgirls*?

KIERYN MCKAY earned her PhD in English from the University of Sydney. She is an independent researcher and an invested equity practitioner who works to engage socioeconomically disadvantaged students in literature, film, and creative practice.

References

Bannon, Lisa. "Parody or Publicity Stunt?" *Globe and Mail*, October 25, 1997.

Berkley, Elizabeth. "Elizabeth Berkley on Late Show (1995)." Interview by David Letterman, *Late Show with David Letterman*, CBS, September 13, 1995. YouTube, 06:21.

Brook, Tom. "*Showgirls* Re-release." *Film 96*, BBC Archive, April 22, 1996. 04:28. https://www.facebook.com/BBCArchive/videos/557407107965657/?comment_tracking=%7B%22tn%22%3A%22O%22%7D.

Calcutt, Andrew, and Richard Shepherd. *Cult Fiction: A Reader's Guide*. London: Prion Books, 1998.

Clifford, James. "On Collecting Arts and Culture." In *Out There: Marginalization and Contemporary Cultures*, edited by Russell Ferguson, Martha Gever, Trinh T. Minh-ha, and Cornel West, 141–69. Cambridge, MA: MIT Press, 1990.

Dole, Robert. "Road to the White House 1996: Dole Campaign Speech." May 31, 1995. 22:11. https://www.c-span.org/video/?65642-1/dole-campaign-speech.

Dyer, Richard. *The Culture of Queers*. New York: Routledge, 2001.

———. "It's Being So Camp as Keeps Us Going." In *Only Entertainment*. New York: Routledge, 1992. First published in 1976.

Ebert, Roger. "Killer Babes Who Strip for Stardom; Imagine *All about Eve* in the Nude." *Record*, September 22, 1995.

Ewing, William E. *The Body: Photographs of the Human Form*. San Francisco: Chronicle Books, 1994.

Feasey, Rebecca. "'Sharon Stone, Screen Diva': Stardom, Femininity and Cult Fandom." In *Defining Cult Movies: The Cultural Politics of Oppositional Taste*, edited by Mark Jancovich, Antonio Lázaro Reboli, Julian Stringer, and Andy Willis, 172–84. Manchester: Manchester University Press, 2003.

Gabriel, Trip. "*Showgirls* Crawls Back as High Camp at Midnight." *New York Times*, March 31, 1996.

Gallagher, Danny. "Professional *Showgirls* Commentator David Schmader Talks about the Perfect Storm of Suck." *Dallas Observer*, April 14, 2015. https://www.dallasobserver.com/arts/professional-showgirls-commentator-david-schmader-talks-about-the-perfect-storm-of-suck-7182008.

Genette, Gérard. *Paratexts: Thresholds of Interpretation*. Translated by Jane E. Lewin. Cambridge: Cambridge University Press, 1997.

Gershon, Gina. "*Showgirls* Q&A | Paul Verhoeven & Gina Gershon." Interview by David Lim. *Total Verhoeven*, Film Society of Lincoln Center, New York, November 16, 2016. YouTube, 33:03. https://www.youtube.com/watch?v=vj7JB_Otn3A.

Gibsone, Harriet. "My Guilty Pleasure: *Showgirls*." *Guardian*. March 19, 2014. https://www.theguardian.com/film/filmblog/2014/mar/19/showgirls-my-guilty-pleasure.

Grannell, Joshua. "Film Is a Drag: Peaches Christ and *Showgirls*." Interview by Walter Crasshold. *Ex-Berliner*, February 9, 2015. https://www.exberliner.com/stage/peaches-christ-showgirls.

Gray, Jonathan. *Show Sold Separately: Promos, Spoilers and Other Media Paratexts*. New York: New York University Press, 2010.

Gunning, Tom. "The Cinema of Attractions: Early Film, Its Spectator and the Avant-Garde." In *Early Cinema: Space, Frame, Narrative*, edited by Thomas Elsaesser, 56–62. London: British Film Institute, 1990.

Hardie, Melissa Jane. "Loose Slots: Figuring the Strip in *Showgirls*." *Xtext* 1 (1996): 24–35.

Iley, Chrissy. "Limping over the Shock Barrier." *Sunday Times* (London), January 7, 1996.

Kempley, Rita. "*Showgirls*: Strip Sleaze." *Washington Post*, September 22, 1995.

Kidwell, April. "Laura Heywood Interviews April Kidwell." Interview by Laura Heywood. *Laura Heywood: Interviews* (podcast). May 6, 2019. https://laura.libsyn.com/laura-heywood-interviews-april-kidwell.

Klein, Naomi. *No Logo*. London: Flamingo, 2000.

———. "Sex Sells? Not the Way *Showgirls* Is Peddling It." *Toronto Star*, April 27, 1996.
Klinger, Barbara. *Melodrama and Meaning: History, Culture, and the Films of Douglas Sirk*. Bloomington: Indiana University Press, 1994.
Leland, John. "Base Instinct." *Newsweek*, September 25, 1995.
Levin, Gary. "Ad's Basic Instinct: Show-It-All and Sell." *Variety*, September 11, 1995. https://variety.com/1995/film/features/ads-basic-instinct-show-it-all-and-sell-99130051.
Lippit, Akira Mizuta. "Half-Star: *Showgirls* and Sexbombs." *Film Quarterly* 56, no.3 (2003): 33–35.
Martin, Ann. "Editor's Note: *Showgirls* Round Table." *Film Quarterly* 56, no.3 (2003): 32.
Maslin, Janet. "$40 Million Worth of Voyeurism." *New York Times*, September 22, 1995.
Massey, Doreen. "The Spatial Construction of Youth Cultures." In *Cool Places: Geographies of Youth Cultures*, edited by Tracy Skelton and Gill Valentine, 121–29. London: Routledge, 1998.
McNary, David. "*Showgirls* to Lead Box Office." *United Press International*, September 22, 1995. https://www.upi.com/Archives/1995/09/22/Showgirls-to-lead-box-office/9996811742400.
Means, Sean P. "*Showgirls*: No Pulse Peep Show." *Salt Lake Tribune*, September 24, 1995, E6.
MGM Entertainment. "*Showgirls*: Advance 8 Minute Preview." YouTube, 08:24, 1995. https://www.youtube.com/watch?v=y-YU21gO3r8.
———. "*Showgirls* 1995 Rare VHS Promo Reel Trailer | Kyle MacLachlan | Gina Gershon | Paul Verhoeven." YouTube, 03:22, 1995. https://www.youtube.com/watch?v=uZ8cFZozkYw.
———. "*Showgirls* (1995) Teaser Trailer." YouTube, 00:29, 1995. https://www.youtube.com/watch?v=ADL7PqkechY.
———. "*Showgirls*—1995 (Trailer)." YouTube, 01:59, 1995. https://www.youtube.com/watch?v=kDJdLxpdU40.
———. "*Showgirls* Teaser Trailer." YouTube, 00:49, 1995. https://www.youtube.com/watch?v=8203A7ARJ_M.
———. "*Showgirls*—Trailer." YouTube, 01:53, 1995. https://www.youtube.com/watch?v=gszDLDFwcLk.
"My Guilty Pleasure." *Guardian*, March 17–May 2, 2014. https://www.theguardian.com/film/series/guilty-pleasure.
Nayman, Adam. *It Doesn't Suck: Showgirls*. 2nd ed. Toronto: ECW, 2018.
Osterweil, Ara. "A Fan's Notes on Camp, or How to Stop Worrying and Learn to Love *Showgirls*." *Film Quarterly* 56, no. 3 (2003): 38–40.

Persall, Steve. "A High-Priced Peep Show." *St. Petersburg Times*, September 22, 1995.
Pinsker, Beth. "All Tell, No Show: *Showgirls* Blurs the Lines between R, NC-17 Ratings." *Austin American-Statesman*, August 21, 1995.
Puig, Claudia. "*Showgirls* Nets Fans with Hot Spot on Web." *Los Angeles Times*, September 20, 1995. https://www.latimes.com/archives/la-xpm-1995-09-20-ca-47890-story.html.
Rife, Katie. "Elizabeth Berkley Accepts the *Showgirls* She Cannot Change." *AV Club*, June 29, 2015. https://www.avclub.com/elizabeth-berkley-accepts-the-showgirls-she-cannot-chan-1798281228.
Robertson, Pamela. "Introduction: What Makes the Feminist Camp?" In *Guilty Pleasures: Feminist Camp from Mae West to Madonna*, 1–22. Durham, NC: Duke University Press, 1996.
Ross, Andrew. "Uses of Camp." In *No Respect: Intellectuals and Popular Culture*, 135–70. New York: Routledge, 1989.
Rudnick, Paul, and Kurt Anderson. "The Irony Epidemic." *Spy*, March 1983, 92–98. https://www.scribd.com/doc/51476375/Spy-Magazine-March-1989.
Sandler, Kevin S. "The Naked Truth: *Showgirls* and the Fate of the X/NC-17 Rating." *Cinema Journal* 40, no. 3 (2001): 69–93.
Schmader, David. "Episode 254: *Showgirls*." Interview by Mike White. *The Projection Booth* (podcast), January 18, 2016. http://www.projectionboothpodcast.com/2016/01/episode-254-showgirls.html.
———. "The Greatest Movie Ever Made." *Showgirls: V.I.P. Edition*. MGM Entertainment, 2004. DVD, 131 min.
Sconce, Jeffrey. "I Have Grown Weary of Your Tiresome Cinema." *Film Quarterly* 56, no. 3 (2003): 44–45.
———. "Introduction." In *Sleaze Artists: Cinema at the Margins of Taste, Style, and Politics*, edited by Jeffrey Sconce, 1–16. Durham, NC: Duke University Press, 2007.
———. "'Trashing' the Academy: Taste, Excess, and an Emerging Politics of Cinematic Style." *Screen* 34, no. 4 (1995): 371–93.
Shaw, Jessica. "Party Girls: *Showgirls* and *Pride and Prejudice*." *Entertainment Weekly*, March 22, 1996. https://ew.com/article/1996/03/22/party-girls-showgirls-pride-and-prejudice.
Sontag, Susan. *Notes on "Camp."* London: Penguin, 2018. First published in 1964.
Span, Paula. "Every Dog Has Its Day." *Washington Post*, April 19, 1996. https://www.washingtonpost.com/archive/lifestyle/1996/04/19/every-dog-has-its-day/9dee17e6-a8b6-4073-bdbd-1dea89a54e4e.
Szalai, Jennifer. "Against 'Guilty Pleasure.'" *New Yorker*, December 9, 2013. https://www.newyorker.com/books/page-turner/against-guilty-pleasure.

Thompson, Gary. "*Showgirls* Rates a Chorus of Boos." *Philadelphia Daily News*, September 22, 1995.
Tinkcom, Matthew. *Working Like a Homosexual: Camp, Capital, Cinema*. Durham, NC: Duke University Press, 2002.
Turan, Kenneth. "The Naked Truth about *Showgirls*." *Los Angeles Times*, September 22, 1995. https://www.latimes.com/archives/la-xpm-1995-09-22-ca-48657-story.html.
Verhoeven, Paul. "*Showgirls* Q&A | Paul Verhoeven & Gina Gershon." Interview by David Lim. *Total Verhoeven*, Film Society of Lincoln Center, New York, November 16, 2016. YouTube, 33:03. https://www.youtube.com/watch?v=vj7JB_Otn3A.
Williams, Linda. "*Showgirls* and Sex Acts." *Film Quarterly* 56, no. 3 (2003): 40–41.
Williams, Linda Ruth. "Nothing to Find." *Sight and Sound* 6, no. 1 (January 1996): 29–30.
Wurzburger, Andrea. "In Honour of Its 25th Anniversary: The Most Memorable Lines from *Showgirls*." *People*, September 23, 2020. https://people.com/movies/showgirls-anniversary-best-quotes.

Notes

1. Ara Osterweil, "A Fan's Note on Camp, or How to Stop Worrying and Learn to Love *Showgirls*," *Film Quarterly* 56, no. 3 (2003): 38.

2. Quoted in Ann Martin, "Editor's Note: *Showgirls* Round Table," *Film Quarterly* 56, no. 3 (2003): 32.

3. Kenneth Turan, "The Naked Truth about *Showgirls*," *Los Angeles Times*, September 22, 1995, F1+, https://www.latimes.com/archives/la-xpm-1995-09-22-ca-48657-story.html; Lisa Bannon, "Parody or Publicity Stunt?," *Globe and Mail*, October 25, 1997, C2.

4. Adam Nayman, *It Doesn't Suck: Showgirls*, 2nd ed. (Toronto: ECW, 2018), xi.

5. In a highly publicized campaign speech, Dole courted his conservative base by attempting to reinvigorate a perennial moral panic around Hollywood's "depraved" influence on America's children. See Robert Dole, "Road to the White House 1996: Dole Campaign Speech," May 31, 1995, 22:11, https://www.c-span.org/video/?65642-1/dole-campaign-speech.

6. MGM Entertainment, "*Showgirls* (1995) Teaser Trailer," YouTube, 00:29, 1995, https://www.youtube.com/watch?v=ADL7PqkechY.

7. MGM Entertainment, "*Showgirls* Teaser Trailer," YouTube, 00:49, 1995, https://www.youtube.com/watch?v=8203A7ARJ_M.

8. For the green-band theatrical trailer, see MGM Entertainment, "*Showgirls*—1995 (Trailer)," YouTube, 01:59, 1995, https://www.youtube.com/watch?v=kDJdLxpdU40.

For the restricted red-band theatrical trailer, see MGM Entertainment, "Showgirls—Trailer," YouTube, 01:53, 1995, https://www.youtube.com/watch?v=gszDLDFwcLk.

9. Originally featuring Czech model Ilona Novackova, Stano's "Sense" was first published a year earlier on the cover of William E. Ewing's *The Body: Photographs of the Human Form* (San Francisco: Chronicle Books, 1994).

10. See Gary Levin, "Ad's Basic Instinct: Show-It-All and Sell," *Variety*, September 11, 1995, https://variety.com/1995/film/features/ads-basic-instinct-show-it-all-and-sell-99130051.

11. Michael F. Siegel quoted in Claudia Puig, "*Showgirls* Nets Fans with Hot Spot on Web," *Los Angeles Times*, September 20, 1995, F41, https://www.latimes.com/archives/la-xpm-1995-09-20-ca-47890-story.html.

12. MGM Entertainment, "*Showgirls*: Advance 8 Minute Preview," YouTube, 08:24, 1995, https://www.youtube.com/watch?v=y-YU21gO3r8.

13. Elizabeth Berkley, "Elizabeth Berkley on Late Show (1995)," interview by David Letterman, *Late Show with David Letterman*, CBS, September 13, 1995, YouTube, 04:46–05:42.

14. Gérard Genette, *Paratexts: Thresholds of Interpretation*, trans. Jane E. Lewin (Cambridge: Cambridge University Press, 1997), 1.

15. Ibid., 2.

16. Jonathan Gray, *Show Sold Separately: Promos, Spoilers, and Other Media Paratexts* (New York: New York University Press, 2010), 48.

17. John Leland, "Base Instinct," *Newsweek*, September 25, 1995, 88.

18. Roger Ebert, "Killer Babes Who Strip for Stardom; Imagine *All about Eve* in the Nude," *Record*, September 22, 1995; Linda Ruth Williams, "Nothing to Find," *Sight and Sound* 6, no. 1 (January 1996): 30; Steve Persall, "A High-Priced Peep Show," *St. Petersburg Times*, September 22, 1995, 3; Beth Pinsker, "All Tell, No Show: *Showgirls* Blurs the Lines between R, NC-17 Ratings," *Austin American-Statesman*, August 21, 1995, 52.

19. Janet Maslin, "$40 Million Worth of Voyeurism," *New York Times*, September 22, 1995, C1; Rita Kempley, "*Showgirls*: Strip Sleaze," *Washington Post*, September 22, 1995, D07; Sean P. Means, "*Showgirls*: No Pulse Peep Show," *Salt Lake Tribune*, September 24, 1995, E6. It is also worth noting that while Sharon Stone's triumph in *Basic Instinct* is often seen as a counter-example of Berkley's critical failure, much of Stone's success is also attributed to her looks. See Rebecca Feasey, "'Sharon Stone, Screen Diva': Stardom, Femininity and Cult Fandom," in *Defining Cult Movies: The Cultural Politics of Oppositional Taste*, ed. Mark Jancovich, Antonio Lázaro Reboli, Julian Stringer, and Andy Willis (Manchester: Manchester University Press, 2003), 172–84.

20. Despite its reputation as a critical and financial bomb, *Showgirls*' box office status is somewhat debatable. Certainly, it underperformed on MGM/UA's expectations,

earning only $8.1 million in ticket sales in its first weekend (just over half of *Basic Instinct*'s $15.1 million opening draw a few years earlier). In a broader perspective, however, *Showgirls'* box office performance is mediocre at worst: it ranked second nationally and claimed the highest per-theatre gross on its opening weekend, and it remains the highest grossing NC-17 cinematic release of all time.

21. Quoted in David McNary, "*Showgirls* to Lead Box Office," *United Press International*, September 22, 1995, https://www.upi.com/Archives/1995/09/22/Showgirls-to-lead-box-office/9996811742400.

22. Quoted in Chrissy Iley, "Limping over the Shock Barrier," *Sunday Times* (London), January 7, 1996, 41. Verhoeven has had much to say about MGM's marketing slant in the twenty-five years since the film's release. Most notably, he bemoaned:

> I remember seeing the first trailers which were promising this is the most erotic movie that you've ever seen in your life and I was already amazed. . . . The promise of MGM to the audience this was going to be way, way beyond *Basic Instinct*, much more erotic . . . much more sex, I mean it was completely false. I mean, really the movie is anti-erotic. It's really about using . . . sexuality to make money. That was not said. They didn't use that in the campaign but that would have been honest from the beginning.

Paul Verhoeven, "'*Showgirls*' Q&A Paul Verhoeven & Gina Gershon," interview by David Lim, *Total Verhoeven*, Film Society of Lincoln Center, New York, November 16, 2016, YouTube, 11:39–12:41, https://www.youtube.com/watch?v=vj7JB_Otn3A.

23. MGM Entertainment, "*Showgirls* 1995 Rare VHS Promo Reel Trailer Kyle MacLachlan Gina Gershon Paul Verhoeven," YouTube, 02:09–02:14, 1995, https://www.youtube.com/watch?v=uZ8cFZozkYw. While overtly promotional, the prerelease video screener betrays the studio's cognition that its initial campaign had fallen flat. Toeing a careful line between fact and conviction and working hard to promote the now widely condemned film with a straight face, it boldly claims that *Showgirls* "swept the country" yet evidences it as "the most talked about movie of our time" by shrewdly attesting talk volume while sidestepping talk content, reeling between clips from *The Tonight Show*, *Entertainment Tonight*, *CNN News*, and others in short, sharp, substance-free bursts: "Have you heard about this movie called *Showgirls*?" / "Strip goes legit" / "*Showgirls*" / "Joe Eszterhas" / "*Showgirls*" / "This is *Showgirls*" / "*Showgirls*" / "It's called *Showgirls*. . . ."

24. The *Showgirls* VHS promotional poster ("SENSUAL. CONTROVERSIAL. AVAILABLE.," January 1996) can be viewed at https://www.filmaffinity.com/au/filmimages.php?movie_id=461751.

25. Quoted in Trip Gabriel, "*Showgirls* Crawls Back as High Camp at Midnight," *New York Times*, March 31, 1996, 43.

26. Quoted in ibid.

27. Naomi Klein, *No Logo* (London: Flamingo, 2000), 79; see also Naomi Klein, "Sex Sells? Not the Way *Showgirls* Is Peddling It," *Toronto Star*, April 27, 1996, L3.

28. Massey coins this phrase to describe the specified practices of Yucatec Mayan youth cultures across physical and virtual spaces. Doreen Massey, "The Spatial Construction of Youth Cultures," in *Cool Places: Geographies of Youth Cultures*, ed. Tracy Skelton and Gill Valentine (London: Routledge, 1998), 125.

29. Andrew Ross, "Uses of Camp," in *No Respect: Intellectuals and Popular Culture* (New York: Routledge, 1989), 149.

30. The participatory allure of the film's script is realized both by the interactive camp audience depicted here and also by proliferating catalogues of *Showgirls'* "best quotes" and the like, first brought to being by *Edge* magazine's "Top 25 Lines from *Showgirls*" as early as 1996 and continuing today. Gabriel, "*Showgirls* Crawls Back," 43; see also, for example, Andrea Wurzburger, "In Honour of Its 25th Anniversary: The Most Memorable Lines from *Showgirls*," *People*, September 23, 2020, https://people.com/movies/showgirls-anniversary-best-quotes.

31. Tom Gunning, "The Cinema of Attractions: Early Film, Its Spectator and the Avant-Garde," in *Early Cinema: Space, Frame, Narrative*, ed. Thomas Elsaesser (London: British Film Institute, 1990), 56–62; Susan Sontag, *Notes on "Camp"* (London: Penguin, 2018, first published 1964), 16.

32. Sontag, *Notes on "Camp,"* 9.

33. Osterweil, "A Fan's Notes on Camp," 39.

34. See the early passage, only a one-minute screen duration, in which Nomi, having burst from the Riviera, traverses six lanes of traffic to an empty car space vacated by the pickup that kept her belongings. Distressed, Nomi batters a nearby car roof and, after a brief physical altercation with the car's owner, vomits in the car park. Taken aback at the force of Nomi's reaction ("Jesus!"), the car's owner proffers the comforting gesture of a hand to her shoulder ("Hey . . ."), but Nomi bats it away ("NO!") and runs back onto the busy road. Rescued by the stranger ("Hey!") and pulled to the roadside, Nomi is deflated. She presses her forehead against the stranger's, lingers for a brief moment of intimacy, and slumps into a tearful embrace.

35. Sontag, *Notes on "Camp,"* 16. This reading draws as much from Pamela Robertson's notion of feminist camp. See Pamela Robertson, "Introduction: What Makes the Feminist Camp?," in *Guilty Pleasures: Feminist Camp from Mae West to Madonna* (Durham, NC: Duke University Press, 1996), 1–22.

36. Sontag, *Notes on "Camp,"* 22.

37. Quoted in Gabriel, "*Showgirls* Crawls Back," 43.

38. Ibid.

39. Sontag, *Notes on "Camp,"* 32.

40. Most notably Peaches Christ's annual drag gala "Night of 1,000 Showgirls" (which ran in San Francisco from 1998 to 2018) and April Kidwell's feminist camp satires *Showgirls! The Musical!* (premiering off-Broadway in 2013, San Francisco in 2016) and *I, Nomi* (San Francisco 2018, off-Broadway 2019). Neither Christ nor Kidwell subscribes to ironic readings of *Showgirls*. Interviewed in 2015, Joshua Grannell (Peaches Christ) drew a clear delineation between the kind of participatory fandom arising at his drag festivities and the kinds of cult viewing entertained by Buckley's party: "I call it the best movie ever made. Believe it or not, I'm not being cheeky. Our audiences genuinely love *Showgirls*. There's not sort of this ironic twist. We're not hate-watching that film." Kidwell locates her own feminist camp cathexis to *Showgirls* in Nomi's survivalist narrative: "I revere this character and this person, I feel empathy for them. . . . I understand the grittiness of this, the darkness and the humanity." As Kidwell explains, *Showgirls! The Musical!* and its mash-up derivation, *I, Nomi*, parody their source material in service of satire. Each show is, she states, "like those films [*Showgirls* and *I, Tonya*], a very over the top and hilarious commentary on the exploitation of women in this [entertainment] industry." Joshua Grannell, "Film Is a Drag: Peaches Christ and *Showgirls*," interview by Walter Crasshole, *Ex-Berliner*, February 9, 2015, para 4, https://www.exberliner.com/stage/peaches-christ-showgirls; April Kidwell, "Laura Heywood Interviews April Kidwell," interview by Laura Heywood, *Laura Heywood: Interviews* (podcast), May 6, 2019, 14:33–15:20, https://laura.libsyn.com/laura-heywood-interviews-april-kidwell.

41. Jeffrey Sconce, "'Trashing' the Academy: Taste, Excess, and an Emerging Politics of Cinematic Style," *Screen* 34, no. 4 (1995): 372.

42. Klein took a sardonic view, also insisting that *Showgirls* was only ever "rented on video as a joke," grossly oversimplifying fannish camp presentations by *Showgirls'* spontaneous "second wave." Klein, "Sex Sells?," L3.

43. For more on this, see Kevin S. Sandler, "The Naked Truth: *Showgirls* and the Fate of the X/NC-17 Rating," *Cinema Journal* 40, no. 3 (2001): 85.

44. Both iterations of the theatrical rerelease poster ("The Girls Are Back in Town," February 1996 and "The Babes Are Back in Town," April 1996) can be viewed at MGM's Media and Licensing archive: https://clips.mgm.com/posters.

45. Maslin, "$40 Million Worth of Voyeurism," C1.

46. Means, "*Showgirls*," E6.

47. Gary Thompson, "*Showgirls* Rates a Chorus of Boos," *Philadelphia Daily News*, September 22, 1995, 48.

48. Sconce, "'Trashing' the Academy," 374.

49. Quoted in Paula Span, "Every Dog Has Its Day," *Washington Post*, April 19, 1996, G01, https://www.washingtonpost.com/archive/lifestyle/1996/04/19/every-dog-has-its-day/9dee17e6-a8b6-4073-bdbd-1dea89a54e4e/.

50. Interviewed in Tom Brook, "*Showgirls* Re-release," *Film 96*, BBC Archive, April 22, 1996, 02:06–02:14, https://www.facebook.com/BBCArchive/videos/557407107965657/?comment_tracking=%7B%22tn%22%3A%22O%22%7D.

51. Quoted in Shaw, "Party Girls: *Showgirls* and *Pride and Prejudice*," *Entertainment Weekly*, March 22, 1996, 21.

52. David Schmader, "The Greatest Movie Ever Made," *Showgirls: V.I.P. Edition*. MGM Entertainment, 2004, DVD.

53. The excision of the rape scene is perhaps Schmader's most active intervention. One assumes he does so to preserve a sense of *badfilm* fun. Schmader notes that audiences semifrequently resist its omission, on the basis he is "robbing it of its power." He defends it thus: "Fuck you. Are you talking to me about preserving the integrity in *Showgirls*?" David Schmader, "Episode 254: *Showgirls*," interview by Mike White, *Projection Booth* (podcast), January 18, 2016, 01:05:27–01:05:39, http://www.projectionboothpodcast.com/2016/01/episode-254-showgirls.html.

54. Quoted in Danny Gallagher, "Professional *Showgirls* Commentator David Schmader Talks about the Perfect Storm of Suck," *Dallas Observer*, April 14, 2015, https://www.dallasobserver.com/arts/professional-showgirls-commentator-david-schmader-talks-about-the-perfect-storm-of-suck-7182008.

55. Sconce, "'Trashing' the Academy," 382.

56. As a columnist for the *Stranger*, Schmader's supposed "surprise" here may be somewhat disingenuous, given the predominance of the studio's second-wave campaign in the cultural sphere by the time he first viewed the film. Schmader, "*Showgirls*," 00:59:01–00:59:10. For more on the authenticating motive of the fan chronotope, drawing on Mikhail Bakhtin, see James Clifford, "On Collecting Arts and Culture," in *Out There: Marginalization and Contemporary Cultures*, ed. Russell Ferguson, Martha Gever, Trinh T. Minh-ha, and Cornel West (Cambridge, MA: MIT Press, 1990), 156.

57. Ross, "Uses of Camp," 153; Matthew Tinkcom, *Working Like a Homosexual: Camp, Capital, Cinema* (Durham, NC: Duke University Press, 2002), 11–14.

58. Ross, "Uses of Camp," 153.

59. Barbara Klinger, *Melodrama and Meaning: History, Culture, and the Films of Douglas Sirk* (Bloomington: Indiana University Press, 1994), 134.

60. Robertson, "Introduction," 122.

61. Ibid., 4. My emphasis.

62. Melissa Jane Hardie, "Loose Slots: Figuring the Strip in *Showgirls*," *Xtext* 1 (1996): 34.

63. Ann Martin, "Editor's Note," 32. *Film Quarterly's* pioneering "*Showgirls* Round Table" was the first published collection dedicated to the film, assembling seven brief but vital reflections on *Showgirls* and its still-evolving cultural status. The Round Table's significant contribution to *Showgirls* scholarship is reflected by its republication in full in the current volume.

64. Osterweil, "A Fan's Notes on Camp," 38, 39. Like Osterweil, several of the Round Table authors adopt a playful, personal, purposeful performativity to interrogate and unpack their critical reflections on the film. See, for example, Jeffrey Sconce's apologetic "confessional mode," Jeffrey Sconce, "I Have Grown Weary of Your Tiresome Cinema," *Film Quarterly* 56, no. 3 (2003): 44.

65. Osterweil, "A Fan's Notes on Camp," 38, 39.

66. Ibid., 39–40.

67. For Rudnick and Anderson, the "irony epidemic" began twenty years earlier still, with Sontag's essay, the coextensive rise of Pop Camp, and (shortly later) Robert Venturi's *Learning from Las Vegas* forming ironic camp's "big bang"—a view shared by Andrew Ross and Pamela Robertson. As Robertson explains, by problematizing the question of taste Warhol and Pop provided context; Sontag's essay, while flawed, lent publicity and established currency; Venturi deployed, exemplified, furthered. For Robertson (and Andrew Ross before her), it was this critical combination that "outed" and "heterosexualized" camp, eventually mainstreaming ironic camp sensibilities. Paul Rudnick and Kurt Anderson, "The Irony Epidemic," *Spy*, March 1983, 92–98; see Robertson, "Introduction," 3–22; see also Ross, "Uses of Camp," 135–70. For earlier examples of camp essentialism, see, for example, Richard Dyer, "It's Being So Camp as Keeps Us Going," *Only Entertainment*, 1976, reprinted in Richard Dyer, *The Culture of Queers* (New York: Routledge, 2001). Sconce, "'Trashing' the Academy," 380.

68. Rudnick and Anderson, "Irony Epidemic," 96.

69. Osterweil, "A Fan's Notes on Camp," 40.

70. See Robertson, "Introduction," 4; see also Ross, "Uses of Camp."

71. Tinkcom, *Working Like a Homosexual*, 189.

72. Osterweil's desire for a more marginal subject might be more easily satisfied by the collective camp response(s) to *Showgirls* emergent in the decades after her writing—for example, the widely attended screenings for London's 2011 Fringe! queer film festival and Cinespia's twenty-year anniversary celebration at Los Angeles's Hollywood Forever cemetery in 2015. Elizabeth Berkley famously attended the latter, thanking the four-thousand-strong crowd for offering her a magical "full-circle moment" by finally providing "the sweetness of a screening with a crowd that embraced it." Quoted in Katie Rife, "Elizabeth Berkley Accepts

the *Showgirls* She Cannot Change," *AV Club*, June 29, 2015, https://www.avclub.com/elizabeth-berkley-accepts-the-showgirls-she-cannot-chan-1798281228.

73. Ross, "Uses of Camp," 169.

74. Tinkcom, *Working Like a Homosexual*, 1.

75. Ibid., 2.

76. Ibid., 5.

77. Ibid., 2, 26.

78. Ibid., 4. My emphasis.

79. Andrew Calcutt and Richard Shepherd, *Cult Fiction: A Reader's Guide* (London: Prion Books, 1998), xvi.

80. Osterweil, "A Fan's Notes on Camp," 38.

81. Ross, "Uses of Camp," 136. Original emphasis.

82. Linda Williams, "*Showgirls* and Sex Acts," *Film Quarterly* 56, no. 3 (2003): 40; Akira Mizuta Lippit, "Half-Star: *Showgirls* and Sexbombs," *Film Quarterly* 56, no. 3 (2003): 33.

83. "My Guilty Pleasure," *Guardian*, March 17–May 2, 2014, https://www.theguardian.com/film/series/guilty-pleasure.

84. Jennifer Szalai, "Against 'Guilty Pleasure,'" *New Yorker*, December 9, 2013, https://www.newyorker.com/books/page-turner/against-guilty-pleasure.

85. Harriet Gibsone, "My Guilty Pleasure: *Showgirls*," *Guardian*, March 19, 2014, https://www.theguardian.com/film/filmblog/2014/mar/19/showgirls-my-guilty-pleasure.

86. Jeffrey Sconce, "Introduction," in *Sleaze Artists: Cinema at the Margins of Taste, Style, and Politics*, ed. Jeffrey Sconce (Durham, NC: Duke University Press, 2007), 2.

87. Gina Gershon, "*Showgirls* Q&A Paul Verhoeven & Gina Gershon," interview by David Lim, *Total Verhoeven*, Film Society of Lincoln Center, New York, November 16, 2016, YouTube, 26:35–26:41, https://www.youtube.com/watch?v=vj7JB_Otn3A&ab_channel=FilmatLincolnCenter.

88. Osterweil, "A Fan's Notes on Camp," 38.

4 BADNESS

ADRIAN MARTIN

In 2015, at a distance of two decades, Paul Verhoeven reflected on his intentions in making *Showgirls*. It was "a political film, but never in a pedantic way, like a professor giving a course on politics. . . . I think I overestimated the way in which the public generally sees and understands films. I thought they would get this side of it, but they didn't see it. I thought it would be droll, that people would be amused. Nothing of the kind." Then Verhoeven changed direction in his auto-commentary. "However, when the black costume designer is raped in the most brutal way imaginable, it's clear that I show the reverse side of the whole thing, as if to say: 'This is really how things are behind the show.'"[1] To my mind, Verhoeven's own hesitation—is it a droll comedy or a shattering, dramatic exposé?—is eloquent and its resonances worth exploring, particularly in relation to what a "show" is in cinema and what it can mean to go "behind the show."

1

On Spanish television, I stumble on a dubbed version of *Staying Alive* (1983), the sequel to *Saturday Night Fever* (1977). John Travolta again plays aspiring dancer Tony Manero—now less mired in the gritty sociological problems that kept him down first time around. *Staying Alive* is a showbiz musical full of melodramatic intrigue, and I am in time for the second half of the movie, with its intensive rehearsals of *Satan's Alley*—the spectacular stage presentation unveiled in the final scenes.

As I rewatch and enjoy the inspired, all-out craziness of *Staying Alive*—with its athletic bodies making extravagant leaps all over this New York stage, covered in smoke and driven by power disco—I think, "This is an awful lot like *Showgirls*," only twelve years earlier. As far as I am aware, this affinity or resonance has been little noted in the critical literature on either film. As a matter of fact, there is very little critical literature of any decent kind to be consulted on *Staying Alive*. And, as I'm working on this essay for a book on the much-maligned *Showgirls*, I have to stop and wonder: Why isn't there a book on the even more maligned *Staying Alive*? "Universally panned by film critics," Wikipedia tells me. "On review aggregator website Rotten Tomatoes, the film has a rare approval rating of 0%." Or, logically, a rare disapproval rating of 100 percent.

But there's no mystery in this, really. *Saturday Night Fever* had been a film "split," from birth, in its production and in its reception—half neorealist urban drama, half canny sales pitch for the tentacular disco phenomenon of the 1970s—and this uneasy friction was publicly reflected in everything from the testimony of its director (John Badham, going for the realist angle) to those brave critics (including, at the time, eighteen-year-old me) who wanted to "redeem" the movie from everyone who so blithely dismissed it as merely flash superficiality and consumerist "marketing." People such as the leftie student in a late 1970s class I tutored, who stood in front of the theaterette's projector beam as the Bee Gees medley played over the final credits of *Saturday Night Fever* and protested, "This is a bloody K-tel commercial!"

With *Staying Alive,* however, there was, and remains, no split or friction to get the discourse rolling. It is a "cleaned-up" sequel, directed by Sylvester Stallone (with a singing part for his brother Frank), hugely successful at the box office during its initial release window, starring a Travolta who, by 1983, was turning less neoreal with every on-screen instant. This film just never had a chance with the critics, who knew what they expected to see—and duly got it. Whether you enjoy the movie or not, the case is closed. As William Routt noted in one of his brilliant commentaries on B or trash cinema, "A certain attitude . . . attempts to direct all of the possible responses to 'trash' into a single smug channel where everyone feels secure in their tastes, confirmed in the knowledge that they know what is bad, at least"; such smugness is for "the kind of people who need desperately to feel superior to something."[2] *Staying Alive* got that channel humming, for sure.

Showgirls, in 1995, was an altogether different case. It arrived as a Paul Verhoeven film, an "auteur" work in the wake of *RoboCop* (1987) and *Basic Instinct* (1992), and a lot was riding on it. But it confounded the receptive audience of aficionados who anticipated something else entirely—either the "moral drama" that a lavish prepublicity campaign, stoked by the director's eager personal involvement, had promised, or at the very least a savage social satire on the level of *Sweet Smell of Success* (directed by Alexander Mackendrick, 1957). The film certainly did *not* arrive with a heroic, *maudit* aura; it had not been interfered with or recut by any producer or studio. It was exactly whatever it intended itself to be. In the event, *Showgirls* was not only about badness—it was, in itself, apparently very bad and completely trashy.

"How can I even begin to describe the awfulness of the new Paul Verhoeven film, *Showgirls*?" That was the first sentence of my review, broadcast over Australian radio in October 1995.[3] It sounds assertive and confident—bullish, even—but it betrays a note of uncertainty, self-doubt. I had a problematic task in front of me: how to make coherent sense of the film's pieces and levels, its assumed intentions and their subsequent on-screen effects, and how to separate whatever expectations people were bringing to it from its real project. But what *was* this project? And, since I had started off on such a strong note of evaluation or opinion-mongering, how was I to account for and prove this announced *awfulness*? Was this badness really so self-evident? Or was it something I was imposing through blinkers of various kinds?

What the quick comparison between *Staying Alive* and *Showgirls* unveils is the existence of at least two kinds of badness in the cultural sphere. The supposed *obvious* badness of *Staying Alive* is of the type that most viewers of the time perfectly accurately forecast: garish, commercial, mainstream trash. The film itself is deemed bad—which, in the case of *Staying Alive,* is mirrored or doubled by the show within the show, *Satan's Alley,* deemed ultra-bad but presented by Stallone "straight," without critical distance or irony of any kind. Throw it in the bin or yuck it up as camp—in the final instance, both these responses to the film, both "uses" of it, agree on its inherent, fixed nature as bad art, as bad pop culture.

But *Showgirls* was such a puzzling phenomenon in 1995 that it threw everybody for a loop—and inadvertently fertilized the ground that gave rise to its collective, in-depth discussion (for or against) ten, fifteen, or twenty-five years down the track. This was a *disputed* badness, only ambiguously trashy. There could be something—or nothing—"behind the show," as Verhoeven put it. The postmodern blankness or gnomic puzzle of its stance, its unclear attitude toward its own material, came to be mirrored in proud post-*Showgirls* events like Harmony Korine's ultra-self-conscious and mannered *Spring Breakers* (2012).

There is a third attribute of badness in cinema that is highly relevant to *Showgirls,* and also to its ambiguity: let's call it *embedded* badness.[4] Embedded badness occurs when a frame, usually invented for the occasion, is placed around a work—a song within a film, a play within a film, a stage spectacular within a film, a film within a film—and the work is *marked off* as bad within a larger context that is precisely presenting, commenting on, and possibly sending up this badness. A prime example would be the ludicrously overwrought, entirely generic typical Bruce Willis action movie, of which we see a small portion in Robert Altman's Hollywood satire *The Player* (1992).

But *Goddess*, the Las Vegas stage spectacular of *Showgirls* that is so in harmony with *Satan's Alley* in *Staying Alive*—what are we going to make of that? *Showgirls* posed a problem in 1995 because it so rapidly split its interpretive community along the lines of defining and agreeing on its accursed share of badness and happily continues to do so. The relation between the embedded show and the overall film that frames it seems, to some viewers, unclear. Or perhaps that relation is completely nonexistent, as in the case of *Staying Alive*: there is, effectively, no difference in aesthetic status between the show and the show within the show.

What follows is not a textual account of *Showgirls* itself but the proposal of a framework and a history we might use to understand and approach these questions. It aims, above all, to split the question of badness *in* films from the question of badness *of* films, since the latter category so quickly invites us to wallow in dubious but self-satisfied criteria of taste, invariably snobbish or condescending, and too many a priori assumptions of what constitutes and differentiates good and bad movies.

2

Embedded badness is an identifiable device deployed in specific ways across media. TV formats (from Clive James onward) where a cool host or panel of commentators introduce clips from around the world to jeer at them handle this kind of embedding game with no trouble whatsoever. (This material used to be poached predominantly from Japanese TV; now YouTube serves up as much as anybody needs from all over the globe.) The frame lines distinguishing good from bad and smart from stupid are crystal clear, guaranteed by the particular televisual *dispositif* or setup. And the spectator is in no doubt as to where to line up, if they so wish, in that guillotine division of judgmental taste.

In cinema, it's a bit harder. Embedded badness is always a gamble for any filmmaker. Who wants to bore an audience and risk alienating and losing viewers with a protracted display of what they paid money precisely *not* to see and hear? Even if the satirical/critical point is clear—and it's usually *very* clear right from the get-go, as in Robert Altman's *Prêt-à-Porter,* made just a year before *Showgirls,* with its instantly ludicrous parade of fashion designs—the toll on the public can be mighty. Why bother showing what is bad, beyond the somewhat brittle pleasure of feeling superior to it?

Two strategies predominate in the cinematic embedding of badness: do it as fast, as elliptically, and as economically as you possibly can, or put a surprising plot spin on its consequence.

Since at least the 1930s and the coming of sound, bad actors (and their bad acting performances) tend to be the easiest to show without too much difficulty or ambiguity. When Jack Benny saunters onstage as a foppish Hamlet in Ernst Lubitsch's *To Be or Not to Be* (1944), intoning those famous words of the title, or when John Barrymore hams like mad in Howard Hawks's *Twentieth Century* (1934), we—along with our representatives, the disapproving spectators handily positioned on the sidelines inside the movie—easily know what's what. There is no undue lingering on these shows of badness; they are established and then immediately absorbed into other larger offstage problems such as, in Lubitsch, the deployment of amateur theater to fight Nazi occupiers in Poland.

Bad music—bad songs, in particular—constitute a far dicier proposition. Let's set aside the excessively obvious (and sometimes facile) cases where someone in a movie sings completely out of tune or off-key while believing they sing wonderfully (Candice Bergen in Alan J. Pakula's *Starting Over*, 1979); or when the stage technology fucks up, resulting in an orgy of mic squealing or distorted, poorly mixed instrumentation (the ultraloud cymbal that, every few bars, obliterates the charming punk band rendition of "Jingle Bells" in Charles Band's *Trancers*, also known as *Future Cop*, 1984). We are talking about songs—perhaps in their entirety, from go to whoa—that are performed and presented and that constitute a spectacle of some sort. Films (of any kind) are in the business of serving up spectacles, and here is where the conundrum of badness begins.

Let's consider what is, for me at least, among the central—and most ambiguous—vocal performances in all of cinema: Jennifer Jason Leigh in *Georgia* (also released in the year of *Showgirls*, 1995) holding the stage in an enormous, packed auditorium for a whole eight minutes as she belts out a relentlessly cyclical, musically very simple Van Morrison tune titled "Take Me Back." I find this scene hypnotic and extraordinary. Others find their teeth jangling by about the second verse and wonder why director Ulu Grosbard felt compelled to shine such inordinate light on such an awful display of low to no talent. In its dramatic context, Leigh as Sadie is the eternal loser (problems with addiction, money, and bad boyfriends) in comparison with her fabulously successful folk-rock star sister Georgia (Mare Winningham). Everything hinges on how deluded Sadie may—or may not—be in her dogged pursuit of a career based on a harder-edged musical style. Grosbard maintains the open question whether Sadie's performances are good or bad right though the closing sequence, which intercuts the two sisters, in two very different venues, singing the same American standard, "Hard Times Come Again No More." Personally, I prefer Sadie's snarling rendition!

The "Take Me Back" example (and the range of published reactions to it) demonstrates to what extent the very varied musical tastes of individual spectators are hard, if not impossible, to aggregate. It's rarely enough for a movie character to simply burst forth singing a type of music deemed inappropriate for the specific dramatic or comic setting—heavy metal, folk, country 'n' western, punk, whatever it may be—because there is always sure to be a diehard fan in the real movie audience who takes offense at such slander of their beloved genre. Robert Altman—whose name is destined to arise often in any consideration of cinema's badness—straddled all sides of this problem. *Nashville* (1975) is, like *Showgirls*, a super-ambiguous case where the country songs (many composed by the actors themselves) seem to be offered as bad schmaltz, yet—due in no small part to the conviction with which they are delivered—some end up becoming not bad at all, to some spectators at least. In his final film, the delightful *A Prairie Home Companion* (2006), you can almost feel the exact moment at which Altman decides to drop his satirical pose and henceforth love any and every musical gift his troupe serves up, including Lindsay Lohan's spiritedly obscene, spontaneous desecration of the classic "Frankie and Johnny."

We are all familiar with that staple of both film and television comedy whereby, in an audition montage sequence, an off-key singer squawks a few bad notes and is cut dead by a bell or sometimes literally yanked out of the frame—a trope that became the structuring principle of that long-running Theatre of Cruelty known as *The Gong Show* (1976–1989, revived 2017), a true ode to badness as masterminded by Chuck Barris.[5] That standard sudden death gag is exemplary of the kind of savage condensation frequently wielded by cinema when it must contemplate badness. Cameron Crowe's music-based films provide many examples of this phenomenon—for example, in *Say Anything* (1989), when Lili Taylor strums a few acoustic bars of her monotonal composition —"Joe lies, Joe lies, Joe lies . . . when he cries"—in the "complaint rock" genre, as Alicia Silverstone names this mode in *Clueless* (1995). Any more than ten seconds of that tune and someone in the movie audience may decide they like it!

3

But what if the embedded bit of bad art turns out to be, in fact, good? This is the game that Jerry Lewis plays in *The Patsy* (1964): a famous comedian dies before the beginning of the story and a team of grumpy entrepreneurs reason that, with the right training, they can turn anybody into an instant replacement star—even the hapless bellboy (Lewis as Stanley Belt) who wanders into the room at that precise instant. The film is then a serial succession of spectacular failures: Stanley cannot successfully sing, dance, act, tell jokes, nothing. The internal paradox involved here (as a *Cahiers du cinéma* collective cannily pointed out in 1968) is that, in the process of Stanley proving that he cannot perform like Jerry Lewis, Lewis (as actor-director) demonstrates his absolute mastery of hilarious cinematic gags involving the discombobulation of props, physical gestures, space, and so on.[6]

Within the fiction, the situation resolves itself when Stanley, in the framework of a live television skit, suddenly throws away his training and improvises a Chaplinesque bit of proletarian, back-alley pathos. By becoming "somebody who has enough mastery over his own skills to be able to imitate Chaplin perfectly," Stanley's journey in *The Patsy* thereby represents the "mathematical proof" that Lewis "can make people laugh at the failure of 'Chaplin' to imitate Lewis and, on top of that, playing the character of an actor imitating Chaplin, he will be funny only to the spectators *inside* the film itself."[7] The much-vaunted reflexivity of 1960s pop modernism, a trope we could define as making a framing structure evident, takes a few baroque turns in that logic—but this is reasonably typical in cases of embedded badness. Even something as sophisticated as *The Patsy* finds itself flipped two decades later in Martin Scorsese's *The King of Comedy* (1982), where Lewis (playing a TV talk show host) is literally usurped by a younger comedian (Robert De Niro as Rupert Pupkin) whose long-rehearsed, live-to-air monologue poses a conundrum of badness or brilliance to match "Take Me Back" in *Georgia*.[8]

If bad art can't be good, necessarily, can it at least become, within the twists of the plot, a *success*? This is the premise that Mel Brooks made immortal (as well as highly profitable) in his original version of *The Producers* (1967), which rightly deserves (for a change) the tag of a "cult movie" that slowly accrued its devoted fan audience. Let's remind ourselves of how its premise works: a producer realizes he can make more money from a flop than from a hit, so he hires a very strange artiste who creates, in inspired innocence, a grotesquely tasteless and inappropriate musical titled *Springtime for Hitler*. Alas, the reaction of its opening night audience switches from aghast horror to uncontainable hilarity at this apparently camp masterpiece. Now the show is a big success, and that's a big problem for its producers.[9]

Sometimes there's a turnabout: against all odds, the bad art magically metamorphoses into something good, even great. In another baroque marvel of pop culture, in 2004 the fourth season of Larry David's television series *Curb Your Enthusiasm* managed to combine *The Producers* (literally) with *The Patsy* (allusively). Mel Brooks sees Larry perform at a stand-up comedy club and decides, with total, unshakable conviction, that he has found the ideal casting for the role of Max Bialystock in the latest musical run of *The Producers*—even though this ever-grumbling actor-writer is not especially gifted in the singing and dancing departments and seems indifferent even to learning the spoken lines. It is revealed only late in the season, twelve episodes later, that Brooks and his wife, Anne Bancroft, hope, through this counterintuitive casting, to sink the property for good and finally be free of it—a mirror of *The Producers'* own basic premise. On opening night, in the season's final episode, Larry cracks up onstage (having been spooked by the curse of a disgruntled audience member played by Stephen Colbert) and forgets his lines. People start leaving the auditorium in disgust—just as Mel and Anne had planned. Suddenly, Larry steps forward as himself and offers an inspired, impromptu stand-up monologue that delights the crowd and persuades them to stay. Then the musical kicks back in (several numbers whizz by in a montage), with its new star now seemingly blessed with extraordinary showbiz talents and showered with applause at bow time.

Another reversal of this type is offered by one of the most beautiful and surprising of all teen movies, Nobuhiro Yamashita's *Linda Linda Linda* (2005). For around 110 minutes, we see snatches (amid other plotlines) of the desultory rehearsals of a motley group of rather alienated, unhappy schoolgirls; we figure that surely, when the school concert arrives, they will scarcely be able to get it together to perform a single number well. A depressing Australian quasi-memoir movie, Alex Proyas's *Garage Days* (2002) delivers this very scenario. It is the exact opposite to, say, Richard Linklater's *School of Rock* (2003), a comedy earnestly devoted to the "good pedagogy" that trains a disparate bunch of kids to hit the stage and groove together triumphantly—an outcome we never doubt will happen, unless external factors contrive to impede it. In *Linda Linda Linda,* there is nothing but doubt or apprehension of the worst.

Come the day, Son (Bae Doona) nervously approaches the mic, the camera onstage with her, observing her close and in profile, once the guitarist has strummed the first power chord of the Blue Hearts' punk anthem "Linda Linda Linda." Sweating, Son gives the opening lyrics all she's got, and then the four-to-the-floor drumbeat kicks in. The surprise arrives with a perfectly placed cut to a vantage point behind Son's head:

incredibly, the entire audience of grotty schoolkids is going wild, jumping up and down and dancing, filling the whole frame with their Dionysian energy. It has the joyful force of a transformation, a metamorphosis sweeping up its characters and their embedded audience alike.

However, the *Linda Linda Linda* happy ending is rarer in contemporary cinema and television than the "unfathomable success" punch of *The Producers*, which plays to our postmodern sense either that bad art can somehow be reclaimed (against its will) as enjoyable camp or that the mass audience is, at large, so stupid it can no longer tell the difference between good and bad, and hence is likely to embrace anything. *Starting Over* has this cynical premise as a filigree in its plot: Jessica's composition may be awful—certainly in the eyes of Phil (Burt Reynolds), who shoots us a knowing, reflexive, disdainful look in the mirror—but it becomes a hit, and the women that Phil later tries to date tend to hum it gleefully, one of them even giving it a Dolly Parton-style country lilt. The Australian film *The Wannabes* (2003), Nick Giannopoulos's follow-up to his wildly successful *The Wog Boy* (2000), appears to meld Mel's golden idea of 1967 with a situation pinched from, of all places, Jean-Luc Godard's *Prénom Carmen* (1983), itself an already bent take on Prosper Mérimée and Georges Bizet: a bunch of crooks seeks to ingeniously hide their mansion robbery underneath a super-bad one-off act for kids, but the show becomes inexplicably popular instead.

Between 2015 and 2016, global culture spontaneously produced a weird sign o' the times: two separate films, one French (*Marguerite*) and the other British (*Florence Foster Jenkins*), both based on the historic personage of Florence Foster Jenkins; a decade earlier, the same thing had happened in theater with the productions *Glorious!* and *Souvenir*. Jenkins (1868–1944) was an American socialite and wealthy patron of the arts who also fancied herself a singer, and duly put herself on the stage, on disc, and on film over the course of two world wars. But her tuneless voice and outlandish, self-designed costumes were the starring attractions, and the audience derision of her became, as legend has it, a spectator sport. Wikipedia informs us that—in what is presumably an early manifestation of twentieth-century camp—"she became a prominent musical cult-figure in New York City during the 1920s," and her celebrity fans included Cole Porter, Lily Pons, and Enrico Caruso. It is an odd tale, the details of which (such as the mental illness sometimes imputed to Jenkins) biographers understandably grapple over, but it's the kind of hook that filmmakers love to grab and fictionalize in any direction they see fit.

In the French fashioning of her life, Xavier Giannoli's *Marguerite*, much is made of the avant-garde appropriation of the Jenkins figure: in Dadaist cabarets, Marguerite (Catherine Frot) is the living symbol of a wonky and decadent bourgeois culture, held up in blistering irony. But Marguerite, seemingly unaware of the reaction she causes and perfectly deluded as to her own talents, is party to these anarchic spectacles. The entire film turns, uneasily, on the extent, or the very existence, of that delusion: in a queasy scene of dramatic reversal, she plays a recording of herself to her appropriators and seems suddenly aware of the role she has been playing for them all this time. When this switch comes, Giannoli asks us to feel sympathy for Marguerite and only scorn for the uppity avant-gardists—the exact opposite of where the story starts out.

Stephen Frears's rendition, *Florence Foster Jenkins* starring Meryl Streep, sticks closer to the historical record and uses the real names. Frears states that, having visited the recorded archives of this self-styled diva (which are sampled in the final credits), he was drawn to the project because Jenkins, as a figure, seemed to him both ridiculous and adorable, even admirable. His film is an ingenious attempt to sustain the equilibrium of that double perspective. Its complexity is indicated by the way it virtually opens with a pianist complaining about "some

Saint-Saëns bullshit"—that is, considering it sickly, sentimental, and facile pop classical music—and ends by incorporating this same music into its own uplifting score. As in *Marguerite* but more sharply, the driving question of the script is: how did Florence remain so unaware of her own badness as a singer?

Frears and screenwriter Nicholas Martin diversify the reasons and responses: there are those who shut up about the reality of the situation because they benefit from Jenkins's financial patronage (this group includes Arturo Toscanini) or payment for services (her accompanist); those who conspire in her "training" but avoid any public affiliation with her (the singing coach); and those who could expose her but are denied access to her salon performances (professional music critics, portrayed either as a dastardly lot of vicious hacks or as lackeys who can be easily bought off). When it comes to audience types among Florence's fans, there's a similarly wide range: little old ladies with hearing problems; hepcat artists who derive a camp laugh from it all; vulgar audience members who hear no badness and just like the show; and punters who take it as a virtuosic comedy act. Holding the film together is the ambiguous character of Jenkins's companion and manager, St. Clair Bayfield (1875–1967, played by Hugh Grant), himself a failed actor who benefits economically from his ongoing arrangement with Florence but—true to his word—has never laughed at her delusion and in fact devotes himself body and soul to enabling her dream to materially persist. His stated feelings for her appear quite genuine, and the film winds around to being a touchingly unlikely love story.

4

The thoroughly deluded figure whose personal pluck, eccentric charisma, and career drive we are ultimately asked to value above any objective judgment of their art is the basis of Tim Burton's highly influential *Ed Wood* (1994), about the B movie director Edward D. Wood Jr. (1924–1978). Burton took a big gamble devoting himself to this figure who, by the mid-1990s, had been well and truly colonized by the "so bad it's good" cult in movie exhibitions across many countries. It would have been very easy to make a facile comedy in which Wood is the butt of every joke. *Ed Wood* plants no external points of reference (as *Twentieth Century* does) to indicate a judgment on its main character's zany ways, such as keeping the camera rolling no matter what accident happens and never shooting anything twice. The hero's charm is infectious: Johnny Depp (who wisely commented, in interviews of the time, that he couldn't have played Wood if he assumed the guy was just an incompetent idiot or a failure) presents him as all smiles, manic gesticulations, and boyish cheer, like one of the many lovable figures populating the 1940s screwball mosaics of Preston Sturges.

More significantly still, Burton's film takes the tack of adding a special quality of 1990s cinema that was uncannily in tune with a larger vogue in the burgeoning self-help industries: the invitation to immerse ourselves in, identify with, and approve Wood's magnificent *dream* of himself—no matter how nutty that dream may be. Jenkins's deathbed vision in Frears's film—singing perfectly (we hear Streep's real voice), lavishly costumed, beautifully lit, bowing deep before a rapt, adoring audience—is, on this level, on par with Burton's conjuring of the 1956 premiere of Wood's *Plan 9 from Outer Space* (why are opening nights such a consistent staple of this genre?), when the director bounds into the theater and runs up the aisle like an irrepressible superstar.

Both Ed Wood and Florence Jenkins, as presented in these films, are innocents; we are asked to adore their naivete, their one-eyed vision, their undaunted determination to project their movie in a lavish picture palace or take the stage at Carnegie Hall before a full house. As well, we are asked to applaud their basic goodness as people: their spontaneous acts of charity, fidelity to their friends and assistants, and the ability to draw together an inclusive, nonbiological "family" comprising all manner of social misfits (sexual misfitting—transvestism, queerness, "free love"—is an almost constant feature of movies in this mode). Frears even throws into this stew a dash of salutary patriotism during the wartime effort: Florence gives hundreds of free tickets for her big concert to soldiers on leave (who show up drunk and begin jeering her, but end up cheering her on).

Let us note the intriguing recurrence of this trope at the end of the *Showgirls* documentary *You Don't Nomi* (directed by Jeffrey McHale, 2019): the ultimate willingness of Elizabeth Berkley to introduce a screening of the film before its twenty-first-century "cult" audience—despite some evident puzzlement or discomfort (evident, at least, to my eyes) on her part at having to adopt this posture—signals her inherently agreeable nature as a good sport. In this context, to be a good sport means to agree to the badness foisted on you! A similar scene concludes James Franco's *The Disaster Artist* (2017), a film, owing much to *Ed Wood*, about the making of Tommy Wisseau's "bad movie" classic *The Room* (2003): Franco-as-Wisseau takes the stage after the premiere (another premiere!) of *The Room* and—perhaps with Paul Verhoeven's retroactive rap on *Showgirls* in mind—declares in light of the audience's reaction, "I'm glad you liked my comedic movie. Exactly how I intend it." In this case, it is the enduring value of Wisseau's tie to his best friend, Greg Sestero (Dave Franco)—doubled by the real-life brotherly casting—that rises up and triumphs over any cultural issue of goodness or badness. This, and the testamentary cry "We followed our dream."

Even more richly than for its standard auteur connection, *Ed Wood* can be networked with the other projects by the screenwriting team of Scott Alexander and Larry Karaszewski, who have made a specialty out of the biopics of larger-than-life eccentrics situated somewhere within the capacious sphere of showbiz: a renegade publisher in *The People vs. Larry Flynt* (1996), an enigmatic comedian (Andy Kaufman) in *Man on the Moon* (1999), a washed-up TV star (Bob Crane) in *Auto Focus* (2002), an "outsider" or "naive" artist (Margaret Keane) in *Big Eyes* (2014).[10] But the most outstanding work they have done, in my view, is the script for Craig Brewer's *Dolemite Is My Name* (2019), which stars Eddie Murphy as Rudy Ray Moore (1927–2008).

This subject was, again, risky to tackle: the self-financed "blaxploitation" movies that Moore made and starred in throughout the 1970s swim in a cultural space far below most canons of cinema and far away from all criteria of respectability, depth, and seriousness. Moore himself is an extraordinary but also disconcerting performer, especially on first contact: we may find ourselves wondering, before we get hooked (or prematurely unhook ourselves), whether he's for real, whether he's genuinely in control of his style and his intensity—whether, in short, he's an artist worth the name, and whether his projected character of the super-dude Dolemite can be considered a genuine creation. The central sequence of *Dolemite Is My Name* shows a sex scene in Moore's inaugural movie venture that goes disastrously wrong as it is being shot—the set starts falling apart—but miraculously metamorphoses into a knowing and winning form of comic artifice. In that nutshell of a sequence, the film hands us its fine critical appreciation of Moore's artistry.

Dolemite Is My Name owes something to *Baadasssss!* (2003)—Mario Van Peebles's tribute to his father Melvin's milestone independent production *Sweet Sweetback's Baadasssss Song* (1971)—which in turn owes much to Burton's *Ed Wood*. But Brewer and his collaborators push beyond the by now typical species of behind-the-scenes comedy involving on-set mistakes and difficulties, diminishing finances, and administrative obstacles. The trope of the makeshift family becomes—as, fleetingly, for Van Peebles—a matter of an entire community; as soon as this collective aspect kicks in, not only on the production side but, even more importantly, in what we see of the promotion, exhibition, distribution, and reception processes, *Dolemite Is My Name* becomes a genuinely populist manifesto. The final scene, in which Moore strides out into the street to personally entertain those customers impatiently waiting for the next screening session of *Dolemite*, is indelible.

5

It takes less than seventy seconds of Mia Hansen-Løve's DJ-chronicle *Eden* (2014) to whip through a kaleidoscope of received opinions concerning *Showgirls*—akin to what Stephen Fears spread out over 110 minutes of *Florence Foster Jenkins*. Hansen-Løve, we are reliably informed in Adam Nayman's book *It Doesn't Suck: Showgirls*, is a "great and devoted fan" of *Showgirls*.[11] This action-packed segment in *Eden* will take far longer to properly evoke in writing than it does to watch and hear it in the film itself; yet I believe it deserves a thicker and more context-informed description than the bare script pages Hansen-Løve provided to Nayman before the film's production. In this densely packed scene, one of its axes, as a radiograph of cultural attitudes, is—inevitably—the reputed badness of *Showgirls* and the various stances, related to differences in temperament, lifestyle, and value system, that can be adopted in relation to it.[12]

A recurring secondary figure in *Eden*, Arnaud (played by highly recognizable character actor Vincent Macaigne, often praised for his excessive performance style), is obsessed with Verhoeven's film. The year is *circa* 2000. As the scene begins, the *Showgirls* DVD ends on a widescreen TV in a messy lounge room crammed with books and posters for Daft Punk and similar acts. As we learn, this is the third time that Arnaud has forced his tight-knit group of eight friends in the club/music milieu to watch the film—although it seems he needs to get them drunk or stoned to achieve this ("You take advantage of our exhaustion," one of them cheerfully remarks).

Arnaud's own position is unmovable and, to him, irrefutable, pronounced in a calm, clear voice: "*Showgirls*, a masterpiece." His pals burst into laughter at this clearly oft-heard proclamation. Someone yells, "Junk!" Someone else ironically comments off-screen, "Better than *Texas Chain Saw Massacre*." There is a lightning-fast discussion of Berkley's abilities as an actor: the remark "She can run for Worst Actress Ever" is countered by "She won a Razzie." Since this is not apparently shared cultural capital among French youth in 2000 ("A what?"), the reference is handily glossed: "Oscars, but negative."

Arnaud, still hovering in standing position at the TV set like a cinema studies pedagogue, heads into the interpretive fray: "Find her performance slightly over-the-top?" "A little," somebody replies, as everybody again laughs. "It's intentional," Arnaud continues. "Verhoeven directed her like that to emphasize his vision. He wanted grotesque." Off-screen interjection at this point: "He got it." Arnaud perseveres: "He targeted American vulgarity." Finally, he gets a little exasperated: "I've shown it to you three times, and you still don't get it?" A guy sunk deep into the sofa takes another drag on his cigarette, which may be a spliff, and replies that it is "Time to move on"—meaning to find another, better film to worship.

Arnaud, finally relinquishing his oratorical pose, takes a seat but delivers his final verdict: "That film is a masterpiece." He adds, in a quieter tone to the woman beside him, a curious qualification: "A '90s masterpiece." *Eden*'s hero, Paul (Félix de Givry), then intervenes in the discussion to play devil's advocate: "I'm in the middle. Critics were wrong to trash it. It's still Verhoeven, but not his best." An auteurist speaks! Arnaud looks a little relieved to get at least this much backup.

What's really going on in this scene, beyond a simple referencing of a period through one of its most famous/notorious pop culture markers? Hansen-Løve's work has a dual tendency: while aiming for a minimalist, flat, all-over tone and construction like Robert Bresson, she also explores a naturalism in character psychology and behavior and a busy, everyday realism of normal incidents as they unfold, such as friends hanging out together—this scene, for instance, could well have been based on an actual incident in her life. She is hence constantly trying to find emblematic moments that are true to (or, at least, expressive of) individual psychologies, while also capturing a certain time- and place-bound constellation of cultural values, attitudes, and experiences.

In this light, Arnaud's friends, it is clear, do not think he is being exactly sincere in his extravagant love of *Showgirls*: they assume it must be his running social gag, his studied, perverse provocation. It's true that whenever we glimpse Arnaud in *Eden*, he's behaving as an outrageous joker. I, however, choose to believe that he sincerely means what he says in this particular scene: *Showgirls* is a masterpiece. I wonder why his conviction on this point is so hard to take, to believe in, whether by the characters in Hansen-Løve's film or by many of *Showgirls*' viewers and commentators.

And there's more. In Hansen-Løve's chronicle of this generation of DJs, club-goers, and music makers—more or less her own generation, since the script is cowritten by her older brother, Sven Hansen-Løve, and based on his life experiences as a DJ from 1992 to the present—the polar opposite to the type of spiky joviality represented by Arnaud comes in the form of a more central character, Cyril (Roman Kolinka). This figure, based on the real-life graphic artist Mathias Cousin, is heavily marked, from his first appearance, as someone plagued by depression;

in the course of time, the major event in *Eden*, discreetly tucked away off-screen in a Bressonian ellipsis, is his suicide. Almost every time we encounter Cyril in the mosaic movements of the film's plot, he is shutting down, opting out, pushing others away emotionally, and withdrawing behind his own hard, bitter shell.

So, in the overall semantic and naturalistic psychological system of *Eden*, how will Cyril react to *Showgirls*? Not with sympathy, laughter, or irony, as his companions in that makeshift lounge cinematheque do, but *angrily*. Seated on the floor slightly apart from his friends, almost right in the corner of the room, he shakes his head in stern negativity at every word Arnaud speaks and even has to cover his eyes to blot out this collective mania. When the film is described as "junk," he offers a corrective: "Trash, even." It is he who calls Berkley the "Worst Actress Ever." When Paul somewhat defends the film, Cyril explodes: "It's just a piece of shit. You're all crazy!" And as he picks up his coat and storms out of the apartment, he mutters, "I've wasted enough time with your crap, Arnaud." Then the scene, in its diminuendo, morphs into a discussion of the now absent Cyril and his difficulties relating to women. To Arnaud, he's either a "total misogynist" or a "faggot"—but nobody tweaks to the possibility that he's actually suffering from depression. Cyril's specific and extreme problem with *Showgirls* functions, in *Eden*, as a type of symptom or sign.

6

Few commentators take *Showgirls* out on the line of flight that would link it profoundly to the most radical cases of collapse or indistinction between embedded spectacle and framing spectacle in cinema history (or, at least, as much of that history as I know): John Cassavetes's *The*

Killing of a Chinese Bookie (two versions, 1976 and 1978, clearly an influence on the dressing room scenes of *Showgirls*) and Abel Ferrara's *Go Go Tales* (2008)—films in which the question of badness (of the various stage performers: strippers, dancers, comedians, musicians, magicians) is never explicitly raised by anybody inside the story, nor even implicitly posed by the total narration or presentation of that story by the director. They are special, near-miraculous works precisely to the extent that they manage to suspend this question of value or evaluation likely to arise in the heads of most spectators.

Isn't *all* interpretation, all criticism, ultimately a case of framing, a particular "gaze," as Routt would say? And doesn't some framing, by definition, embed what it labels to be bad solely within the terms it constructs? Perhaps there is no such thing at all as *obvious* badness, only the act of "calling out," calling it up, bringing it into existence. Perhaps nothing is *less* obvious, in the final instance, than badness; there is only ever the cultural clinch that agrees to point at something and recognize it, in a communal gesture, as bad.[13]

A last anecdote: trying to persuade a German university classroom in 2014, during a course on critical method, that Pitof's *Catwoman* (2004) is a really good film—rather than the "turkey" it is frequently assumed to be—led to two full weeks of impenetrable resistance and suspicion from most of my students. They kept shouting at me about "bad script, bad acting, bad effects," as if all these properties were entirely self-evident—and that to believe otherwise was simply and solely perverse. The students came to regard me in the same way that Arnaud's friends regard him in *Eden*!

I confess that this depressing experience has indelibly shaped my own attitude to badness in cinema as something that desperately needs to be redefined, reclaimed, and redeemed. So, roll on, *Showgirls*!

ADRIAN MARTIN is an arts critic, lecturer, and audiovisual essayist based in Spain and Adjunct Professor of Film and Screen Studies at Monash University. He is author most recently of *Mise en Scène and Film Style: From Classical Hollywood to New Media Art*; *Mysteries of Cinema: Reflections on Film Theory, History and Culture 1982–2016*; and *Once upon a Time in America*.

References

Aumont, Jacques, Jean-Louis Comolli, André S. Labarthe, Jean Narboni, and Sylvie Pierre. "A Concise Lexicon of Lewisian Terms." In *Frank Tashlin*, edited by Claire Johnston and Paul Willemen, 89–115. Edinburgh: Edinburgh Film Festival, 1973. (First published in *Cahiers du cinéma* 197 [January 1968]: 58–63.)

Chauvin, Jean-Sébastien, and Stéphane Delorme. "L'ironie est un art perdu: Entretien avec Paul Verhoeven" [Irony Is a Lost Art: Interview with Paul Verhoeven]. *Cahiers du cinéma* 715 (October 2015): 6–19.

Martin, Adrian. *Mysteries of Cinema: Reflections on Film Theory, History and Culture 1982–2016*. Perth: University of Western Australia Publishing, 2020.

Nayman, Adam. *It Doesn't Suck: Showgirls*. 2nd ed. Toronto: ECW, 2018.

Perkins, V. F. "Badness: An Issue in the Aesthetics of Film." *Movie: A Journal of Film Criticism* 8 (2019): 34–37. https://warwick.ac.uk/fac/arts/film/movie/8_badness.pdf.

Routt, William D. "Bad for Good." *Intensities* 2 (November 2001). https://intensitiescultmedia.files.wordpress.com/2012/12/routt-bad-for-good.pdf.

Notes

1. Jean-Sébastien Chauvin and Stéphane Delorme, "L'ironie est un art perdu: Entretien avec Paul Verhoeven" [Irony Is a Lost Art: Interview with Paul Verhoeven], *Cahiers du cinéma* 715 (October 2015): 12 (my translation).

2. William D. Routt, "Bad for Good," *Intensities* 2 (November 2001), https://intensitiescultmedia.files.wordpress.com/2012/12/routt-bad-for-good.pdf.

3. Unpublished review from my archive. I tell the story of my total turnaround on *Showgirls* in my *Mysteries of Cinema: Reflections on Film Theory, History and Culture 1982–2016* (Perth: University of Western Australia Publishing, 2020), 353–70.

4. There is a formidable body of work in literary theory, spanning at least six decades, on structures of embedding in novels, short stories, and so forth. I leave it to others, better equipped in this tradition, to relate the insights from that critical work to the manifestations of badness in cinema.

5. Note the uncanny rhyme between Barris's weird 1984 "fictional autobiography" *Confessions of a Dangerous Mind* (filmed in 2002 by George Clooney from a script by Charlie Kaufman) and *Showgirls* screenwriter Joe Eszterhas's even weirder self-satire, *An Alan Smithee Film: Burn Hollywood Burn* (1997): both are tortured, self-debasing, shame-filled apologies for having foisted cultural trash upon the world.

6. Jacques Aumont, Jean-Louis Comolli, André S. Labarthe, Jean Narboni, and Sylvie Pierre, "A Concise Lexicon of Lewisian Terms," in *Frank Tashlin*, ed. Claire Johnston and Paul Willemen (Edinburgh: Edinburgh Film Festival, 1973), 89–115. The original appears in *Cahiers du cinéma* 197 (January 1968): 58–63.

7. Ibid., 102–103 (translation amended from the original French, 60–61).

8. There exists an intriguing subgenre twisting around the enigma of unfunny comedy, or "anti-comedy" as it is called; Miloš Forman's *Man on the Moon* (1999) and Rick Alverson's *Entertainment* (2015) are prime examples. The driving question of these films is less "Is this act good or bad?" than "Am I meant to be laughing and where is this act coming from?"

9. Lubitsch's *To Be or Not to Be* is clearly Brooks's main source of inspiration for *The Producers*: he remade it as a quasi-musical in 1983.

10. Films about naive art constitute a special subcategory of the "ambiguous badness" genre; Fritz Lang's *Scarlet Street* (1945) stands at the helm of this tradition.

11. Adam Nayman, *It Doesn't Suck: Showgirls*, 2nd ed. (Toronto: ECW, 2018).

12. In *The Clouds of Sils Maria*, made the same year as *Eden* by Hansen-Løve's former partner Olivier Assayas, the corresponding scene shows Kristen Stewart and Juliette Binoche, representing actors of two generations, vigorously arguing over a space opera 3D blockbuster—an imaginary, faux fragment generated by Assayas himself, similar to *The Player*'s action insert.

13. For a very different argument, see V. F. Perkins, "Badness: An Issue in the Aesthetics of Film," *Movie: A Journal of Film Criticism*, no. 8 (2019), 34–37, https://warwick.ac.uk/fac/arts/film/movie/8_badness.pdf.

5 *SHOWGIRLS, SHOWGIRLS 2,* AND THE FATE OF THE EROTIC THRILLER

BILLY STEVENSON

Of all the erotic thrillers of the 1980s and 1990s, *Showgirls* was perhaps the least likely to spawn a sequel.[1] In popular and critical discourse, Paul Verhoeven's 1995 film was associated with endings. It was seen as marking the end of the NC-17 rating experiment since it was neither hard core enough to satisfy audiences looking for a mainstream pornographic fix nor titillating enough in the way that it distributed and exhibited female bodies to justify the NC-17 allure, featuring only a single simulated sex scene. Accordingly, in a review for the *Washington Post,* Desson Howe noted that while the film was rated NC-17, "some people . . . keep their clothes on."[2] In addition, *Showgirls* was seen as marking the end of Elizabeth Berkley's bid at a serious cinematic career and came close to halting the Hollywood life of Verhoeven, who would make only two more films in the studio system.

More pressingly for this chapter, *Showgirls* was seen as marking the finitude of the erotic thriller itself. In her groundbreaking study of the erotic thriller, Linda Ruth Williams follows Jim Collins's account of genre formation in *Architectures of Excess: Cultural Life in the Information Age.*[3] Collins argues that genres evolve across three discrete phases: an "initial period of consolidation"; a "'Golden Age,' in which the interplay of by now thoroughly stabilized sets of stylistic features and audience expectations is subject to elaborate variations and permutations"; and, finally, a "dissolve into either self-parody or self-reflexivity."[4] Both the second and third phases involve a certain element of self-reflexivity. The implication of Collins's schema is that this self-reflexivity is aesthetically productive in the second phase, where it produces "elaborate variations and permutations," but far more derivative and predictable in the third phase, which is "generally described in terms of all-purpose decline."

Within the evolution of the erotic thriller, Williams positions *Showgirls* at the cusp between this second and third phase.[5] This means that *Showgirls* apotheosized the aesthetic aspirations of the erotic thriller but also exhausted them. More specifically, it means that *Showgirls* took the self-reflexivity of the erotic thriller and transformed it from a source of aesthetic innovation into a source of aesthetic stagnation. This perception of *Showgirls* affords it a unique position in the history of 1980s and 1990s cinema more generally, if we accept the broader claim that the erotic thriller was particularly attuned to this moment in film history.

While writers have identified a vast range of influences operating on the erotic thriller, from film noir to the demise of the Hays Code, from *giallo* to the rise of art house erotica, most agree that the genre, at its peak, was coterminous with the 1990s. In "The Rise and Fall of the Erotic Thriller," Ryan Lambie notes that "by the end of the 90s, the American erotic thriller, in popular terms, was effectively spent,"[6] while R. Barton Palmer notes in 1994 that it was already "the most popular genre of the 90s," partly due to the way it invoked the "popular taste for noir narrative" in American culture.[7] In a more recent opinion piece in *Vice*, Christina Newland agrees, observing that "these overheated Hollywood crime dramas . . . are now mostly ignored or forgotten entirely"—an even more striking fact given their heyday, when, as Williams notes, they "were *the* most discussed films and amongst the highest earners."[8] Significantly, Williams emphasizes that the erotic thriller didn't merely dominate the box office but was a constant point of reference in film criticism at the time.

In combination, these perspectives suggest that the erotic thriller was seen as hegemonic of the 1990s both at the time and during the present day. Yet in an era of rampant 1990s nostalgia, the erotic thriller has been one of the few film genres that remain resistant to reboot culture. While there has been a recent wave of neo-erotic thrillers that acknowledge the 1990s heyday, these are typically lacking in the explicit erotic content that defined the genre in the first place (in the case of *Deep Water, A Simple Favor, Greta,* or *The Voyeurs*) or else reimagine the erotic thriller as a more intersectional comment on race and sexuality (in the case of the 2010s "thot horror" movement, which starts with *Obsessed,* a remake of *Fatal Attraction,* and includes *No Good Deed* and *When the Bough Breaks*). Writing at the time, Williams predicted that the erotic thriller would be evanescent and framed her project as an effort to configure a cinematic era before it disappeared entirely: "This book has partly been fueled by the impetus to map this fast-fading film history before it is forgotten."[9] While the idea that a stylistic period could be "forgotten" might seem absurd from the vantage point of today's reboot culture, the fact remains that the erotic thriller has never been revived with the same simulacral detail as other comparable 1980s and 1990s genres. Whereas horror films (*The Thing*), buddy films (*Point Break*), and action films (*Rambo*) have been remade, nobody has had the audacity to attempt to try to reboot *Indecent Proposal* or *Fatal Attraction,* let alone *Showgirls.* The closest we have come is *Deep Water* since it continues the erotic thriller as a lineage of Adrian Lyne films stretching back to the mid-1980s, although most critics concurred that this 2022 update served only to clarify just how thoroughly the genre is a figment of the past. In her review for the *New York Times,* Jeannette Catsoulis notes that "on paper," Lyne "seems [like] the perfect choice to direct" the film but that this merely makes it a more "baffling return," especially because, like so many neo-erotic thrillers, "there's surprisingly little sex" now that the genre has lost its former pride of place as the cutting edge of soft-core porn access.[10]

The dearth of erotic thriller reboots rendered it all the more provocative when Rena Riffel, who plays Penny Slot in *Showgirls,* directed a sequel in 2011, *Showgirls 2: Penny's from Heaven,* based on her character in the original film.[11] Riffel's film is too amateur to be called low budget, instead operating entirely outside the studio system and often playing like an anthology of home movies or a series of YouTube tributes to *Showgirls,* with very little connection or cohesion between many of its main incidents. If *Showgirls* received critical opprobrium, then *Showgirls 2* went largely beneath the critical radar, partly because it hasn't even garnered the same cult response as Verhoeven's film. On IMDb, *Showgirls 2* has a rating of 1.8 stars out of 10, based on only 657 votes, and it wasn't even reviewed by enough critics to garner a Rotten Tomatoes rating, despite scoring 11 percent in the user section of the website, this time based on a mere 52 viewers.

Riffel's film, and its relation to Verhoeven's film, forms the focus of my chapter, along with their shared relation to the perceived demise of the erotic thriller as a whole. *Penny's from Heaven* responds to some of the questions that have been posed around the erotic thriller, especially the questions of why it was so emblematic of the 1990s, and why it has been so resistant to reboot culture. Lambie offers two possible reasons for the decline of the erotic thriller but is skeptical of accepting either of them unequivocally. First, Lambie suggests, erotic thrillers arose in part to counteract internet pornography, rendering them redundant as internet pornography evolved beyond any erotic spectacle that cinema could command. Second, Lambie speculates that the rise of right-wing values in American culture produced a prurience that precluded the erotic thriller as a mainstream genre.[12] Verhoeven has voiced agreement with both of these options, suggesting that *Showgirls* was ultimately *too* attuned with public taste, resulting in "the most realistic movie I've ever made in the United States."[13]

Interestingly, Lambie is more dismissive of the first option than the second. Yet the rise of internet pornography seems like an intuitive challenge to the hegemony of the erotic thriller, especially since so many erotic thrillers set out to make a case for the cinematic as a category of pleasure, by way of wide-screen perspectives, lush mise-en-scènes, and complex negotiations with the cinematic past. This heritage is particularly emphatic in *Showgirls*, which combines the spectacles of neo-noir, melodrama, and the musical to create a genre hybrid that originates with the erotic thriller but also exceeds it. If, as Williams argues, *Showgirls* marks a cusp between the second and third eras of the erotic thriller, it is by collapsing the erotic thriller into a more indiscriminate concatenation of cinematic style.

More specifically, erotic thrillers often played as conscious cinematic claims to the male gaze and as dramatizations of the two roles that female bodies have traditionally played in Hollywood cinema: "erotic [objects] for the characters within the screen story, and as erotic object for the spectator within the auditorium, with a shifting tension between the looks on either side of the screen."[14] Laura Mulvey's understanding of the male gaze as a dynamic entity that traverses and unifies diegetic and nondiegetic space centers on "the device of the show-girl," which "allows the two looks to be unified technically without any apparent break in the diegesis." The erotic thriller was peculiarly invested in the interplay of male gazes that operate in the film and the male gazes that operate in the audience—and in how film teaches men in the audience how to see and teaches women in the audience how to maximize being seen.

The infrastructural significance of the "show-girl" in reconciling the diegetic space of the film's fictional world and the nondiegetic space of the audience is embedded in Mulvey's hyphenation of the name. Williams points out that the posters for *Showgirls* parsed the word in a similar way, placing a lithe fragment of Berkley's body between "Show" and "Girls": "A noun becomes a verb; a statement of content (this will be a movie about showgirls) becomes a promise (this movie will show us girls, revealing what's hidden behind the poster's black concealments)."[15] As a figure of the male gaze, the "show-girl" conceals and reveals, generating the scopophilia that Mulvey identifies as the erotic basis of the male gaze. While this scopophilia may be organized around the female body, it also exceeds the female body, at least within Mulvey's psychoanalytic scheme, since "scopophilia [is] one of the component instincts of sexuality which exist as drives quite independently of the erotogenic zones."[16]

Within Mulvey's account, the "show-girl" therefore exists as the cusp where the male gaze is detached from the female body and generalized into a broader scopophilic principle. This corresponds to the cusp that *Showgirls* occupies between the second and third stages of the erotic thriller. As Williams notes, films made during the second stage, such as *Basic Instinct* and *Sliver*, were quite frank about depicting sexuality and genitality. By contrast, *Showgirls* features only one sex scene and largely dissociates sexuality from genitality, de-emphasizing the eroticism of the naked female body by placing it within a broader scopophilic milieu that is depicted through Las Vegas, thereby subsuming the Strip and its "smiling snatches" into the perpetual tease of genitality. Part of the film's curious depiction of Las Vegas is that it is never primarily presented as a gambling city—or at least not in a traditional sense. While Nomi might lose at the jackpots in the opening scene, the Las Vegas economy, as Joe Eszterhas and Verhoeven present it, is dependent on musical theater and live performance, both in the "highbrow" form of the showgirl revues and the "lowbrow" form of the city's stripteases.

The real gamble in this iteration of Las Vegas doesn't lie in the casinos but in the way that the film thematizes the male gaze as a scopophilic pleasure in and of itself, effectively crafting a film in which scopophilia becomes its own object, resulting in a second-order scopophilia in which the audience is encouraged to invest erotic pleasure in looking at themselves looking.

Verhoeven and Eszterhas's decision to transform the libidinal economics of the erotic thriller into the subject of their erotic thriller means that *Showgirls* both exemplifies and exhausts the genre, explaining both its allure as it was being promoted and its subsequent failure at the box office: "Thus *Showgirls* overtly read sexuality as commodity, never as romance. . . . Perhaps the most shocking thing about *Showgirls* is the sheer crudity of the erotic economics upon which these images rely."[17] This results in a situation in which "explicitness is judged as an effect of quantity rather than quality . . . a 131-minute testament to Roland Barthes' famous 'Woman is desexualised the moment she is stripped naked.'"[18] Yet Williams's insistence that *Showgirls* is essentially "made-for-the-living room masturbation fare which briefly tries to pass itself off as theatrical-class" belies the extent to which these erotic economies are embedded within the hypercinematic style of the film.[19] Certainly, as Williams argues, erotic thrillers thrived at the video store, where they formed a bridge between the regular selection and the "back room" typical of independent stores and small chains, while the straight-to-video market drove the nomenclature of erotic thriller titles toward "two shocking elements into one come-on message" that would be immediately alluring on a VHS sleeve.[20] Yet the erotic thriller also mounted a case for cinematic experience in the grandest of wide-screen modes, a process that culminated with *Showgirls,* which presents the male gaze both as a spectacle in and of itself and as a spectacle that can be appreciated only at a cinematic scale.

To some extent, Williams acknowledges that the erotic thriller represents an argument for the cinematic. Early in her book, she condenses the genre to a single question: "When contemporary mainstream sex cinema works to the limits of what it is allowed to do, what are we allowed to see?"[21] The erotic thriller is only *just* mainstream, even as it negotiates the complex censorial space between what is deemed acceptable in cinemas, at video stores, and within the privacy of home viewing. In doing so, it enacts a peak continuum between the multiplex and the video store, evoking and enacting a finitude to cinematic experience as it was understood at this moment in time. Within this broader milieu, *Showgirls* functions as an apotheosis of this anxiety about the relation between the multiplex and the video store experience and attachment. On the one hand, *Showgirls* had the most pronounced VHS and DVD afterlife of any of the erotic thrillers of the 1990s, really gaining traction only once it had entered the home viewing market, due in part to Verhoeven's inability to turn the new NC-17 rating into a cinematically viable classification.[22] Yet *Showgirls* is the most expansive of all the major erotic thrillers in its cinematic ambitions, offering a series of panoramic, wide-screen spectacles that both replicate and demand the scale of a multiplex spectatorial experience, reflecting Verhoeven's experiment in discerning whether "sexual material," especially that of the erotic thriller, "could be treated in an adult fashion with a large-scale theatrical release."[23]

No surprise, then, that Williams sees "Las Vegas as a metaphor for Hollywood" in *Showgirls* since the film takes place, in its entirety, en route to Los Angeles.[24] Nomi's ambitions are ultimately cinematic, but the film suggests that Hollywood, and the traditional film industry, can no longer command the cinematic intensity needed to mitigate against a world in which cinema has increasingly been displaced by its own medial supplements, such as VHS, straight-to-VHS, and home viewing experiences. Verhoeven therefore uses the hyperreal space of Las Vegas to enact a hypercinematic spectacle in which cinema itself, and the male gaze that has traditionally animated cinema, is turned into the ultimate spectatorial and erotic situation. Since the male gaze was typically coded as white, this turns the white naked female body into a source of cinematic salvation, as Verhoeven constructs a series of elaborate tableaux around Nomi, Cristal, and the erotic space between them. As in most of the erotic thrillers that came out around this time—especially those penned by Eszterhas—*Showgirls* is less invested in lesbian sexuality on its own terms than as a heightened address to, and defiant subversion of, the male gaze that animates so much of the film, at least when it focuses on the relationship between Nomi and Cristal, the main emotional backbone of the screenplay.

In fact, *Showgirls* contains a more genuinely queer vision of lesbian sexuality in its interstitial spaces, framing lesbianism largely as an intersectional category that can't be understood in terms of the rapport between remunerative white female bodies, so thoroughly have these been co-opted by the Hollywood apparatus. The first source of lesbian sexuality occurs among the working-class women at the strip club where Nomi initially gets work. While these women address the male gaze of both the audience and their clients, they do so too crudely and uncouthly for the likes of the erotic thriller. As working-class women, they work too hard for the gaze, meaning that their cruisy sexual energy, and their invitation to Nomi to "party" with them, is largely dissociated from Nomi's rapport with Cristal. The second and more pervasive source of lesbian sexuality occurs between Nomi and Molly Abrams, a Black-Hispanic woman played by Gina Ravera, who becomes Nomi's confidante, ally, and roommate.

In the *Fatal Attractions* podcast, Matthew Turner reiterates the widespread notion that the erotic thriller has fallen on hard times, noting that "modern versions these days (for example Beyoncé in *Obsessed* or Rosario Dawson in *Unforgettable*) seem to fall flat and don't strike a chord with audiences," while also noting that at least *Showgirls* is never "lying to itself" in its economy of erotic scale.[25] It is telling that Turner references Beyoncé and Dawson as an index of the erotic thriller's decline, since while there may have been multiple other halfhearted remakes, these are the two most prominent films to feature nonwhite actresses. As Turner intuits, the erotic thriller doesn't really make sense with nonwhite leads, or at least with leads who are decisively or emphatically identified as other than white, since its subject matter, preoccupation, and anxiety are that of the male gaze as it has been defined from classical Hollywood up to the present day. While the erotic thriller is erotic, it is not exotic, meaning that Molly's presence in *Showgirls*, and her rapport with Nomi, introduces an uncanny element from the start. As with the strippers, the addition of an element—there, class; here, race—that offsets the hegemony of the white female body lies outside the ambit of the genre, meaning that Nomi's rapport with Molly is largely unprocessed by the film's spectacular apparatus. Although Molly and the strippers play a key role in facilitating Nomi's spectacular trajectory, they are conspicuously and structurally absent from that trajectory as it unfolds.

Between the stylized lesbianism of Nomi and Cristal and the subsumed lesbianism of Nomi, Molly, and the strippers, a complex dialogue emerges in which lesbianism itself becomes coterminous with the film's anxieties and aspirations about the role of cinematic spectacle within American media. Lesbian sexuality becomes a kind of limit case for the erotic thriller—proof, on the one hand, of how eloquently it can turn the male gaze into a subject matter, but also proof that this gaze, and its cinematic coordinates, have clear demarcations and limitations. Since the erotic thriller is so preoccupied with a "one-sided gaze," as Newland puts it, its writers and directors tend to be "more concerned with exploiting—and then condemning—the feminine wiles of its women, rather than offering genuine sensuality."[26] In the process, lesbian sexuality becomes a limit case for the sensuality of cinema itself, offering lesbianism both as a horizon of unimaginable sensuality and as a study in erotic metrics that turns out to be surprisingly banal, bland, and by the numbers. As Lee Wallace notes, David Lynch's *Mulholland Drive* took this aspect of the erotic thriller even further than *Showgirls*, using a stylized lesbian sex scene to suggest the demise of cinema as both medium and form by taking "the classical cinematic conflation of homosexuality and spectacle to formal extremes."[27] Only *Mulholland Drive*, within Wallace's scheme, has exceeded *Showgirls* in its extension of the erotic thriller form, which will prove critical to its quotation in the opening act of *Showgirls 2*.

To fully grasp the significance of this citation, however, the style of *Showgirls 2* needs to be set against that of Verhoeven's film. Throughout *Showgirls*, Nomi's trajectory is counterpoised with that of Penny, a stripper who never makes her way into the big time and who ends up living with James, Nomi's onetime lover, played by Glenn Plummer. Between Nomi, Penny, and James, three distinct types of spectacle emerge within Verhoeven's vision of Las Vegas. First, there is the spectacle of the strip club, which is framed as both an impoverished cinematic experience and an impoverished iteration of the erotic thriller. Second, there is the indie circuit, represented by James's original dance piece, which he initially writes for Nomi but ends up conceding to Penny after Nomi refuses to stay with him. Finally, there is the hypercinematic spectacle of Cristal's show and the infrastructure that supports it. While this show contains elements of striptease, they are subsumed into a much more ambitious theatrical extravaganza, situated in a theater in which the patrons are kept at an appropriate distance from the performers, who never come into direct contact with them.

The opening scene of *Showgirls* immediately indicates that Nomi is more aligned with this cinematic third space in the film as she moves contiguously from one increasingly stylized space to the next, with the help of the hyperactive body movements that she will eventually put to the service of Cristal's show. In the opening scene, a tracking shot takes us through a mall car park to a Las Vegas sign, while a series of hyperactive movements—Nomi taking her knife out of her holster, a car swerving to the side of the road, Nomi hitting the man giving her a lift—quickly bridges the distance between the highway and the Las Vegas Strip. From there, Verhoeven moves rapidly from the Strip to the interior of a casino, where Nomi wins big and then runs outside and onto the road, where she is nearly hit by a car, before collapsing into Molly's arms. Then we move to Nomi and Molly having dinner. Nomi's body language becomes even more frenetic and manic, propelling us six months ahead, when Nomi is now living with Molly and on her way to watch Cristal's show at the Stardust theater, where she imitates the motions of the dancers as she gazes on from the audience.

It takes only ten minutes of the film for Las Vegas, and its role in the American cultural landscape, to be telescoped into the show playing at the Stardust and the spectacle of Cristal's body. From this point onward, the postmodern extravagance of the Strip is never extricable from the show, which radiates an ultra-cinematic decor and a taste for immaculate and grandly scaled mise-en-scènes that grow more dramatic as the film proceeds. Nomi's dance moves become the haptic vocabulary required to sustain this ever-increasing sense of spectacle, enabled by a consumer environment that is always a little too intrusive and a little too oversized, forcing Nomi to strain herself to accommodate it. From the hyperactive way she doles ketchup onto her meal during her first night with Molly, to the enormous bags of chips that she shares with Molly, to the lollipop ring that she sucks on during a pivotal early scene, Nomi is continually striving to fit her body language to spectacle as an economy of scale. The film's camerawork follows suit, adopting a dizzying array of dollies, pans, and tracking shots that mirror Nomi's body language even as they offset and disorient her position in space even further, forcing her to work doubly hard to keep up with their gymnastic contortions.

This economy of scale culminates with the Stardust, whose cavernous proscenium is pointedly contrasted to the theater-in-the-round of the strip club where Nomi initially finds work. Verhoeven stages multiple scenes to emphasize the enormous scale of this space, especially when it is empty or when only the cast and crew are in the audience, since it is during these moments that its coordinates ramify most vividly. While erotic spectacle might take place in this theater, the theater itself is largely de-eroticized and instead used as an objective correlative for the erotic economics of the film itself. The point is succinctly made midway through the film, when Nomi agrees to do an extra gig for a group of wealthy businessmen who have come to Las Vegas to participate in a boat show. Cristal puts Nomi onto this opportunity, and for a moment it seems as if Nomi will be subjected to some kind of egregious sexual humiliation for having dared to speak out of turn to Cristal. Yet Nomi abruptly refuses the sexual overtones of the businessmen, leaving the focus of the scene on the cavernous opening shot of the boat show, which replicates the sight lines, scale, and spectacular imperative of the theater, but attaches it to an even more explicit market imperative. This boat show is the biggest space in the film we see outside the theater, and it serves to demystify the theater, offsetting the shadowy spaces of the Stardust's proscenium with a series of precisely cataloged and curated boats reaching as far as the camera can see.

The revelation of the boat show is that the white female body functions in the same way as these gleaming white nautical crafts. Nomi may be shocked at the comparison, and artistic director Zack Carey, played by Kyle MacLachlan, may tell her that he is shocked as well, but Zack's protestations turn out to be another manifestation of the proscenium, uttered onstage in between rehearsals. Like the boats in the show, the white female body is venerated as a consumer object above all, resulting in three key performances at the Stardust that are oddly divested of erotic energy. All three of these spectacles play as Busby Berkeley inflected through exploitation cinema, as the classical coordinates of the early Hollywood musical are paired with a more lascivious and explicitly sexual sense of spectacle. Yet where Berkeley's writhing configurations of female bodies were erotic, suggesting a series of bodily combinations that couldn't be directly represented from within the Hays Code, Verhoeven's elaborate sequences jettison eroticism in favor of a franker and more mercenary sexuality. While Berkeley's sequences suggest an indefinite number of erotic combinations, Verhoeven's sequences close down the possibility of further erotic extension, focusing on the breasts, in particular, as the only sexual spectacle of any significance or stable market value.

All three of these pivotal sequences venerate the breasts through Cristal's body, which emerges only as a function of the elaborate choreographic set pieces that constitute the "act." The first sequence, which also forms Nomi's first experience of Cristal, takes place at the top of a volcano, where the dancers move in time to a Technicolor-styled vista of lava, magma, and bright red and yellow hues. In this sequence, Cristal emerges from the volcano, literally and figuratively "hot" as she enters the final part of the dance with calculated abandon. However, this "hotness" has started to dissipate by the second sequence, which transplants the veneration of Cristal's body to a more stylized church-like environment, clad in cool tones and blue hues. This time, Cristal ascends from the stage, rather than onto the stage, clasping herself in a crucifix-like position as the dancers continue the sequence without her. The third sequence culminates this newfound coldness with a stylized sadomasochistic display, in which the actors roam around the stage on motorcycles and Cristal descends, clad in leather bondage gear, as a fetish object, entirely devoid of the "heat" of the original volcano dance sequence.

The entire trajectory of *Showgirls* is bound up in the progression of these three dance sequences. In moving from the volcano to bondage, Cristal is gradually shorn of erotic "heat" and instead subsumed into a more explicitly scopophilic imperative. In the first sequence, Cristal's presence sends a heat wave out through the dancers, entrancing the audience with what it must be like to touch her. By the third sequence, she is being touched and manhandled by all the dancers, who manipulate her body with a more sadistic and scopophilic attitude. Concomitantly, the sequences mark a movement from classical Hollywood to the erotic thriller. While the volcano sequence contains female nudity, it is stylized in such a way as to be plausible in certain mid-century genres, such as the sword-and-sandal epic, adventure film, or ethnographic film. By the time we arrive at the bondage sequence, however, there can be no doubt that we are in the realm of the erotic thriller, with its focus on tastefully curated and expertly managed kink. Finally, the progression of the three dance sequences correspond to Nomi's—and the audience's—perception of Cristal. Taken together, the three sequences map a rise and fall, in which Cristal's body is lifted onto the stage, lifted above the stage, and then deposited back onto the stage once more. Each of these moments marks a critical juncture in Nomi's relation to Cristal—she first sees her during the volcano sequence, first realizes how far she must go to get a part during the religious sequence, and then pushes

Cristal down the stairs after the bondage sequence, ensuring she gets Cristal's part in turn.

When Nomi takes on Cristal's role, the cycle starts again, as Nomi now finds herself the star of the volcano sequence, and Verhoeven repeats the backstage reception of Cristal earlier in the film shot for shot, with Nomi now occupying Cristal's place. The economy of this cycle, and the rotation of this trilogy of Stardust pieces, reflect the economy with which the erotic thriller internalizes the spectacular language of classical Hollywood. Every erotic thriller, *Showgirls* insists, co-opts the cinematicity of classical Hollywood to broker a connection to the 1990s by way of an intensified male gaze that turns back on itself as the final testament to the pleasures of cinematic experience. Where *Showgirls* differs is by explicitly presenting this process *as* a cycle, effectively turning the spectacular logic of the erotic thriller into its subject matter. Neither quite a deconstruction nor a consummation of the erotic thriller, *Showgirls* instead enacts the metrics of the erotic thriller, allegorizing its own condition of production even as it refuses to allow its audience quite enough critical distance for irony. Both more excessive and more corporate than any other images to circulate through the erotic thriller, Verhoeven's spectacles are continually co-opted by corporate forces within the film, resulting in an executive aesthetic that manages as much as it massages the audience.

The erotic thriller is therefore, first and foremost, an argument for cinema, explaining why it has declined so dramatically in the last twenty years. While most genres of the 1980s and 1990s have been rebooted in some way, these reboots have generally been dependent on a plethora of new viewing platforms. By contrast, the erotic thriller really ramifies only as a cinematic spectacle or in a media ecology in which cinema still holds a hierarchical relationship to VHS, DVDs, and other subsidiary media. While Williams notes that the erotic thriller was peculiarly obsessed with the synergy between the multiplex and the video store, this synergy was predicated on the precarious supremacy of the multiplex as the site at which the broad strokes of the erotic thriller were anchored and established. Even erotic thrillers that were made for the small screen gained much of their titillating allure from the way in which they evoked this multiplex milieu, encouraging home audiences to recognize that they were experiencing the total panoramic sweep of the erotic thriller from the comfort of their couches, transforming the genre into the first major venue for the home theater experience.

The postcinematic milieu of the 2010s is therefore precisely what the erotic thriller was steeling itself against, meaning that any attempt to reboot the erotic thriller must take into account the conditions of production that preclude its ongoing existence in the present. This is the project of *Showgirls 2,* which plays less as a traditional sequel and more as an alternative version of the trajectories outlined in the original film. There, Nomi's path led her toward an intensified cinematic spectacle in the form of the Stardust proscenium while Penny's path led her toward a more impoverished spectacle that was associated both with the original world of the strip club and with James's indie dance performance. While James may have originally composed this performance for Nomi, he was forced to rebrand it for Penny after Nomi rejected his advances. An indie, art house impulse was therefore subsumed into the denuded cinematic spectacle of Penny's downward mobility. This convergence is explored further in *Showgirls 2: Penny's from Heaven,* which is named after Penny, features Penny as protagonist, and was written and directed by Rena Riffel, who performs Penny in *Showgirls.*

The first scene of *Showgirls 2* starts with the dance piece that James composed for Nomi, foregrounding this convergence of indie and striptease impulses—and the corresponding movement away from the cinematic slick of *Showgirls*—from the very outset. While James may have composed this dance for Penny, he is now presented in the guise of a striptease customer, watching her perform it for him as he speaks crudely and exploitatively about the way her body looks. The discerning dance curator of the original film is long gone, as is the cinematic milieu that his indie credentials briefly glimpsed. Instead, Riffel situates us in a grungy, amateur, ugly environment that deliberately sets itself against the executive assurance of Verhoeven's elaborate mise-en-scènes. Barely competent, but also very long, *Showgirls 2* consistently resists the idea of mise-en-scène itself, retreating so far from the proscenium shots of *Showgirls* that most of its spaces are discontinuous with one another and very difficult to parse or process on their own terms. If the shooting locations weren't so random, they might conceivably be drawn from Riffel's own daily routine and living spaces, but there's just enough variety to prevent even that vicarious semblance of homeliness, as Riffel quickly cloaks her scenes in darkness whenever they come too close to a sense of place.

As a result, *Showgirls 2* is devoid of even the most cursory sense of Las Vegas in its opening scenes, which is just as well, since Riffel quickly continues the westward momentum that drove Verhoeven's film. Just as Nomi was in Las Vegas en route to Los Angeles and headed for the City of Angels in the final scene, so Penny decides to head to Los Angeles as well, hitching a ride to Hollywood to try to get a job as a professional dancer. In Verhoeven's film, Nomi gets a lift from the same man who drives her to Las Vegas in the first place and repeats many of the same gestures when she gets into his car, creating a circular narrative logic that suggests that Las Vegas has already exhausted the cinematic spectacle she is hoping to achieve on the West Coast. These final moments of *Showgirls* replay the entire film as camp, and Riffel continues that gesture. In doing so, she ruptures the executive style of *Showgirls*, permitting the audience a critical distance that mitigates against the all-encompassing sight lines of the Stardust. Moreover, by completing

Nomi's fantasy of Los Angeles, *Showgirls 2* effectively removes it as fantasy, presenting a vision of Los Angeles that is devoid of even the most residual of cinematic cues, let alone the grand stardom that Nomi is hoping to find.

In its own way, *Showgirls 2* thus forms part of a wider corpus of works that, in the 2010s, attempted to envisage how Los Angeles might appear after cinema, now that the cinematic medium has lost some of its hegemony within American popular culture. While Penny might head to Los Angeles to try to avoid the convergence of indie and striptease imperatives we see in the opening scene, she is never able to recapitulate the grand cinematic scale of the original film, but instead finds herself cast as a dancer for a television program. In fact, the most emphatic cinematic citations occur during the transition from Las Vegas to Los Angeles and proceed through three distinct stages. First, Penny decides that she needs to move to Los Angeles after a client reduces her screen aspirations to a fetish, ogling her while referring to himself as "Mr. Movie Producer." Second, Penny hitches a lift with the same man who provided Nomi with a lift in the original film, pulling out a casting director's business card from between her legs before her driver reveals that this director is one of his relatives. Finally, after a series of spatially incoherent sequences, Penny "arrives" in Los Angeles much as Laura Elena Harring's character arrives in Los Angeles at the start of *Mulholland Drive,* stumbling awkwardly down a street before Riffel cuts to an image of the Mulholland Drive street sign that replicates and reiterates the beginning of the eerie title sequence in David Lynch's film.

Interestingly, Penny is wearing a blonde wig during this scene, meaning that she encapsulates Harring's character both at the beginning of the film, when she is named Rita, and at the end of the film, when she is named Camilla Rhodes. Lynch's fantasy of Los Angeles exists between those split identities—one a regular name, one named after Rita Hayworth—while the central lesbian sex scene in *Mulholland Drive* intensifies and condenses the vocabulary of the erotic thriller to try to reconcile these two conceptions of what Hollywood represents. As Wallace notes, however, Lynch is never able to effect this reconciliation, effectively exhausting the erotic thriller, and its dependence on lesbian optics to rehabilitate the male gaze, by generating "[a] rapid series of present tense and assorted flashback scenes . . . all of which assist the claims of lesbian continuity but continue to test the viewer's apprehension of a consistent storyworld."[28] Continuing to test continuity, the lesbian sex scene in *Mulholland Drive* becomes a kind of epilogue to *Showgirls*' efforts to use the erotic thriller as a limit case in both cinematic continuity and the viability of cinema itself as a continuing medium and space. By recapitulating this entire fantasy dissolution as camp, and by situating it in an impoverished milieu composed mainly of darkness, *Showgirls 2* indicates that the fears of the erotic thriller have indeed come to pass, leaving their lesbian images free-floating and decontextualized.

Showgirls 2 enacts the conditions of productions that led to the demise of the erotic thriller. This process is encapsulated in the way Riffel handles the three key Stardust spectacles of the original film. Whereas *Showgirls 2* is quite scrupulous about revisiting the key moments from the original, these three performances are compressed into a single relatively short scene. Like the volcano sequence, this represents our first sustained introduction to the key spectacular space of Riffel's film, which now takes the form of a cramped television studio rather than an expansive proscenium. Like the scene in the church, this sequence involves a dancer undermining another dancer by scattering rhinestones beneath her feet. Finally, this tableau recalls the bondage sequence by setting the events in play that lead to Penny taking over the main role and graduating into the star attraction.

By compressing these three spectacles, however, Riffel defuses their spectacular imperative, partly because it was impossible for any one of them to have been further intensified without lapsing into banality and self-parody. In contrast to the Stardust, the television studio is tightly shot, drably furnished, and drably lit. While the scene starts with a few symmetrical configurations of bodies that briefly recall the Busby Berkeley style of the Stardust sequences, these are quickly undercut by the rhinestone incident, which devolves the scene rather than being incorporated into its broader choreography, as occurs in Verhoeven's version. Not only does the dance fall apart, but it dissolves into the space that should be occupied by the audience, in a visceral reminder that this tight theatrical space is addressing a televisual demographic. Whereas the empty space of *Showgirls* brimmed with spectacular potential, the empty space in this scene is neither theatrical nor cinematic, instead invoking a televisual audience whose absence denudes the dance scene, rather than intensifying or revivifying it.

Finally, this collapse of the cinematic coordinates of the original film disrupts the male gaze that the erotic thriller aimed to rehabilitate as the last vestige of cinematic spectacle. After the dancer falls to the floor in Riffel's version, the best candidate to replace her is actually one of the gay cast members, who makes a convincing bid to don the dress and become the lead of the show. Although he is initially rebuffed by the "commonsense" artistic director, turns out the two have slept together, despite the latter exuding the hangdog heterosexuality typically associated with straightness in the original film. The guardian of the male gaze in *Showgirls* is now used to collapse male and female bodies, as the gay dancer outs himself as transgender to quell any residual concerns about having a "male" lead. Finally, this sequence is shifted to a flat-screen television, where Penny is watching the scene unfold.

This final shift is the last ingredient in Riffel's dissolution of the residual cinematic coordinates of the scene and its residual appeal to the male gaze. While the television program broadcasts live, meaning it is plausible that the accident has gone to air, it's less likely that the events that have transpired on the sidelines, involving the trans dancer and the artistic director, have been captured on the screen, partly because they occur on the fringes of the space that is being filmed. Yet Penny appears to have internalized their import, situating the entire scene in a strange zone between diegetic and nondiegetic space that Shane Denson has identified with the "crazy cameras" typical of a postcinematic environment: "imaging apparatuses, both physical and virtual—[that] seem not to know their place with respect to the separation of diegetic and non-diegetic planes of reality . . . [and that] therefore fail to situate viewers in a consistently and coherently designated spectating-position."[29] By retreating from the classicism of *Showgirls* to the craziness of this new media regime, Riffel elegantly articulates the erotic thriller as an argument for cinema, and for the dependence of cinema on the male gaze, that no longer computes in a postcinematic world. While *Showgirls,* like *Mulholland Drive,* made one last extravagant bid for this spectacular logic, *Showgirls 2* proves why that bid was always destined to fail, as fantasmastic as pennies from heaven, forming a final grace note on the erotic thriller as a whole and its cinematic border conditions.

BILLY STEVENSON earned his PhD in Literature and Film Studies from the University of Sydney. His recent work appears in *Senses of Cinema, Post-Cinema: Theorizing 21st-Century Film,* and *ReFocus: The Films of Paul Schrader.*

References

Barton-Fumo, Margaret, ed. *Paul Verhoeven: Interviews*. Jackson: University Press of Mississippi, 2018.

Catsoulis, Jeannette. "*Deep Water* Review: Love and Loathing in New Orleans." *New York Times*, March 17, 2022. https://www.nytimes.com/2022/03/17/movies/deep-water-review.html.

Collins, Jim. *Architectures of Excess: Cultural Life in the Information Age*. London: Routledge, 1995.

———. "Genericity in the Nineties: Eclectic Irony and the New Sincerity." In *Film Theory Goes to the Movies*, edited by Jim Collins, Hilary Radner, and Ava Preacher Collins, 242–63. New York: Routledge, 1993.

Denson, Shane. "Crazy Cameras, Discorrelated Images, and the Post-perceptual Mediation of Post-cinematic Affect." In *Post-cinema: Theorizing 21st-century Film*, edited by Shane Denson and Julia Leyda, 193–232. Falmer: Reframe, 2016. https://reframe.sussex.ac.uk/post-cinema/2-5-denson/.

Howe, Desson. "*Showgirls*." *Washington Post*, September 22, 1995. http://www.washingtonpost.com/wp-srv/style/longterm/movies/videos/showgirlsnc17howe_c02e6a.htm.

Lambie, Ryan. "The Rise and Fall of the Erotic Thriller." Den of Geek, July 16, 2012. https://www.denofgeek.com/movies/22017/the-rise-and-fall-of-the-erotic-thriller.

Mulvey, Laura. "Visual Pleasure and Narrative Cinema." In *The Norton Anthology of Theory and Criticism*, edited by Vincent B. Leitch, William E. Cain, Laurie A. Finke, Barbara E. Johnson, John McGowan, and Jeffrey J. Williams, 2181–92. New York: W. W. Norton, 2001.

Newland, Christina. "The Gruesome Demise of the 90s Erotic Thriller." *Vice*, December 20, 2017. https://www.vice.com/en_us/article/xwvjz3/the-gruesome-demise-of-the-90s-erotic-thriller.

Palmer, R. Barton. *Hollywood's Dark Cinema: The American Film Noir*. Farmington Hills, MI: Twayne, 1994.

Riffel, Rena, dir. *Showgirls 2: Penny's from Heaven*. Rena Riffel Films, 2011.

Turner, Matthew, host. "Episode 038: *Showgirls*." *Fatal Attractions* (podcast), July 6, 2018. https://fatalattractions.libsyn.com/episode-038-showgirls.

Verhoeven, Paul, dir. *Showgirls*. Carolco Pictures, Chargeurs, United Artists, 1995.

Wallace, Lee. *Lesbianism, Cinema, Space: The Sexual Life of Apartments*. London: Routledge, 2011.

Williams, Linda Ruth. *The Erotic Thriller in Contemporary Cinema*. Bloomington: Indiana University Press, 2005.

Notes

1. Paul Verhoeven, dir., *Showgirls* (Carolco Pictures, Chargeurs, United Artists, 1995).

2. Desson Howe, "*Showgirls,*" *Washington Post*, September 22, 1995, http://www.washingtonpost.com/wp-srv/style/longterm/movies/videos/showgirlsnc17howe_c02e6a.htm.

3. Linda Ruth Williams, *The Erotic Thriller in Contemporary Cinema* (Bloomington: Indiana University Press, 2005); Jim Collins, *Architectures of Excess: Cultural Life in the Information Age* (London: Routledge, 1995).

4. Jim Collins, "Genericity in the Nineties: Eclectic Irony and the New Sincerity," in *Film Theory Goes to the Movies*, ed. Jim Collins, Hilary Radner, and Ava Preacher Collins (New York: Routledge, 1993), 246.

5. Williams, *Erotic Thriller*, 172.

6. Ryan Lambie, "The Rise and Fall of the Erotic Thriller," Den of Geek, July 16, 2012, https://www.denofgeek.com/movies/22017/the-rise-and-fall-of-the-erotic-thriller.

7. R. Barton Palmer, *Hollywood's Dark Cinema: The American Film Noir* (Farmington Hills, MI: Twayne, 1994), 168.

8. Christina Newland, "The Gruesome Demise of the Erotic Thriller," *Vice*, December 20, 2017, https://www.vice.com/en_us/article/xwvjz3/the-gruesome-demise-of-the-90s-erotic-thriller; Williams, *Erotic Thriller*, 2.

9. Williams, *Erotic Thriller*, x.

10. Jeannette Catsoulis, "*Deep Water* Review: Love and Loathing in New Orleans," *New York Times*, March 17, 2022, https://www.nytimes.com/2022/03/17/movies/deep-water-review.html.

11. Rena Riffel, dir., *Showgirls 2: Penny's from Heaven* (Rena Riffel Films, 2011).

12. Lambie, "Rise and Fall."

13. Margaret Barton-Fumo, ed., *Paul Verhoeven: Interviews* (Jackson: University Press of Mississippi, 2018).

14. Laura Mulvey, "Visual Pleasure and Narrative Cinema," in *The Norton Anthology of Theory and Criticism*, ed. Vincent B. Leitch, William E. Cain, Laurie A. Finke, Barbara E. Johnson, John McGowan, and Jeffrey J. Williams (New York: W. W. Norton, 2001), 2186–87.

15. Williams, *Erotic Thriller*, 171.

16. Mulvey, "Visual Pleasure," 2184.

17. Williams, *Erotic Thriller*, 174.

18. Ibid., 171.

19. Ibid., 175.

20. Ibid., 9.

21. Ibid., 3.

22. Ibid., 168.

23. Ibid.

24. Ibid., 172.

25. Mathew Turner, host, "Episode 38: *Showgirls*," *Fatal Attractions* (podcast), July 6, 2018, https://fatalattractions.libsyn.com/episode-038-showgirls.

26. Newland, "Gruesome Demise."

27. Lee Wallace, *Lesbianism, Cinema, Space: The Sexual Life of Apartments* (London: Routledge, 2011), 99.

28. Ibid., 111.

29. Shane Denson, "Crazy Cameras, Discorrelated Images, and the Post-perceptual Mediation of Post-cinematic Affect," in *Post-cinema: Theorizing 21st-century Film*, ed. Shane Denson and Julia Leyda (Falmer: Reframe, 2016), http://reframe.sussex.ac.uk/post-cinema.

FIFTY SHADES OF *SHOWGIRLS* 6

BETTER LIVING THROUGH MEDIATION

MELISSA HARDIE

During an appearance on *Saturday Night Live* to promote the movie, Dakota Johnson said of the novel *Fifty Shades of Grey* that it was the kind of book that "made you want to never touch your mother's Kindle."[1] In her comment, Johnson evoked complex generic crossovers and generational anxieties at work in the film and, more generally, at work in film. Johnson plays Anastasia Steele, a *naive* indoctrinated in the arts of erotic pleasure by entrepreneur Christian Grey. This scheme and its implicit taboos place it in a historicized past, as it vaunts forms of erotic socialization historically familiar but frowned on in the present. Temporal dislocation is implicit also in the book's gestation as a fan fictional exercise, an elaboration of the *Twilight* saga created in a promiscuous loop of decentered authoring termed "prosumption," where author and readers collaborate as producers and consumers.[2] In her accounting for the success of the book and subsequent series, Eva Illouz notes the novel's "high retrievability through the Internet and e-reading devices."[3] As such, the fan fiction–novel–Kindle iterations of the film's gestation threaten to overwhelm that orderly progression of media styles and mediations that is otherwise assumed in accounts of ecologies where media fight for space in an otherwise overpopulated domain.

Accounts of this space as a domain of contest are not new, and one way to characterize the persistence of some forms of media has been to see those as "residual," still around but not very dynamic. The term *residual media* appears in Charles Acland's edited volume *Residual Media* and riffs on Raymond Williams's description of dominant, residual, and emergent culture.[4] In launching the film version of *Fifty Shades of Grey*, Johnson's comment demonstrates the hauntological power of superannuated media as well: situating her generation as fastidiously seeking distance from the prior one, Johnson's comment positions the novel as an object that describes a generational uneasiness over the "handoff" between mother and daughter, or mentor and mentee, or (more abstractly) between media: book, Kindle, film. Wanting to represent the novel through Kindle-delivered remediation exacerbates rather than mitigates the problem, where the alliance between novel and Kindle has been a way for the residuum to reassert itself in medial terms.

But this assertion is equally striking in generic terms. Johnson's comment rises above an ordinary moment of mediatic intergenerational disquiet when you remember that her mother is Melanie Griffith (*her* mother was Tippi Hedren). So in a more explicit way than usual, an oedipal disquiet about where the mother's hand has gone and what the mother's hand has done is mapped onto competing genealogies: a technological genealogy that articulates a generational relationship between the codex to the movies memorialized in the Kindle as a print+screen digital reading device and a cinematic genealogy that draws a line from Tippi Hedren, the 1960s late Freudian heroine of Alfred Hitchcock's *Marnie* (1964), to her daughter Melanie Griffith, the 1980s mostly screwball star of *Working Girl* (1988), and finally to Johnson, the ingenue fan of the literary in *Fifty Shades of Grey* (2015).[5]

In this scenario, *Fifty Shades of Grey* offers a perverse rewriting of Mike Nichols's *Working Girl* (1988). In that film, Tess McGill (Melanie Griffith) bests rival Katharine Parker (Sigourney Weaver) for the affections of the suggestively named Jack Trainer (Harrison Ford), her mentor. She does this by being genuinely ingenuous but *also* by learning to emulate and succeed in the place of the older woman. The utter conventionality of this scheme in generic terms is offset by its unpredictably comic and consequently cruel lampooning of the "driven" older woman. That comedy is in marked contrast to the earlier films it parodies, such as Jean Negulesco's *The Best of Everything* (1959), where the impossibility of a place of respite for either woman in this contest is darkly augured by Parker's counterpart Amanda Farrow (Joan Crawford) abruptly quitting the contest to make a lugubrious yet fervid descent into suburban life.[6]

These medial and generic turns center this article as it claims that *Fifty Shades of Grey* and *Showgirls* are alike, even "*exactly* alike" (my emphasis), to quote Cristal Connors in the earlier film. I was reminded of the reception of *Showgirls* when I observed the reception of Sam Taylor-Johnson's *Fifty Shades of Grey* twenty years later. Like *Showgirls, Fifty Shades of Grey* was pilloried on its release and found to be extravagantly lacking in quality or merit, a joke, a preposterous put-up job—a scam. There's a better critical discourse for resisting these evaluations than I believed there was in 1995, and so I won't bother doing what I did then, which was to parse contemporary critique in a deconstructive way to find pressure points of resistance and real interest; these days there's a more efficient set of mental habits by which to circumvent such critical labors.[7] *Fifty Shades of Grey,* like *Showgirls,* is an interesting film, and, like *Showgirls,* its interest was only dimly augured in its reviews.

But it would be equally a detour to assume that this similarity in their reception was the only reason that one made me think of the other. Such a correlation might make sense in a critical practice more guided by reception than mine is or by one as interested in representation as I used to be, but in neither rests the case for a seemingly counterintuitive connection between the two films. Were it not for a kind of pressing comparison elicited by the sense of something alike between them, you might think they are, broadly speaking, opposites. The palettes of the films are as different as you could imagine: *Fifty Shades of Grey* is, as its name insinuates, a largely monochromatic, grayscale vision of secluded modernity; even in his lair of sexual depravity, sadist Christian Grey (Jamie Dornan) decks out his "torture chamber" in muted tones.[8] By contrast, *Showgirls'* palette offers blisteringly rich, saturated colors, outré scenery, and a seeming dissolution of the distinction between public and private space, boldly asserted by the use of neon palm trees to decorate and illuminate Zack Carey's (Kyle MacLachlan) bachelor pad. Paul Verhoeven's Euro vernacular, street cinematic is a world away from Taylor-Johnson's pseudo-literary chamber drama, where exterior shots are gray and opaque and interiors are coldly modernist, both stark and unambiguous yet murky and ambiguous by virtue of the chromatic calibrations implied by the plural noun *shades*. Despite its promise of sexual adventure, *Fifty Shades of Grey* represents sexuality as fastidious, and at its most extravagant, epicurean. In *Showgirls,* sexuality is florid and flagrant, unmanageable and visceral at the same time that it is manipulated in schemes every bit as devious as the later film's. Performances in *Fifty Shades of Grey* are likewise well mannered, whereas in *Showgirls* they are famously out of bounds, even ludicrous. While now we might see the theatrical excesses of *Showgirls* as Brechtian and estranging in deeply deliberate gestures of anti-realist style, at the time of their releases both films were held to be poorly judged and tedious in precisely these particulars and in rather similar ways; judged bland beyond vanilla, *Fifty Shades of Grey* was reviewed by Jack Halberstam on the Bully Bloggers website as "Fifty Shades of Zzzzzzzzz."[9]

But these contrasting mise-en-scènes are deceptive. Both films open with the introduction of a young woman out of her depth, stumbling into a scene beyond her own cognizance. In the case of *Showgirls,* unworldliness is registered by being the too easy victim of a con and thus by defeat in intellectual contest. Nomi Malone (Elizabeth Berkley) is outsmarted by Jeff (Dewey Weber) in an elementary scam, and her vulnerability establishes her as an ingenue despite her streetwise mannerisms and style. Her fall is metaphorical and intellectual, establishing a point of departure from which she requires pedagogical support. *Fifty Shades of Grey*'s ingenue, Anastasia Steele (Dakota Johnson), is new to the sexual though versed in its intellectual apprehension, a virginal literature major who falls into erotic thrall, literally, after stumbling into the office of her seducer. The film does not endeavor to articulate the erotic and the educational; her progression is into a world of entrepreneurial verve personified by Christian Grey, her putative mentor and seducer. Grey's character is Patrick Bateman repackaged for the post-crash teens of the new century; what, ironically, was critiqued as sociopathic and outré in *American Psycho* is domesticated as rogue and temperate in its subsequent outing.[10] Anastasia's *Bildung* is experienced through her creating, negotiating, and consenting to a contractual relationship with Grey as a form of allegorical enlightenment. This highly novelistic, quasi-Richardsonian plot paradoxically renders her academic knowledge intractably useless in both the commercial and the erotic scenarios Grey contrives. She is equally at sea in the world of entrepreneurial capitalism and the world of "straight" perversity; the pairing of the two is not subtle.

By contrast, Nomi's apparent dislocation from models of bourgeois literary self-creation is matched by what (after Eve Sedgwick) I call her "thinkiness," the sense that her movement around the screen, as around Las Vegas, is driven by calculation or intellectual heat.[11] Despite her duping early in the film, she is above all a thinker, proto-algorithmically calculating risk and benefit in her career progression and scamming where appropriate to advantage herself. Her relationships are transactional even when the value of the transaction is superseded by rich, affective opportunity, and the film unselfconsciously endorses folding affective benefit into schemes because, like Nomi, it purports and values no more ennobling social formation. There is no "outside" to the world of contrivance and calculation Nomi encounters in Vegas, a point made clear when her romantic interest and boss Zach Carey is revealed as casually complicit in a work opportunity that turns out to be a form of deceptive pimping. Nomi's *Bildung* therefore depends on her realization that the distinction between her past and her present isn't the nature of the exchanges but the environment of duplicity, or scamming, through which these exchanges are brokered. As such, her sentimental education is supported by the "thinkiness" of the scammer economy.

It seems unlikely that Joe Eszterhas and Paul Verhoeven had Barbara Loden's 1970 drama *Wanda* in mind as they scripted their main character, Nomi, negotiating the vernacular modernism of Las Vegas. Wanda's apparently purposeless drift in the American landscape considers the wandering woman as stranded and abject in the midst of masculine schemes and calculations. But a series of such abjected female wanderers in French cinema in particular more certainly ghosts Nomi's arrival and departure from our screen, such as the heroine of Agnès Varda's 1985 *Sans toit ni loi* (*Vagabond*).[12] Mona Bergeron (Sandrine Bonnaire) succumbs to the vicissitudes of precarity before the film even begins, and the film finds context, if not meaning, for her predicament. Such unassailable and cruel separation from the holding mechanisms that selectively define contemporary well-being is Nomi's predicament at the beginning of *Showgirls,* as copious commentary on the implications of her pseudonymous first name has stressed.[13] So when she thrives, the perplexity of this turnaround requires reconsideration of the terms of the bind in which she finds herself. That reconsideration needs to address some of the founding misalliances or misattributions of the film. For example, the fact that a prodigiously talented physical performer is maligned as second-rate or even incompetent aligns with the film's focus on Nomi's "thinkiness" as the work of locating the self in schemes advanced by others.

Showgirls' revision of the plot of female rivalry and supersession is interesting partly for the way it dramatizes the acquisition of the knowledge necessary to establish rivalry. Whereas Eve Harrington (Anne Baxter) in *All about Eve* knows in some preternatural way how to emulate her idol to the point of their mutual annihilation, Nomi learns through the movie how to do something similar to Cristal Connors, but it annihilates neither woman.[14] As she watches backstage rivalries, she hones her capacity to *be* a rival, essential for survival in the scamming economy. By contrast, *Fifty Shades of Grey* is interested in the legalistic parsing of contracts between heterosexual parties; its rivalry or contests are as "chambered" or closeted as *Showgirls'* are public, rehearsed on the stage, and privately concluded in the threshold space between front and back—the stairway.[15] Whereas Nomi is a self-starter, Anastasia is groomed for what passes for success in the late capital domain of enterprise. Of course, that its contestants, Anastasia and Christian, are ultimately alike is *Fifty Shades of Grey*'s comic premise: the sadist becomes ever more supplicant as he entreats the masochist to accept the terms of his contract, terms that are whittled into fifty shades of negotiation. But this alikeness is ironic, a reduction of parties to the insinuation of parity or simplicity. *Showgirls,* by contrast, proliferates versions and counterexamples: visually, with mirrors and symmetries; diegetically, through subplots and structural repetitions; and stylistically, with highly figured grounds for every figure. *Showgirls'* visually recursive style offers a heterogeneously centripetal drive for its insistent performativity: style moves tensely inward as actions (for example, dancing) are propulsively outward-bound.

Cristal Connors (Gina Gershon) says Nomi and herself are "exactly alike." As Adam Nayman notes, in this scene Verhoeven "violates the

180-degree rule," and in so doing he "convey[s] the effect of 'two women talking to themselves.'"[16] Nayman's reading of the "violation" comports with or even installs his book's larger thesis, that Eszterhas's script is in a dialectical relation to Verhoeven's mastery: "The contrast between the overstatement of the dialogue and the subtlety of the direction mirrors the contrast in the performance styles of Berkley and Gershon, which is more evident than ever—and which is the exact same dynamic that's supposed to be playing out between the two characters. Good filmmaking propping up bad screenwriting: a bad actress dragging down a good one. It's all in plain view."[17]

Nayman's account relies on the opposition between good and bad that underwrites his revisionist reading of the "so bad it's good" aesthetic of *Showgirls*. Rather than see this opposition as dissolved by the camerawork, it could be understood temporally as well as spatially: the bad actor is not yet good, the good actor declines to bad. Instead of static categories, they are immiscible and at times indistinguishable: "exactly alike." Or, put another way, instead of hidden "in plain view," this interplay is plainly visible precisely because it establishes the film's pedagogy.

Nayman's substitution of a dialectical struggle between director and writer attempts to create an auteur-based genealogy different from the one I've identified as centered on media ecology. One of the interesting things about historical criticism of *Showgirls* is the way it allies the film to the "erotic thriller"—most notably, of course, *Basic Instinct*, which Verhoeven made with Eszterhas three years earlier. But of course, *Showgirls* is not really a thriller: both in its reliance on the figure of the jaded ingenue and in its lack of plot suspense, it bears scant resemblance to the earlier film. What it does share with *Basic Instinct* is a "thinky" female protagonist who pairs sexual athleticism with a presence in the world centered by intellectual action. Where it differs from *Basic Instinct* is not in the erotic, then, but in the way Nomi is physically present in the film; as Nayman notes, there is a gulf between the clinical, chilly precision of Catherine Tramell (Sharon Stone's murderess in *Basic Instinct*) and Nomi's floundering, what Nayman calls "frantic acting."[18] Nayman quotes one reviewer, for instance, collapsing Nomi's floundering with Berkley's: "She can't act, but watching her try to act, to do the thing acting is rumored to consist of, is moving."[19]

The pairing of Verhoeven and Eszterhas as contesting authors of the earlier film facilitates the generic sleight of hand or scamming involved in interposing this masculine dyad as the referent of the "violation," as it likewise "violates" a rule, in this case a rule of genre. But the effect is better managed generically as an index of the film's focus on how similarity or alikeness isn't merely apparent but rather is cultivated, thought out. When Cristal says they are "exactly alike," her comment isn't merely an observation but an instruction and, in line with the cinematic effect of the rule violation, a seduction as well. Here, unlike in the labored post-PC seduction scenes between Grey and Steele, violation still has the power to formally instate the queer possibility afforded by rule-breaking. It is a formal registration of the chaotic "flailing" of genre that Nomi's purportedly accidental off-tempo physical comedy similarly registers, where the unbidden generic intersection is not with the thriller but with screwball comedy.[20] While it's perfectly clear in *Fifty Shades of Grey* that Anastasia Steele is a character drawn from screwball, that Nomi Malone is likewise drawn is less obvious, but her physicality expresses precisely the chaotic reordering of plot, event, and narrative on which the screwball depends.[21] As we see later in the film, in her satisfying pummeling of rapist Andrew Carver, Nomi has either acquired or always had a physical balance outside the frame of the "frantic" floundering described earlier, a poise and gift for timing the film ascribes to her "thinky" relationship to career jockeying. She bides her time in this battle with Carver as she bides her time before sabotaging

Cristal to take the lead in *Goddess*. And it's her timing that delivers the punches, comic and dramatic.

Both *Fifty Shades of Grey* and *Showgirls* deliver the erotic intermingled with the screwball in a fashion that modulates the generic attributes of screwball comedy—what Andrew Sarris, for instance, defines as sex comedy without the sex.[22] In both cases physical comedy is integral to their performances, and both films aroused distaste partly because the ensemble "erotic screwball" is designed to ward off as much as incite libidinal interest, much like the Kindle handled by the mother threatens to extinguish erotic appetite. In *Fifty Shades,* Anastasia literally falls over as she enters the offices of Grey; in *Showgirls,* Nomi's exuberant dancing is essentially comedic, and the comedy centers on the gap between intellect and action. James Smith (Glenn Plummer) notes of Nomi that "she thinks she can [dance]." In fact, Nomi is too "thinky" to dance "well." Bringing together slapstick and the erotic in both films elicits disgust and distaste, perhaps because it introduces slapstick into the realm of the sexual, where it sits most uncomfortably. Henri Bergson notes that the comic relies on the repetition available to mechanical reproduction arising within the human, and the mechanization of the erotic unsettles it as a serious domain and similarly fractures the "serious" film.[23]

It's only after a set of shots that reproduce the violation of the 180-degree rule that Cristal says to Nomi, "We are exactly alike." Their exact alikeness, erotically, is managed by the film's careful drive to ensure erotic interest is reciprocal: what sets these two apart from the otherwise predatory sexuality on display is its minutely staged reciprocity. This means also that their erotic interest, exactly matched, avoids inexact or surplus erotic "value" that would then be displaced in commercial transactions. Contractually speaking, there is no consideration and as such no contract. Their exact alikeness, comedically, is in their capacity to match mismatchedness: that very compatibility of the good and bad, subtle and vulgar, overt and covert that Nayman identifies in the shot. Leo Bersani identifies "analogy without similitude" as a specific quality of certain metaphors where "the likeness between [the] terms is faint, remote, incongruous."[24] Separating this definition from more extreme examples of dissimilarity or far-fetchedness, "whether the similitude is easily perceptible or wholly unexpected, it is presumed to be real, and we are expected to come to recognize the likeness. Such metaphors function as epistemological accretions."[25] Cristal's comment to Nomi flails the generic, oedipal mirroring of films of female rivalry in favor of a pleasure in "learning likeness." A similar lesson arrives through the comparison of these two films as they elicit anxiety over similarity in mediatic and generational terms. This association can helpfully "screwball" the logic of diminishing return that otherwise obtains when deviations of genre and mediatic slippage are domesticated into schemes of reproduction rather than learned to be read as reciprocations between styles and forms that are similar.

Postscript: Shade Is a Mediation

In Ottessa Moshfegh's *My Year of Rest and Relaxation* (2018), her lethargic ingenue dreams her way through time.[26] Sleep itself becomes a form of periodization, a year, and her dreams are contoured around periodization's restorative potential as a form of mediation. Sleep is not merely an occupation of time and space but an engagement with it. When not asleep, she passes the time watching films repeatedly and repetitively; her preference, for the films of Whoopi Goldberg and Harrison Ford, expresses a wish for visibly generic performances, rather than high culture. As a recent escapee from a high-end art gallery and soon to become an avant-garde art project herself, the narrator's deeply driven attachment to videotape is rooted in particular urban and social encounters. She finds her tapes on sale at the Rite Aid where she otherwise gleans medications prescribed in her pseudo- rather than psychoanalytic relationship with a shrink. She enjoys the banality of the most everyday commodities in distinction to, well, distinction itself.

One way to read her quest for sequestration is as an ironically privileged—that is, economically and culturally facilitated—desire to seek *refuge* from forms of class and racial privilege. These forms of privilege are just about to become newly or differently visible to her white, bourgeois peers: set on the verge of 9/11, this novel, an unambivalent riposte to the hip, faux-Bourdieusian anatomies of Bret Easton Ellis and others as they historicized this scene, interests itself in another world, that of the generic. It's no surprise, then, that one of the videos she encounters and devours is *Showgirls*. By 2000 it has traversed the scandal of its release and the derogation of its aesthetic ambitions; it has been rereleased as a videocassette and circulated all the way to the discount bins and cut-price shelves of the local drugstore. Although the narrator expresses preferences (for actors, genres, styles), the video serves the purpose of demonstrating mediation itself and as such is notionally fungible, a video substitutable for any other video. Like sleep, videos take time and space and harbor this heroine in mediation itself.

Her sleep, in this sense, performs the same function as Nomi's wandering, although in this scenario the wander is through the matter of mediation itself. In this sense, its dense complexity is orthogonal to the transparency and parsability of the contracted engagement between Anastasia and Christian. Of course, contracted engagements are libidinal because they promise endless proliferation and endless deferral: more clarification, more debate, more qualification. This kind of contract is the one Moshfegh's protagonist enters when she herself becomes the medium of an art project that "capitalizes" on her torpor. But Moshfegh's heroine's sequestration ultimately offers the video itself, the matter and material of the film, as a way to immerse herself in its mediations, and for all the assumption that the film selection is somewhat random, she has merely found a new delivery system for the "perfect" film, nestled among the discards and abjected objects of millennial culture, of which *Showgirls* was, perhaps, the supreme example. Her engagement with *Showgirls*' mediated form twists again the screwball logic of the film: recognizing its inhibiting rather than libidinal representation of sexually explicit performance (*circa* 1995), it comes to resemble instead the more opaque quality of mediation *itself* as a way to slow down and make less clear the film's relation to the world it purportedly addresses. Another way to say this: *Showgirls*' historical fate is congealed into those material forms of circulation contemporary with its release and initial derogation. Unlike the example offered by *Fifty Shades of Grey*'s similarly incarcerated heroine, the slumbering, drug-dependent heroine of *My Year of Rest and Relaxation* re-creates a domestic scene to transpose as tired and inert those very elements that animate *Showgirls*.

MELISSA HARDIE is Associate Professor of English at the University of Sydney. Her recent work appears in *Australian Humanities Review, Textual Practice, Film Quarterly,* and *Angelaki*. Her most recent book chapter (with Amy Villarejo) is on the 1978 Briggs Initiative and the television drama *Family,* in *Television Studies in Queer Times*. She is editor of the Oxford University Press series Approaches to the Novel.

References

Acland, Charles R., ed. *Residual Media*. Minneapolis: University of Minnesota Press, 2007.
Bergson, Henri. *Laughter: An Essay on the Meaning of the Comic*. Translated by Cloudesely Brereton and Fred Rothwell. Mineola, NY: Dover, 2005.
Berlant, Lauren. *Cruel Optimism*. Durham, NC: Duke University Press, 2011.

———. "Genre Flailing." *Capacious: Journal for Emerging Affect Inquiry* 1, no. 2 (2018): 156–62.

Bersani, Leo. *Thoughts and Things*. Chicago: Chicago University Press, 2015.

Critton, Benjamin. *Evil People in Modernist Homes in Popular Film*. Vol. 1. New Haven, CT: B. Critton, 2010.

Devereux Herbeck, Mariah. *Wandering Women in French Film and Literature: A Study of Narrative Drift*. New York: Palgrave Macmillan, 2013.

Gehring, Wes D. "Screwball Comedy: An Overview." *Journal of Popular Film and Television* 13, no. 4 (1986): 178–85.

Halberstam, Jack. "Fifty Shades of Zzzzzzzzz by Jack Halberstam." Bully Bloggers, February 25, 2015. https://bullybloggers.wordpress.com/2015/02/25/fifty-shades-of-zzzzzzzzzz-by-jack-halberstam.

Hardie, Melissa Jane. "Loose Slots: Figuring the Strip in *Showgirls*." *Xtext* 1 (1996): 24–35.

Harron, Mary, dir. *American Psycho*. Lions Gate Films, 2000.

Illouz, Eva. *Hard-core Romance: Fifty Shades of Grey, Best-sellers, and Society*. Chicago: University of Chicago, 2014.

Jagose, Annamarie. "Thinkiest." *PMLA* 125, no. 2 (March 2010): 378–81.

Mankiewicz, Joseph L., dir. *All about Eve*. 20th Century Fox, 1950.

Moshfegh, Ottessa. *My Year of Rest and Relaxation*. New York: Vintage, 2018.

Nayman, Adam. *It Doesn't Suck: Showgirls*. Toronto: ECW, 2014.

Negulesco, Jean, dir. *The Best of Everything*. 20th Century Fox, 1959.

Nichols, Mike, dir. *Working Girl*. 20th Century Fox, 1988.

Puar, Jasbir K. *The Right to Maim: Debility, Capacity, Disability*. Durham, NC: Duke University Press, 2017.

Sarris, Andrew. *You Ain't Heard Nothin' Yet: The American Talking Film, History and Memory, 1927–1949*. Oxford: Oxford University Press, 1998.

Saturday Night Live. "Season 40, Episode 14." NBC, February 28, 2015.

Sedgwick, Eve. *Fat Art, Thin Art*. Durham, NC: Duke University Press, 2004.

Shahinyan, Diana. "Talk Dirty to Me: *Venus in Furs, Fifty Shades of Grey*, and the Erotics of Contract." *Law and Literature* (forthcoming).

Taylor-Johnson, Sam, dir. *Fifty Shades of Grey*. Universal Pictures, 2015.

Verhoeven, Paul, dir. *Showgirls*. Carolco Pictures, Chargeurs, United Artists, 1995.

Williams, Raymond. *Marxism and Literature*. Oxford: Oxford University Press, 1977.

Notes

1. *Saturday Night Live*, "Season 40, Episode 14," NBC, February 28, 2015; Sam Taylor-Johnson, dir., *Fifty Shades of Grey* (Universal Pictures, 2015).

2. On this evolution see Eva Illouz, *Hard-core Romance: Fifty Shades of Grey, Best-sellers, and Society* (Chicago: University of Chicago, 2014), 20–21.

3. Ibid., 17.

4. Charles R. Acland, ed., *Residual Media* (Minneapolis: University of Minnesota Press, 2007); Raymond Williams, *Marxism and Literature* (Oxford: Oxford University Press, 1977).

5. I'm leaving Dakota Johnson's father (Don Johnson) out of the equation for now. He became involved with Melanie Griffith when he was Tippi Hedren's costar in *The Harrad Experiment* (1973); Griffith was fourteen. Mike Nichols, dir., *Working Girl* (20th Century Fox, 1988).

6. Jean Negulesco, dir., *The Best of Everything* (20th Century Fox, 1959).

7. Melissa Jane Hardie, "Loose Slots: Figuring the Strip in *Showgirls*," *Xtext* 1 (1996): 24–35.

8. Grey's lair evokes the aesthetic described by Benjamin Critton in *Evil People in Modernist Homes in Popular Films*, Vol. 1 (New Haven, CT: B. Critton, 2010), a fanzine devoted to this phenomenon, whose name is self-explanatory.

9. Jack Halberstam, "Fifty Shades of Zzzzzzzzzz by Jack Halberstam," Bully Bloggers, February 25, 2015, https://bullybloggers.wordpress.com/2015/02/25/fifty-shades-of-zzzzzzzzzz-by-jack-halberstam.

10. Mary Harron, dir., *American Psycho* (Lions Gate Films, 2000).

11. Eve Sedgwick, *Fat Art, Thin Art* (Durham, NC: Duke University Press, 1994), 160. Lauren Berlant's work on Sedgwick's "thinkiness" in *Cruel Optimism* (Durham, NC: Duke University Press, 2011) extracted and enriched this term usefully for me. Annamarie Jagose has another take in her tribute to Sedgwick, "Thinkiest," *PMLA* 125, no. 2 (2010): 378–81.

12. For a comprehensive overview of this figure in French cinema, see Mariah Devereux Herbeck, *Wandering Women in French Film and Literature: A Study of Narrative Drift* (New York: Palgrave Macmillan, 2013).

13. On the global biopolitics informing such holding mechanisms and their socioeconomic selectiveness, see Jasbir K. Puar, *The Right to Maim: Debility, Capacity, Disability* (Durham, NC: Duke University Press, 2017). My thanks to an anonymous reviewer for drawing this book to my attention.

14. Joseph L. Mankiewicz, dir., *All about Eve* (20th Century Fox, 1950).

15. On the inter-implication of heterosexuality and contractual engagement in *Fifty Shades of Grey,* see Diana Shahinyan, "Talk Dirty to Me: *Venus in Furs, Fifty Shades of Grey,* and the Erotics of Contract," *Law and Literature* (forthcoming).

16. Adam Nayman, *It Doesn't Suck: Showgirls* (Toronto: ECW, 2014), 71–72.

17. Ibid., 72.

18. Ibid., 37.

19. Anthony Lane, "Starkness Visible," *New Yorker,* October 9, 1995, 95, quoted in Nayman, *It Doesn't Suck,* 11.

20. For more on the "flailing" genre, see Lauren Berlant's definition of "genre flailing" as "a mode of crisis management that arises after an object, or object world, becomes disturbed in a way that intrudes on one's confidence about how to move in it." The term can apply equally to Nomi's generic transformation into action hero in response to the genuine crisis created by Molly's assault and to the difficulties experienced by formally constrained readings of *Showgirls* through genre. Lauren Berlant, "Genre Flailing," *Capacious: Journal for Emerging Affect Inquiry* 1, no. 2 (2018): 157.

21. For an account of screwball that foregrounds this "screwy" aspect of chaotic reordering by drawing on its ties with baseball usage ("any pitched ball that moves in an unusual or unexpected way"), see Wes D. Gehring, "Screwball Comedy: An Overview," *Journal of Popular Film and Television* 13, no. 4 (1986): 178–85.

22. Andrew Sarris, *You Ain't Heard Nothin' Yet: The American Talking Film, History and Memory, 1927–1949* (Oxford: Oxford University Press, 1998).

23. "The attitudes, gestures and movements of the human body are laughable in exact proportion as that body reminds us of a mere machine." Henri Bergson, *Laughter: An Essay on the Meaning of the Comic,* trans. Cloudesely Brereton and Fred Rothwell (Mineola, NY: Dover, 2005), 39.

24. Leo Bersani, *Thoughts and Things* (Chicago: Chicago University Press, 2015), 65.

25. Ibid.

26. Ottessa Moshfegh, *My Year of Rest and Relaxation* (New York: Vintage, 2018).

THE INSTABILITY OF EVIL 7

DOUBLE TROUBLE AND THE WORKING GIRL

MEAGHAN MORRIS

Hypocrite lecteur, — mon semblable — mon frère!
You — hypocrite Reader, — my double — my brother!

—Charles Baudelaire, "Au lecteur" / "To the Reader," *Les Fleurs du mal / Flowers of Evil*

The projective mutual accusation of two mirror-image men, drawn together in a bond that renders desire indistinguishable from predation, is the typifying gesture of paranoid knowledge. "It takes one to know one" is its epistemological principle, for it is able, in Melville's phrase, to form no conception of an unreciprocated emotion. . . . And its disciplinary processes are all tuned to the note of police entrapment.

—Eve Kosofsky Sedgwick, *Epistemology of the Closet*

In her study of *Twins in Contemporary Literature and Culture*, Juliana de Nooy issues a twofold challenge to critical work on the theme of duality.[1] First, she rejects the reductive premise (shared especially by psychoanalytic readings) that there is "a single, underlying meaning to the appearance of twins in our storytelling" such as "the mirror stage, narcissism, the uncanny, separation anxiety, sibling rivalry," and so on.[2] For de Nooy, twins and doubles offer "multiple entry points" to our cultural preoccupations rather than a single key. Their stories form "a whole variety concert," and so an analysis of specific "conjunctions of gender and genre" is required instead of treating these figures as functionally the same across genres.[3] Second, by studying twins and doubles in twentieth-century novels and popular cultural texts (thrillers, horror films, and queer comic fiction), de Nooy contests the idea that contemporary narratives "represent the decline into triviality of a great Romantic theme." To demonstrate the vitality of the innovation that occurs as twin tales are transformed for new audiences, she focuses on particular clusters, repeated patterns, and "storytelling habits" that interest her.[4]

This approach is invaluable for thinking about the role of doubling in Paul Verhoeven's *Showgirls* (1995) and Pitof's *Catwoman* (2004), two films that not only fail epically to merit inclusion in any great Romantic canon but have a well-documented history of being viewed *generically* as list-worthy "worst films"; both scooped the Golden Raspberry awards (the "Razzies") for badness in the years of their release.[5] The threat of triviality, even the fear of a projected hypocrite reader, presses intimately in a project like this: a poem by Kathleen McConnell ("Flex and Stretch: The Inevitable Feminist Treatise on *Catwoman*") pillories the prospect of a redemptive pop cultural reading of female self-empowerment in a "vicious social fiction" while stylishly performing the academic moves such a treatise could entail.[6] My entry point is work rather than empowerment, and my interest lies in the struggles that form a narrative transition rather than with the perfunctory blazon of victory with which most Hollywood films now conclude. Nevertheless, there is an issue of propriety here, a set of decisions to make about where and how to set critical boundaries. Is it right, is it *meaningful* to draw on the legacy of great nineteenth-century literature, as I have in my epigraphs above, to frame an approach to films widely regarded as cinematic dross?

It is easy in Cultural Studies to sneer this question away, but more is to be learned at an entry point by seeking an answer. Here, de Nooy's emphasis on storytelling "habits" and their refashioning in conjunctions of genre and gender (along with race and class in my chosen films) opens a space for enquiry in which research questions arise. Take genre: is there a way of motivating a combination of *Showgirls* with *Catwoman* that relies on more than a putative aesthetic badness, a female stars–male director nexus, early box office failure, and a camp reception culture that has loved one film (*Showgirls*) but not the other?[7] I will argue that these films do have a meaningful connection in a conjuncture where Hollywood's preoccupation with "working girls" in the transforming economies of the 1980s and 1990s intersects with a historically deep cluster of "orphan" stories about doubling.[8] The literary historian Karl Miller attests that "a proximity which is sometimes an identity" between the orphan and the double has, with "secrecy and terror over all," depicted for two centuries "the place of the individual in one or more of the environments which befall him."[9]

Both Polly Ann Costello / Nomi Malone (Elizabeth Berkley) in *Showgirls* and Patience Phillips (Halle Berry) in *Catwoman* are orphans, and at the outset both are trying to survive low-level jobs in the girlie image sectors (erotic dancing and cosmetics respectively) boosted by the casino capitalism unleashed in the 1980s by Reaganomics, with its cultural industries trickling down "champagne wishes and caviar dreams" to working people.[10] This is the harsh, aspirational class environment that befalls both Nomi and Patience. However, in film-marketing terms they inhabit different genres while sharing that online pop grouping as "bad." *Showgirls* is a backstage musical of sorts, with Nomi (the creation of runaway Polly Ann) tempted by a Bad Twin, star showgirl Cristal Connors (Gina Gershon); the moral status of their relationship remains unstable until Nomi provisionally decides it through her narrative trajectory.[11] A sideline of DC's Batman franchise, *Catwoman* is a superheroine origin story told as a fairy tale; after being killed for overhearing the toxic secret of Beau-line, an addictive skin cream, Patience is granted through "magic and metamorphosis" a second life, abilities, and an alter ego / Bad Twin as Catwoman.[12] With her beauty, new confidence, and fighting skills, Catwoman then faces an Evil Twin in the murderous model-entrepreneur Laurel Hedare (Sharon Stone), forming a triangulated field of doubled doubles. Further questions arise at this point. What happens to the myth of the double through gendering in these aesthetically marginal films with their differing legacies? Then, for the purposes of a queer historiography willing to trace relationships exceeding the boundaries of film industry and camp consumption discourses alike, how might we describe the genre in which this encounter of *Showgirls* with *Catwoman* takes place?

In what follows, I approach these questions through the problem of *similarity* posed by the double in proximity to the orphan, including the way in which the unsettling relationship of resemblance between alternative versions of the "bad," "evil," and/or "wicked" pole of a gendered duality ("good girl / bad girl," for instance) is explored in these films along with the "secrecy and terror" regulating labor in the capitalist enclaves that these films represent. Similarity emerges as a problem about *shades* of difference in stories of doubling because it arises as an issue for reflection (both in dialogue and for "the reader" or spectator) at points in a story where action decisions must be made. It follows that what will count as evil in the social fiction of each film is not defined at the outset but will rather be tested in the work that storytelling performs.

The concept of the double also floats in an unstable semantic field of bifurcation. Miller identifies an inner duality in that "doubles may appear to come from outside, as a form of possession" (associated traditionally with supernatural evil and death) or "from inside, as a form of projection" apt for a modern culture of individual psychology.[13] This instability has foundational force: "the double stands at the start of that cultivation of uncertainty by which the literature of the modern world has come to be distinguished."[14] Cultivation is a productive process, and the neatness of any dualism is blurred by distinctions that proliferate in ways shaped by context in every instance of usage (an aleatory potential suppressed by reductive critiques of the binary mode as "bad"). Not all dualisms take the form of an "either/or" opposition, and conjunctive possibilities ("and/and") hover to complicate those that do.[15]

Consider, then, the uncertainty subtending the variety of English translations of the famous "doubling" last line of Charles Baudelaire's "To the Reader," the liminary poem of *Flowers of Evil* (1857). For most of its length, the poem describes the horrific realm of vice and sin ruled by the demon, Satan Trismegistus, who infiltrates "our" bodies and minds with stupefying fumes of torment and obsession. Then, in the last two lines of the final stanza (here in Roy Campbell's translation), a swivel to direct address identifies the worst of evils:

C'est l'Ennui! L'oeil chargé d'un pleur involontaire,
II rêve d'échafauds en fumant son houka.
Tu le connais, lecteur, ce monstre délicat,
— Hypocrite lecteur, — mon semblable, — mon frère!

Boredom! He smokes his hookah, while he dreams
Of gibbets, weeping tears he cannot smother.
You know this dainty monster, too, it seems —
Hypocrite reader! — You! — My twin! — My brother![16]

In an online compilation of translations of this poem the intractably French phrase "*mon semblable,*" invoking likeness or similarity, becomes "my fellow," "my twin," "my like!," "my double," and "my likeness"; elsewhere, it becomes "my alias."[17] This familiar problem of translation initiates uncertainty *in* English between different forms of similarity and their relationship, in turn, to the kinship aggressively projected in the closing enunciative action between the "I" of the text and "you," the reader. Borrowing Baudelaire's last line in French for line 76 of "The Burial of the Dead" in *The Waste Land* (1922), T. S. Eliot added an exclamatory English vocative to highlight this forceful act of interpellation: "You! hypocrite lecteur! — mon semblable, — mon frère!"[18]

In an extended reading of "To the Reader," Ross Chambers suggests that the poem's modernity and "tremendous *critical* power" in relation to the social and textual hypocrisy of the emerging bourgeois society of mid-nineteenth-century France stem largely from the fact that it posed the question of *sameness* and thus of "kinship, resemblance, and metaphor" along with that of duplicity.[19] In so far as "we," Baudelaire's readers today, may indeed know the yawning indifference of a sniveling state of boredom that keeps us consuming amid atrocities ("the reign of evil," in Chambers's phrase), a question of *com*plicity may also arise for us.[20] In which case, the poem's sudden splitting of its inclusive "we" into the accusatory "I–you" at the end of the poem opens a rhetorical corridor toward the *mutual* projection of bonding that typifies "paranoid knowledge" ("it takes one to know one") for Eve Sedgwick in her reading of Herman Melville's *Billy Budd*.[21] Along this corridor, as Allyson Booth observes in her study of *The Waste Land*, Eliot borrows Baudelaire's line and repeats his act of "breaking the frame" between poet and reader to zero in himself on any reader's "secret acknowledgment" of complicity: in Booth's paraphrase, "Stop kidding yourself, the speaker demands; you know you're as bad as the rest of us."[22]

While rarely breaking the frame (or "the fourth wall" in cinema) with direct address to the audience, a scene performing *for* the spectator an assertion of similarity from one man to another, usually villain to hero ("we're alike, you and I"), is a recurring feature of Hollywood action cinema, and I ask below what happens when a *question* of similarity or sameness arises between women who are rival doubles (*Showgirls*) or across the divided interiority of one woman (*Catwoman*).[23] However, for clarifying the conjunction of gender and genre shared by these films, Eliot's uptake of Baudelaire's poem is also of interest because of what it does to "the frame" understood in broader terms. Taught for generations to students of English literature worldwide, *The Waste Land* severed the accusatory last line from the demon-infested Hell of "To the Reader," releasing it into a floating life as a tag. At the same time, it replaced what Booth calls the "gothic horror" of Baudelaire's Ennui with the debris-strewn "Unreal City," where boredom rules "the mild insufficiency" of a modern everyday life.[24]

This desiccated life with its dull premonitions of apocalypse is also *trivial* and substantially feminized. Baudelaire's Hell is bestial, classically writhing with scorpions, hounds, jackals, vultures, snakes, and worms; like Satan, the vice of Ennui is male, and only a simile invoking "the martyred breast of an ancient whore" marks a femininity excluded from this poem's fraternal address ("My brother"). Eliot no less homosocially echoes this disgust at the aged female body in the figure of the blind seer Tiresias, "an old man with wrinkled dugs" (Tiresias having been turned into a woman for seven years by the wrath of the goddess Hera). However, Eliot's wasted city with its dead commuters, cheerless flats, and pubs at closing time is abuzz with stereotypically petty feminine concerns: travel plans, fortune-telling, a bad cold, bedchamber decor, hairstyling, chess, "nerves," bad sex ("Well now that's done: and I'm glad it's over"), and mean-girl prattle about husbands, dental work, and abortion pills. The paranoid doubling gesture to the reader is muted in *The Waste Land*, which famously engages instead with the sociocultural duality of that "great divide" between high and low aesthetics that the poem *performs* with virtuoso ambivalence; Baudelaire's line is just one of the fragments of (fraternal) literary art shored in this intensely class-conscious poem against the vitality of mass culture ("O O O O that Shakespeherian Rag") in a feminized everyday life.[25] In the process of this muting, *The Waste Land* in its high modernist moment helps to affirm that "decline into triviality of a great Romantic theme" that de Nooy contests.

In *Doubles*, Miller uses "him" advisedly to designate the individual because within the scope of his literary history "few women are awarded doubles," although many romantic heroines are orphans.[26] How, then, might the gendered experience of such recent fictional characters as Nomi Malone and Patience Phillips figure in relation to these classic masculine imaginaries of doubling and division? In Hell they would barely be visible: Nomi is merely a youthful sometime whore-in-denial while Patience mincing about in her shredded leather catsuit would make a risible demon indeed (one "in dire need of real evil," as a reviewer remarked of Margot Robbie's "minxy" Harley Quinn in David Ayer's 2016 *Suicide Squad*).[27] In contrast, both could plausibly reside in the Unreal City, perhaps adding a little passion to scenes of sexual faking (Nomi) and loud party-spoiling (Patience). Agreeing with Miller that "female twins and doppelgängers are virtually absent from legend and literary history," de Nooy points out that they become "standard fare" in the twentieth century, with most stories foregrounding a good girl–bad girl contest and "the problems of telling them apart."[28] Beyond a commonplace triviality, however, as products of a recent (and no less masculine) cinematic imaginary of feminism, Nomi and Patience bring a *childish* quality to their struggles with evil within as well as without. Early in the film, Nomi, in a moment of frustration, throws a tantrum, smashing her food all over the table when her rescuer Molly Abrams (Gina Ravera) asks about her past; sweet Patience scribbles "Sorry" on a take-out coffee cup and a paper bag to make up for bad behavior (standing up a date and stealing jewels respectively).

I want to suggest that this shared streak of infantilism locates the heroines of *Showgirls* and *Catwoman* in a particular cluster of orphan–double stories concerning the motherless child. Drawing on Anne Freadman's argument that genre involves "a set of habits, or a tradition, of solutions" to a *problem* of representation, de Nooy notes that while some nineteenth-century concerns articulated by the double remain important with different inflections today (such as unconscious desires, the dangers of narcissism, the fear of the monstrous), in late twentieth-century twin tales about women "their good and evil is overwhelmingly understood in sexual terms."[29] In female orphan versions of such tales, however, that dislocation from family that makes the orphan represent for Miller the contingent placing of the individual in an environment that "befalls" him is compounded by a felt absence of maternal care that makes *sexualization* one of many external forces to which young women learn to respond with an unstably experimental performance. Given the power of this force, and what Yvonne Tasker calls the "insistent equation" in Hollywood "between working women, women's work and some form of sexual(ised) performance," the problem of representation that such stories address may be one of formulating a woman's values and life experience in other than sexualized terms.[30]

Motherless: That Bad Eartha

The one twentieth-century female figure to whom Miller devotes an analysis is Norma Jeane (Mortensen) Baker / Marilyn Monroe (1926–62): "a real orphan who was also an imaginary one, and who played the part to perfection."[31] However, Miller is interested in the Monroe imagined by Norman Mailer in *Marilyn: A Biography* (1973) and *Of Women and Their Elegance* (1980). A more directly eloquent exemplar of motherless child duality from mid-century American popular culture was Monroe's African American friend, the singer, dancer, actress, and writer Eartha Mae Keitt / Eartha Kitt (1927–2008), who crossed a barrier for Black American actresses by playing Catwoman in the 1967 third season of the ABC television series *Batman*.[32] Famously heralded by Orson Welles as "the most exciting woman in the world" when he cast her in *Time Runs*, the theater piece in his European revue called "An Evening with Orson Welles" (1950), Kitt has also been called "the institution of cabaret personified not to mention the most fatally feline femme fatale of them all."[33] She is also "the original material girl" (for her lusciously camp, gold digger performance of such 1950s hit songs as "Santa Baby" and "Just an Old-Fashioned Girl," and "Champagne Taste" in 1965) and "pop music's first 'world music' figure" for her ability to sing songs in several languages.[34] Kitt wrote three autobiographies: *Thursday's Child* (1956), *Alone with Me: A New Autobiography* (1976), and *I'm Still Here: Confessions of a Sex Kitten* (1989). At different stages in her life, these told and retold the story of how she became a world-famous performer from her poverty-stricken South Carolina origins as a "yella gal" rejected by her Black sharecropper community as well as an unknown White father, then abandoned by her Black and Cherokee mother at around the age of three to labor in the house and the cotton fields for a family who beat, starved, and abused her. In the last autobiography, she explains that Welles's compliment came offhand when she asked him for guidance in her role as Helen of Troy. He prefaced it with, "Don't ask stupid questions, you stupid child."[35]

Journalists loved to recycle the "most exciting woman" tag, but in her writings and interviews Kitt relished the child persona. She used it wittily to parry charges of risqué behavior ("I can't understand it, I'm just an innocent little girl") and, in a flagrantly camp mode of comedy, to take the edge off her erotic objectification as a woman of color performing mainly for White audiences, even as she transgressed the rigid 1950s mores ostensibly shared by the latter in the United States.[36] Her early filmed performance of "I Want to Be Evil," a sung soliloquy included on the 1956 LP *That Bad Eartha,* is as unsettling of mid-twentieth-century American sexual and racial hypocrisy in its irreproachably cute way as the gothic horror of "To the Reader" was in its genre, time, and place.[37] Filmed mostly in close-up direct to camera, peeking at us in complicity across the back of a couch with her hair in beribboned bunches and a leopard throw snarling beside her, she ranges teasingly between "little girl mischief" images of evil ("I wanna be wicked, I wanna tell lies / I wanna be mean, and throw mud pies") and a dream of dissipation offered to the viewer by a prim and proper miss who longs to lose her virginity ("my unspoiled gender").[38] At the same time, in her life story as reworked over decades in interviews as well as in her books, the trauma of the child Eartha Mae who felt "hated" by White and Black people alike gave rise in performance to a cosmopolitan adult double, the globally desirable "Eartha Kitt."[39] The relationship between these two personae varies across her work but is always explicit: "Ironically, I think of Eartha Kitt as practically nothing. . . . She is so very far removed from the basic nature of Eartha Mae that I can—and do—think of her in the third person. She's she, not me. She's a name on a marquee."[40] At the same time, she claimed Eartha Kitt as her creation, saying in a 2006 interview, "Both of us think it's a lot of fun, that this urchin child that nobody wanted is doing this. They told me, 'You're nothing,' and so I made nothing into something."[41]

Early in her career, when African Americans were struggling for basic human rights, Kitt's subjective fluidity (for *Ebony* magazine, her "indefinitive personality") and her resistance to aesthetic racialization as a "Negro entertainer" were criticized in the Black press, while the gossip magazine *Confidential* salaciously exposed her interracial love life.[42] Later, a different kind of notoriety followed her criticism at a

White House lunch in 1968 of the Vietnam War's impact on poor Black urban communities; targeted by the Federal Bureau of Investigation and Central Intelligence Agency, she was unable to work in the United States for a while but won the admiration of a new generation of Black activists.[43] In a third phase, her articulate empathy for all "oppressed, depressed and . . . accused people" and her support for civil rights and marriage equality as well as her sexually provocative stage persona saw her heralded as a gay icon.[44] As the author of her own life legend, however, "Eartha Kitt" the storyteller forged space throughout to insist that Eartha Mae's story was a quest for affection and acceptance as a human rather than about the achieved glamour and transgressive confidence of Eartha Kitt the star. Conceptualizing through her writing the role of the double in a public performance space was one way in which she strove to solve the problems of self-presentation that "befell" her as a woman of color working transnationally across the racialized cultural industries of the mid-twentieth century.

Following Gilles Deleuze, I see Eartha Kitt here as an intercessor, an intermediary persona able to create a *series* from otherwise distinct and unconnected terms.[45] Kitt's performances as well as her storytelling offer us an entry point for the later conjunction of "champagne dreams" in which *Showgirls* and *Catwoman* pose social and representational problems. Her imprint in the latter film is direct: not only did her 1967 version of Catwoman inform Halle Berry's interpretation (in particular with Kitt's sonic signature, that impressively rolling "purr-fect"), but she hosts *The Many Faces of Catwoman,* a documentary about the history of the character and the actresses who had played her that features on the 2005 wide-screen edition of Pitof's film.[46] The resonance of Kitt's nomadic life as a dancer and an intimate club performer with Nomi's story (and Berkley's performance) in the big-stage world of *Showgirls* decades later is more oblique. Forming across her autobiographies and interviews, it vibrates through a wealth of detail about the experiences of a young woman striving to succeed in show business while struggling with exploitation and prejudice. Such details could be seen as backup for Verhoeven's claims to realism in *Showgirls,* or as clichés artfully drawn from the rich backstage mythology of theater; for Kitt's biographer, key aspects of her stories are "fanciful" but attest in their persuasiveness to her "power of self-invention."[47] None of these plausible descriptions diminish the capacity of Kitt's "legending" (to borrow again from Deleuze) to mediate *Showgirls* and *Catwoman* by connecting their stories of doubling to a wider gendered history that helped to shape the twentieth-century cultural industries.[48]

"Alone with Me": The Orphan Indefinitive

We hear Nomi Malone before we see her. *Showgirls* opens with the sound of traffic flowing over a black screen in which the dusky pink title appears, then over another black screen we hear the purposeful clicking of a pair of women's boots, crunching the surface too rapidly to signify a man. As a snowy parking lot and highway come into view against a mountain backdrop, a studded and fringed black leather jacket topped with a head of golden hair enters, left arm swinging, in rear shot from the right. The crunching continues as the camera follows the jacket flouncing, strong shouldered, toward the road. As the head turns left in profile, the camera swivels front on to frame a young woman licking heavily glossed and outlined lips in front of a road sign to Las Vegas. She turns away, and the camera follows her toward the side of the road as she moves deeper into the shot and starts to hitchhike. The focalization shifts to powerful glutes and long legs in light blue jeans, and a very large suitcase that this woman handles with ease. The crunching stops when she puts the suitcase down. Another metonym completes her figure as she turns to face the traffic: again in close-up from the rear, her right arm goes out, and a beautifully painted thumbnail is defined against oncoming cars.

Showgirls is commonly invoked in the media by a still of a near-naked Nomi onstage, often licking the pole that she uses for her show at the Cheetah's club. This directs us indexically to the place-based story of a young woman doing whatever it takes to become a dancer in the spatial hierarchy of Las Vegas show business (Cheetah's strip joint, indie Crave Club, elite Stardust Casino) and thus to the debates about sexuality and representational "taste" that preoccupy much coverage of the film. This is the primary story that writer Joe Eszterhas claimed was about "moral values and spiritual choices" and that Verhoeven quipped could be titled *All about Evil,* clearly referring to the abuse of dancers and the gang rape of Molly led by her idol Andrew Carver (William Shockley), but also claiming an old-money Hollywood lineage for the film by linking the war of succession between Nomi and Cristal to that between the young pretender Eve Harrington (Anne Baxter) and the aging diva Margo Channing (Bette Davis) in Joseph L. Mankiewicz's *All about Eve* (1950).[49] The opening scene of *Showgirls,* however, initiates a framing story about a solitary woman's movement *between* "different places." The suitcase, the boots, and the highway are defining features here, as the crunching carries us to a familiar liminal space that is charged with gender and genre questions.

In *Doubles,* Miller calls his chapter about orphans "Forlorn," and from his literary corpus he uses "the white face at the window" as an emblem of the vulnerability and queer freedom of the orphan that signifies "both exclusion and escape" for people with families.[50] In media culture today, an image of any woman alone on the road creates a similar ambivalence, prompting hermeneutic questions ("who is she?" "where is she going?" "why is she alone?") that gain piquancy if our social knowledge tells us she might be at risk of harm. In narrative cinema, these converge in genre expectations: will this be a horror film, a thriller, a rape revenge or serial killer story, a quest, perhaps a rom-com, even a feminist road movie? Sound and visual cues constrain these possibilities, while ratings and publicity guide the viewer in advance, but the potential for shock is always there. An unsettling reflection on this is Cindy Sherman's "Untitled Film Still #48" (1979), in which the highlighted figure of a smoothly coiffed blonde with her hands clasped behind her, modest in a white blouse, check full skirt, and childish little white socks waits with a suitcase just this side of the bend in a deserted and darkening road.[51] We have no clue what is coming round the bend. From behind in mid-shot she looks defenseless, out of place in the rural landscape, her natural habitat a homeware commercial. The scene is truly frightening, however, because we receive no answers to our questions other than whatever expectations the image bounces back to us, and while we may fear for the woman there is no one else in sight, and any predatory gaze is ours.

At the outset, Nomi's stride, the strength in her shoulders and legs, and the way she handles that suitcase predict that is she is ready for evil to befall her on the road (as the next scene confirms when she whips out a knife to control the music as well as the man in the car that picks her up). The DVD commentator David Schmader compares Nomi's style in this first scene to that of a Martian who looked up hitchhiking in a dictionary and tried to do it.[52] I don't see that. The combination of hyperfemininity (curls, lips, those nails) with powerful movement in a woman alone on the road is arresting, but it also appears on the gorgeous pulp cover of the 1958 Four Square paperback edition of *Thursday's Child*. On the right in the middle distance, a Black girl in pedal pushers and a tight pink top marches with a strikingly upright carriage alone along a scrubby dirt road, suitcase in hand beneath a vast, dusty sky. The sense of danger is muted by the large figure of a lovely woman in the left foreground, turning sensuously toward us in a pearl silk dress. Hyper-femininity in 1958 is a matter of breasts, prominent on both figures. In between these figures is an "indefinitive" space of sky and road, a void in time for narrative to fill; we must read to learn that the strong backs of the girl hiking in the past toward her future and her older double, the "exciting" woman gazing at us now, are shaped by a life of labor—first in the cotton fields, then in dance.

This image condenses two journeys made in the 1930s by little Eartha Mae. The first is on a "long dark dusty road" in South Carolina that she wanders homeless as a toddler seeking shelter with her mother and baby sister.[53] This road goes "down, down, down" to "what seemed like hell," and the evils haunting the road are spirits, bogey men, and the "bulging eyes" of the cotton glaring as she passes by. Once settled on the Stern family farm, she is abandoned by her mother when the latter's new man erases Eartha Mae from their lives: "there was no me, as far as he was concerned."[54] The second trip is by train. At seven or eight, she is sent for by an aunt in Harlem on her mother's death; this time she carries a little suitcase.[55] Kitt later described her life of servitude in between as part of "that era of black purgatory between the abolition of slavery and the beginning of the civil rights movement in the fifties," and her arrival in New York as "discovering the twentieth century." On this threshold in time, however, "black magic and evil" cross from the "netherworld" and the rural past to animate the bright blue fire that leaps from a terrifying gas stove.[56]

Eartha Mae's solitude is explained directly in the first five chapters of *Thursday's Child*: in her abandonment she is orphaned not only by contingency but by legacies of racial capitalism that infiltrate "secrecy and terror" into the formative depths of a little girl's life. Nomi's backstory of domestic violence, in contrast, is withheld for most of *Showgirls*.

The second scene in the car stresses her unusual name ("My mom was Italian"), and hints drop throughout the place-based story that begins when the driver steals her suitcase on arrival in Las Vegas: from "different places," with "no family" or Social Security number, she flinches when casually called "Pollyanna." Only after Nomi has crossed to the dark side herself do we learn that Polly Ann is a runaway with a long rap sheet (for prostitution, drugs, and assault) whose father suicided after killing her mother. Brutally delivered by Zack with his hands around her throat ("You're going to be a big star"), this revelation with its threat of forced labor brings us back to the framing story: after "kicking the shit" out of Andrew Carver with a killer pair of boots, Nomi hitchhikes on the scrubby desert highway to Los Angeles. Reunited with her suitcase when the same driver picks her up, she whips out her switchblade once more as they pass a billboard promoting the "Goddess" persona she is leaving behind in Las Vegas.

Nomi shares with Eartha Mae/Kitt a "no me" experience and a "know me" project formed by violent social traumas dispersed in American life. As several critics note, the name "No-mi" combines an erasure of self with a claim for recognition.[57] When Nomi tells the driver at the end that what she won in Las Vegas was "me," she effects a transition from the first reading of her name to the second; in Las Vegas, Polly has *become* a Nomi who is a subject of self-knowledge. The gap between internal doubles closes for now, although Polly's past waits for Nomi in bureaucratic files down the road. The storyteller in *Thursday's Child,* in contrast, intensifies the dissociation between Eartha Mae and the star Eartha Kitt whose creation is a theme of the story. As the last chapter begins, "I" recounts arriving in Las Vegas in 1954 to perform at El Rancho. Driving in from the airport, she sees a huge sign that "spelled a name that I could not make a complete identification with—EARTHA KITT."[58] Rather than ending the autobiographical project to "know me," the author will work with her readers on the problem of indefinitive identity for two more volumes.

Patience in *Catwoman* has a "nobody" rather than a "no me" problem. Halle Berry's voice-over tells us up front that Patience has no family; her obituary would describe "the unremarkable life of an unremarkable woman, survived by no one." Reviewers rejoiced in calling Patience "mousy"; sexuality-averse in body-smothering clothes, she is shy and anxious to please, and except for a couple of office pals she is alone in her "consistently ordinary" life of work, sleepless nights thanks to party animal neighbors, and moments spent painting.[59] In a rare bit of excitement, she climbs out of her window to rescue a cat, and a passing policeman, Tom Lone (Benjamin Bratt), saves her from falling to her death. When she learns that Beau-line turns flesh to a stony substance that disintegrates without use of the cream, Laurel's henchmen flush her like waste through the factory's disposal pipes into the ocean. Brought back to life by that cat (Midnight, an Egyptian Mau), Patience acquires feline powers, a hot new style, an extrovert second personality as Catwoman, and a problem of grasping the relationship between her (old) "good" and (new) "bad" selves. The exquisitely evil Laurel, an ice-blonde aging model with "skin like living marble," refuses to the end in their final fight to take her opponent seriously: "just a scared little girl playing dress up. Nobody. Nothing."

Unlike Nomi, Patience has no personal backstory to explain why a little girl might have been scared. Catwoman, of course, has a deep archival story: first appearing for DC as "the Cat" in the *Batman* comic in spring 1940, with her regular alter ego, cat burglar Selina Kyle, taking shape in 1950, she crosses in many variations among comics, television, graphic novels, and cinema.[60] An outsider to Selina mythology (an innovation that Catwoman fans did not like), the figure of Patience nonetheless emerges from a media past. Pitof's film creates a pictorial background for her story by slow panning during the credits across images (later repeated within the fiction as on websites and in photos) of "cat ladies" through the ages, following the "feline migration" of the sacred Mau from ancient Egypt, China, and Rome to New York. Next we see Patience dead, not by the side of a road but floating drowned in deep water with her long hair waving like weeds, a cliché of commercial photography.[61] An aerial traveling shot of a generic Unreal City then swoops around corporate towers, down through *Working Girl* space, and spirals into any mall-space whatever, where Patience apologetically bumps into people as she rushes to work: "I was supposed to be an artist by now. Instead, I was designing ads for beauty cream."

Both *Showgirls* and *Catwoman* compose allusions that their European directors perhaps expected anglophone audiences to appreciate. Dutch master Paul Verhoeven invoked German expressionist painting of the Weimar period to situate the "hyperbolic" style of *Showgirls*, backing off quickly when an American audience laughed, and yet those stills of Nomi smiling toothily as she licks her stripper's pole blend right in to George Grosz's vision of the sex slaves of capitalist hell in his *Panorama (Down with Liebknecht)* of 1919.[62] The celebrated French visual effects specialist Pitof (Jean-Christophe Comar) is from another generation: with *The City of Lost Children* (1995) and *Alien Resurrection* (1997) among his technical credits, his debut as a director, *Vidocq* (2001), was the first feature shot with a high-definition digital camera.[63] A graphic designer herself, Patience dwells in a glossy realm of hypertextuality rather than the Batman archive of the DC Universe, to which *Catwoman* links with the reference-spotting fetishism of internet fan culture: the opening montage, for example, has the Mau arriving in New York in DC Catwoman's birth year, 1940. The most significant links to spot, however, are to Michelle Pfeiffer's version of Catwoman in Tim Burton's *Batman Returns* (1992).

In the synchronic aesthetics of referencing, Pfeiffer's blonde Selina Kyle is an elder double of Berry's Black Patience in more ways than one. A headshot of Pfeiffer in her catsuit floats down as a *mise en abyme* of their kinship among the photos that fall around Patience in the library of her mentor, Ophelia Powers (Frances Conroy), and within the racial contrast embodied by the actresses the similarities between their characters are marked. Both Selina and Patience are single, sexually frustrated and repressed respectively, and live alone in personalized apartments. Both women are put-upon workers killed by capitalists. As Tim Burton puts it, his Selina is "a very beaten down secretary" thrown out of a window by industrialist Max Schreck (Christopher Walken) when she discovers his plan to drain energy from Gotham City.[64] Before being flushed out to sea by Laurel, Patience is bullied by her petulant boss George Hedare (Lambert Wilson), Laurel's husband. Both women are revived by a clowder of cats: Selina is nibbled back to life while Patience receives an infusion of Midnight's breath. Both become sexually aggressive, whip-cracking fighters. Both set off on a revenge mission, with the difference noted by Catherine Driscoll that while Selina is "personally transformed," smashing up her hyper-pink flat and converting a "Hello There" neon sign into "Hell Here" before sewing a black catsuit, Patience is "possessed" by a cat goddess, owns a catsuit she has been too modest to wear, and will experience recurring bouts of being a confident version of her old sweet self.[65] In this respect, Burton's Selina/Catwoman is a product of what Miller calls the "modern" understanding of duality as psychologically based, while Patience crosses into the world of Eartha Mae, where spirits move among us and a Catwoman purring like Eartha Kitt boldly prowls the city's rooftops.

Another difference is that Selina has a mother who belittles her on an answering machine about her "lowly" job status, while Patience reproaches herself for not fulfilling her artistic ambition. From this we know through the chain of references that Patience is a motherless child.[66] Lightly touched on in Pitof's film, this potential of Catwoman's origin story would be explored in season 3 (2016–17) of the Warner Bros. TV series *Gotham,* with Selina (Camren Bicondova) left in an orphanage at the age of five by her mother, Maria Kyle (Ivana Miličević), herself an orphan and a thief who returns after eleven years only to scam Selina. Orphan trauma structures the "secrecy and terror" of the entire Batman universe, with its repeated staging of the primal scene in which the child Bruce Wayne witnesses the murder of his parents, and with other cases of doubling triggered by family violence. In *Batman Returns,* the Penguin / Oswald Cobblepot double (one of the "freaks" who bring Baudelaire's Hell into most renditions of Gotham) was pushed into the drains as a baby by his parents. With no family and no Batman in her life, Patience will achieve a resolution of the "difficulty with duality" that Pfeiffer's Selina discusses in a romantic moment with Michael Keaton's Bruce Wayne. Unlike Selina/Catwoman, who remains anguished in *Batman Returns,* but much like Nomi, who develops a livable "me," Patience embraces the subjective fluidity between her original self ("very good") *and* Catwoman ("bad as I wanna be"). Alone with herself, her "nobody" becomes an *indefinitive* somebody.

Working Double

While *Showgirls* sits with *Catwoman* in my favorite-film archive, there is an imbalance in my affections. *Showgirls* transcends any social context of my viewing (if you dislike it, I think the problem lies with you), but I love *Catwoman* best when I watch it alone. This is not a "guilty pleasure" but a private joy. Sharing the film, I wince from an other's point of view at those CGI glitches (in some sequences Catwoman parkours like a frog), crass stereotypes (the "gay" and "man-hungry" office pals), and vapid scripting moments ("freedom is power," ouch). Watching alone, these flaws fade as I exult in Patience calling her boss an "untalented, unethical egomaniac" in front of the whole office and Patience smashing up the party that nightly deprives her of sleep. Infused with Mau spirit but not yet fully transformed into her own doppelgänger, Patience acts out visceral fantasies from a professional woman's overworking life; I have nursed *exactly* those fantasies for decades in journalism and academia. If *Showgirls* is about dilemmas facing oppressed female labor, *Catwoman* treats similar themes in a different social setting and a vengeful fairy-tale mode.

The conditions of access to paid work for women—bullying, humiliation, unpaid overtime, violence, sexual exploitation, unrequited emotional work, and expendability—are pervasive concerns for both films. Around the focal events of murder, rape, and forced labor that affect the key protagonists, both films sketch social landscapes littered with the petty submission rituals typical of the labor regime that the anthropologist David Graeber calls "managerial feudalism."[67] In *Showgirls*, Penny (Rena Riffel) is initiated at Cheetah's with equivocal jokes about giving the boss a blow job, while Nomi at the Stardust has to ice her nipples for the director Tony Moss (Alan Rachins), a micromanagement of her person later enforced by his lieutenant, the choreographer Marty Jacobsen (Patrick Bristow). The vulnerability of women in this regime is underscored by the confidence contrast between Nomi's Black friend James Smith (Glenn Plummer), who shows off by quitting his "flunky" job as a parking attendant just to keep talking to Nomi, and Molly, also Black, without whose costumier skills the Stardust show would fall apart but who fears that Cristal could fire her because of Nomi's rudeness.[68] In *Catwoman*, workplace relations figure in sketchier terms, but the core narrative of death and rebirth is triggered by George's abusive demand that Patience work till midnight to vary the shade of red in her artwork, while the cowed obsequiousness of her colleagues is exposed when they cheer her en masse for telling George off and losing her job. The patriarchal cast of this feudalism is emphasized when, in a nicely gratuitous aside, Ophelia Powers sniffs that "male academia" denied her tenure after twenty years of work as a professor.

The cinematic conjunction of gender and genre in which these visions of working life appeared, however, is historically specific. Along with their lineages in, respectively, the erotic thriller (Adrian Lyne's *Fatal Attraction*, 1987; Verhoeven's *Basic Instinct*, 1992) and the live-action comic strip movies of the 1990s, both *Showgirls* and *Catwoman* participated in a particular configuration of cinematic discourse about women, work, and self-making that was shaped in the 1980s.[69] Romances such as Lyne's *Flashdance* (1983), Mike Nichols's *Working Girl* (1988), and Garry Marshall's *Pretty Woman* (1990) refracted the shifting gender roles, class mobility challenges, and Whiteness politics initiated during and outlasting Ronald Reagan's presidency (1981–89). Chris Jordan writes that in this "watershed period in Hollywood history," Reagan's mobilization of a "success ethic" that rested on "moral merit and self-made status" brought an emphasis on how worthy individuals might reshape their lives in accord with White suburban family ideals, shaping "trends in the film industry and its movies that continue today."[70]

Labor in the romances of this period involved a semiotically fine-tuned mode of gendered role performance that opens a path to upward mobility ("cross-class dressing" for Yvonne Tasker).[71] As the socially critical, often downbeat tenor of 1970s New Hollywood receded in a burst of glamour coupledom, big hit soundtracks, and frothy old Hollywood rescue fantasies (shadowed, for the most part silently, by the HIV-AIDS epidemic), the "Reagan backlash" films that followed had radiant actresses exuding a contagious joy through the gauntlet of humiliation that the scripts made their characters run.[72] They were what Elspeth

Probyn called "winking" fantasies of improbable success that offered intimate feelings of possibility ("you!") while avowing their dream factory status: "Welcome to Hollywood! What's your dream?" asks Happy Man (Abdul Salaam El Razzac) to open and end *Pretty Woman*. Coining the term *choiceoisie* to capture the idea of women's agency then emerging with postfeminism, Probyn pointed out that multiple images loaded with discursive memories of love, family, and children were winking at us, saying, "We know the choice is already made—'what's fundamental hasn't changed.'"[73]

Duality in the Reagan-era rom-coms may involve disguise, but it does not project a double or cultivate uncertainty. On the contrary, duality has a steering function defined by a rigid template for choice. A popular craze for personal impression management ("dress for success") did powerful hegemonic work in that era, and stark binary oppositions between social destinies were laid out pedagogically in details of dress and comportment.[74] Alex Owens (Jennifer Beals) in *Flashdance*, a thickly clad welder by day and a near-naked dancer by night, dreams at home in her leg warmers of studying ballet. *Pretty Woman*'s "fidgety" streetwalker Vivian Ward (Julia Roberts), a natural moral aristocrat, is transformed by deportment lessons and an "obscene" shopping budget into a high-class beauty fit to marry a millionaire. In the most didactic film of all, *Working Girl*'s Staten Island secretary, Tess McGill (Melanie Griffith), masquerades as her Wall Street boss Katherine Parker (Sigourney Weaver) when hard work fails to get her "head for business" recognized; we learn to "rethink the jewelry" and that recessively femme "big hair" must make way in business for blunt-cut "serious" hair.[75] Aesthetic advice helped heroines to reconcile career and money successfully with love and sex, as Helen Gurley Brown promised women "starting with nothing" in her 1982 bestseller, *Having It All*.[76] However, as Elizabeth G. Traube notes of *Working Girl*, the outcomes were circumscribed: "Tess achieves *moderate* success through the intervention of a paternal protector" while Katherine, the woman qualified to rise to the top, is discredited.[77] In these films, choice is *definitive* (it determines a life path) and formed by an erotics of male tutelage. Tess is taught deal preparation by Jack Trainer (Harrison Ford), who becomes her lover. In *Flashdance*, the factory owner Nick Hurley (Michael Nouri) persuades his employee/lover Alex to accept his nepotism while *Pretty Woman*'s Vivian has three tutors: her client (Richard Gere), an elderly capitalist (Ralph Bellamy), and the hotel manager (Héctor Elizondo).

It was within this conjunction of sociopolitical and film industry trends with storytelling habits that *Showgirls* and *Catwoman* "failed" as films about working women. Nomi and Patience understand the pragmatics of serious hair: Nomi tamps her locks down to bash Andrew Carver while Patience bobs, burnishes, and straightens hers to start a new life as Catwoman. However, both films broke the template of "choice" and "having it all" in several ways. Neither Nomi nor Patience shows any interest in reconciling work and sex with love. Sex *is* work for Nomi, and while she angrily refuses to be defined as a "whore" and resists coercion to deliver sexual perks, she freely seduces Cristal and Zack to further her career. Nomi loves Molly, but, having avenged her, she must leave Molly behind for another new start, and she does so in good spirits. Respectable Patience ends up dumping love *and* work when as Catwoman she is freed from containment by "the rules of society" (as Ophelia Powers puts it). Having enjoyed a night with Tom Lone, she discards him affectionately ("you'll always be in my heart") to practice freedom open-endedly in and for itself.

This is unusual. In her study of the "hypervisibility" of heterosexual single women in media from the mid-1990s, Anthea Taylor argues that "rarely is a single woman in popular culture shown to be entirely reconciled to her singleness, itself one of the ways in which the threat she poses is managed."[78] While Michelle Pfeiffer's feisty Selina grieves that she could not live with herself and Bruce Wayne in his castle, "mousy" Patience embraces her single life as a double ("alone with me"). *Showgirls* for its part breaks decisively with the pattern that ends *All about Eve* with marriage and retirement for Margo while Eve is forced into coupledom with creepy critic Addison DeWitt (George Sanders); Cristal sheds a tear at Nomi's departure, but she will head off happy with her "real nice settlement." More complex than character-based allegory, then, is how both films confront the genre-defining problem of representing trajectories for women who pursue what Eartha Kitt once called a "feeling for tomorrow" ("I was not looking for anything definite, but I wanted to see beyond yesterday, to have a feeling for tomorrow") without producing closure on any definitive social path or role—or, for that matter, on the choice of death by Grand Canyon that ended the heroines' drive for freedom in Ridley Scott's *Thelma and Louise* (1991).[79]

Personal development in *Showgirls* and *Catwoman* is not driven by patriarchal tutelage. Zack tells Nomi how to pronounce "Versace," and Patience thanks Lone for seeing her as special, but heterosexual men in both films are primarily a "narrative 'problem,'" as Tasker notes with reference to *Showgirls*.[80] They just cause trouble, even as lovers. Rather, what Miller calls the "proximity" between the orphan and the double in these films allows learning to take place through inner struggles and moments of care or tutelage from other women. Ophelia Powers calls Patience "child" while Nomi has "Mama" Bazoom (Lin Tucci) at Cheetah's; even Cristal gives Nomi a tissue after her humiliating audition, and in both films the orphan's key formative relationship is with an older woman who is a "diva" or established star in her industry. Development also occurs in acts of mimetic creativity. When Nomi first sees Cristal onstage, the latter is performing "the iconic 'Showgirls' hand flutter"; Nomi mimics her and makes the flutter her own. Possessed by a spirit, Patience does not have to copy the moves of a cat (Halle Berry did that), but she does need to learn what a Catwoman can do: Powers pushes her off a balcony to show that she can fall safely from a height, and Midnight inspires her to squeeze through prison bars.[81]

In opening paths for female orphan survival and self-invention, the two films draw differently on double mythology. In *Showgirls*, doubling is a compositional principle. Noting that "ideas of reflection and doubling are present at every level of the filmmaking," Adam Nayman cites the hand movements of Nomi and Cristal at lunch, dual given and stage names (Penny/Hope), the "follow my lead" rehearsal method, details of mise-en-scène, and matching sequences, notably Nomi's lap dance and pool sex with Zack.[82] For Nayman, however, reflection is the dominant *model* of doubling, and he sees the mirror as a looping device that stops progression. The twin hitchhiking scenes that open and end the film then suggest that Nomi may be "fated to keep returning to square one."[83] In *Catwoman*, mirrors are restrictively associated with Laurel as "the evil force of industrialised femininity."[84] Patience has only a functional mirror at home, but signifying mirrors abound in her workplace: the front region of Hedare Beauty displays mounted photographs and Warholian multiples of Laurel that she sees taken down for shots of her young replacement Drina (Kim Smith).[85] Two back spaces have no mirrors: the busy open-plan office where the designers work and, off-site, the dark metallic factory pouring poison into jars and waste into the sea. A third back space is an industrial storage gallery of Laurel portraits high up on the tower's mechanical floor. After killing George, Laurel restores images from her collection to the front region and projects her Beau-line launch speech on a massive screen in a meeting room; shot in close-up from the front, Laurel is doubled within the frame by her own inflated image.

While mirrors are necessary in films about performance work, Nayman's view of their role in *Showgirls* is marked by the psychoanalytic thought that de Nooy regards as reductive. Before Jacques Lacan theorized the foundation of the Imaginary in the mirror phase, Otto Rank proposed in 1914 that the double signifies a blocked capacity for love in Stellan Rye's horror film about an ambulant mirror reflection, *The Student of Prague* (1913), and a "presumptuous desire" to stay young in Oscar Wilde's novel *The Picture of Dorian Gray* (1890), in which Gray's aging is transferred to his portrait.[86] The act of destroying the double in these stories with narcissistic male protagonists results in the death of the self. In the dream factories of femininity today, however, youthfulness is a form of capital with immediate bearing on financial longevity rather than personal vanity. In *Showgirls*, the line manager Gay Carpenter (Michelle Johnston) advises Nomi on her first day at work to "figure out a job and a man for later on." Nomi needles Cristal about aging, but Cristal knows this means Nomi wants her job; her self-esteem is intact at the end of the film while Nomi's is enhanced rather than back at "square one." As a reverse Dorian Gray, Laurel in *Catwoman* conforms more closely to Rank's model. Beau-line keeps Laurel resembling her photographs, but when she falls to her death, after glimpsing in a window's reflection the ravines cracked into her marble face by Catwoman's whip, her surviving portraits remain forever young.

Another stock figure of doubling, the "dual personality," is foregrounded in *Catwoman* but ignored in the competitive world of *Showgirls*, where people adopt masks and aliases with singularity of purpose. In an unfortunate passage of dialogue, Ophelia Powers expounds the "duality in all women" to Patience while a graphologist assures Lone that the two "Sorry" texts are by different women, one an "insecure . . . people-pleaser" and the other "self-confident, almost angry." Patience still thinks in the singular, asking whether as Catwoman she won't be

Patience anymore. Ophelia reassures her that she is both: this is an "and, and" mode of duality, not an "either/or." While some critics found this an annoying sign of a "refusal to commit" to the transformation of Patience, this reiterates an orthodox portrayal of Catwoman as a force for gray in Batman's black-and-white ethical world.[87] Always a serial figure, she generates multiple variations including Patience, "Eartha Kitt," and many Selina Kyles.

More illuminating than reflection or personality tropes of the desire to have a "feeling for tomorrow" that both *Showgirls* and *Catwoman* explore is the temporal emphasis in Freud's suggestion that the double may incorporate "the unfulfilled but possible futures" that we cling to in fantasy, and "all the strivings of the ego which adverse external circumstances have crushed."[88] While for Freud this incorporation involves culturally and psychically "primitive" materials (all active and present in Eartha Mae's modernity), his formulation shifts attention away from a "Self" caught in a repetitive logic of composition and toward the imaginative *projects* that doubling narratives make possible. In the course of striving to see beyond the adversities of yesterday, both Nomi and Patience are twice represented gazing at something beyond themselves that invites them to dream of a different tomorrow. These scenes play variations on familiar motifs that mark affective events in cinema. One is a scene of women window-shopping, and the other is an urban rooftop panorama.

Anne Friedberg has shown that from the mid-nineteenth century, the shop window displaced the mirror's centrality as "a site of identity construction," then was in turn "displaced and incorporated" by the cinema screen.[89] In *Showgirls,* identity work happens triadically between Nomi, Molly, and the siren call of a Versace dress that pulls Nomi up short at a window in the mall. Molly offers to double the black bandage held together with studs, but for Nomi buying the "original" marks a break with the precarity of her past ("I've got the money") and holds the promise of a classier life ("I never had a dress like that"). The commodity magic works: hours after buying the dress, Nomi gets an audition at the Stardust. In the comparable scene in *Catwoman,* Sally is helping Patience carry her things away from the office after being fired when Patience is drawn to a window displaying the jeweled claw necklace glimpsed in the opening sequence as having Catwoman provenance and a history of being stolen. Patience does not have the money, but a remarkable shot layered from inside the window shows the reflection of the necklace framing Patience's face outside the window, as though the commodity itself is "trying on" a potential Catwoman. Patience looks great on the necklace, and in a moment of cinematic magic, she feels her tomorrow as Catwoman *and* a jewel thief while behind her Sally is fainting from the toxins in the evil commodity, Beau-line.

These are complex scenes, and, as Driscoll points out in reference to *Catwoman,* neither film is developing "an anti-beauty culture narrative."[90] Rather, they pull away from the Reagan working girl pattern in which women "choose" beauty in class-conscious ways and practice aesthetics instrumentally with the social goal of having it all. Sally in *Catwoman* is comic because she does precisely this with her moisturizer fetish and manic husband quest. In *Showgirls,* beauty is a craft involving specialist knowledge, like Molly's touch with a needle and Nomi's artistry with nails. Through shop windows, the aesthetic power of a commodity lures Nomi and Patience alike with the *feeling* of a possible future. A question of genre then arises with this *promesse du bonheur.* What lies ahead? How does a story end well within what Miller calls "the annals of the orphan and the singleton" if a *woman* drawn by aesthetic power chooses to cultivate uncertainty, or simply the feeling of freedom?

A twilight rooftop invites reflection on these questions. In *Catwoman,* Patience sits cross-legged in jeans and loafers atop a narrow building in a run-down quarter of the Unreal City after learning her new identity. Within what Mick LaSalle rightly called the "dark elegance" of this film, this scene stands out for its muted, tonal beauty.[91] Far from the glassy towers, Patience nests in a pocket of an older industrial economy with its tawny buildings, serried rows of dark windows, crazy ladders, and faded lettering on a hotel wall. A "director's dreamscape," the rooftop in superhero films grounds a master perspective; Batman uses it to foresee events and map paths to action.[92] In this scene, Patience is more like the orphan super-soldier Max Guevara (Jessica Alba) in the TV series *Dark Angel* (2000–02), who rests on Seattle's Space Needle at night after the struggles of her day. However, Patience ignores the urban vista, haptically stroking the leather cat mask passed on to her by Ophelia and caressing Midnight beside her. The plan she forms is limited and personal: to find out who killed her, and why. A cut with an upbeat musical burst transitions to open-toed stilettoes walking along a ledge as Catwoman sashays in full costume toward the scene of the crime.

Another hip-swinging "cat-walk" ends the film, with Catwoman cracking her whip against a full moon. The punning humor eluded critics who wanted the film to be unintentionally funny or to tut-tut about Halle Berry's "swaying rear end."[93] The gender and genre problem faced by *Catwoman* surfaces most clearly in response to Berry's closing voice-over: "To live a life untamed and unafraid is the gift that I've been given, and so my journey begins." This line aroused scorn for Catwoman's "moral neutrality" ("she doesn't kill anyone, so what is she going to do with her powers? . . . grrrrrrl stuff"); her failure to become a "social justice crusader" ("rebel without a cause"); and her unheroic sense of freedom ("to wander around on city rooftops wearing nothing but a leather bra and a matching pair of pants").[94] Action movie demands subtend these criticisms while memories of Eartha Kitt playing the first Black Catwoman as an amoral, stylish, and deliciously bitchy free spirit seem distant even when critics recall her performance to better deride Halle Berry's. Leaving aside the issue of whether Catwoman in her screen iterations is reliably a *crusader* (as Eartha Kitt's sexy but sadistic crime queen certainly was not), a story about a shy, stifled Black woman acquiring a charismatic glamour-puss as a double (the story of *Thursday's Child,* in fact) surely should not need to further motivate its joy in freedom. Considered as a working girl film, however, *Catwoman* offers a humorous, feminized fantasy of a picaresque license to go off and do whatever ("grrrrrrl stuff") that may speak to any over-worker who has lain awake facing an unreasonable deadline set in unpaid overtime by a tyrannical boss who won't admit their own mistakes. In action movie rhetoric, this fantasy could be called *Catwoman: Escape from Creative Industries.*

Nomi's story could be subtitled *Beyond the Casino Economy.* A twilight rooftop scene reveals the form of her economic fantasy while initiating a moral transition. With support from Zack, she has just been chosen as Cristal's understudy despite the diva's hostility. From behind, we watch her gazing out over the Las Vegas Strip from the hood of a bright yellow car perched at the edge of a high parking lot. The fabled red and gold feathers of the Flamingo sign unfurl before her while in the distance The Mirage hotel-casino complex projects three gold words, *Mirage,* across Nomi's horizon. As the camera moves slowly around her, catching Caesars Palace on her left, she picks up an illicit hamburger, takes a bite, and sighs as her curls stir gently in the breeze. Nomi's dream future as a star in this town is coming close in this moment, although The Mirage suggests that the prospect may not be as lovely as it seems. After this lyrical interlude, events take a nasty turn. Nomi learns that James has given up his dreams of choreography and that Cristal has nixed her promotion. When a gloating Cristal calls her "slave girl" onstage, Nomi saves her dream by pushing Cristal down the stairs, breaking her hip and doubling the job strategy endorsed by Cristal herself: “If someone gets in your way, step on ’em.” As the ambulance pulls away, from behind we see Nomi remove her black wig to reveal her tamped-down blonde hair. Sliding around to the front once again, the camera focuses in close-up on Nomi’s painted face as her red lips form an unmistakably evil smirk.

This moment does not end Nomi’s self-invention; she will leave the “casino film” genre that gives form to her place-based story and go back on the road. However, the sequence that begins on the rooftop and ends below with the smirk marks an issue that both films address. A violent femme and an anarchist thief respectively, Polly-Nomi and Patience-Catwoman are not moral heroines in the Reagan success ethic’s terms, but neither are they “deadly” in the concentrated mode of the ancestral women of film noir. Rather, the twinning of each of their less than perfect characters around issues of access to paid labor explores the capacity of women to *do* evil sporadically and with intent, rather than to incarnate it sexually (“the devil’s gateway”) as an essence.[95] In both films, it is the role of the diva, Cristal and the undoubtedly deadly Laurel, to pressure Nomi and Patience to decide the moral tendency of their lives, in the process highlighting the limited ways in which the events that “befall” these women are critically recognized *as* evil.

Unreciprocal: The Diva’s Ennui

In *Confessions of a Sex Kitten* (1989), Kitt tells an illuminating story about one of her first hits. Written by June Carroll and Arthur Siegel for Leonard Sillman’s Broadway revue *New Faces of 1952*, “Monotonous” is a boasting song about “the ennui of an international courtesan,” according to Kitt’s biographer, John L. Williams.[96] Kvetching that “Life could not be drearier / If I lived in Siberia,” the singer begins by inviting the listener ("Everyone"/you!) to identify with her boredom: "Everyone gets into a dull routine / If they don't get a chance to change the scene / . . . I'll tell ya what I mean."[97] There follows a witty list of extravagant gifts fictionally offered to the femme fatale by such famous men as Johnnie Ray, King Farouk, Harry Truman, Chiang Kai-shek, and Gayelord Hauser. She dismisses each one: "Monotonous!" Then still in her twenties and recently returned from Europe, Kitt knew some of these men (Jacques Fath did style her dresses) and had contact with others (T. S. Eliot sent her roses in delight at being named).[98] The line "Sherman Billingsley even cooks for me" sniped at a New York club owner accused of racism by Josephine Baker, and Williams notes that this "was the show's one carefully coded allusion to the fact that their star was an African-American."[99]

According to Kitt, the song was inspired by a conversation she had with Carroll, Siegel, and Ronny Graham about an incident at Churchill's club in London. Passing a table of "very distinguished men," she overheard them discussing her nationality when one dismissed her with a racist slur. Upset, she ran offstage after three songs. The owner persuaded her to face the men in person. She spent an evening of "fun and laughter" at their table, and when one of them escorted her home she asked if he still endorsed that slur: "Flowers flooded my apartment the next day."[100] Her biographer overlooks this story, casting doubt on her claim that she also choreographed and designed the final staging of the song.[101] Yet "Monotonous" is avowedly based on Kitt's legending (she did stop traffic in Istanbul, and wealthy men did shower her with gifts), and the version that she performs across four chaise longues as the closing solo in the 1954 film *New Faces* combines her lithe power as a dancer with such a scorching vocal performance of disdain that I have no doubt this is *her* riposte to abuse by "very distinguished men."[102]

The taut ferocity of Kitt's performance of contempt for the blandishments of the world ("A camel once walked a mile for me") twists a difference into the femme fatale figure that the lyrics explicitly invoke. May Ann Doane argues that in the texts of modernity, the femme fatale was "not the subject of power but its *carrier*"; "overrepresenting" a body given an agency not subject to her conscious will, "she has power *despite herself*."[103] The way Kitt uses her body in "Monotonous" more closely evokes Georges Sadoul's description (cited by Doane) of the *diva* in early Italian cinema: "exaggerated movements of the hips and arms, with the head thrown back, her hair suddenly spilling down her back, contortions, rolling eyes."[104] Kitt's hair is bobbed in harmony with the clean lines of her matador pants, but the extravagance of her muscular arm and shoulder gestures, the controlled flaunting of her head and neck as she "contorts" between poses across the chaise longues, and an accent on the whites of her eyes all resonate with the style of Lyda Borelli that Sadoul had in mind. This is not an influence. Kitt's movement was trained in the African dance theater of Katherine Dunham. However, on film both styles draw on a stage tradition of vamping that came through silent cinema and endures in camp today; *diva* means "goddess," and the arm-bending, hip-thrusting style of the *Goddess* show in *Showgirls* descends from this tradition. The twist that Kitt brings to "Monotonous" is a hostile energy that sizzles with "conscious will." She *wields* her refusal as power, ordering one suitor to "take back" his offering of the Taj Mahal. She boasts of her femme fatale reputation, "*but*," she sings, her agency is rather expressed by a violent yawn that "comes up" like thunder (and perhaps other bodily exhalations).

What kind of ennui is this? For Williams, the courtesan image entails the cliché "jaded," but there is nothing weary in Kitt's delivery.[105] She is "almost angry" (to take a phrase from *Catwoman*), a woman hating her entrapment by the luxury in which she is complicit. Baudelaire's

Ennui involuntarily leaks tears as he smokes and yawns, but Kitt's courtesan *willfully* spits air as she gyrates across a lovely excess of chaise longues. Her conspicuous consumption is so fantastic ("He bought me the Black Sea for my swimming pool") that her interpellation of "everyone" caught in a dull routine is manifestly comic, yet with the mirage of similarity she also proffers—to us, hypocrite listeners—the allure of a "change of scene" that might bring our boredom intimately closer to hers. We are invited to share the diva's ennui, or to earn (if you dare identify *here* as "brother") her scorn.

The refusal to reciprocate performed in this song is the contrary of Vivian's promise at the end of *Pretty Woman* that she will rescue her prince "right back." A revolutionary moment in modernist popular culture, the song shaped Eartha Kitt's public image for much of her career. She was portrayed as a cold, hard gold digger in real life: the composer Murray Grand reportedly said, "She sang 'I Wanna [*sic*] Be Evil'—and she was!"[106] Called "shrewish" and "disdainful of her own race" in the accusations cited by *Ebony* magazine, Kitt protested that she was "not cold—just a little numb sometimes. Courtesy of my childhood."[107] Music critic Stephen Holden sensed another disposition: "Ms. Kitt, like so many divas before her, seemed driven by an unquenchable anger."[108]

Holden points to a recurring tension ("so many divas") between performers' life experiences, their representation, and public demand for a return on our investment in the goddess. For Eve Sedgwick, such a demand takes paranoid form within the mutual projection of a bond; a "fatal symmetry" is produced by a mode of knowledge that cannot conceive of an unreciprocated emotion.[109] Sedgwick writes of "mirror-image men" in literature and life, but the bond between a goddess and her fans in popular culture partakes of a comparable fatality: what Sedgwick calls "the note of police entrapment" sounds for the diva who fails to reciprocate the passion that sustains her. Kitt knew this in 1976, when she gave thanks that no press witnessed her hysterical rejection ("What do you *want* from me?") of a stepsister who called out "Eartha Mae, do you remember me?" at Carnegie Hall in 1974. They would have seen "Eartha Kitt" cruelly spurn her "long-lost" family. But Kitt the writer insists (taking control of her legend) that it was Eartha Mae who screamed as the stranger smashed through the "mental armor" hiding the motherless child "suspended" in the diva: "until that evening . . . no one ever got to Eartha Mae through Eartha Kitt. Never."[110]

Showgirls and *Catwoman* portray working girls with *practical* knowledge of this conceptual incapacity in others. Their livelihood depends on handling demands for a reciprocity they do not feel in conditions that they have not set but to which they are constrained to consent. For Ross Chambers, Baudelaire's Ennui was the worst of demons because of his complicity in an evil *regime*: as the earth became a shambles, his yawning could swallow the world ("*Il ferait volontiers de la terre un débris / Et dans un bâillement avalerait le monde*"). This is the kind of complicity that gives Cristal and Laurel their power in industries run by very unpleasant men. Both are jaded, angry divas facing age as an inexorable enemy. Cristal, however, keeps faith with her fans to "show them what they want to see"; a realist, she still loves living her champagne dream and admits only at the end that she is tired and has merely "stepped on" her rivals to get to the top—where she looks the other way or joins in the fun as other women are brutalized. Laurel is a fairy-tale evil queen who burns with fury: she kills the scientist who created her magic youth potion, murders her husband to take over the company, frames Catwoman for both deeds, and plots to disfigure masses of women if they stop using her product. Tired of yawning, she wants to run the evil regime.

In both films, an encounter between the diva and the orphan posits their similarity then draws out a divergence as the younger woman gets a feeling for a new tomorrow. In *Showgirls*, this occurs in Cristal's failed seduction of Nomi at lunch. Modulating subtly between medium and extreme close-ups of the women's faces as their attraction and hostility fluctuate, this scene plays out the classic paranoid accusation: "You and me, we're exactly alike." Cristal puts this to Nomi after they bond over "Doggy Chow" nostalgia in their similar black leather jackets, evoking similar pasts of poverty and struggle. When Cristal segues into flirting about Nomi's breasts, however, the symmetry breaks down. Nomi confides that she didn't like feeling "like a hooker" at the Cheetah's, as though Cristal will commiserate like a friend. Cristal mentors Nomi that both of them are "whores," as though Nomi is her younger self; "it takes one to know one" grounds her certainty. The fatality here is that Cristal cannot imagine what she does not know about Nomi's past. Her own story of self-fabrication using paint and a surgeon to transform "dingy brown hair and little bitty tits" recalls Gurley Brown's coy suburban model of the "mouseburger" ("a near loser who got to be a winner"), not trauma and a violent life on the run.[111] Nomi spits, "I'll never be like you." She is right. Her actions continue to double Cristal's only until Molly is hurt and Nomi swerves from the path of complicity.[112]

Disconcerting to Cristal, Nomi's anger also puzzles many critics in ways that enable debate about Berkley's performance: was she a bad actor overdoing every scene or an ingenue who obeyed instructions to act hyperbolic?[113] I have a different question: exactly how is a woman who has survived a parental murder-suicide and a juvenile life of crime *supposed* to behave? It baffles me how rarely Berkley's performance is linked to the story of Polly Ann's trauma. Verhoeven has rightly called Polly/Nomi an "edgy, nearly psychotic" character; that "*nearly*" is an achievement, and her struggle for secure subjectivity is a triumph over the evil that the feminist philosopher Claudia Card calls "terrorism in the home."[114] In the realm of aesthetic realism, let alone hyperbole, why wouldn't such a woman carry a knife and threaten to use it? Smash things up after being robbed of all she owns? Hit back at men who importune her and repel people's efforts to "help"? For Schmader, all this is grist for snide amusement at Nomi's "bizarre" responses ("why touch something you can kick?"; "overreact much?"), as though she should act like a nice college girl at one of his shows.[115] Nayman, a sympathetic critic, speculates that Nomi's past use of crack may explain the "wild extremity" of *Berkley*'s performance.[116] Why is that more plausible than recognizing that she plays an angry trauma survivor who is hypervigilant, who struggles to keep it together, and who tries to form ties through her double without being quite sure how that is meant to be done?

Recognition is crucial to creativity in stories of the similar and the double. In action films, the likeness accusation poses a problem of self-knowledge to the hero, who must work out how he differs from the villain by recognizing what they share. Laurel in *Catwoman*, however, cannot conceive of a likeness to anyone but herself. In the hilarious final "die hard" fight between the diva and the orphan, two iconic actresses—symmetrical as famous beauties while contrasting in the fiction as a White supermodel in cocktail pants and a Black superheroine in leather—smash, kick, and poleax each other through Laurel's giant vanity tableaux. When Catwoman issues a childish insult from the ceiling ("You're a fake!"), Laurel rips back action movie options as she waves a gun around: "what are you? A hero? A thief? A freak?" Serial Catwoman could claim any of these roles, but she reveals herself now as Patience: "It was me you flushed down the pipes." As befits an instance of the Sharon Stone singularity, Laurel is unimpressed. An older, harder, sexually neglected version of *Basic Instinct*'s ice pick killer, a Catherine Tramell stripped back to that driving force of unquenchable anger, Laurel reveals that she herself is now a freak who "can't feel a thing."

There is no mystery about the differences between these similarly "free, independent and unnatural" women: Laurel tries to kill Catwoman while Catwoman tries to save Laurel.[117] Laurel doesn't learn: frozen in self-interest, she fatally persists in dismissing Catwoman as "nobody." Catwoman learns to limit her own indefinitiveness ("I might not be a hero but I'm certainly not a killer") and to act to help others; glimpsing a Beau-line ad from her prison cell, she tells Midnight, "It's not just about me anymore." These women are twinned, however, in their *roles* as victims of corporate masculinity. Like Molly in *Showgirls*, the supermodel and the artist do essential labor in their industry but are treated by management as disposable. Driscoll points out that Laurel is the one to make feminist quips in this film ("I'm a woman, Lone. I'm used to doing all kinds of things I don't want to do").[118] Defending Patience to George, Laurel also shows that she could have been a good boss; trapped in a stereotype of what a model can do, her narcissism is "necessitated" (as Sandra M. Gilbert and Susan Gubar suggest of the wicked queen in Snow White stories) by a state from which all "outward prospects have been removed."[119] Laurel and Catwoman diverge, however, in their grasp of women's power under patriarchy. Catwoman finds it in solitary freedom, walking away from it all, but Laurel confuses power with conformity: "I was everything they wanted me to be. I was never more beautiful, never more powerful, and then I turned forty and they threw me away."

Laurel is evil by any standards, both in character and in deed.[120] A late capitalist upgrade of the wicked queen, instead of eliminating rivals for her status as "the fairest of them all," she plans to profit from "every" woman's desire to be as beautiful as she can be. Her evil is radical in the Kantian sense: envisaging the mass mutilation of women who stop buying her product, she "subordinates rational humanity to nonmoral, instrumental ends which are based in [her own] self-love."[121]

Her stability in this respect is matched in *Showgirls* only by the vicious Andrew Carver, whose pitiless misogyny inflicts "significant harm" on Molly. While significant harm is a philosophical criterion distinguishing evils from wrongs, Claudia Card in *The Atrocity Paradigm* more stringently defines evils as "foreseeable intolerable harms produced by culpable wrongdoing," emphasizing their severity: "Evils tend to ruin lives, or significant parts of lives."[122] This clearly applies to the disfiguring of Beau-line users and to murder, as well as to the rape of Molly in *Showgirls*. Laurel's bitter speech then floats a question toward us and the critical networks in which films and life stories are connected: can we, do you, consider what has happened *to* Laurel "evil" in any way? Despite preserving at an insane cost the looks she needs for her job, she has succumbed to a *systemically* ageist sexism whereby a woman becomes obsolete in the marketplace on an arbitrary date.

This is a question, not a proposition. For Card, inequalities and discrimination are not evils, however wrong they may be, and unlike most workers made redundant Laurel retains the lifestyle of a diva who would never have refused the Taj Mahal.[123] However, we are not asked to sympathize with her self-pity (performed with peak glamour in a black negligee on a rich leather couch), but we are offered a moment to consider its causes. In sharp contrast with the elitism of "moral merit" in the Reagan working girl films, *Catwoman* shares with *Showgirls* a focus on how labor abuse structurally *generates* evils in gendered ways—a concern more explicitly pressing in social contestation today than it was when these films first appeared.

Breaking the Frame

In *Thursday's Child*, Kitt writes that after returning to South Carolina for the burial of her aunt, she fled back to Paris to avoid trying out at the

Blue Angel nightclub in New York: "in Paris I had broken through the barrier between public and artist. I could not face the idea of not succeeding. . . . I got a ticket on the S.S. *America* to return to my world of safety where I knew I was loved."[124] For Card, intolerable harm deprives people of the basics that make life worth living, and these include "affective ties with other human beings; the ability to make choices and act on them; and a sense of one's own worth as a person."[125] Eartha Mae's childhood was shaped by one of the atrocities that preoccupy Card ("American slavery" with its severing of kinship ties for victims *and* their descendants), then spent enduring another, the "private atrocity" of child abuse.[126] Kitt's writings explore with heart-stopping clarity the long, arduous process of quelling her sense of worthlessness through a double that could sustain a spectacular public career and help manage dissociation (give or take a little numbness) by forming intense affective ties with a collectivity of fans: "Whenever I walk out on a stage, I'm begging for affection. My best directors have always been my fans, sitting in that audience."[127]

In their sleaze, casual brutality, and glitz, the fictional worlds of *Showgirls* and *Catwoman* seem lightweight by comparison. Kitt's intercession nonetheless reveals the burden of genre expectations and storytelling patterns still being negotiated by these stories of female orphans working in late twentieth-century cultural industries. That dislocation from family combined with a refusal of the coupling closure typical of "postfeminist" Hollywood cinema allows the protagonists to experiment with sexuality while also developing other priorities—subjectivity for Nomi, freedom for Patience—that give value to their lives, as the quest for affection did for Eartha Mae/Kitt. They achieve this in social environments that do not, in fact, "befall" them as vulnerable individuals (as Miller writes of his literary orphans) but rather *produce* their vulnerability in a structured and formative way. Unlike Miller's "white face at the window," the solitary Black girl marching on a country road with a suitcase, the blond woman hitchhiking alone, and the dead woman floating in deep water evoke destinies generically predictable for those figures—and fates that their stories resist.

This resistant quality is produced by actor labor as well as the audience activity emphasized in Cultural Studies. My emphasis has been on some long-running continuities as well as the changes at work in a particular "conjunction of gender and genre" (in Juliana de Nooy's words) that formed as the Reagan era in Hollywood made way for the new intensities of managerial feudalism in cultural industries. Change does not spring from directorial vision or representation moves alone, and the ever-negotiable boundary between imagined and actual worlds is highly porous when actors play performers or interpret stories that they intimately *know*. The way that queer communities infiltrate that boundary to celebrate *Showgirls* is amply documented now. The acclaim of four thousand fans at the 2015 Cinespia outdoor screening in Los Angeles gave Berkley the affirmation of love and "safety" that Eartha Kitt needed from her public in Paris sixty years earlier, and *You Don't Nomi* (2019) features performers from *Showgirls! The Musical!* who elaborate the film in extreme-diva mode, with April Kidwell recounting how playing versions of Berkley helped her own recovery from sexual assault.[128] The capacity of a film to get *involved* in people's lives is made possible not simply by "identification" with an image or a gaze but through a kinaesthetic and empathic mobilization of sensations that commingle performer and audience experience.[129]

Actors share with everyone else the mix of idiosyncratic memory-images with community-based forms of common sense that makes cinema intelligible for spectators, and memory-work (and memories *of* work) is embodied in performance as it is in the eventfulness of what Kara Keeling calls audience "affectivity."[130] I have focused on Eartha

Kitt's essays in self-invention and survival because across all her work she wrote "the story" that people who cope with cruelty and marginalization intimately know while giving an account of a twentieth-century popular cultural formation that illuminates the longevity of the struggles still marked in films about "show business" decades later. Other performers amplify this story. Gina Ravera, for example, has spoken of the "deeply unpleasant and painful nine-hour ordeal" of filming the rape sequence in *Showgirls* while Sharon Stone's compelling delivery of Laurel's "thrown away" speech in *Catwoman* draws on more than our awareness that work for women in Hollywood, as for models and dancers, tends to dry up at a certain age.[131] At the age of forty-three, Stone suffered a massive stroke: she made *Catwoman* midway through a seven-year recovery, during which her treatment as a disabled person was, she has said, "brutally unkind" ("I'd been this very bright and shiny thing, and then I got a ding in my fender and suddenly I just wasn't bright and shiny any more").[132]

Recently, Halle Berry has spoken eloquently about how Hollywood's economy throws away women of color. Studios blamed *Catwoman* for their own choice to "set back female superheroes in films for more than a decade," and the film was disgraced for failing to fulfill the promise of widening representation that its publicity made to Black and Latino audiences; the story was set in a fantasy world where "race does not exist," thereby regressing from Eartha Kitt's 1967 satire on race-blindness in the "hair bomb" episode ("Catwoman's Dressed to Kill") when she turned White socialites' hairdos into afros at a fashion award for Batgirl.[133] However, Berry's Oscar for *Monster's Ball* (2002), comically clutched as she accepted her Razzie for *Catwoman*, figures in retrospect as one of her major disappointments.[134] She hoped that the Oscar would make way for other Black women to win and that great scripts would come her way, but neither of those things had occurred.

Reflecting on this in an interview in 2020, she casually used the very line with which Patience farewells Tom Lone in the default White wasteland that Catwoman could inhabit only in parkour mode: "there was no place for someone like me."[135]

Yet, as with *Showgirls*, something of Freud's "unfulfilled but possible futures" filters through the *event* of this troubled film in the long history of diverse struggles "to forge a way out of no way" (as Berry puts it) in hostile contexts of cultural production. De Nooy calls attention to the different inflections that "twin tales" have today alongside the concerns with unconscious desire, narcissism, the monstrous, and (I would add) evil inherited from the nineteenth century. In the women's stories I have considered, the orphan figure still implies the regimes of "secrecy and terror" that interest Miller, but the double is a creative means whereby the orphan can make a livable self and shape a "feeling for tomorrow" in a world beyond enclosure by the patriarchal family. These are stories of working lives, of abuses that are systemic rather than randomly individual, of chosen kinship, of queer pedagogies and life lessons with angry divas, and of a practical rather than paranoid engagement with the limits of complicity in a given social economy.

They are also stories of survival into an open future of uncertain everyday life. Nomi and Catwoman achieve a modus vivendi, a happy ending, but they cannot discard their pasts as Polly (a legal record) and Patience (a valued self); there is no triumphal closure or "cure" for the fractures of their experience. For Eartha Kitt, this would be fortunate; preserving duality was the key to survival in "the commercial world" she knew. The diva and the orphan could protect each other from being devoured, and in *Alone with Me* she reflected that the tragedy of Marilyn Monroe was that "somewhere along the line, Marilyn lost Norma Jeane" and no longer differentiated her *self* from the name on the marquee, and "how does one go about treating or helping a marquee?"[136] In Kitt's last autobiography, published when she was sixty and had raised to adulthood a much-loved daughter of her own, it is Eartha Mae who speaks unequivocally and in conclusion as "I": "The conflict between Eartha Kitt and Eartha Mae continues but nowadays Eartha Kitt always wins. She is the stronger, the bread-winner. I'm still here, and my one-woman show will go on, with both of us interpreting life as we feel it."[137]

If this "still being here" and "going on" involves trivialization of that great Romantic theme of the double, then it is not a matter of decline but rather an expansion of the theme's capacity to articulate women's manifold experiences of the sometimes hellish vagaries of modern life once their stories do not end with marriage, or no longer end because they do not marry. Living as well as interpreting that life continues to be an art as well as an achievement.

MEAGHAN MORRIS is Professor of Gender and Cultural Studies at the University of Sydney. She is author of *The Pirate's Fiancée: Feminism, Reading, Postmodernism*; *Too Soon Too Late: History in Popular Culture*; and *Identity Anecdotes: Translation and Media Culture*.

References

Alter, Ethan. "'Showgirls' at 25: Gina Ravera Discusses the Cult Movie's Most Controversial Scene." Yahoo! Entertainment, September 23, 2020. https://www.yahoo.com/entertainment/showgirls-gina-ravera-controversial-scene-paul-verhoeven-220338697.html.

Anderson, Jeffrey M. "Tall Tail." Combustible Celluloid, July 19, 2004. https://www.combustiblecelluloid.com/2004/catwoman.shtml.

ART by Bastiaan Mol. "Eartha Kitt Sings Swedish and Talks about Her Gay-Fans." YouTube, 5:43, June 9, 2009. https://youtu.be/ciHv4qUH1Ok.

Basevich, Elvira. "Modern Representations of Evil: Kant, Arendt, and the Devil in Goethe's *Faust* and Bulgakov's *The Master and Margarita*." In *Philosophical*

Approaches to Demonology, edited by Benjamin W. McCraw and Robert Arps, 242–56. New York: Routledge, 2017.
Baudelaire, Charles. *Les Fleurs du mal*. Project Gutenberg. Released July 1, 2004. https://www.gutenberg.org/ebooks/6099.
Bell, Linda A. "Challenging the Genteel Supports of Atrocities: A Response to *The Atrocity Paradigm*." *Hypatia* 24, no. 1 (2009): 123–40.
Blackwelder, Rob. "Cat Camp Fever." SPLICEDwire, July 23, 2004. http://splicedwire.com/04reviews/catwoman.html.
Bonnaud, Frédéric. "The Captive Lover—An Interview with Jacques Rivette." Translated by Kent Jones. *Senses of Cinema* 79 (September 2001). First published in French, 1998. http://sensesofcinema.com/2001/jacques-rivette/rivette-2/.
Booth, Allyson. *Reading the Waste Land from the Bottom Up*. New York: Palgrave Macmillan, 2015.
Brooks, Daphne A. "Planet Earth(a): Sonic Cosmopolitanism and Black Feminist Theory." In *Cornbread and Cuchifritos: Ethnic Identity Politics, Transnationalization, and Transculturation in American Urban Popular Music*, edited by Wilfried Raussert and Michelle Habell-Pallán, 111–25. Tempe, AZ: Bilingual Review Press, 2011.
Burgos, Ryan. "*Showgirls* (1995) Behind the Scenes Interviews: Joe Eszterhas." YouTube, 2:08, April 15, 2018. https://www.youtube.com/watch?v=v2g4Dngr9-U.
Calder, Todd. "The Concept of Evil." In *Stanford Encyclopedia of Philosophy*, Summer 2020 ed., edited by Edward N. Zalta. https://plato.stanford.edu/archives/sum2020/entries/concept-evil.
Card, Claudia. *The Atrocity Paradigm: A Theory of Evil*. Oxford: Oxford University Press, 2002.
Chambers, Ross. *The Writing of Melancholy: Modes of Opposition in Early French Modernism*. Translated by Mary Seidman Trouille. Chicago: University of Chicago Press, 1993.
"Charles Baudelaire's *Fleurs du mal / Flowers of Evil*." Accessed February 23, 2019. https://fleursdumal.org/poem/099.
Chell, Samuel. "Eartha Kitt: Purr-Fect & in Person at the Plaza." All about Jazz, March 29, 2009. https://www.allaboutjazz.com/eartha-kitt-purr-fect-and-in-person-at-the-plaza-by-samuel-chell.
Chinitz, David. "T. S. Eliot and the Cultural Divide." *PMLA* 110, no. 2 (March 1995): 236–47.
Collier, Aldore D. "Halle Berry Is 'Purrrfect' as She Cracks the Whip in Movie *Catwoman*." *Jet*, July 26, 2004, 56–61.
Daniher, Colleen Kim. "Yella Gal: Eartha Kitt's Racial Modulations." *Women & Performance: A Journal of Feminist Theory* 28, no. 1 (2018): 16–33.

Davis, Nicole. "Up on the Roof: 16 Classic Rooftop Scenes on Film." BFI, July 20, 2018. https://www2.bfi.org.uk/news-opinion/news-bfi/lists/rooftop-scenes-film.

DeCandido, Keith R. A. "Purr-fectly Mediocre—*Catwoman*." Tor, May 25, 2018. https://www.tor.com/2018/05/25/purr-fectly-mediocre-catwoman.

Deleuze, Gilles. *Negotiations, 1972–1990*. Translated by Martin Joughin. New York: Columbia University Press, 1995.

De Nooy, Juliana. *Twins in Contemporary Literature and Culture: Look Twice*. London: Palgrave Macmillan, 2005.

Dixon, Wheeler Winston, and Richard Graham. *A Brief History of Comic Book Movies*. New York: Palgrave Macmillan, 2017.

Doane, Mary Ann. *Femmes Fatales: Feminism, Film Theory, Psychoanalysis*. New York: Routledge, 1991.

Driscoll, Catherine. "Superheroine: Women as Martial Artists in Early Twenty-First Century Cinema." In *Women Willing to Fight: The Fighting Woman in Film*, edited by Silke Andris and Ursula Frederick, 161–77. Newcastle: Cambridge Scholars, 2007.

"Eartha Kitt a Friend to the Gay Community." *On Top Magazine*, December 28, 2008. http://www.ontopmag.com/article/2961/Eartha_Kitt_A_Friend_To_The_Gay_Community.

Ebony. "Why Negroes Don't Like Eartha Kitt." December 1954, 29–38. EBSCOhost.

Eliot, T. S. *The Waste Land*. Poetry Foundation. Accessed March 9, 2020. https://www.poetryfoundation.org/poems/47311/the-waste-land.

Ewing, Jeffrey A. "Women as 'the Devil's Gateway': A Feminist Critique of Christian Demonology." In *Philosophical Approaches to Demonology*, edited by Benjamin W. McCraw and Robert Arps, 75–92. New York: Routledge, 2017.

Feuer, Jane. *The Hollywood Musical*. 2nd ed. Bloomington: Indiana University Press, 1993.

Film at Lincoln Center. "*Showgirls* Q&A: Paul Verhoeven & Gina Gershon." YouTube, 33:03, March 1, 2017. https://www.youtube.com/watch?v=vj7JB_Otn3A.

Flora, Carlin. "Eartha Kitt: She Growls, She Purrs." *Psychology Today*, September 1, 2006. https://www.psychologytoday.com/intl/articles/200609/eartha-kitt-she-growls-she-purrs.

Freadman, Anne. "Reflexions on Genre and Gender: The Case of *La Princesse de Clèves*." *Australian Feminist Studies* 12, no. 26 (1997): 305–20.

Freud, Sigmund. "The Uncanny." In *Art and Literature*, The Pelican Freud Library, Vol. 14. Translated by James Strachey. London: Penguin, 1985.

Friedberg, Anne. *Window Shopping: Cinema and the Postmodern*. Berkeley: University of California Press, 1994.

Gilbert, Sandra M., and Susan Gubar. *The Madwoman in the Attic: The Woman Writer and the Nineteenth Century Literary Imagination*. 2nd ed. New Haven, CT: Yale University Press, 2000.

Gleiberman, Owen. "'You Don't Nomi': Film Review." *Variety*, June 9, 2020. https://variety.com/2020/film/reviews/you-dont-nomi-review-showgirls-elizabeth-berkeley-paul-verhoeven-1234628623/.

Goffman, Erving. *The Presentation of Self in Everyday Life*. New York: Doubleday, 1959.

Gonsalves, Rob. "*Catwoman*." Rob's Movie Vault, July 23, 2004. https://robsmovievault.wordpress.com/category/comic-book/page/7/.

Graeber, David. *Bullshit Jobs: A Theory*. London: Allen Lane, 2018.

Gurley Brown, Helen. *Having It All: Love, Success, Sex, Money Even If You're Starting with Nothing*. New York: Simon & Schuster, 1982.

Hammergren, Lena. "Embodied Spectatorship? Interpreting Dance Reviews around 1900." *Nordic Theatre Studies* 29, no. 1 (2017): 8–24.

Hanley, Tim. *The Many Lives of Catwoman: The Felonious History of a Feline Fatale*. Chicago: Chicago Review Press, 2017.

Harrison, Mark. "How the 1990s Changed Comic Book Movies." Den of Geek, March 7, 2019. https://www.denofgeek.com/movies/how-1990s-changed-comic-book-movies/.

Hendricks, Nancy. "1980s." In *Popular Fads and Crazes through American History*. Vol. 2: *Modern Pop: 1960s–2010s*, 497–574. Santa Barbara, CA: Greenwood, 2018.

Holden, Stephen. "Forever Feline, Forever Fierce." *New York Times*, December 26, 2008. https://www.nytimes.com/2008/12/27/arts/music/27kitt.html.

Horner, Harry, and John Beal. *New Faces*. DVD. 20th Century Fox. 1954.

Ide, Wendy. "*Suicide Squad* Review—in Dire Need of Real Evil." *Guardian*, August 7, 2016. https://www.theguardian.com/film/2016/aug/07/suicide-squad-review-bad-film-margot-robbie-jared-leto.

"I Want to Be Evil Lyrics." AZLyrics. Accessed February 23, 2020. https://www.azlyrics.com/lyrics/earthakitt/iwanttobeevil.html.

Jack, Adrian. "Obituary: Eartha Kitt." *Guardian*, December 27, 2008. https://www.theguardian.com/music/2008/dec/26/eartha-kitt-obituary.

Jamal, Hakim A. "Eartha Kitt Wins Hearts of Black People." *Los Angeles Free Press* 5, no. 184 (January 26, 1968): 8. https://jstor.org/stable/community.28039698.

Jordan, Chris. "Gender and Class Mobility in *Saturday Night Fever* and *Flashdance*." *Journal of Popular Film and Television* 24, no. 3 (1996): 116–22.

———. *Movies and the Reagan Presidency: Success and Ethics*. Westport, CT: Greenwood, 2003.

Keeling, Kara. *The Witch's Flight: The Cinematic, the Black Femme, and the Image of Common Sense*. Durham, NC: Duke University Press, 2007.
Kitt, Eartha. *Alone with Me: A New Autobiography*. Chicago: Henry Regnery, 1976.
———. *I'm Still Here: Confessions of a Sex Kitten*. London: Sidgwick & Jackson, 1989.
———. "I Want to Be Evil." Composed by Raymond Taylor and Lester Judson. RCA Records, 1953.
———. *That Bad Eartha*. LP. RCA Victor Records, 1956.
———. *Thursday's Child*. New York: Duell, Sloan and Pearce, 1956.
Kuersten, Erich. "All Clawed up and Nowhere to Go." *Acidemic Journal of Film and Media*, August 10, 2004. http://acidemic.com/id24.html.
Lambie, Ryan. "10 Remarkable Things about Catwoman." Den of Geek, August 1, 2013. https://www.denofgeek.com/movies/10-remarkable-things-about-catwoman/.
LaSalle, Mick. "A Feisty, Feminist Feline with a Taste for Sushi, Leather and, Most of All, Revenge." *SFGate*, July 23, 2004. https://www.sfgate.com/movies/article/A-feisty-feminist-feline-with-a-taste-for-sushi-2739485.php.
Lerner, Jeffrey, dir. *The Many Faces of Catwoman*. New Wave Entertainment, 2005.
Lippit, Akira Mizuta. "Half-Star: *Showgirls* and Sexbombs." *Film Quarterly* 56, no. 3 (2003): 33–34.
Masters, Charles. "French 'Vidocq' a High-Definition First." *Hollywood Reporter*, February 15, 2000. https://web.archive.org/web/20090523161903/http://www.allbusiness.com/services/motion-pictures/4941598-1.html.
McConnell, Kathleen. "Flex and Stretch: The Inevitable Feminist Treatise on *Catwoman*." In *Pain, Porn and Complicity: Women Heroes from Pygmalion to Twilight*, 79–96. Hamilton, ON: Wolsak & Wynn, 2012.
McCracken, Grant. *Big Hair: A Journey into the Transformation of Self*. Woodstock, NY: The Overlook Press, 1996.
McHale, Jeffrey, dir. *You Don't Nomi*. XYZ Films, Grade Five Films, 2019.
Miller, Karl. *Doubles: Studies in Literary History*. Oxford: Oxford University Press, 1985.
Molloy, John T. *The Woman's Dress for Success Book*. New York: Warner Books, 1978.
"'Monotonous' Lyrics." Genius. Accessed February 23, 2020. https://genius.com/Eartha-kitt-monotonous-lyrics.
Montgomery, Hugh. "How *Showgirls* Exposed the Rot of Our Misogynistic Culture." BBC Culture, July 15, 2020. https://www.bbc.com/culture/article/20200714-how-showgirls-told-the-truth-about-americas-foul-misogyny.
Nayman, Adam. *It Doesn't Suck: Showgirls*. 2nd ed. Toronto: ECW, 2018.
Noriega, Chon. "A Whisper of Satire." *Film Quarterly* 56, no. 3 (2003): 36–38.
"Pitof: Biography." Internet Movie Database. Accessed September 16, 2020. https://www.imdb.com/name/nm0685759/bio?ref_=nm_ov_bio_sm.

Pitof, dir. *Catwoman*. Warner Bros., Village Roadshow Pictures, and Di Novi Pictures, 2005.

Probyn, Elspeth. "Choosing Choice: Images of Sexuality and 'Choiceoisie' in Popular Culture." In *Negotiating at the Margins: The Gendered Discourses of Power and Resistance*, edited by Sue Fisher and Kathy Davis, 278–94. New Brunswick, NJ: Rutgers University Press, 1993.

Rank, Otto. *The Double: A Psychoanalytic Study*. Translated and edited by Harry Tucker Jr. Chapel Hill: University of North Carolina Press, 1971.

Razzie Channel. "Halle Berry Accepts Her RAZZIE® Award." YouTube, January 14, 2011. https://youtu.be/U-7s_yeQuDg.

Rosen, David. "The Night Josephine Baker Never Got Her Steak." *Black Star News*, October 7, 2015. https://www.blackstarnews.com/us-politics/justice/the-night-josephine-baker-never-got-her-steak.html.

Schmader, David. "The Greatest Movie Ever Made." Audio Commentary. In *Showgirls*. Directed by Paul Verhoeven. Carolco Pictures, Chargeurs, United Artists, 1995.

Sconce, Jeffrey. "I Have Grown Weary of Your Tiresome Cinema." *Film Quarterly* 56, no. 3 (2003): 44–45.

Sedgwick, Eve Kosofsky. *Epistemology of the Closet*. Berkeley: University of California Press, 1990.

Setoodeh, Ramin. "How Halle Berry Fought Her Way to the Director's Chair." *Variety*, September 2020. https://variety.com/2020/film/news/halle-berry-bruised-directing-toronto-film-festival-1234762255/.

Sherman, Cindy. "Untitled Film Still #48." MoMA, 1979. https://www.moma.org/collection/works/56994.

Singgih, Pierce. "How the Fourth Wall Takes You Deeper." Film School Rejects, December 21, 2018. https://filmschoolrejects.com/how-the-fourth-wall-takes-you-deeper/.

Sontag, Susan. "Notes on Camp." In *Against Interpretation and Other Essays*, 275–92. New York: Delta, 1966.

Steinem, Gloria. *Marilyn: Norma Jeane*. New York: Henry Holt, 1988. Kindle.

Strange, Susan. *Casino Capitalism*. Oxford: Basil Blackwell, 1986.

Sura, Oona. "#GuiltyPleasureConfessional: Halle Berry's 'Catwoman' Is Pure Purrrfection." Black Nerd Problems, November 22, 2017. https://blacknerdproblems.com/guiltypleasure-catwoman/.

Szalai, Jennifer. "The Complicated Origins of 'Having It All.'" *New York Times*, January 2, 2015. https://www.nytimes.com/2015/01/04/magazine/the-complicated-origins-of-having-it-all.html.

Tasker, Yvonne. *Working Girls: Gender and Sexuality in Popular Cinema*. London: Routledge, 1998.
Taylor, Anthea. *Single Women in Popular Culture: The Limits of Postfeminism*. London: Palgrave Macmillan, 2012.
Thomas, Kevin. "A Catnip High." *Los Angeles Times*, July 23, 2004. https://www.latimes.com/archives/la-xpm-2004-jul-23-et-catwoman23-story.html.
Tirado, Fran. "The Enduring Legacy of Eartha Kitt, a Subversive Icon Targeted by the CIA." *Vice*, December 26, 2017. https://www.vice.com/en_us/article/8xvqbv/the-enduring-legacy-of-eartha-kitt-a-subversive-icon-targeted-by-the-cia.
TooFab. "Elizabeth Berkley Embraces 'Showgirls' 20 Years Later." YouTube, 6:37, June 29, 2015. https://youtu.be/tk8XR3U71D0.
Traube, Elizabeth G. *Dreaming Identities: Class, Gender, and Generation in 1980s Hollywood Movies*. London: Routledge, 1992.
Vallance, Tom. "Eartha Kitt: Singer and Actress with a Difficult Reputation Who Was Described as 'The Most Exciting Woman on Earth.'" *Independent*, December 27, 2008. https://www.independent.co.uk/news/obituaries/eartha-kitt-singer-and-actress-with-a-difficult-reputation-who-was-described-as-the-most-exciting-1212439.html.
Verhoeven, Paul, dir. *Showgirls*. Carolco Pictures, Chargeurs, United Artists, 1995.
———. *Showgirls: Portrait of a Film*. New York: Newmarket Press, 1995.
Walden, Celia. "Set in Stone." *Sun-Herald Sunday Life*, October 11, 2020.
Warner, Marina. *From the Beast to the Blonde: On Fairy Tales and Their Tellers*. London: Vintage Books, 1994.
———. *Once upon a Time: A Short History of Fairy Tale*. Oxford: Oxford University Press, 2014.
Whaley, Deborah Elizabeth. "Black Cat Got Your Tongue? Catwoman, Blackness and the Alchemy of Postracialism." *Journal of Graphic Novels and Comics* 2, no.1 (2011): 3–23.
Wikipedia. "List of Films Considered the Worst." Accessed February 28, 2010. https://en.wikipedia.org/wiki/List_of_films_considered_the_worst.
Williams, John L. *America's Mistress: The Life and Times of Eartha Kitt*. London: Quercus, 2013.
Wogan, Terry. "Eartha Kitt—Emotional Interview, Part 2." *Wogan*, BBC One, 9:51, September 11, 1989. https://www.youtube.com/watch?v=5rodWxy17C8.
———. "Eartha Kitt—'I Want To Be Evil' & Emotional Interview, Part 1." *Wogan*, BBC One, 5:59, September 11, 1989. https://www.youtube.com/watch?v=OmSWVqpb-No&t=0s.

Notes

1. Juliana de Nooy, *Twins in Contemporary Literature and Culture: Look Twice* (London: Palgrave Macmillan, 2005), xiv.

2. Ibid., xiv, 2.

3. Ibid., 4, xiv.

4. Ibid., xiv.

5. See Wikipedia's aggregated "List of Films Considered the Worst," accessed February 28, 2020, https://en.wikipedia.org/wiki/List_of_films_considered_the_worst.

6. Kathleen McConnell, "Flex and Stretch: The Inevitable Feminist Treatise on *Catwoman*," in *Pain, Porn and Complicity: Women Heroes from Pygmalion to Twilight* (Hamilton, ON: Wolsak & Wynn, 2012), 79–96.

7. *Catwoman* attracted some reviews in the "so bad it's good" mode: Rob Blackwelder, "Cat Camp Fever," SPLICEDwire, July 23, 2004, http://splicedwire.com/04reviews/catwoman.html; Oona Sura, "#GuiltyPleasureConfessional: Halle Berry's 'Catwoman' is Pure Purrrfection," Black Nerd Problems, November 22, 2017, https://blacknerdproblems.com/guiltypleasure-catwoman. Other critics struggled to represent its mixed qualities: "much better than it had to be and a lot better than many Internet critics, eager to hate it, wanted it to be" wrote Rob Gonsalves, "*Catwoman*," Rob's Movie Vault, July 23, 2004, https://robsmovievault.wordpress.com/category/comic-book/page/7/. See also Jeffrey M. Anderson, "Tall Tail," Combustible Celluloid, July 19, 2004, https://www.combustiblecelluloid.com/2004/catwoman.shtml; and Keith R. A. DeCandido, "Purr-fectly Mediocre—*Catwoman*," Tor, May 25, 2018, https://www.tor.com/2018/05/25/purr-fectly-mediocre-catwoman/.

8. See Yvonne Tasker, *Working Girls: Gender and Sexuality in Popular Cinema* (London: Routledge, 1998).

9. Karl Miller, *Doubles: Studies in Literary History* (Oxford: Oxford University Press, 1985), 39.

10. Nancy Hendricks, "1980s," in *Popular Fads and Crazes through American History, Vol. 2: Modern Pop: 1960s–2010s* (Santa Barbara, CA: Greenwood, 2018), 502. See Susan Strange, *Casino Capitalism* (Oxford: Basil Blackwell, 1986).

11. See Jane Feuer, *The Hollywood Musical*, 2nd ed. (Bloomington: Indiana University Press, 1993), 15–22. *Showgirls* departs from Feuer's classic backstage model by pillorying rather than "glorifying" American entertainment. Ibid., 90–91.

12. Marina Warner, *Once upon a Time: A Short History of Fairy Tale* (Oxford: Oxford University Press, 2014), 19–43.

13. Miller, *Doubles*, 416.

14. Ibid., viii.

15. De Nooy also recognizes "doubtful" doubles, between whom "either their resemblance is uncertain, their very existence is in question, or they are considered of dubious worth or quality"—for example, Ivan Reitman's film *Twins* (1988) with Danny DeVito and Arnold Schwarzenegger cast as siblings. De Nooy, *Twins*, 139.

16. This English version is from a 1952 translation by Roy Campbell, https://fleursdumal.org/poem/099.

17. See "Charles Baudelaire's *Fleurs du mal / Flowers of Evil*," accessed February 23, 2019, https://fleursdumal.org/poem/099. "My alias" is from Ross Chambers, *The Writing of Melancholy: Modes of Opposition in Early French Modernism*, trans. Mary Seidman Trouille (Chicago: University of Chicago Press, 1993), 128.

18. T. S. Eliot, *The Waste Land*, Poetry Foundation, accessed March 9, 2020, https://www.poetryfoundation.org/poems/47311/the-waste-land.

19. Chambers, *The Writing of Melancholy*, 125. *Flowers of Evil* was partially censored in 1857.

20. Ibid., 123.

21. Eve Kosofsky Sedgwick, *Epistemology of the Closet* (Berkeley: University of California Press, 1990), 100.

22. Allyson Booth, *Reading the Waste Land from the Bottom Up* (New York: Palgrave MacMillan, 2015), 74.

23. Pierce Singgih, "How the Fourth Wall Takes You Deeper," Film School Rejects, December 21, 2018, https://filmschoolrejects.com/how-the-fourth-wall-takes-you-deeper.

24. Booth, *Reading the Waste Land*, 74–75.

25. On the younger Eliot's attitudes to mass culture and the role played by Ezra Pound in editing *The Waste Land* toward a more hostile view of the popular, see David Chinitz, "T. S. Eliot and the Cultural Divide," *PMLA* 110, no. 2 (March 1995): 236–47.

26. Miller, *Doubles*, 52.

27. Wendy Ide, "*Suicide Squad* Review—in Dire Need of Real Evil," *Guardian*, August 7, 2016, https://www.theguardian.com/film/2016/aug/07/suicide-squad-review-bad-film-margot-robbie-jared-leto.

28. De Nooy, *Twins*, 49–50.

29. Ibid., 162–63. See Anne Freadman, "Reflexions on Genre and Gender: The Case of *La Princesse de Clèves*," *Australian Feminist Studies* 12, no. 26 (1997): 305–20.

30. Tasker, *Working Girls*, 3.

31. Miller, *Doubles*, 369. Abandoned before birth by her father, and left as a baby to grow up in foster homes and an orphanage for a time, Marilyn Monroe was an "imaginary" orphan insofar as her mentally ill mother, Gladys Baker née Monroe, was

not dead as Monroe claimed in her early studio years but confined to an institution. Gladys Baker outlived her daughter by twenty-two years. See Gloria Steinem, *Marilyn: Norma Jeane* (New York: Henry Holt, 1988), 187.

32. The identity of Eartha Kitt's biological father was never officially clarified. However, the family name to which she was attached in early life was "Keitt"; see John L. Williams, *America's Mistress: The Life and Times of Eartha Kitt* (London: Quercus, 2013), 16, on the headstones in the graveyard between the small towns of North and St. Matthews in South Carolina. In some accounts of her life, "Keitt" becomes "Keith." See Adrian Jack, "Obituary: Eartha Kitt," *Guardian*, December 27, 2008, https://www.theguardian.com/music/2008/dec/26/eartha-kitt-obituary.

33. Samuel Chell, "Eartha Kitt: Purr-Fect & in Person at the Plaza," All about Jazz, March 29, 2009, https://www.allaboutjazz.com/eartha-kitt-purr-fect-and-in-person-at-the-plaza-by-samuel-chell.

34. Carlin Flora, "Eartha Kitt: She Growls, She Purrs," *Psychology Today*, September 1, 2006, https://www.psychologytoday.com/intl/articles/200609/eartha-kitt-she-growls-she-purrs; Colleen Kim Daniher, "Yella Gal: Eartha Kitt's Racial Modulations," *Women & Performance: A Journal of Feminist Theory* 28, no. 1 (2018): 17. On Kitt's "sonic cosmopolitanism," see Daphne A. Brooks, "Planet Earth(a): Sonic Cosmopolitanism and Black Feminist Theory," in *Cornbread and Cuchifritos: Ethnic Identity Politics, Transnationalization, and Transculturation in American Urban Popular Music*, ed. Wilfried Raussert and Michelle Habell-Pallán (Tempe, AZ: Bilingual Review Press, 2011), 111–25.

35. Eartha Kitt, *I'm Still Here: Confessions of a Sex Kitten* (London: Sidgwick & Jackson, 1989), 81. All quotations are from this edition.

36. Kitt's response to the mayor of Los Angeles who claimed to be outraged by her performance for Greek royalty at the Mocambo in Hollywood, 1953, cited in Williams, *America's Mistress*, 139. See Kitt's account of the incident in *Alone with Me: A New Autobiography* (Chicago: Henry Regnery, 1976), 206–207. All quotations are from this edition.

37. Eartha Kitt, "I Want to Be Evil," comp. Raymond Taylor and Lester Judson (RCA Records, 1953); Eartha Kitt, *That Bad Eartha*, LP (RCA Victor Records, 1956).

38. Cited in Tom Vallance, "Eartha Kitt: Singer and Actress with a Difficult Reputation Who Was Described as 'The Most Exciting Woman on Earth,'" *Independent*, December 27, 2008, https://www.independent.co.uk/news/obituaries/eartha-kitt-singer-and-actress-with-a-difficult-reputation-who-was-described-as-the-most-exciting-1212439.html. See "I Want to Be Evil Lyrics," AZLyrics, accessed February 23, 2020, https://www.azlyrics.com/lyrics/earthakitt/iwanttobeevil.html.

39. Cited in Williams, *America's Mistress*, 234.

40. Kitt, *Alone with Me*, 4. In her sixties, Kitt sang a growling version of "I Want to Be Evil" on British television before giving a tearful account of her early life and the Eartha Mae/Eartha Kitt relation to chat show host Terry Wogan. See the two-part interview: Terry Wogan, "Eartha Kitt—'I Want To Be Evil' & Emotional Interview, Part 1," *Wogan*, BBC One, 5:59, September 11, 1989, https://www.youtube.com/watch?v=OmSWVqpb-No&t=0s; and Wogan, "Eartha Kitt—Emotional Interview, Part 2," *Wogan*, BBC One, 9:51, September 11, 1989, https://www.youtube.com/watch?v=5rodWxy17C8.

41. Flora, "Eartha Kitt."

42. "Why Negroes Don't Like Eartha Kitt," *Ebony*, December 1954, 29, 32. On the role of race in Kitt's aesthetic strategies, see Daniher, "Yella Gal." See also Williams, *America's Mistress*, 156–57, 261–62. For her own view of public curiosity about the racial identity of her lovers, see Kitt, *Alone with Me*, 216–17.

43. See Kitt, *Alone with Me*, 237–66; Williams, *America's Mistress*, 257–64. An activist reaction at the time is Hakim A. Jamal, "Eartha Kitt Wins Hearts of Black People," *Los Angeles Free Press* 5, no. 184, January 26, 1968, 8, https://jstor.org/stable/community.28039698. A recent view is Fran Tirado, "The Enduring Legacy of Eartha Kitt, a Subversive Icon Targeted by the CIA," *Vice*, December 26, 2017, https://www.vice.com/en_us/article/8xvqbv/the-enduring-legacy-of-eartha-kitt-a-subversive-icon-targeted-by-the-cia.

44. See "Eartha Kitt a Friend to the Gay Community," *On Top Magazine*, December 28, 2008, http://www.ontopmag.com/article/2961/Eartha_Kitt_A_Friend_To_The_Gay_Community; and ARTbyBastiaanMol, "Eartha Kitt Sings Swedish and Talks about Her Gay-Fans," YouTube, 5:43, June 9, 2009, https://www.youtube.com/watch?v=ciHv4qUH1Ok.

45. Gilles Deleuze, *Negotiations, 1972–1990*, trans. Martin Joughin (New York: Columbia University Press, 1995), 124–25. This is the simplest version of the concept of "intercessor" (translated by Joughin as "mediators"), which is rendered more strictly in Deleuze's later works.

46. Aldore D. Collier, "Halle Berry Is 'Purrrfect' as She Cracks the Whip in Movie *Catwoman*," *Jet*, July 26, 2004, 58.

47. Verhoeven, cited in Adam Nayman, *It Doesn't Suck: Showgirls*, 2nd ed. (Toronto: ECW, 2018), 124; Williams, *America's Mistress*, 12.

48. Deleuze, *Negotiations*, 125–26. Deleuze takes the word *legending* from the Québécois filmmaker Pierre Perrault, and in his own usage it refers to "the movement of constitution of a people" in minority discourse.

49. Ryan Burgos, "*Showgirls* (1995) Behind the Scenes Interviews: Joe Eszterhas," YouTube, 2:08, April 15, 2018, https://www.youtube.com/watch?v=v2g4Dngr9-U.

50. Miller, *Doubles*, 39–40.

51. Cindy Sherman, "Untitled Film Still #48," MoMA, 1979, https://www.moma.org/collection/works/56994. Thanks to Melissa Hardie for bringing this image to my attention.

52. David Schmader in *You Don't Nomi*, directed by Jeffrey McHale (XYZ Films, Grade Five Films, 2019), 7:56–8:05.

53. Eartha Kitt, *Thursday's Child* (New York: Duell, Sloan and Pearce, 1956), 3. All quotations are from this edition.

54. Ibid., 13.

55. Ibid., 11–12.

56. Kitt, *Alone with Me*, 25–26, 45–47.

57. Akira Mizuta Lippit, "Half-star: *Showgirls* and Sexbombs," *Film Quarterly* 56, no. 3 (2003): 34. See also Chon Noriega, "A Whisper of Satire," *Film Quarterly* 56, no. 3 (2003): 37; and Jeffrey Sconce, "I Have Grown Weary of Your Tiresome Cinema," *Film Quarterly* 56, no. 3 (2003): 44–45. On the possibility of a self-aggrandizing "no . . . *me*," see Nayman, *It Doesn't Suck*, 33.

58. Kitt, *Thursday's Child*, 243.

59. A vicious example is Erich Kuersten, "All Clawed up and Nowhere to Go," *Acidemic Journal of Film and Media*, August 10, 2004, http://acidemic.com/id24.html.

60. See Deborah Elizabeth Whaley, "Black Cat Got Your Tongue? Catwoman, Blackness and the Alchemy of Postracialism," *Journal of Graphic Novels and Comics* 2, no. 1 (2011): 3–23. See also Tim Hanley, *The Many Lives of Catwoman: The Felonious History of a Feline Fatale* (Chicago: Chicago Review Press, 2017).

61. See the Getty Images iStock website for 105 "most popular" photos on the subject "women drowning underwater floating on water." https://www.istockphoto.com/photos/women-drowning-underwater-floating-on-water?mediatype=photography&phrase=women%20drowning%20underwater%20floating%20on%20water&sort=mostpopular.

62. Film at Lincoln Center, "'Showgirls' Q&A: Paul Verhoeven & Gina Gershon," YouTube, 7.20–8.55, March 1, 2017, https://www.youtube.com/watch?v=vj7JB_Otn3A.

63. "Pitof: Biography," Internet Movie Database, https://www.imdb.com/name/nm0685759/bio?ref_=nm_ov_bio_sm; Charles Masters, "French 'Vidocq' a High-Definition First," *Hollywood Reporter*, February 15, 2000, https://web.archive.org/web/20090523161903/http://www.allbusiness.com/services/motion-pictures/4941598-1.html.

64. Cited in Hanley, *The Many Lives of Catwoman*, 106.

65. Catherine Driscoll, "Superheroine: Women as Martial Artists in Early Twenty-First Century Cinema," in *Women Willing to Fight: The Fighting Woman in Film*, ed. Silke Andris and Ursula Frederick (Newcastle: Cambridge Scholars, 2007), 169.

66. Marina Warner points out that in fairy tales "the absence of the mother . . . is often declared at the start, without explanation, as if none were required." Marina Warner, *From the Beast to the Blonde: On Fairy Tales and Their Tellers* (London: Vintage, 1994), 210.

67. David Graeber, *Bullshit Jobs: A Theory* (London: Allen Lane, 2018).

68. Ibid., 28–30.

69. On the erotic thriller, see Billy Stevenson's chapter in this volume. On 1990s live-action comic book movies, see Wheeler Winston Dixon and Richard Graham, *A Brief History of Comic Book Movies* (New York: Palgrave Macmillan, 2017), 10–14; and Mark Harrison, "How the 1990s Changed Comic Book Movies," Den of Geek, March 7, 2019, https://www.denofgeek.com/movies/how-1990s-changed-comic-book-movies/.

70. Chris Jordan, *Movies and the Reagan Presidency: Success and Ethics* (Westport, CT: Greenwood, 2003), 3–4. These trends lasted because reforms in taxation, company ownership, and marketing, as well as new technologies of distribution (MTV arrived in 1981), gave rise to huge conglomerates pitching product with cross-media synergies to the widest possible public. On the "success ethic," see Elizabeth G. Traube, *Dreaming Identities: Class, Gender, and Generation in 1980s Hollywood Movies* (London: Routledge, 1992). In the 1990s, the "moral merit" template was translated into Black community settings and adapted to different concerns with gender and class by such films as Reginald Hudlin's rom-com *Boomerang* (1992) and Robert Townsend's comedy *B.A.P.S.* (1997), both starring Halle Berry.

71. Tasker, *Working Girls*, 39–47. See also Chris Jordan, "Gender and Mobility in *Saturday Night Fever* and *Flashdance*," *Journal of Popular Film and Television* 24, no. 3 (1996): 116–22.

72. *Pretty Woman* refers in general terms to the need for "safety" in a sex work setting with a display of colorful condoms when the protagonists first meet. Once the couple begins to bond emotionally, we do not see these again.

73. Elspeth Probyn, "Choosing Choice: Images of Sexuality and 'Choiceoisie' in Popular Culture," in *Negotiating at the Margins: The Gendered Discourses of Power and Resistance*, ed. Sue Fisher and Kathy Davis (New Brunswick, NJ: Rutgers University Press, 1993), 281, 285.

74. Formulated by Erving Goffman in *The Presentation of Self in Everyday Life* (New York: Doubleday, 1959), impression management was translated into a best-selling pedagogical program in the late 1970s by John T. Molloy. See his *The Woman's Dress for Success Book* (New York: Warner Books, 1978).

75. On the New York snobbery surrounding big hair, and on Melanie Griffith's "blunt" cut, see Grant McCracken, *Big Hair: A Journey into the Transformation of Self* (Woodstock, NY: The Overlook Press, 1996), 125, 169.

76. Helen Gurley Brown, *Having It All: Love, Success, Sex, Money, Even If You're Starting with Nothing* (New York: Simon & Schuster, 1982).

77. Traube, *Dreaming Identities*, 112. My emphasis.

78. Anthea Taylor, *Single Women in Popular Culture: The Limits of Postfeminism* (London: Palgrave Macmillan, 2012), 10.

79. Kitt, *Thursday's Child*, 68.

80. Tasker, *Working Girls*, 152.

81. Owen Gleiberman, "'You Don't Nomi': Film Review," *Variety*, June 9, 2020, https://variety.com/2020/film/reviews/you-dont-nomi-review-showgirls-elizabeth-berkeley-paul-verhoeven-1234628623. Berry mentions watching hours of video and reading *National Geographic* to learn how cats move in *The Many Faces of Catwoman*, directed by Jeffrey Lerner (New Wave Entertainment, 2005), 24:28. See also Hanley, *The Many Lives of Catwoman*, 218.

82. Nayman, *It Doesn't Suck*, 7–9.

83. Ibid., 40.

84. Driscoll, "Superheroine," 169.

85. On the front and back regions of everyday life performance, see Goffman, *The Presentation of Self*, 109–40.

86. Otto Rank, *The Double: A Psychoanalytic Study*, trans. and ed. Harry Tucker Jr. (Chapel Hill: University of North Carolina Press, 1971), 3–7, 18, 77.

87. See Hanley, *The Many Lives of Catwoman*, 226, and the remarks by Jeph Loeb (comic book writer and former executive at Marvel TV) in Lerner, *The Many Faces of Catwoman*. On the refusal to commit, see DeCandido, "Purr-fectly Mediocre."

88. Sigmund Freud, "The Uncanny," in *Art and Literature*, The Pelican Freud Library, vol. 14, trans. James Strachey (London: Penguin, 1985), 358.

89. Anne Friedberg, *Window Shopping: Cinema and the Postmodern* (Berkeley: University of California Press, 1994), 66.

90. Driscoll, "Superheroine," 169.

91. Mick LaSalle, "A Feisty, Feminist Feline with a Taste for Sushi, Leather and, Most of All, Revenge," *SFGate*, July 23, 2004, https://www.sfgate.com/movies/article/A-feisty-feminist-feline-with-a-taste-for-sushi-2739485.php.

92. Nicole Davis, "Up on the Roof: 16 Classic Rooftop Scenes on Film," BFI, July 20, 2018, https://www2.bfi.org.uk/news-opinion/news-bfi/lists/rooftop-scenes-film.

93. Hanley, *The Many Lives of Catwoman*, 220. See also Blackwelder, "Cat Camp Fever," and Ryan Lambie, "10 Remarkable Things about Catwoman," Den of Geek, August 1, 2013, https://www.denofgeek.com/movies/10-remarkable-things-about-catwoman.

94. These quotations are from, respectively, Kuersten, "All Clawed Up"; Whaley, "Black Cat," 15; and Lambie, "10 Remarkable Things about Catwoman."

95. Jeffrey A. Ewing, "Women as 'the Devil's Gateway': A Feminist Critique of Christian Demonology," in *Philosophical Approaches to Demonology*, ed. Benjamin W. McCraw and Robert Arps (New York: Routledge, 2017), 75–92. While evil is depicted in these films as an everyday force, it is fully intentional; it is never "banal" in Hannah Arendt's sense of the mindless and unimaginative.

96. Williams, *America's Mistress*, 119.

97. "'Monotonous' Lyrics," Genius, accessed February 23, 2020, https://genius.com/Eartha-kitt-monotonous-lyrics.

98. On T. S. Eliot, see Williams, *America's Mistress*, 287n7.

99. Williams, *America's Mistress*, 124. See David Rosen, "The Night Josephine Baker Never Got Her Steak," *Black Star News*, October 7, 2015, https://www.blackstarnews.com/us-politics/justice/the-night-josephine-baker-never-got-her-steak.html.

100. Kitt, *Confessions of a Sex Kitten*, 112–13. On the chaise longues, see Kitt, *Thursday's Child*, 214–16, and Kitt, *Alone with Me*, 187–88.

101. Williams relies on an account by Sillmann that belittles Kitt's role: *America's Mistress*, 120–21.

102. Harry Horner and John Beal, *New Faces* (DVD. 20th Century Fox, 1954).

103. Mary Ann Doane, *Femmes Fatales: Feminism, Film Theory, Psychoanalysis* (New York: Routledge, 1991), 2, emphasis in original. A significant example of the femme fatale as "carrier" that is relevant to the performance tradition informing *Showgirls* is the figure of the "false" Maria in Fritz Lang's *Metropolis* (1927). As the vamp-robot double of the saintly human Maria (Brigitte Helm), false Maria's gyrating, lascivious, yet puppet-like dance drives the mob into a frenzy of destruction at the command of her maker, Rotwang (Rudolf Klein-Rogge). My thanks to an anonymous reviewer for pointing this out.

104. Cited in Doane, *Femmes Fatales*, 125–26. A glimpse of Lyda Borelli performing this style is available on https://www.youtube.com/watch?v=AN3u-PxwAbY&list=WL&index=2.

105. Williams, *America's Mistress*, 118, 120.

106. Vallance, "Eartha Kitt." On Kitt as a gold digger, see Stephen Holden, "Forever Feline, Forever Fierce," *New York Times*, December 26, 2008, https://www.nytimes.com/2008/12/27/arts/music/27kitt.html. For her view of this inability to distinguish her "stage" from her "real" personality, see Kitt, *Confessions of a Sex Kitten*, 213.

107. *Ebony*, "Why Negroes Don't Like Eartha Kitt," 30.

108. Holden, "Forever Feline."

109. Sedgwick, *Epistemology of the Closet*, 98–100.

110. Kitt, *Alone with Me*, 1–6.

111. Jennifer Szalai, "The Complicated Origins of 'Having It All,'" *New York Times*, January 2, 2015, https://www.nytimes.com/2015/01/04/magazine/the-complicated-origins-of-having-it-all.html.

112. For Verhoeven, "she is saved, redeemed. It is sort of a Christian morality tale." *Showgirls: Portrait of a Film* (New York: Newmarket Press, 1995), 22.

113. The first reading sees Nomi's performance as an example of "failed seriousness"; Susan Sontag, "Notes on Camp," in *Against Interpretation and Other Essays* (New York: Delta, 1966), 287. Admiration for Berkley within the second reading came from Jacques Rivette in 1998: "that actress is amazing!" Frédéric Bonnaud, "The Captive Lover—An Interview with Jacques Rivette," trans. Kent Jones, *Senses of Cinema* 79 (September 2001), first published in French, 1998, http://sensesofcinema.com/2001/jacques-rivette/rivette-2.

114. Verhoeven cited in Hugh Montgomery, "How *Showgirls* Exposed the Rot of Our Misogynistic Culture," BBC Culture, July 15, 2020, https://www.bbc.com/culture/article/20200714-how-showgirls-told-the-truth-about-americas-foul-misogyny; Claudia Card, *The Atrocity Paradigm: A Theory of Evil* (Oxford: Oxford University Press, 2002), 139–65.

115. David Schmader, "The Greatest Movie Ever Made," Audio Commentary. In Paul Verhoeven, dir., *Showgirls* (Carolco Pictures, Chargeurs, United Artists, 1995); and his comments in McHale, *You Don't Nomi*.

116. Nayman, *It Doesn't Suck*, 88.

117. LaSalle, "A Feisty, Feminist Feline."

118. Driscoll, "Superheroine," 169.

119. Sandra M. Gilbert and Susan Gubar, *The Madwoman in the Attic: The Woman Writer and the Nineteenth-Century Literary Imagination*, 2nd ed. (New Haven, CT: Yale University Press, 2000), 37.

120. On philosophical debates about evil action and personhood, see Todd Calder, "The Concept of Evil," *Stanford Encyclopedia of Philosophy*, Summer 2020 ed., ed. Edward N. Zalta, https://plato.stanford.edu/archives/sum2020/entries/concept-evil/. The evil character of Laurel trails the neo-noir screen aura of the actress; Lambie's "10 Remarkable Things about Catwoman" sardonically lists "Sharon Stone is evil" as one of those ten things.

121. Elvira Basevich, "Modern Representations of Evil: Kant, Arendt, and the Devil in Goethe's *Faust* and Bulgakov's *The Master and Margarita*," in *Philosophical Approaches to Demonology*, ed. Benjamin W. McCraw and Robert Arps (New York: Routledge, 2017), 243.

122. See Calder, "The Concept of Evil"; Card, *The Atrocity Paradigm*, 3.

123. "Not all injuries to dignity leave permanent or deeply disfiguring scars, even if they leave permanent memories and are just cause for resentment." Card, *The Atrocity Paradigm*, 105. For a critique of this position, see Linda A. Bell, "Challenging the Genteel Supports of Atrocities: A Response to *The Atrocity Paradigm*," *Hypatia* 24, no. 1 (2009): 123–40.

124. Kitt, *Thursday's Child*, 177. Her later accounts of this moment change slightly as her legending takes different directions. In *Thursday's Child*, Kitt goes to Hotel Gallia in Paris (181). In *Alone with Me*, the ship is the *Queen Elizabeth*, the hotel is the same, and "I was absolutely alone" (158–59). In both accounts she has run out of money in New York. In *Confessions of a Sex Kitten*, she finds Mary Chase, manager of Kitt's friend Josh White, installed in her suite on the *Queen Elizabeth*, probably at her expense. Mary insists that they go to the Plaza Athénée, "one of the most expensive hotels in Paris" (76–78).

125. Card, *The Atrocity Paradigm*, 16.

126. Ibid., 15–16 and 5–6, respectively.

127. Flora, "Eartha Kitt." On reading the autobiographies for insight into "the mechanics of producing Eartha Kitt," see Daniher, "Yella Gal," 19.

128. TooFab, "Elizabeth Berkley Embraces 'Showgirls' 20 Years Later," YouTube, 6:37, June 29, 2015, https://youtu.be/tk8XR3U71D0.

129. See Lena Hammergren's account of "embodied spectatorship" as a kinaesthetic and empathic mode of reception whereby "perception of another's action is also experienced as one's own movement/sensation." Lena Hammergren, "Embodied Spectatorship? Interpreting Dance Reviews around 1900," *Nordic Theatre Studies* 29, no. 1 (2017): 15. My thanks to Megan Wood for drawing this article to my attention.

130. Kara Keeling, *The Witch's Flight: The Cinematic, the Black Femme, and the Image of Common Sense* (Durham, NC: Duke University Press, 2007), 19–24.

131. Ethan Alter, "'Showgirls' at 25: Gina Ravera Discusses the Cult Movie's Most Controversial Scene," Yahoo!Entertainment, September 23, 2020, https://www.yahoo.com/entertainment/showgirls-gina-ravera-controversial-scene-paul-verhoeven-220338697.html.

132. Celia Walden, "Set in Stone," *Sun-Herald Sunday Life*, October 11, 2020, 8–9.

133. Hanley, *The Many Lives of Catwoman*, 222; Whaley, "Black Cat," 15–16. On the ethnic publicity, see also Collier, "Halle Berry Is 'Purrrfect.'"

134. Razzie Channel, "Halle Berry Accepts Her RAZZIE® Award," YouTube, January 14, 2011, https://youtu.be/U-7s_yeQuDg.

135. Ramin Setoodeh, "How Halle Berry Fought Her Way to the Director's Chair," *Variety*, September 2020, https://variety.com/2020/film/news/halle-berry-bruised-directing-toronto-film-festival-1234762255/.

136. Kitt, *Alone with Me*, 230.

137. Kitt, *Confessions of a Sex Kitten*, 275.

PART II
CONVERSATIONS

THE ACCIDENTAL SHOWGIRL 8

REMINISCING WITH PERFORMER AND PIONEER FEMINIST LYNNE HUTTON-WILLIAMS

JANE CHI HYUN PARK AND SHAWNA TANG

Introduction

This piece brings together a series of conversations from May to August 2019 that gender and cultural studies scholars Shawna Tang and Jane Park had with Lynne Hutton-Williams about her experiences as a trapeze artist turned showgirl from the 1950s to the late 1960s. Lynne traveled and performed all over the world—first as a trapeze artist touring fair dates and shrine circuses around the United States, and then as various combinations of trapeze artist, dancer, and showgirl at the Latin Quarter nightclub in New York and the Casino du Liban in Lebanon, as well as a number of engagements in Europe and Japan. In 1964, she had a six-month stint in Las Vegas as a showgirl. We highlight this brief period in her life to provide an alternative historical narrative alongside the readings of *Showgirls* in this volume.

In what follows, we try to paint a picture of what it was like for Lynne to work as a showgirl in a period that saw rapid shifts in gender roles with the advent of second-wave feminism—the generation critiqued by third-wave feminism, whose style and sensibilities are on sharp display in *Showgirls*. It considers her transition from performing as a highly skilled trapeze artist in the circus to inhabiting the showgirl's "unskilled" body at nightclubs, cabarets, and ballets. In particular, it explores the complex ways that her growing feminist consciousness and later activism influenced her performances—as a woman, as queer, as a British American expat, and as a singularly "tough broad"—onstage and offstage.

The fluid and fragmented nature of Lynne's memory, our own personal interests and investments in her story, and the multiple interviews we conducted—in different settings, times, and states of mind—are reflected in our interview notes. We have structured these notes chronologically, highlighting topics that emerged organically from our meetings together, which often involved eating and drinking and, on a few occasions, looking through Lynne's photo albums together.

The article is divided into three sections. In the first section, we introduce ourselves, our relationship to Lynne, and our respective interests in her story. The second section provides a time line of Lynne's professional life, from her time in the circus to her move to Australia. The last section reconstructs conversations from our interviews, using Lynne's time line and photos, and focuses primarily on her time in Las Vegas.

The Interviewers

Jane Chi Hyun Park

When *Showgirls* was released in 1995, I was a young Korean American feminist who had just graduated from Brown University, then and now a famous bastion of the culture wars. Third-wave feminism was at its height—we listened to Ani DiFranco, Queen Latifah, and Bikini Kill, read Susan Faludi's *Backlash* and Clarissa Pinkola Estés's *Women Who Run with the Wolves*, went to performances by Guerrilla Girls, and discussed postcolonial feminism and Donna Haraway's "A Cyborg Manifesto" over coffee. Some of my fellow feminist students stripped at the local bars to "subvert the male gaze." I don't recall any of them liking

Showgirls. Instead, the movie was celebrated by my gay male friends who claimed it as a fabulous example of camp, resplendent with the exquisite performances of those perfectly proportioned and excessively objectified women Lynne calls "the failed divas of the world."

I met Lynne several years ago through my colleague and mentor Meaghan Morris, but it wasn't until I moved into the same neighborhood in 2016 that Lynne and I grew close. We bonded over our new pets—Lynne's kitten and my puppy quickly became great friends—ate dumplings from the local Chinese restaurant with Chardonnay from Lynne's never-ending supply, and discussed our experiences as American expats in Australia.

I soon discovered that Lynne's attitudes toward feminism (positive) and the United States (negative) were much stronger and clearer than my own—I think, in large part, due to the tremendous struggles she faced as a fiercely independent, observant young woman who managed to make a precarious living as a beautiful and talented performer in an often sexually exploitative industry. Perhaps for this reason, my questions tended to circle around the seeming contradictions between her emerging feminist consciousness and her attitudes toward the labor she performed as a "sex object."

Shawna Tang

I come to *Showgirls* as a cultural stranger, unaware of its status as a cult classic in the anglophone world and alien to the bewildering casinoscape of Las Vegas. In 1995, when *Showgirls* was released, I was a freshman at the National University of Singapore, where feminism was quite absent from my social science curriculum. As I began this project, removed from *Showgirls* culturally and contextually, I couldn't help but wonder: was I alone in missing out?

Among my friends who are more pop culture savvy, two had recollections of watching the movie. Both had watched bootleg copies of *Showgirls* bought and smuggled home from Johor Bahru (JB) in Malaysia and Hong Kong. Off the cuff, they said, "The movie isn't bad but was quite controversial in the '90s" and "JB was the go-to source for all things banned in Singapore. Or maybe it played at the Yangtze Theatre." Yangtze, an old Singaporean institution, had by the mid-1990s become known as a "softcore cinema" frequented by older male retirees.[1] Until it closed for good in 2016, Yangtze was not a venue for a broad audience. Is this why *Showgirls* was never a cultural phenomenon in Singapore, censored as it was in mainstream cinema and screened only in the musty halls of Yangtze? It is from these knowledge interstices that *Showgirls* is for me both an abstracted object and a site of anthropological interest.

When I found out that Lynne, my new friend, was a showgirl in 1960s Las Vegas and had been in dialogue with Jane for a *Showgirls* research project, I joined in their conversation, curious about the cultural phenomenon that *Showgirls* never was in Singapore. My keen questions, stemming mostly from barely disguised ignorance, were generously welcomed by Jane and Lynne. Unwittingly, I became a part of their expansive conversation.

As a gender and cultural studies scholar, I am interested in questions of affective labor in relation to the work of a showgirl. How did Lynne, the avowed feminist, regard and not regard her labor as a showgirl? As a queer Singaporean who grew up in a heteronormative environment, I wondered what sort of queer possibilities and same-sex intimacies existed for a lesbian woman in the seedy, male-dominated context of Las Vegas in the mid-twentieth century.

As a new friend of Lynne, someone I bonded with over death and grief (she having lost her partner and I my mother in recent years), my interest has been from the start simply about getting to know her. Her life trajectories put into sharp relief the contrast of my own, and her geographies of living exist at the limits of my own imagination. Las Vegas, among the many worlds Lynne found herself in, was a place my adventurous mother always longed to visit but didn't, and so a vision of life in Las Vegas through Lynne's lens seemed both serendipitous and significant.

Time Line

March 20, 1938	Lynne Hamilton Hutton-Williams is born in England.
1942	Lynne, her sister Carol Hutton-Williams, and their mother move to Sarasota, Florida, to live with Lynne's maternal grandmother.
1944–1950	Carol and Lynne begin acrobatic training by circus professionals when Sailor Circus, a children's circus founded by Bill Rutland, provides lessons at their school.
1950–1952	Carol (then known as Carol Brent) and Lynne join the Hollywood Sky Ballet and apprentice as trapeze artists under owners John and Phyllis Gibson. The troupe tours fair dates around the country.
1952–1953	The sisters perform professionally with the Hollywood Sky Ballet.
1953–1956	Lynne joins Harold Alzana's high-wire act and tours fair dates and shrine circuses nationally.
1956–1961	Lynne performs as an aerialist at the Latin Quarter, New York.
1961–1962	Lynne moves to London, which becomes her home base, then takes a job working as a hairdresser on a merchant navy ship.

1962–1964	Lynne performs as a trapeze artist and showgirl at the Casino du Liban, near Beirut.
1964	Lynne performs as a showgirl at the Dunes, Las Vegas.
1964–1966	Lynne performs as a showgirl at Le Ballet de Bentyber, Paris, touring Barcelona, Stockholm, and Monaco.
1966–1968	Lynne performs as a showgirl in the Magic Show, touring all cities in Japan.
1968–1973	Lynne returns to London, works as a London Tourist Authority registered guide, and meets her future partner, Robyn Kemmis.
1973	Lynne and Robyn move to Sydney.

From Circus to Cabaret

"A Modern-Day Coliseum"

Lynne began acrobatic lessons at age six and performed in trapeze soon after receiving training by professionals from Sailor Circus (see fig. 8.1). *Lynne appears in a short documentary about this circus produced by Warner Bros. called* Under the Little Big Top *(directed by André de la Varre, 1953). Sarasota was the home of Ringling Bros. and the setting for the film* The Greatest Show on Earth *(directed by Cecil B. DeMille, 1952), in which Lynne also appears, marching with other children in a street scene. When Lynne was twelve, she and Carol were recruited by the owners of the Hollywood Sky Ballet, John and Phyllis Gibson, to apprentice as trapeze artists and perform around the country.*

Q: How did you end up joining the circus?
I was always a really physical child and started with dance lessons, which led to acrobatic training by circus performers in establishing Sailor Circus—the first children's circus in the USA. I performed a sixty-foot aerial act with partner Bruce Winne [see fig. 8.2]. You have to

8.1 Lynne practicing with Sailor Circus, 1950. Lynne Hutton-Williams personal collection, courtesy of Carol Burman-Jahn.

remember that Sarasota, where we lived, was the home of Ringling Bros. When I was twelve, along with my older sister, Carol, I was scouted to apprentice with the Hollywood Sky Ballet. We toured around the country, living and working communally with people, and performed at different fairs, including the Dallas World's Fair in 1952.

Q: Did you do anything besides trapeze?
Yes—I also did bareback riding acts and trick roping and trained to ride "high school," an equestrian act, on a Lipizzan. Horses were my first

Suspended from the high trapeze, Bruce Winne holds Lynne Hutton Williams as they go through their tryouts for the third renewal of the Sarasota High School Sailor Circus.

8.2 Suspended from the high trapeze: Lynne trying out for the third renewal of Sarasota High School's Sailor Circus. *Sarasota Herald-Tribune*, March 2, 1952.

love. But at five feet six and a half inches, I had perfect proportions for acrobatic work—a good core, long legs, and tight torso—which helped.

Q: What was it like working in the circus?
When people say "it's a circus"—the metaphor is derogatory. The circus is denigrated for its physicality and emphasis on the body. But performing in the circus requires extensive physical training and artistry as well as technical skills. For instance, Carol and I designed the rigging for all of our acts. We told the engineers what to do. You had to design unique choreography, wardrobe, music, and presentation to distinguish your act from others. There is a hierarchy in the circus where clowns are at the bottom—they function as distraction when someone falls because there were no nets until 1956—aerialists on top, animal acts in between. You took the risk; that's the way it was. It was like a modern-day coliseum with bloodthirsty crowds anticipating a fall. We all knew that and worked with it. I stood on my hands a hundred and twenty feet in the air without the wire or nets [see fig. 8.3].

"A Hundred and Twenty Feet in the Air"

Q: Did the climate change after the nets came?
No, not immediately. The risk now is more about injury rather than death. Back then there was the idea that you could die at any moment. We normalized this. There was a pronounced instance of working in the now.

Q: Could you describe the kind of training you got, your daily schedule, and the different kinds of work you did?
We woke up early in the morning and trained. This was the two years that I was apprenticing from age eleven to thirteen. A hundred sit-ups,

8.3 First professional performance in Dallas, Texas, 1952. Carol and Lynne appear in the cradle section. Photographer: Ewing Galloway. Lynne Hutton-Williams personal collection.

a hundred push-ups, get on the trapeze, hang straight, circle the bar, run up the ladder really quickly for one to two hours, breakfast, how to do spotlights, how to build rigging, how to tear it down, stack and load and transport. The day ended when the act was presented [see fig. 8.4].

Q: Were there things you were taught to center yourself?
No, we weren't taught. You really have to be centered, to put it mildly. You were surrounded by this gigantic ocean of fear. You knew that one slip and likely you'd be dead or hurt very badly. That was enough to make you concentrate really well.

Q: Yet you were also performing to a large audience, so your orientation had to be somewhat outward as well as you being so focused.
You are aware that it's a performance, but that awareness is way back there. It's like there, not there. When you are doing it, the only thing you are focused on is what you are doing. It is so narrow. The narrowest you can be, really. And the others are not there.

Q: How do you think that has sort of shaped you? The ability to stay so focused.
I wish it had. I wish I could apply the focus to other areas of life. I am too randomly interested in too many things. I am interested in so many things [*laughs*].

"A Family Feeling"

At age fifteen, Lynne broke her back performing an act with her sister. This was also when she became self-contracting. Lynne never had an agent, which was common for women and people in the circus in general at the time. In 1955, she was recruited by Harold Alzana, a renowned high-wire walker from England, to work in his wire act touring US fair dates and coliseums.

8.4 Hollywood Sky Ballet. *From top to bottom*: Lynne, Sandra Sprangle, Carol, Phyllis Gibson, and Nick O'Connell. Photographer: Ewing Galloway. Lynne Hutton-Williams personal collection.

I didn't have an agent. I joined Harold Alzana. He worked on the Ringling show. I became a part of his act. It's not the same as working for someone. You're never working for one person because you're always a component of an act, which makes you vital and a part of something. You are doing a task, but it's always a collective. There's a big difference. It's always a part of something. There is no way you can do any circus things or trapeze or any of that without total cooperation. It's always working with others. It's fantastic in the circus, and it's been horrible ever since. Because we were like a moving community [see fig. 8.5].

Q: You mentioned how you never actually came out because everybody in the circus was already queer, and so that was the norm.
Well, no, they weren't queer. They didn't care. It wasn't worth talking about at all. Nobody noticed because the important thing was what you could do. Not who you fucked or what your private life was like. Most people did not have a private life. We lived in a gigantic family. But they weren't family—like dominating. There were individuals and families. Families that performed or had their children performing with them in an act—they operated as a family in a small sense, but on a wider level within the group they just saw each other as members of a bigger organization. It was all dependent on what you could do and how you performed.

Q: It's interesting you also described that as your family.
I would describe it as a *family feeling*. It is a collective, close feeling, connected the way families are supposed to be but often [are] not. The really important thing is: can you do a handstand or can't you?

The Lie and the Latin Quarter

At age eighteen, Lynne was working at the Latin Quarter in New York, where she performed a trapeze act.

8.5 Publicity group photo of circus members in the dressing room. Lynne is seated bottom left. Lynne Hutton-Williams personal collection.

Q: A newspaper report of your time at the Latin Quarter says you were part of the famed Wallenda troupe.[2]

Which was a lie. It's not true at all. My sister and I were hired to perform at the Latin Quarter [see fig. 8.6]. And because we were young and didn't have a name established, they had to give it to circus professionals who had a name. So they got the Wallendas in, but we were paid for doing what was our idea. That's what I mean by a lie.

8.6 Lynne performing at the Latin Quarter, New York, 1961. Photographer: Pat Rich. Lynne Hutton-Williams personal collection.

Q: You've mentioned you worked with Liberace at New York's Latin Quarter. . . . Can you tell us a bit about what that was like?
He was a really nice guy. He was a person of superb generosity, super kind, a rarity in that kind of showbiz. He gave every person in the cast one of his albums at the end of the show, and on an everyday basis he treated people very openly and always with kindness.

Q: Would you consider this period—working in New York's night-spots—a retirement from the circus?
Most people don't retire. You *transition* out of the circus as you get older and your body gets weaker.

Transitioning from Circus Professional to Hairdresser, Dancer, and Showgirl: Beirut, Europe, Japan, Las Vegas

In 1961, Lynne took some time off to sail with the merchant navy to South Africa, working as the ship's hairdresser. A year later, she was recruited by Charley Henchis to perform at the Cabaret du Liban near Beirut.

Q: What was Beirut like?
I worked at the Casino du Liban, thirty kilometers from Beirut [see fig. 8.7]. In my act, I came down from a wire through a jagged hole in the ceiling cut by tin snippers. A man had to guide me through the hole and wire me up every performance. He had to be very careful, or I could have been decapitated.

There was an incident. I hardly ever talk about this. Not long after we arrived and before we opened the show, I was living in Beirut with a couple of showgirls and the main diva—she was the star of the show, right? But the other showgirl was living in Jounieh [a coastal city north of Beirut], which is near the big casino where we were working. So we

8.7 The cast at Casino de Liban, where Lynne performed as dancer and showgirl. Lynne is pictured top row, standing third from left in yellow and red headgear. Lynne Hutton-Williams personal collection.

wanted to live there rather than pay the thirty or forty dollars to go by taxi from Beirut out to the casino. . . . Public transport was very unreliable and strange. So we got a place out there, and there was an accident. One morning I woke up, and the other two were still sleeping, and I knocked on the door. I had a room of my own, and they had a room together. And I opened the door and they were both sort of lying. . . . They had gassed themselves with the heater.

I went into action mode and dragged one off the bed, but she was dead. She was the star of the show. I dragged the other off the bed, all the way out to the balcony because I knew that she would need air. So I was giving her CPR and rising above the concrete railing of our veranda and yelling and trying to get people's attention. And finally someone heard and came rushing over with some people we didn't know from the village. The ambulance came and the whole bit. The woman survived—they had to pack her in ice. They saved her life. Then I went back to Beirut. I thought, I'm going to have a real problem getting out of here alive. I got a flat in Beirut and made the commute to work.

Q: You were still doing trapeze but in a cabaret. How was that different?
It was totally different. It wasn't dangerous; it wasn't anything. If a dancer was needed or a showgirl was needed and I would still fit into that, I always said yes. I was trying to support myself—transitioning from circus so whatever came along that was possible to do, I did without having to resort to prostitution. I managed to keep going on for quite a while.

Instability aside, it was wonderful. I was in a different country. I was having a nice time. It was good when I had proper contracts with a beginning and an end, and in that interim period when that was happening, I was really happy. It was fun because I knew everything was going well. And I felt like everything, more or less, was in control in my area. And it was a great thing to do. But the times away from contracts, it was so precarious. Precarious is everybody's life today. That was my life then.

It was a survival thing for me. It just happens to women in that situation that I was, sort of in transition, kind of looking pretty most of the time. So, therefore, people were working out ways to use me. I was outside the circus and was contracted with independent dancing companies, a ballet company for a while, which was not a conventional ballet but a cabaret ballet. If I got offers, I viewed them as an opportunity, and I did what I could, and I tried to keep going.

In the period from 1961 to 1964, Lynne continued her transition from trapeze artist to dancer and showgirl. The Paris-based Ballet de Bentyber, to which Lynne was contracted, toured Barcelona, Stockholm, and Monte Carlo, where the troupe attended Grace Kelly's wedding. Lynne did all of the hair for the ballet members using her training as a hairdresser and met Rudolf Nureyev, Maria Callas, and Aristotle Onassis. Her account is a fascinating glimpse of how the mobile world of show business and entertainment overlaps in this time with the high gods of modernism [see fig. 8.8].

Q: Tell us about your geographies of work and living.
From the time that Carol and I stopped working together on the same shows, I was always on my own, just making my way. Going from contract to contract and booking to booking. Usually I was seen some place by a producer or director, and they approached me. Said, "We're doing a show in blah blah, and we want you to be in that." And then they'd send me a contract. And a plane ticket. And off I'd go. So that's the way it worked for me, most of the time, during that period.

I moved from Beirut to Europe to Japan. In Japan, I was recruited to perform as a showgirl for the Magic Show—a magic variety show that toured all the cities in Japan. This was an exciting cross-cultural experience. Performers were housed with local families and immersed in the local culture, which I loved [see fig. 8.9].

Q: And in Monte Carlo, you went to Grace Kelly's wedding?
Yes, and I did the hair of everybody, of the whole company. At the Monte-Carlo Sporting Club, I was swimming, and Nureyev was in the pool; Callas and Onassis were sitting alongside. I was diving—I

8.8 Lynne in her dressing room about to go onstage in Las Vegas. Lynne Hutton-Williams personal collection.

8.9 Lynne in Japan. Lynne Hutton-Williams personal collection.

could dive well then. Afterward I was chatting to Nureyev, and Onassis asked us to join them for a drink. But Nureyev went off, and I had one drink with Onassis and Callas; that's it. I was a great Maria Callas fan. She had a tiny dog, pulling its ears—she seemed kind of depressed. Men did not do well by her. Onassis asked me about myself; then I pissed off.

The Accidental Showgirl

It was in this period of transition that Lynne found herself working as an "accidental showgirl" in Las Vegas. In 1964, she was sent to Vegas to complete a six-month contract in which she had originally been hired to perform elsewhere, thus finding herself in a city and situation she had not chosen.

Working in Vegas

Q: How did you get this job?
I got the job because I had a contract for Las Vegas for a period of about six months. Somehow my original contract fell through, and the only place I could be sent to that this person had anything to do with, this person who hired me, was Las Vegas. Because he had connections with the Dunes hotel and he didn't want to pay me out my contract for nothing. So that is why I said I was an accidental showgirl. That's how I got there. That's the story [see fig. 8.10].

Q: Can you describe what a typical day was like for a showgirl?
I'd be sharing accommodations with one or two other women, and we'd go for breakfast about 8:30 a.m. or 9:00 a.m. We'd have eggs and bacon; there was no whole food awareness! You went with the girls, seldom alone.

Then you'd go to rehearsal every single day. That took two and a half to three hours, then we'd go out for lunch. That was self-supplied, you had to use your own money. Then at 2:00 p.m. you'd do the show. It would last about one and a half to two hours. Then you would have a snack and go on to do the evening show, two shows a day. After that you would go to watch another show, the competition, or one that you'd heard about. You'd party, check out the competition, get new ideas for yourself. It was your whole life.

8.10 Dressing room shot of Lynne in Las Vegas. Lynne Hutton-Williams personal collection.

You'd have dinner after that, maybe with a close friend who was not a showgirl or another performer, whoever was around. It was socially fluid. We all felt like a group. You'd get home about 1:00 a.m.

Q: How were showgirls treated at the workplace?
As a showgirl we were always both treated quite well on some levels but then very poorly regarded on others. We were treated well in the sense

of . . . on a personal level of "Oh, you are so beautiful" and this and that, these kinds of very artificial and fake compliments. And not treated well otherwise. So that contradiction was always there.

It was really not glamorous at all. I mean even pay was delayed and nobody gave a shit. On a business level . . . the management and the choreographers needed to get what they wanted out of every single person. It was a work necessity to get that from each one. They would come in as you were actually in rehearsal and add little extra twists of commentary for each one.

But it's also hard to explain. The sexual expectations were not overt, but they were pervasive. Nobody refused to give a blowjob, ever. For example, I could have asked for a raise but never did because I didn't want to be pawed. You always got hit on by all sorts of men and learned how to deflect it. In everyday life this was not overt from stagehands and helpers, but every time you went out for lunch, there would be whistling, street stuff. It was normalized. We expected it and coped with it.

Q: Can you describe some of your friendships with the showgirls?
Well, you would have a preference for the company of some girls. But you always knew you were going to say goodbye when the show ended. Our relationships were not like those that people who live in towns can have. The last show was always really sad. You couldn't form deep friendships the way settled people do. This applies to show business in general.

But yet, there could be an extraordinarily deep sense of familialism in the circus. People stayed linked over generations in the circus world, like a clan based on shared occupation and expertise. The showgirl world did not have that; there was no family feeling at all. It's a strange level to have to operate on for a long period of time.

As a showgirl, your body was an object of surveillance. It was very different from being accustomed to experiencing the body as an object of appreciation, as in circus. It was a loss. I felt it was demeaning.

8.11 Las Vegas showgirls, backstage. Lynne Hutton-Williams personal collection.

Q: It's also a time when your feminist sensibility became a lot more sharpened through your encounters with certain texts at the bookstore. Did that feminist sensibility help or hinder your relationships or friendships in that space?

Probably helped. I mentioned feminist books to those who would want to hear the things I was reading. For instance, I would be carrying a book around and have my nose in it all the time. And people would be then either interested or not. The only friend I made that I can recall is someone who read a lot. Other people, I think, were scared of me. It was always work, work, work.

When we were together at a show, for example, and the girls were backstage and dressing together and doing all that makeup stuff. It was friendship by association and support for each other. They were very, very friendly and careful and willing to share with each other. If you needed something, they would help. If you fell, they would be right there to see that it wasn't too bad or whatever [see fig. 8.11].

Q: Was it about supporting each other to put up a good performance?
Oh, just general support in being there. But performance-wise there were some jealousies too. Some people couldn't believe I could be a showgirl because I wasn't the type. My legs were too short. I am in absolutely perfect proportion for an acrobat or a trapeze artist but certainly not for a showgirl. You have to have very long legs in proportion to the rest of the body because that is what is going to get the attraction of the male gaze. That's what the job is to start with.

Q: You've said how some of these women were single mothers and were really struggling.
Well, anyone who had a child had a really, really hard time. They didn't last long. The children were usually with the mothers of the showgirls, and they were sending money home all the time.

Showgirl Labor

Q: How much did you make? Do you remember?
Quite a bit. I think it was something like three hundred fifty dollars a week. They had to pay me the money that I had signed for [in] the original contract. It wasn't my fault that I wasn't doing the work that I should have been doing. So they still paid me the money I would have got for

performing as a trapeze artist while I was working as a showgirl. But no one else was getting what I was getting. The other showgirls were getting one hundred dollars a week or something. That was still a lot. I finished my contract and that was the end of that.

Q: What was the most outrageous outfit you had to wear as a showgirl? Do you remember?
Or didn't? [*laughs*] Okay, what was most outrageous? I am going to have to describe some clothes, aren't I? I had a very tall wig in that photo you've seen and it was a very outrageous wig. And it was the only one. Other people had other wigs made for them. My wig was very tall because I was small—that is, next to the other girls who all got in because of their height and beauty rather than anything else. I don't consider myself particularly small.

Q: What's the difference between dancing and being a showgirl? Can you describe the show?
The dancers are the action people. They come out and do things. Showgirls only display their bodies. They can develop a unique style of undressing, but they're not supposed to dance. After a while it becomes nothing but pure presentation for you. So it's like work and non-work. Because you are timekeeping but you are not really working. You are just presenting. Onstage, when the dancers are performing, usually the showgirls are offstage entirely or they will be the spectacle or the backdrop to the dancers. And then the showgirls will be promoted one after the other at some point in any big display.

Q: How are showgirls chosen?
From the managerial point of view of the show, they are chosen for their body lengths, their boob size, and their long legs. That is all you need, and a beautiful face, that goes without saying. That is all you need to be a

showgirl. But a dancer has to be trained and needs to be choreographed and all of that to make a show with them. A showgirl you can just take from anywhere, more or less. . . .

But they're not unskilled, of course, in reality. They were doing things all the time onstage. They develop their own ways, working to do the presentation, which is: I am a body and it's for you. "I'm yours." One way or another that's the message. And "I'm available" [*laughs*]. So you're not doing "emotions"—you're just *showing* your body.

Q: Showgirls! That makes sense. How did you feel performing onstage?
Well, you are making yourself into this object that is part of a larger object. And it's mostly fun. It's more fun than it is work in some sense. Even the actual work of presentation itself is kind of okay. You get feedback all the time. If the show is good, you take a share of that. It's pleasurable. It's very odd. But I mean of course when you get feedback from the audience, despite the fact that it's because of your nude body, you still feel some kind of an ego rush. But at the same time, you know how dreadful it is. It's a two-feeling situation.

Q: Can you describe the energy of the performance?
It wasn't particularly high energy, but the pleasure came in by being different in the way that you presented, and knowing how to play with the performance in a way to suit yourself as well as give a little bit [of] what was required to keep the job. You know, it was tits and bums, tits and bums. And that's very boring, really. So you had to move a little bit and find a special way to present that.

Q: What was your signature?
No, I did not have that kind of gestural signature. I just did what I thought was . . . you construct it as you go. Well, I thought that was the

best way to do it. It was improvised, and anything done over and over again becomes less interesting.

Q: Was there any sort of training showgirls had to undergo?
There was no training. Most everybody who became a showgirl did have training in dance. But they were not suitable for something they tried out for and got rejected and then decided, "Oh, I'll do this. I'll be a showgirl." That's how it worked. For many of them, that was the main route to being a showgirl.

Q: Were there forms of management surveillance and evaluation of the performance?
No one ever gave you any kind of information or surveillance activity. Not at all. Really in the main, for most people that was the case. When you got hired, people knew what they were getting. It's only in circumstances like mine, for example, when there could have been reason to look at me because I was an accident—I wasn't really a showgirl. But no one did. The hiring was important. Once you got hired, no one [could] tell you how to do your act.

I mean, you might have to modify certain things for yourself, for your own reasons, and occasionally move physically to a different spot to satisfy some outside criteria. But in the main, you had the act and that was it.

Q: Did it not matter how you kicked? Like in the movie, they were told off for not kicking right.
No, because showgirls don't kick in Las Vegas. But dancers do. The dancers have a choreographer, and the choreographer fits into the desires of the management and all the other admin people. And they get the show that the management wants that way. So you would rehearse.

If you were a dancer, you would rehearse, and if you were a showgirl you rehearse. And once that's done, that's it. It's open and it's rote. Then it becomes a day-to-day thing.

Q: Was it mostly mechanical and going through the motions since you also mentioned pleasure?
Yes, you have to find a way to make it pleasurable enough for you to do it. And put up with all the other aspects. If you do that, then you keep yourself going. And it comes back to people liking you more. And you can tell all those things. When you have an audience and they respond.

Q: Did some of this response onstage translate into relationships between showgirls and audience members?
Not to my knowledge. They all had moneyed boyfriends in the end. But they were never looking for that as far as I know. Because it was more frivolous. It was more what happened and you just do that. You know that kind of thing. I didn't know any one showgirl who was there to find the man and the money. In fact, being a showgirl would not be the way to do it if you were interested in that.

Q: Can you recall any shows that were particularly memorable?
Like somebody taking their dick out when they saw it? [*Everyone laughs*] You mean that sort of thing? No, it didn't happen.

Queer Relations

Q: It was a very male-dominated environment. Were you in a relationship with a woman then?
Well, I was always trying [*laughs*].

Q: Well, how were those efforts received?

You'll be surprised at how many women wanted to get away from men. Certain men were really irritating and a pain in the ass. And women were much more open. So I had lots of lovers, really, in those days.

Q: Were any of them showgirls?
Of course, sure.

Q: And what were those relationships like?
Erm . . . well, most of them, when you were traveling and everything, they were short. And I think sexuality is very different when you're young. It's all very kind of flexible. I was always close to someone, and often it was just very nice and maybe didn't involve sex or it did—it didn't matter either way. But I did have lots of lovers.

Q: Did you encounter any predatory women, like Cristal in the movie?
No, I would have wished for them! In my experience as a gay woman, there were always women who were not considered gay but were happy to be a sexual partner. You were in the business of being feminine, and with a one-night stand no one was moralistic. My initiation to sex was a threesome with two other women.

Q: Was there a memorable relationship being in that one place in Vegas for six months?
I didn't have one single relationship.

Q: You just fucked lots of women and everyone else was doing this too?
I don't want to make it sound like it was a sexual frenzy type thing because it wasn't. But people weren't so worried about it.

Q: You were in a peculiar situation because you were contracted for six months. Did you hear of the other showgirls talking about their relationships?

Oh yeah. They all had men that were paying them one way or another. Or trying to get them to bed [*laughter*]. Be their girlfriend or whatever. Maybe there would always be one of them and that would last for a little while, then you would get another one. But it happened with managers, those who attended the shows, the gamblers, and so on. . . .

They were all desirable. They were all accustomed to being continually accosted for their beauty and stalked and perved on and whistled at and all that stuff constantly. So they were open to that, but they were also pursued by people with money all the time.

Mostly they were heterosexual, but then that didn't mean as much in those days. Like, for example, I would never have to state [*in a deep voice*] "I'm a lesbian" [*laughter*]. Women were very amenable to me, liked me, treated me the same, and also fucked me. So it all seemed to work out.

Q: Were you ever accosted by a female audience member?
I don't really think so. I think I adduced at some point or other that someone gay might be interested but never anyone making a real overt display or ask[ing] you out or anything like that. It was all much more subtle with women.

Q: What a surreal experience that must have been on some level. You're queer, in Vegas, and reading feminist literature. . . .
[*Laughs*] Among the heterosexual showgirls, they were all sort of more or less on with the local crooks.

Q: The Mafia?
Yes, and they were selected by them . . . paying them attention and buying them gifts, seducing them. The girls appeared in the show or they were the diva or something, and mobsters would line up and attract

them and have them as girlfriends. And that was kind of standard. You didn't have to be the diva either. I mean, you could have just been one of the girls. Because they were always around. And that was one of the parts that made it so *tacky*—you know, being in Vegas? [*Laughs*] Really quite unattractive, I thought. But that sort of thing does go on in show business generally anyway. But you don't often run into the mob as much as you did [in Vegas]. I mean, it was in the day of Meyer Lansky and all those early people who were very nasty.

Q: Do you remember any in particular? Did any of the mob approach you?
I remember a mob boss buying a nephew an ice cream cone and fawning over him. Carol and her son were visiting from Florida. I can't remember his name. But he was well known. And these people were famous mobsters. They weren't just your average—

Q: They were the celebrity mobsters.
Right. Strength and power. So that was really terrifying, and Carol and I were absolutely horrified.

Coda

Q: Along with the mobsters dating the showgirls, do you have any other visceral memories of Vegas?
It's just that the entire place is so *tacky*! It's like living in a toilet [*laughter*]. It's so corrupt. Gambling is everywhere. Vegas pools it all together in this really close fashion, and there's no way you can avoid having your face pushed into that end of capitalism. Where everything is commodified. It's just horrific. But you have to have the attitude to see it, I

suppose. Some people wouldn't notice and think it was all jolly. It was very violent; it made me feel like I never ever wanted to be in America anymore. That's how horrible it was and how it affects you. That was one of the last jobs I did before I left the US.

Q: It's interesting how you survived that space.
From my own point of view, there wasn't much I could see myself doing where I could have any respect for myself at all. Because I didn't have anything to rely on. I had no schooling; I had nothing. I didn't want to feel that way, and I didn't want to be in that environment. I thought it was a really bad one to be in. That was *it*, though. That was the tail end of my story. I knew I didn't want to spend my time in the US anymore, and I knew I wanted to be out of the industry.

After Las Vegas, Lynne returned to London, where she worked as a London Tourist Authority registered guide, giving tours in Europe to people from all over the world, including the Red Guard. She lived in Bickenhall Mansions, above Yoko Ono and her daughter from her first marriage, whom Lynne sometimes babysat. Occasionally she saw John Lennon and the other Beatles in the lift.

In 1970 she met Australian expat Robyn Kemmis, who became her life partner. Together they played a significant role in the burgeoning feminist movement there, occupying a vacant building in Earlham Street, Covent Garden, which became the base for the first Women's Liberation Workshop. Soon afterward, the couple moved to Sydney, where they continued to advocate for social justice—Robyn in a number of senior management positions at the University of Technology Sydney and in the New South Wales public service, where she eventually became Deputy Lord Mayor of Sydney; Lynne in the Sydney Women's Liberation Workshop, where, with like-minded feminist members, she formed a collective called Control devoted to furthering abortion and reproductive rights for women.

JANE CHI HYUN PARK is Senior Lecturer in Gender and Cultural Studies at the University of Sydney. She is author of *Yellow Future: Oriental Style in Hollywood Cinema*. Her recent work appears in *Educational Philosophy and Theory, Screen Bodies,* and *Inter-Asia Cultural Studies.*

SHAWNA TANG is Senior Lecturer in Gender Studies at the University of Sydney. She is author of *Postcolonial Lesbian Identities in Singapore: Re-thinking Global Sexualities* and editor (with Hendri Yulius Wijaya) of *Queer Southeast Asia*. Her recent work appears in *Continuum, Journal of Gender Studies,* and *Journal of Intercultural Studies.*

References

"Real Swinger." *New York Mirror,* November 26, 1961.

Yip Wai Yee. "Goodbye to Softcore Cinema Yangtze." *Straits Times,* March 1, 2016. https://www.straitstimes.com/lifestyle/entertainment/goodbye-to-softcore-cinema-yangtze.

Notes

1. Yip Wai Yee, "Goodbye to Softcore Cinema Yangtze," *Straits Times,* March 1, 2016, https://www.straitstimes.com/lifestyle/entertainment/goodbye-to-softcore-cinema-yangtze.

2. "Real Swinger," *New York Mirror,* November 26, 1961, 1.

9 "FUCK YOU! PAY ME"

STRIPPER ART AND STORYTELLING SPEAKING BACK FROM THE STAGE

ZAHRA STARDUST

Cinematic representations of striptease in popular culture often repeat narratives of fascination, titillation, or tragedy. They linger on the visual and embodied pleasures of dancing: sequins, lights, choreography. They emphasize the competitiveness in backstage spaces: rivalry, sabotage, and aspirations of fame. The 1995 cult film *Showgirls* is no exception. In this popular fantasy of striptease, women are positioned as pitted against one another, vying for male attention and validation. Dancers are willing to literally push one another down stairs to get to the top. But despite its melodrama, there are some aspects of this renowned stripper revenge classic that remain relevant today. The pervasive themes of *Showgirls* that saturate the film are the tyranny of men's entitlement, an absence of workers' rights, and an inescapable "whorearchy"—a hierarchy of value within the sex industry—that ascribes shame to certain types of sexual labor. In *Showgirls,* women repeatedly repudiate their status as sex workers. Nomi Malone is constantly grappling with her own internalized stigma, repeatedly asserting that she is "not a whore." When she is accused by Cheetah's manager Al with the retort "You're a stripper, don't you get it?" Nomi refutes, "I'm a *dancer.*" These motifs of respectability, shame, gender, and power emerge in strippers' own present-day narratives and cultural production.

Almost thirty years since the release of *Showgirls* (and its official status as "box office bomb" and later revival as a cult classic), a

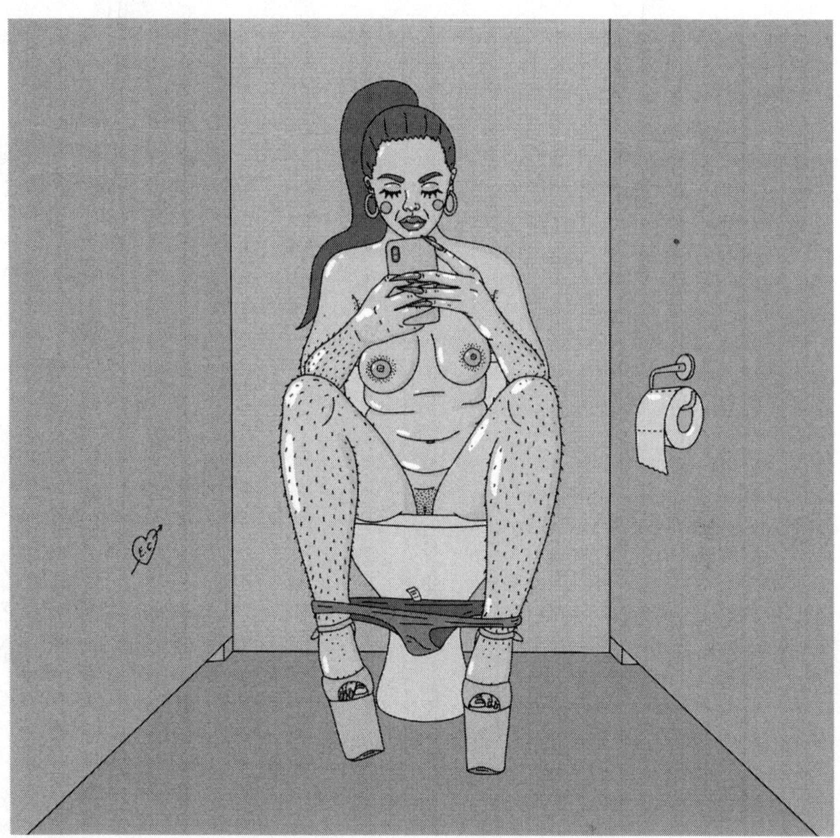

9.1 Backstage showgirl life. Artwork courtesy of Exotic Cancer.

burgeoning body of contemporary literature, arts, and storytelling is thriving from strippers within the industry. These narratives are reframing popular conversations about striptease through the lens of the workers, effectively flipping the gaze to foreground worker experiences and commentary of sexual labor. This time, the spectacle is not the strippers themselves but instead the customers, managers, and media representations. In creating a body of work not simply *about* but instead *by* and *for* strippers, strippers are offering richer contemporary understandings of this labor practice and making demands for cultural, industrial, and legal change.

This chapter showcases popular stripper artists, comedians, and storytellers from Australia whose work has received critical acclaim over the last five years. It considers how the stories, demands, and implorations of these artists engage with dominant narratives told about striptease culture in popular representations such as *Showgirls*. It explores four key emerging themes: male entitlement, gendered labor, consent culture, and structural violence. It situates these local pieces within a growing international movement in both Australia and the United States for workplace rights, law reform, accountability, and justice.

Strippers in the Academy

Increasingly, strippers are part of the academy. In some cases, academics have worked as strippers throughout their under- and postgraduate university degrees and continued on to study their own workplaces. In other cases, academics have commenced work as strippers as part of their research methodologies. Notable examples include cultural anthropologist Katherine Frank, whose book *G-Strings and Sympathy: Strip Club Regulars and Male Desire* draws on her ethnography as an exotic dancer in five strip clubs across the United States. She began stripping "as both a means of earning extra cash for graduate school and as part of a feminist theory project investigating female objectification and body image."[1] Similarly, R. Danielle Egan's book *Dancing for Dollars and Paying for Love: The Relationships between Exotic Dancers and Their Regulars* draws on her work as a podium and lap dancer in

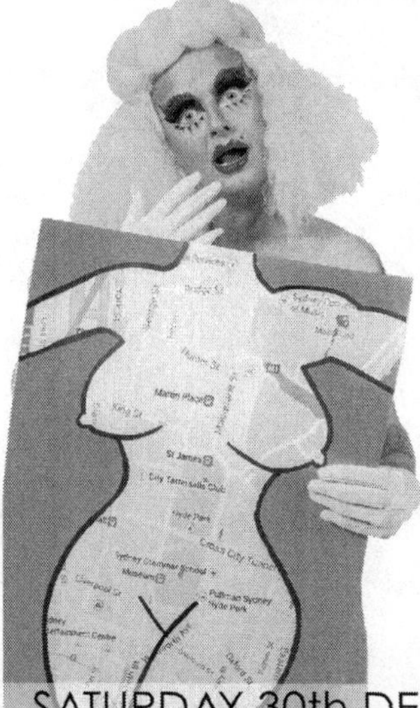

9.2 Poster from Glitta Supernova's solo show *Body Map: The Glitta Supernova Experience*. Image by Chrissie Hall, courtesy of Glitta Supernova.

two clubs in New England, where she juggled roles, "laboriously transcribing interviews, writing detailed field-notes, and learning 'to work' the pole."[2]

In Australia, dancers, strippers, and sex workers have written doctoral theses on various forms of erotic entertainment, such as Lola Montgomery on burlesque, Holly Zwalf on queer leather mommies,

9.3 Glitta Supernova performs in her solo show *Body Map: The Glitta Supernova Experience*. Image by Roberto Duran, courtesy of Glitta Supernova.

Elena Jeffreys on sex worker organizing, Alyssa Kitt on theater performance (forthcoming), Ruby Summers of TØS Journal, and my own PhD on pornography production. Countless other sex workers have contributed to academic literature in fields such as criminology, sociology, law, social work, and performance studies but are not always "out," given the political, personal, and professional risks of studying what is often regarded as "dirty work."[3] My own work draws on my fifteen years of experience working as a stripper across Australia, originally in clubs in Kings Cross, Sydney, and later touring internationally as an Australian Penthouse Pet and Hustler Honey. My work has involved ethnography and qualitative interviews among strippers, pole dancers, burlesque artists, and sex workers in Sydney, and my own art practice includes participation in the sex worker performance troupe Debby Doesn't Do It for Free.[4]

Sex Worker Art, Comedy, and Storytelling

In her book *Strip City: A Stripper's Farewell Journey across America*, Lily Burana laments the "deafening silence" about striptease in accounts of women's history. Stripper stories, she writes, have been lost in part due to the transient nature of the work, but also because of its surrounding stigma. She states: "Stripping is an outlaw profession, with but one prevailing philosophy: Take the money and run. As a result, the long and colorful history of exotic dance is overlooked and under-recorded."[5] Since Burana's reflections in 2002, we have witnessed a cultural shift toward strippers speaking back from the stage. Dozens of stripper memoirs have emerged, detailing the personal and working lives of exotic dancers. High-profile examples from the United States include Heidi Mattson's 1995 *Ivy League Stripper* and Diablo Cody's 2006 *Candy Girl: A Year in the Life of an Unlikely Stripper*.[6] From Australia, former Miss Nude Australia Suzie Q's 2018 *The Stripper Next Door* details her journey from a seventeen-year-old stripper to an international award-winning pole dancer, while Shay Stafford's 2010 *Memoirs of a Showgirl* documents her journey from Brisbane schoolgirl to a professional dancer at the Moulin Rouge and the Lido in Paris.[7]

Some have questioned the value of memoirs in a "confessional culture" where women are expected to perform particular iterations of intimacy. Media scholar Theresa Senft, who worked as a camgirl for her book *Camgirls: Celebrity and Community in the Age of Social Networks*, questions whether such accounts may be "less likely to alienate men than to titillate them."[8] However, more recently, stripper stories have

9.4 Katia Schwartz promotes an evening of stripper storytelling, *Disrobed*. Image courtesy of Sky Sirens.

shifted toward newer forms of media—memes, comics, artwork—that speak to other strippers. Jacqueline Frances's (also known as Jacq the Stripper) *Striptastic! A Celebration of Dope-Ass Cunts Who Like Money*, published in New York in 2017, comprises comics featuring backstage conversations among strippers across the United States as well as bizarre, rude, and absurd quotes from clients. The digital comic illustrations of Melbourne-based stripper artist Exotic Cancer (and her 2020 [2021] comic book, *Shit Men Say in Strip Clubs*) document the mundane, unglamorized, and laborious moments with dry humor, including the poor behavior of clients, the unrealistic expectations of management, and the unpaid emotional labor of workers.[9] Such texts operate more as client shaming boards and stripper support manuals.

In addition, the interactive and participatory nature of online space and the diversification of alternative media platforms has enabled strippers to share stories, art, and advocacy in online spaces. A plethora of new podcasts run by strippers and sex workers have emerged from the Unites States, such as *Yes, a Stripper* (hosted by Onyx Sachi, Daisy Ducati, GiGi Holliday, and A. M. Davies "for folx in and out of the industry"), *The WhoreCast* (hosted by Siouxsie Q, "sharing voices art and stories of American sex workers"), and *Strange Bedfellows* (hosted by Elle Stanger, pitched as "Sex. Politics. Friends."). Film festivals have emerged, such as San Francisco's Sex Worker Film and Arts Festival, as well as—in Amsterdam—a Sex Worker's Opera, "where Sex Workers take back the stage to tell our own stories in our own words."[10]

In Australia, strippers have staged live comedy performances and one-woman shows blending theater and storytelling. Chase Paradise, a stripper from the Gold Coast, toured her debut show, *Ho Life or No Life*, in 2018, selling out tickets at the Melbourne International Comedy Festival. In 2019, the festival featured Bella Green, a nominee for Best Comedy 2018 at Melbourne Fringe, in her stand-up sketch show *Bella Green Is Charging for It*, a journey through "the surprisingly mundane but always hilarious world of sex work, where the heels are high, the carpet is sticky and the customer is probably wrong."[11] London-born, Melbourne-based sex worker Queenie Bon Bon has been a prolific contributor to sex worker arts and culture in Australia, with regular shows since 2014, including *Welcome to the Mystic Hole, Deeply Leisured, Power Up*, and *I Made My Bed, You Lie in It*, in which she takes the audience on multiple journeys though sex work, from the quietly ordinary to the frankly absurd.

Australia's contemporary stripper art and storytelling have developed from a vibrant history of live performance in which sex workers have entertained queer communities.[12] In the 1990s and 2000s, irreverent and iconoclastic events such as Gurlesque, a queer strip club run by two strippers, Sex Intents and Glitta Supernova, created spaces for amateurs and professionals to come together.[13] Glitta's one-woman neo-burlesque shows *Let's Get METAphysical* (2016) and *Body Map* (2017) draw on her experiences as a stripper using camp humor and sexual satire. Glitta performed in Becky Lou's *Seen and Heard* cabaret in 2018 alongside stripper artists Chase Paradise and Frankie Valentine, offering intimate and personal stories about their lives. In addition to cultivating live performance culture, these art practices have contributed to the telling and recording of stripper histories. Frankie Valentine's photographic essay *Risque,* in collaboration with Nelli Scarlet, features pioneering striptease artists and was displayed at the Australian Burlesque Museum.

Other strippers have gone on to create events that combine sex worker storytelling with audience education and peer capacity-building. *Disrobed,* an event run by former stripper Katia Schwartz in Sydney, involves educating the general public on appropriate strip club etiquette, provides audiences with a "respect" package, and includes a closed session for experienced industry workers to share tips and advice with new workers. All events are Auslan interpreted, and counseling services are available in case speakers or participants need support after the sessions.

Sex worker storytelling thus has multiple effects in providing counternarratives to dominant representations, educating audiences, supporting colleagues, and advocating for change. In the *Journal of Australian Studies,* Elena Jeffreys documents how sex workers use our multifaceted and fine-tuned skills in "parading ourselves" for the purposes of public protest and performance.[14] Sex workers, Jeffreys notes, have highly developed skills in performativity, communication, and dress by virtue of sex work itself. These skills are then transferred to the theatrical staging of advocacy messages. The sex worker artist troupe Debby Doesn't Do It for Free is a prime example of this—the Debbies have created visual art speaking on health, stigma, criminalization, policing, and gentrification of sex industry spaces. In their chapter "Staging Decriminalisation: Sex Worker Performance and HIV" in *Viral Dramaturgies*, Elena Jeffreys and Janelle Fawkes describe how sex workers across Myanmar, Cambodia, Canada, South Korea, Thailand, and the United States use performance in ways that expose "harmful policies and practices, [target] policy makers, and successfully [challenge] the authority of anti-sex work narratives."[15]

The Spectacle of Male Entitlement

One of the most significant themes recurring in contemporary stripper art and storytelling in Australia is the exposing of cultures of male entitlement. In *Showgirls*, men are frequently barking demands and orders at female performers. Dancers are referred to as if they were property (Cristal says to Zack, "I'll buy her for you"). Audition processes at the Stardust Casino involve behavior that amounts to sexual harassment, if not assault. At the Cheetah's club, manager Al tells Hope on her first night, "If you want to last longer than a week, you give me a blow job," and that customers are entitled to violate the "they touch, they go" policy if they tip well: "If he gets it out and cums all over you, call the bouncer. Unless he gives you a big tip. If he gives you a big tip, it's ok."

Some feminist analyses of striptease have theorized its gender dynamics with reference to Laura Mulvey's concept of the "male gaze," positioning dancers as objects and clients as subjects. Striptease has been understood quite simply as an example of how, in Mulvey's words, "the determining male gaze projects its phantasy onto the female form

9.5 Tiny men crawl up stripper stilettos, hanging on for life. Artwork courtesy of Exotic Cancer.

which is styled accordingly,"[16] or, as John Berger describes it, "Men look at women. Women watch themselves being looked at."[17] Rachel Shteir writes in *Striptease: The Untold History of the Girlie Show* that "striptease often measured women through the lens of men. Sometimes it illustrated what women wanted those measures to be, and other times it seemed more like a male rebuke of what women lack."[18] *Showgirls* is replete with examples in which men measure, evaluate, and try to "save" women with a complete lack of awareness of their own imbrication in sexist cultures, practices, and structures.

Stripper art and storytelling see this and speak back to this picture. In her work, Katherine Liepe-Levinson argues that rather than strippers being the primary spectacle, customers act as a voyeuristic spectacle themselves. Liepe-Levinson argues that dancers are constantly watching, reading, and evaluating customers' behavior. She notes that "the biggest tipper is often labelled the 'biggest sucker' by customers, managers, and dancers alike."[19] Strippers, who are commonly found in six- to ten-inch stiletto heels, have the advantage of looking down at customers from an elevated platform. In her book *Stripping, Sex, and Popular Culture,* Catherine M. Roach emphasizes the allure of high heels in the "experience of looking down on people from a position of height" and "conferring power because they make you *tall.*"[20]

In Exotic Cancer's work, strippers are represented as almost Amazonian, while male clients are depicted as pathetic, needy, and entitled. They are frequently depicted as tiny people, cockroaches, and maggots. They are portrayed scrambling up giant stripper heels, being dragged along while holding a stripper's ankles, trapped inside the clear stiletto platforms, being caught in giant spiderwebs, and being swallowed by large carnivorous and vulva-esque Venus flytraps. In her custom tarot deck, released in 2022, the Fool card features a man handing over his cash from an automatic teller machine. The machine reads, "LIFE SAVINGS WITHDRAWN. NEW BALANCE: $0.00." Exotic Cancer has rewritten men's narratives to produce a series titled *Honest Tinder Profiles,* where men's biographies have been rewritten to depict their hypocrisy, mediocracy, fragile masculinity, and misogyny. A series of caricatures of male strip club customers features quotation bubbles with common commentary. These include:

"Women go crazy when I go down on them, I have a special technique."
"Oh . . . Will you look at that . . . I have no money!"
"The things that I would do to you are just unimaginable."
"But why can't I kiss you? There's nobody watching!"
"That is why I can't pay you for a dance, I just respect you too much."
"Please can I put one finger in only for two seconds, please."
"Can I have a preview?"
"Can you just spread your asshole for me and stay
in that position for ten minutes?"
"Please don't go! Can you just give me one more
minute!! Can I at least get a hug!"
"Can you put your pussy in my face for $4.50
in coins and the last of my coke?"
"But do you promise to make it worthwhile?"
"You're better than this. You shouldn't be here letting all
these men treat you like a piece of meat . . . How much
money will it take to bring you home and fuck you?"
"But what's your real name?"
"It's not fair that you make me horny but then
won't let me touch your vagina!"
"You have to convince me first, what's so special about you?"
"I have a daughter, you know, so I respect women.
Can I grab your pussy for an extra $10?"

The collation of these quotes into popular comics for the bemusement and enjoyment of fellow strippers further situates strip club customers as spectacles. These comics are *for* strippers. They center the perspectives and experiences of dancers. Sometimes, they provide a sense of solidarity in an industry where, as Jacq the Stripper writes, you have to "prepare for a career with a 90% rate of rejection."[21] But they also act to shame existing customers, educate potential clients, and expose the broader, repetitive patterns of male entitlement to women's bodies,

9.6 Honest Tinder Profiles #4. Artwork courtesy of Exotic Cancer.

their inflated egos, and their delusions of grandeur. Rather than strippers being the punchline of the joke, customers become the entertainment, measured via a stripper worldview.

And strippers, of course, have heard it all before. A recurrent theme in stripper storytelling is the social phenomenon of men who think they are unique, special, or "different" from the other customers. In her one-woman show, Bella Green, a sex worker and ex-stripper from Melbourne, explains, "Every guy that comes into a strip club or brothel thinks he's totally different from every other guy that comes in. They always say, 'You must get some real creeps in here,' and I'm like,

'Actually, they're all pretty much exactly like you.' Sometimes they say, 'People must want you to do really weird shit.' That's how you know that in about five minutes time, they're gonna ask you to do some weird shit."[22]

For many strippers, the joke is these men's total obliviousness and lack of self-awareness of their own narrative. When asked by a journalist what strippers find funny, Chase Paradise replied, "The expectations of men and just their behaviour in regard to sexual entitlement and having to pay for something that they think should be given to them freely."[23] In *Showgirls,* strippers are presented as serial commodities: the dancers are treated as replaceable, and when Nomi becomes Goddess she begins to mimic Cristal's personality. But in strippers' own cultural production, it is the customers who become serial commodities, an endless supply of comical tropes and stereotypes.

For many decades, sex workers have refused cultures of entitlement by insisting on being paid for clients' access to their gendered labor. In *Whores and Other Feminists,* Eva Pendleton describes how, for her, charging money for sex "reverses the terms under which men feel entitled to unlimited access to women's bodies."[24] Dealing with the unrealistic and undeserving expectations of men also serves to build stripper resilience and boundaries. In the face of such ubiquitous and thinly veiled misogyny, strippers effectively develop an intolerance to bullshit. In some cases, it has prepared them for difficult audiences in other contexts. Chase Paradise reflects, "I think one of the things that prepared me the most for comedy is there's nothing a person could heckle at me that I haven't heard before."[25]

Sex workers have been at pains to reiterate that people of diverse genders and sexual orientations seek out sexual services. Recent literature explores the multitude of motivations of women who pay for sexual experiences.[26] At the same time, frequenting strip clubs remains a largely gendered leisure practice. Women customers represented in both Exotic Cancer and Jacq the Stripper's comics also display confusion about consent and boundaries, but they manifest differently. Women are depicted as unruly clients lacking in knowledge of basic strip club etiquette, as judgmental or patronizing customers who assume strippers are lacking in self-respect, and jealous girlfriends who assume that strippers are out to steal their boyfriends. As Exotic Cancer says in an Instagram caption for one comic, "Thinking sex workers are trying to steal your man is like thinking childcare workers are trying to steal your kid."[27]

Although some of the remarks strippers hear can be so unreal as to be laughable, in Exotic Cancer's work, the risk of violence is also present. In one comic, a creepy Uber driver has dropped a stripper off at work and programmed her work and home address into his GPS. Another comic features text messages from men that begin with come-ons and, after receiving no response, end with derogatory slurs and misogynistic threats ("fuk you slut," "Dirty whor"). This kind of escalation is a common pattern in technology-facilitated gendered violence.[28] Stripper art, comedy, and storytelling reveal how strippers are constantly engaged in risk management of customer behavior—anything on a continuum from patronizing savior complexes to overt threats of violence—and how a large part of stripping is not simply the demanding physical athleticism or the performance of hyperfemininity but the constant unpaid and undervalued emotional labor.

Gendered Labor

In the finale of *Ho Life or No Life,* Chase Paradise invites the audience to chant in unison the stripper maxim "Fuck you! Pay me!" This maxim

9.7 a & b Promotional flyer from Bella Green's show *Bella Green Is Charging for It*. Image by Matt Hofmann, design by Vic Hanlon, courtesy of Bella Green.

is a classic example of strippers' explicit rejection of the undervaluing of sexual labor and an active process of denaturalizing the association between femininity and caring work. Contrary to the idea that strippers buy into impossible gendered ideals, strippers demand that their gender performance and caring work be financially compensated. In her book *Bare: The Naked Truth about Stripping,* Elisabeth Eaves reflects

9.7b

on her experiences dancing in Seattle strip clubs. She found that the routine performance of hyperfemininity for work allowed her to deconstruct gendered ideals and meant that she felt less affected by gender stereotypes in her daily life: "I started dressing more modestly outside of work, wearing overalls and loose sweaters. I got all the sexual affirmation I needed now in a few hours a day. I cared less than I had before whether men thought I was attractive or sexy. And I felt now as if I could control when I was looked at and when I wasn't, like turning a faucet on and off. I lapped it up at work, and the rest of the time I shut it down. I was the master of my own transformations."[29]

Eaves makes similar reflections about the emotional labor she performed for men at work: "I saw that for a long time I had lived as though there was a taboo against being confrontational or angry toward men, as though they had a right to patience and tolerance even when they didn't merit it. I had given too much benefit of the doubt before."[30]

Stripping, like other kinds of professions that encompass customer service, involves dealing with male entitlement, toxic masculinities, and paternalism, performing constant emotional and educative labor. Arlie Russell Hochschild describes emotional labor as "having your enjoyment advertised, promised—in essence, sold."[31] In an apt example and often-quoted line from *Showgirls*, Tony from the Stardust Casino demands, "I want to see you dance and I want to see you smile." In response to such commands, stripper art refutes the idea that men are entitled to niceties in addition to nudity. Sex worker memes are replete with in-jokes about time-wasters, the realities of working to pay rent, and the tedious expectation that they will provide not only sexual services but also validation, education, and ego soothing. Exotic Cancer even sells signature accessories for strippers that include key rings reading "I'll be nice if you pay me."

Exotic Cancer's work also documents the laborious aspects of stripping and gendered performance. The comics feature close-up body shots of strippers painting their nails, squeezing pimples, and removing eyelashes. Dancers are depicted with body hair and scars (from both breast implants and cesarean sections). In one comic, a purple-haired dancer is sitting on the toilet counting cash. In another, a dancer is on all fours using a long selfie stick to take the "perfect" butt selfie. Other artwork depicts used tampons, blood-soaked underpants, and quotes about what it is like to clean one's asshole with wet wipes. In contrast to the glamorized fantasy the dancers are expected to fulfill, Exotic Cancer emphasizes the labor involved in meeting these requirements. One comic describes how stripper gowns are meant to be "classy" and "elegant" but in reality are "never washed" and "[smell] like butt sweat and cigarettes." In another, a woman is answering a phone sex hotline that promotes itself as "sexy, horny babes who are just waiting for your call." The client imagines a blond, bare-breasted woman lying in a pink bed in lashes and lipstick. In reality, the woman is answering the call while sitting on the toilet smoking a cigarette with her clothes and tampon wrapper on the floor while her cat uses the kitty litter tray beside her.

Similarly, in Chase Paradise's show, she performs a scene that talks the audience through a lap dance via the mind of a stripper. The scene consists of four steps, all of which involve how to distract a customer when you inevitably need to fart in the middle of a lap dance. Such representations depict the mundane aspects of what is physical shift work. In *Bella Green Is Charging for It*, Bella emphasizes both the physical labor of the work and the precarious income and exploitative pay structures in clubs:

> I think stripping is the toughest job in the sex industry. Strip clubs make you work ridiculously long late-night shifts in incredibly high heels. It's physically taxing—you end up with knee injuries, back injuries, ankle injuries. Strip clubs don't pay you to be there. In fact, they make you pay a "house fee" to work a shift. The majority of your money doesn't come from dancing on the stage, it's from lap dances, and you have to go around to all the dudes in the room and convince them that they should go and have a lap dance with you, while 50 other supermodels are walking around trying to convince them of the same thing. And if you don't make any money, you end up paying a house fee to the club and

9.8 Frankie Valentine performs at the *Baby Got Back* Fringe World show in 2017. Image by John Leonard Photography, Perth, Western Australia.

going home in the negative. It's a sales job and I challenge anyone who thinks stripping is "easy money" to get almost naked, throw on some 7-inch heels and go work the room for ten hours.[32]

The physical labor of striptease is also echoed in the writing of strippers in the United States, who have documented various kinds of unrealistic club requirements. Katherine Frank, when she was working as a stripper for her academic research, was reprimanded by management for wearing the "wrong kind of shoes," three inches instead of five inches.[33] Vicki Funari writes of her experience in peep shows: "Men come in to see 'naked' girls, but it is a carefully dictated nakedness. Each worker must be costumed in high heels, must wear her hair at least below the ears, and her costume may at no moment cover both her breasts and her pubic area."[34] Lily Burana describes the "micromanagement" of class in one strip club in Dallas that prescribes specific kinds of dancing that are acceptable: "The manager . . . impresses on me that 'lewd' dancing—flashing, tugging on my thong, any contact with the customer that goes beyond touching his knees or shoulders for balance—will not be tolerated. . . . No lie, in the office they have a corkboard filled with Polaroid photos of women they've fired, some with the word *lewd* scrawled, [Hester] Prynne-like, under their names."[35]

Stripper art and literature reveal how strippers are required to constantly navigate stringent codes for the gendered performance of class-based ideals of femininity. Stripper bodies are governed by rules regarding costuming, makeup, hair color, fingernails, tattoos, and body shape. These kinds of hierarchies are overt in *Showgirls*, where the one plus-size stripper plays the role of a comedic fat-o-gram, and strippers must choose their names to meet particular alignments of class, gender, and desire. As Al says to Penny, "They want class, dum-dum. They don't want to fuck a Penny. They want to fuck a Heather. Or a Tiffany. Or a Hope. This is a class joint." In addition to the actual work of striptease, this additional labor of performing narrow kinds of feminine sexuality is tedious, repetitive, and unpaid.

Some strippers deliberately engage with such feminine stereotypes in their performance art. In her one-woman show, *Let's Get METAphysical*, Glitta Supernova describes how she fashioned herself for her first striptease by borrowing from the collective style of her 1990s queer punk shared house. In her first show, "I agonized over what to wear and with the help of all my twelve flatmates, meshed a look together from the communal wardrobe." For Glitta, stripping was a site for experimentation: "Stripping is where I discovered femininity. Up till then I was still a tomboy. But from here on I structured my identity into a hypersexualized porn star, I became a self-made monster of femininity. My new hyper-sex persona mutated into a porno parody at queer, punk, and sex parties and from the exhibitionist the performance artist was born. All the lines began to blur and I was able to bring to life a wild feminine shebeast—a rebellion and reaction of the woman we are all supposed to be."[36]

Glitta's self-fashioned hyperfemininity, while it critiques the onslaught of heteronormative, compulsory femininity, operates less as mockery and more as a celebration of the monstrous, rebellious, and unapologetic feminine. Her signature shows include a malfunctioning femme-bot programmed to be the "perfect woman," a horny she-hulk with a giant green fist and a passion for fisting, Miss Piggy's foray into porn with her costar Pot Plant, Smurfette's life as a stripper in Smurfer's Paradise, and a show in which she proudly swings two steaks around between her legs to resemble her labia majora. She declares, "I refuse to submit to age-appropriate attire. Mutton dressed as lamb is my signature look! Ravage me in the ravages of time. My retirement plan is to do prune porn. I will be a prune star! Wanna see my middle-aged spread?"[37]

Amid hilarious stories of backstage drama and hiccups that demonstrate the sometime absurdity of sexual labor, Glitta's work demonstrates how strippers so expertly navigate the demanding codes of striptease without taking on board the sexual hang-ups, body policing, or societal shame that is so steeped in management policies and attitudes.

Consent Culture and Accountability

In our everyday negotiations with customers, strippers develop finely tuned skills in practicing and promoting cultures of consent. Because a

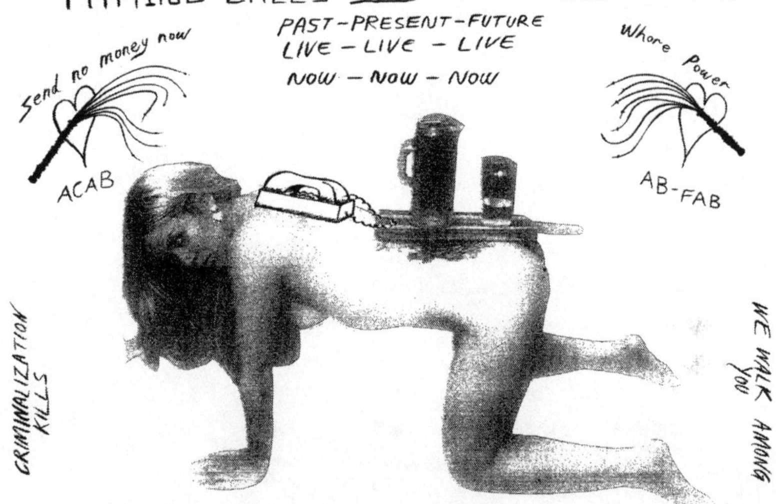

9.9 1800 Stop Slut Shame, T-shirt from Queenie Bon Bon's *Power Up* tour, 2015. Courtesy of Ben Fordree and Queenie Bon Bon.

core part of striptease is negotiating services and maintaining boundaries, consent naturally arises as a theme in sex worker art and performance. In her solo act "The Stripper" that she performed around the globe and that featured at the *Seen and Heard* cabaret, Frankie Valentine shares some of her strip club wisdom for clients. She performs a classic striptease act to a voice-over that offers instructions to audience members on appropriate strip club etiquette:

> Welcome, there are certain rules we would like you to adhere to:
> Feel free to look wherever you like but please don't touch.
> I'll show you mine, don't show me yours.
> Unless my pussy is on fire, kindly refrain from blowing on it.
> Just because I invite you to look at my breasts that
> does not mean that I have daddy issues.
> Just because I invite you to look at my pussy that
> does not mean it yours for the taking.
> Just because I dance for men all night doesn't
> mean I don't eat pussy for breakfast.
> Just because I'm a stripper doesn't mean I'm a slut.
> Just because I'm a slut doesn't mean it's any of
> your motherfucking business.[38]

Frankie's show speaks to common assumptions based on her lived experience dancing at the Men's Gallery in Melbourne. Her narrative dispels assumptions that stripping for men makes one less queer, that in inviting a gaze, strippers are also inviting touch, and that because we remove our clothes for a living, strippers are perpetually sexually available. The warding off unwanted touch is also a theme in the comics of Jacq the Stripper. One comic is direct in its warning: "Touch me again and I'll break your thumbs so badly you'll never be able to masturbate ever again: Consent! It's way sexier than a trip to the ER."[39]

Stripper contributions to promoting and encouraging consent culture are notable because of the legacies of feminist theory that argue that sex workers are unable to consent to sex work. In Queenie Bon Bon's *Welcome to the Mystic Hole* (a journey into "being in your body and other people's"), Queenie describes popular beliefs that sex workers cannot consent to sex because they are being paid:

> They have this belief that the insertion of money into a sexual relationship eliminates the ability to consent. And that sex workers don't "actually" want to be doing sex work, despite what workers themselves might say on the subject. Which really seems wild as I feel sex workers are the people who are most able to negotiate consent in a sexual context. Like we are literally professionals at it. Why are we not being seen as the experts? And they forever say these things like, "If the worker wanted to do it they wouldn't be charging," which is so unreasonable because which entire other workforce are being questioned on if they would turn up to work, regardless of whether they were getting paid or not?[40]

In a practical example, Queenie describes how this attitude manifests in the language of clients: "I wish you would just be like the other guys and be real base level, use language I understand like 'You are a slut' instead of framing it in this gross way like 'How can you sell your body?' I did not sell. I don't even rent it. I'm clearly still using it to maneuver through reality. You know, that's true, because we are here together."[41]

Theorizations of sex work itself as violence and sex workers as selling their whole selves affect sex workers' vulnerability to sexual assault, because sex workers are perceived as less "rape-able." In her rapid evidence review examining interventions that prevent violence against performers in adult entertainment venues, Bonnie Jean Penn finds that "management and venue owners appear disinterested in providing performers with educational and referral resources to therapeutic services."[42] In her book *Sex Workers Unite: A History of the Movement from Stonewall to SlutWalk,* Melinda Chateauvert writes, "Nearly five decades after the sex workers' movement began and almost as many years since the anti-rape movement, 'sluts' (female or male) are accepted in some circles, but prostitutes, whores, and hustlers continue to represent 'a cultural bogeyman.'"[43] In *Showgirls,* when Nomi's roommate is violently sexually assaulted, the club managers prevent Nomi from calling the police and threaten her with her prior offenses. Against this backdrop, strippers have emerged as leading voices in the SlutWalk and #MeToo movements, speaking out about their experiences of sexual violence and harassment (including at the hands of police) and advocating for protection, industrial rights, and safety.[44]

At Melbourne SlutWalk in May 2011, Elena Jeffreys delivered a powerful speech cowritten with Audry Autonomy to twenty-five hundred people who had rallied in front of the State Library Victoria.

> Survivors have had enough! In any city in Australia you can open the paper and see the slut shaming of sex workers who are trying to achieve justice when they are assaulted or raped. For our communities, victim blaming is institutionalized in the criminal justice system. We experience slut shaming individually and on a collective level. As a community, when one sex worker is denied justice, it sends a message that justice will be denied for all. It hurts all of us.
>
> Sexual assault is just as brutal, shocking and criminal in a brothel as it is if it happens in the workplace of a nurse, a police officer, a teacher or a judge. Yet we are told to expect it as some kind of occupational hazard? This is slut shaming! Some people say that all sex work is rape and that sex workers don't understand the difference. This is slut shaming! Governments say that sex work is undesirable and that sex workers and our clients should be punished. This is slut shaming![45]

9.10 Despo Debby, *Wheel of Payment* (Mixed media), 2016. Artwork courtesy of Despo Debby.

Sex workers' unique relationship to consent and our daily opportunities to practice negotiating and maintaining boundaries in the workplace mean that sex workers are well equipped to offer valuable insights in public discussions around consent culture and slut shaming.

Precarious Work, Structural Violence

Sex work is stigmatized work. It has been a strategy within the sex worker movement to destigmatize sex work by emphasizing positive aspects of the job, such as flexibility and autonomy, the diversity of client desires and tastes (which can humanize customers and fracture assumptions of heteronormativity), and the important role sex workers play in providing human connection and intimacy. Many of us have also gone to great lengths to demonstrate how sex work is like other work under capitalism. In one scene of her comedy show, Bella Green reflects on how working in a call center for a bank was more soul-destroying than working in the sex industry: "When I was twenty-one, I'd spent three years taking my clothes off for money and I'd had enough of the instability of sex work. I decided to join the Real World, and that's how I found myself in the most degrading job of my life, my three months working in a call centre for a Big 4 bank."[46]

This comparison is common in international writings by strippers. Erika Langley, for example, talks about feeling phonier and more degraded doing commercial photography work than when she worked in the peepshow at San Francisco's Lusty Lady.[47] However, sex workers have also been quick to assert that we ought not to be expected to perform narratives of empowerment or liberation at work merely to advocate for rights or dignity. In *Revolting Prostitutes: The Fight for Sex Workers' Rights*, Molly Smith and Juno Mac argue that the sex workers' rights movement should maintain distance from the interests of businesses and clients, stating, "We are not here to uplift the figure of the 'sympathetic' client, nor the idea that any client has a 'right' to sex," and reasserting the movement as a collective of workers.[48] Many contemporary stripper comics speak from this unapologetic place.

Strippers have long spoken out against the lack of job security, poor working conditions, and inadequate support mechanisms in the industry, particularly those working as independent contractors in clubs with heavy commissions, stringent rules, fines for dancers, and lack of employment safeguards or grievance policies. Exotic Cancer's work reveals a heavy lament about the downward economic turn of the sex industry, which means that strippers now may earn less than a decade ago. Their comics depict strippers offering support for one another and boosting each other's morale in a context in which hours are long and tips are scarce. In one comic, a dancer complains, "I'm not making much money tonight," and her colleague responds reassuringly, "It's definitely because Mercury is in retrograde."

Notably, the push for industry change has come primarily from Black strippers and strippers of color, who have protested (and been fired for complaining about) structural racism, unfair policies, and discriminatory practices in clubs. In her book *Unequal Desires: Race and Erotic Capital in the Stripping Industry,* Siobhan Brooks describes how "white, middle-class feminists . . . assume all women are afforded the same opportunities for employment in the sex industry" and issues a damning account of the "racial stratification" and "structural and symbolic racism" operating within the exotic dance industry that affect Black and Latina women.[49] Others have described the SlutWalk movement as a "maddening distraction from the systematic and interpersonal violence that women of color face daily."[50] In particular, Black dancers often face disproportionate (or extortionate) house fees, underrepresentation, and sexual harassment. Strippers in New York have criticized the division between "upscale" and "urban" clubs, where upscale clubs primarily hire light-skinned dancers and have unspoken race quotas that cap the number of dark-skinned dancers at any given time, meaning that Black dancers are disproportionately represented in urban clubs that are less profitable.[51]

In 2017, Gizelle Marie spearheaded the New York stripper strike (#NYCStripperStrike) to protest one club's hiring of "Startenders," mostly white social media influencers who worked as "bottle girls" under private contracts and diverted tips away from Black women working as dancers.[52] Strippers continue to organize and unionize to demand fairer working conditions. The documentary *Live Nude Girls Unite!* presents the fight of the workers at San Francisco's famous Lusty Lady in 1996 to end the managerial practice of scheduling only one woman of color per shift.[53] In 2012, dancers won almost US$13 million in a class action lawsuit after claiming three clubs violated state and federal laws by misclassifying them as independent contractors, thereby denying them wages and benefits.[54] Dancers are often required to pay shift fees, locker fees, commissions, and tips for bar staff and security. Even where strippers have won suits to be recognized as employees entitled to a minimum wage, clubs are finding new payment structures to leverage their wages—in some cases requiring them to pay their own hourly rate.[55]

Racerage, an Aboriginal and Torres Strait Islander rapper and artist from Melbourne, has produced work that deals with the income precarity of sex work. Their featured rap track on Simo Soo's "Clown Cars" speaks to the experience of being a broke sex worker:[56]

> Pockets full of lint and air / Barely care coz
> I'm used to my cupboards bare
> Old Mother Hubbard style / No coins clinking for a while
> It's all good—thrifty bitch with some nifty style
> Post FOSAT-SESTA . . . How has it left ya?
> Got me bereft creepin' / Creepin' like Uncle Fester
> This shit ain't funny / Got no smile for no jester
> Plunged into stress / But my fine ass got heft—yeah
> Begging Ancestors / Manifest doll hairs
> Come at me bro / I'm ready now for my blessed years

Racerage's work addresses the impact of US legislation on sex workers internationally and their ability to advertise, provide peer support, and share resources. The Stop Enabling Sex Traffickers Act (SESTA) and Allow States and Victims to Fight Online Sex Trafficking Act (FOSTA, HR 1865) passed in April 2018 made website operators liable if they operate an interactive computer service "with the intent to promote or facilitate the prostitution of another." This legislation has prompted platforms such as Google, Microsoft, and Facebook to amend their terms of service to preclude nudity, sexual content, and sexual services, with an immediate chilling effect on other kinds of sexual speech, including safety mechanisms, health promotion, peer education, advertising platforms, and avenues for sex worker organizing. Sex workers frequently report being banned from online communities simply for the status of being a sex worker, even if their content otherwise complies. Some stripper art directly challenges the "community standards" of social media platforms. In Exotic Cancer's comics, Facebook CEO Mark Zuckerberg's face is pasted over the nipples of strippers. In another comic, men undergo surgery so that their nipples can be donated and transplanted onto strippers' breasts to avoid violating community guidelines. Exotic Cancer and Alicia Amira (founder of Be a Bimbo) have released cropped T-shirts that read "Stop Censoring Sluts"; they donate 10 percent of the price of purchases to the Global Network of Sex Work Projects.

Support Your Local Stripper

Twenty-five years after the release of *Showgirls,* it is not evident that conditions have actually improved for strippers. The movement for strippers' industrial rights has become more publicized in mainstream media, with campaigns to strike, unionize, and protest reported in the United States, Britain, and Australia. However, such industrial actions were already taking place in the era of *Showgirls,* with the push to unionize and bargain for worker rights well underway at the Lusty Lady in 1996–97. While the alignment of sex worker rights with feminist movements for accountability and justice have become more visible, with sex workers at the frontline of #MeToo and SlutWalk movements, sex

9.11 Showgirl zipping up boots. Artwork courtesy of Exotic Cancer.

workers involvement at the forefront of feminist movements is not new. If we listen to contemporary accounts of strippers, the poor working conditions, misogynist management, and customer entitlement so obvious in *Showgirls* do not appear to have dramatically changed. Further, the policies and practices of platforms shutting down sexual speech are limiting avenues for strippers to speak back, organize, support each other, build capacity, and share resources. Even if popular representations of strippers are changing in the public imaginary, the material conditions are not. The fight for basic working conditions remains a constant struggle. It's no surprise that the slogan on one of Jacq the Stripper's T-shirts reads "The one thing all sluts have in common is that we're tired."

In 2019, the Hollywood crime drama film *Hustlers* was released in the United States. The film's cast includes former stripper Cardi B and tells the story of a group of strippers who embezzle money by drugging stock traders and CEOs who visit the club as clients. The film's plot could be read in part as a revenge fantasy where strippers work together to play a system that is so clearly rigged against them. Indeed, in her review, SX Noir describes the film as being "about surviving under capitalism post-2008 financial crash."[57] However, the film still tells stories of striptease within the stereotyped narrative of organized crime and con artists. It reflects similar themes of hierarchy and respectability politics. Aside from the plot, the film raises questions about ethical production of media about marginalized communities. Jacq the Stripper, who was hired to consult on the film and who appears in a brief cameo, expressed anxiety on her Instagram account about "how it got made, who gets paid, who doesn't, and why a Hollywood movie gets to post all over instagram [*sic*] while real workers are getting deleted and censored every day."[58] Further critiques on her feed came from strippers at the Show Palace in New York, where *Hustlers* was shot, who were out of work for a week during the filming and demanding compensation both for their lost income and for being muses who provided inspiration for the film without financial recognition. Following the film premiere, Jacq reportedly spent US$1,800 tipping dancers at the Show Palace to redistribute some of the money lost during the closure of the club. The response drew attention to the fundamentally inequitable distribution of wealth between the film's producers and its subjects. Shot in an industry where income is notoriously precarious, *Hustlers* reportedly made US$33 million on its opening weekend.

Strippers often understand external media representations as profiteering from or appropriating sex work culture. It may be a positive step that Hollywood films are now hiring stripper consultants. However, questions remain about who is invited, whose stories are told, what kinds of power consultants hold in practice, and whether a lone stripper voice is enough in the face of such corporate machinery. Instead of seeking inclusion in mainstream representations, local stripper art, comedy, and storytelling provide countercultural narratives in conversation with one another. Strippers are creating art that resonates with their peers and speaks directly to other sex workers. The work is made *for* strippers. By listening to the voices of strippers themselves, we can contextualize the narrow themes of slut shaming, internalized stigma, and lateral violence that feature in *Showgirls* and the popular link to organized crime that underlies *Hustlers*. Instead, we can turn our lens toward the systems that perpetuate poor working conditions, structural violence, the devaluing of feminized labor, expectations of access to women's bodies, paternalistic desires to rescue, institutionalized racism, and exploitative business structures.

In a context where the most urgent and necessary step is to *listen* to strippers, strippers are being seen but not heard. Audiences may patronize comedy, fringe, and burlesque festivals and, in doing so, financially support the emergence of stripper arts. They may even buy merchandise that promotes good client behavior (Jacq the Stripper's hoodies that read "TIP HER") or that challenges over-regulation of sexual speech (Exotic Cancer and Be a Bimbo's tops that read "Stop Censoring Sluts!"). They may frequent shows that prompt them to critically reflect on their own expectations and assumptions (Chase Paradise's invitation for the audiences to chant out loud in unison "Fuck you! Pay me!") or that school them in boundaries (Frankie Valentine's instructions that "unless my pussy is on fire, kindly refrain from blowing on it"). The more people listen to the stories, experiences, and demands of strippers, the better. These individual acts might be seen as what Jacq the Stripper refers to as "investing in young female entrepreneurs."[59] More collectively, they could be seen as supporting local stripper artists in ways that cultivate community and culture. But these kinds of support remain both individual and consumer based. They cannot make up for the kinds of legal, industrial, and structural change that strippers collectively need. Without structural change that improves the rights and entitlements of strippers as workers, we will simply remain the entertainment. Hollywood films like *Hustlers* (if not *Showgirls*) will take home millions at the box office, sparking a popular hubris about stripper empowerment, without necessarily giving back in material terms to the communities and workers on whom such films are based—indeed, the workers on whose stories, aesthetics, and cultures such films *rely*.

ZAHRA STARDUST is a sociolegal scholar working at the intersections of sexuality, technology, and law. She is a Postdoctoral Research Fellow at the Queensland University of Technology. Her recent work appears in *Porn Studies, Crime, Media, Culture, Social Science and Medicine,* and *International Journal for Crime, Justice and Social Democracy*. She is a former Penthouse Pet, Hustler Honey, and Feminist Porn Awards Heartthrob of the Year, and has toured internationally as a striptease artist, pole dance instructor, aerialist, and sex educator.

References

Anspach, Rachel. "After 5 Months, the #NYCStripperStrike Is Poised to Go Nationwide." Jezebel, March 19, 2018. https://jezebel.com/after-5-months-the-nycstripperstrike-is-poised-to-go-1823835024.

Attwood, Feona. "Dirty Work: Researching Women and Sexual Representation." In *Secrecy and Silence in the Research Process: Feminist Reflections*, edited by Róisín Ryan-Flood and Rosalind Gill, 177–87. New York: Routledge, 2010.

Berger, John. *Ways of Seeing*. London: Penguin, 1973.

Bogado, Aura. "SlutWalk: A Stroll through White Supremacy." In *Gender, Sex, and Politics: In the Streets and between the Sheets in the 21st Century*, edited by Shira Tarrant, 33–37. New York: Routledge, 2015.

Brooks, Siobhan. *Unequal Desires: Race and Erotic Capital in the Stripping Industry*. Albany: State University of New York Press, 2010.

Burana, Lily. *Strip City: A Stripper's Farewell Journey across America*. New York: Miramax Books, 2002.

Caldwell, Hilary. "Women Who Buy Sex in Australia: From Social Representations to Lived Experiences." PhD diss., University of New South Wales, 2018.

Chateauvert, Melinda. *Sex Workers Unite: A History of the Movement from Stonewall to SlutWalk*. Boston: Beacon Press, 2014.

Cody, Diablo. *Candy Girl: A Year in the Life of an Unlikely Stripper*. New York: Gotham Books, 2006.

Cohen, Sascha. "Strippers Are Turning to Old-School Union Tactics to Fight for Fair Wages." HuffPost, June 13, 2019. https://www.huffingtonpost.com.au/entry/strippers-union-fair-wages_n_5cf97c7ae4b06af8b505a2f2.

Cole, Ryan Elizabeth, Elena Jeffreys, and Janelle Fawkes. "The Best Parties Happen under the Bus: The Impact of Lesbian Institutions on Queer Sex Workers in Australia." In *Queer Sex Work*, edited by Mary Laing, Katy Pilcher, and Nicola Smith, 219–31. London: Routledge, 2015.

Corbett, Emma Lea. *The Stripper Next Door*. Sydney: New Holland Publishers, 2018.

Eaves, Elisabeth. *Bare: The Naked Truth about Stripping*. New York: Seal Press, 2002.

Egan, R. Danielle. *Dancing for Dollars and Paying for Love: The Relationships between Exotic Dancers and Their Regulars*. New York: Palgrave Macmillan, 2006.

Eldemire, Summer. "*Hustlers*: Real-Life Strippers Review Jennifer Lopez's Pole-Dancing Performance." *Daily Beast*, September 16, 2019. https://www.thedailybeast.com/hustlers-real-life-strippers-review-jennifer-lopezs-pole-dancing-performance.

Exotic Cancer. *Shit Men Say in Strip Clubs*. 2nd ed. Melbourne: Exotic Cancer, 2021.

Ferguson, Amber. "NYC Strippers Strike: Dancers Say Nearly Naked 'Bottle Girls' Are Grabbing Their Cash, Cite Racism." *Washington Post*, November 3, 2017. https://www.washingtonpost.com/news/morning-mix/wp/2017/11/03/n-y-c-strippers-strike-dancers-say-instagram-star-bottle-girls-are-grabbing-the-cash-cite-racism.

Fileborn, Bianca, and Rachel Loney-Howes, eds. *#MeToo and the Politics of Social Change*. Cham: Springer, 2019.

Frances, Jacqueline. *Striptastic! A Celebration of Dope-Ass Cunts Who Like Money*. New York: Jacqueline Frances, 2017.

Frank, Katherine. *G-Strings and Sympathy: Strip Club Regulars and Male Desire*. Durham, NC: Duke University Press, 2002.

Funari, Vicky. "Naked, Naughty, Nasty: Peep Show Reflections." In *Whores and Other Feminists*, edited by Jill Nagle, 19–35. New York: Routledge, 1997.

Funari, Vicky, and Julia Query, dirs. *Live Nude Girls Unite!* Constant Communication and Others, 2000.

Green, Bella. *Bella Green is Charging for It*. Melbourne International Comedy Festival, 2019. Script provided to author.

Henderson, Margaret. "Pornography in the Service of Lesbians: The Case of *Wicked Women* and *Slit* Magazines." *Australasian Journal of Popular Culture* 2, no. 2 (2013): 159–82.

Herald Sun. "Melbourne International Comedy Festival Comedian Q&A: Bella Green, *Bella Green Is Charging For It*." March 19, 2019. https://www.heraldsun.com.au/entertainment/comedy-festival/qanda/melbourne-international-comedy-festival-comedian-qa-bella-green-bella-green-is-charging-for-it/news-story/f24bce1cea3c95e4d9ca13c05cafaad6.

Hernandez, Ariel. "Poles and Politics: Stripper and Activist Gizelle Marie's Fight for Sex Workers' Dignity." *The Press*, November 27, 2018. https://sashamaslov.com/Poles-and-Politics.

Hochschild, Arlie Russell. "Smile Wars." *Mother Jones* 8, no. 5 (December 1983): 34–42.

House of CT. *Sex Worker's Opera*. 2018. https://www.compagnietheater.nl/programma/sex-workers-opera.

Jane, Emma A. *Misogyny Online: A Short (and Brutish) History*. Los Angeles: Sage, 2016.

Jeffreys, Elena. "Contemporary Sex Worker Cultural Practice in Australia: Sex Workers' Use of Sex Industry Skills in Public Protest and Performance." *Journal of Australian Studies* 30, no. 89 (2006): 113–24.

———, and Audry Autonomy. "Speech at Melbourne SlutWalk, State Library Victoria." May 28, 2011.

———, and Janelle Fawkes. "Staging Decriminalisation: Sex Worker Performance and HIV." In *Viral Dramaturgies: HIV and AIDS in Performance in the Twenty-First Century*, edited by Alyson Campbell and Dirk Gindt, 69–90. Cham: Palgrave Macmillan, 2018.

Kandel, Jason. "Strippers Win $13 Million Settlement in Wage Dispute." NBC Bay Area, November 14, 2012. https://www.nbclosangeles.com/news/local/strippers-win-13-million-settlement-wages-dispute/1942335.

Langley, Erika. *The Lusty Lady: Photography and Texts*. Zurich: Scalo, 1997.

Liepe-Levinson, Katherine. *Strip Show: Performances of Gender and Desire*. New York: Routledge, 2002.

Mulvey, Laura. "Visual Pleasure and Narrative Cinema." *Screen* 16, no. 3 (1975): 6–18.

Pendleton, Eva. "Love for Sale: Queering Heterosexuality." In *Whores and Other Feminists*, edited by Jill Nagle, 73–82. New York: Routledge, 1997.

Penn, Bonnie Jean. "Preventing Violence against Performers in Adult Entertainment Venues: A Rapid Review of Interventions." BSW thesis, University of New South Wales, 2018.

Purcell, Charles. "The Funny Thing about Stripping." *Sydney Morning Herald*, September 18, 2018. Factiva.

Roach, Catherine M. *Stripping, Sex, and Popular Culture*. Oxford: Berg, 2007.

Senft, Theresa M. *Camgirls: Celebrity and Community in the Age of Social Networks*. New York: Peter Lang, 2008.

Shteir, Rachel. *Striptease: The Untold History of the Girlie Show*. Oxford: Oxford University Press, 2004.

Smith, Molly, and Juno Mac. *Revolting Prostitutes: The Fight for Sex Workers' Rights*. London: Verso, 2018.

Soo, Simo (featuring Racerage and Heartattracks). "Clown Cars." Digital track, November 2018. https://simosoo.bandcamp.com/track/clown-cars-feat-racerage-heartattracks.

Stafford, Shay, with Bryce Corbett. *Memoirs of a Showgirl*. Sydney: Hachette, 2010.

Stardust, Zahra. "Critical Femininities, Fluid Sexualities and Queer Temporalities: Erotic Performers on Objectification, Femmephobia and Oppression." In *Queer Sex Work*, edited by Mary Laing, Katy Pilcher, and Nicola Smith, 67–78. London: Routledge, 2015.

Turton, Jonathan. "Inside New York's Stripper Strike." *Dazed*, March 1, 2018. https://www.dazeddigital.com/life-culture/article/39234/1/gizelle-marie-the-woman-leading-new-yorks-stripper-strike.

Notes

1. Katherine Frank, *G-Strings and Sympathy: Strip Club Regulars and Male Desire* (Durham, NC: Duke University Press, 2002), xx.

2. R. Danielle Egan, *Dancing for Dollars and Paying for Love: The Relationships between Exotic Dancers and their Regulars* (New York: Palgrave Macmillan, 2006).

3. Feona Attwood, "Dirty Work: Researching Women and Sexual Representation," in *Secrecy and Silence in the Research Process: Feminist Reflections*, ed. Róisín Ryan-Flood and Rosalind Gill (New York: Routledge, 2010), 178.

4. Zahra Stardust, "Critical Femininities, Fluid Sexualities and Queer Temporalities: Erotic Performers on Objectification, Femmephobia and Oppression," in *Queer Sex Work*, ed. Mary Laing, Katy Pilcher, and Nicola Smith (London: Routledge, 2015), 67–78.

5. Lily Burana, *Strip City: A Stripper's Farewell Journey across America* (New York: Miramax Books, 2002), 135–36.

6. Diablo Cody, *Candy Girl: A Year in the Life of an Unlikely Stripper* (New York: Gotham Books, 2006).

7. Emma Lea Corbett, *The Stripper Next Door* (Sydney: New Holland Publishers, 2018); Shay Stafford, with Bryce Corbett, *Memoirs of a Showgirl* (Sydney: Hachette, 2010).

8. Theresa M. Senft, *Camgirls: Celebrity and Community in the Age of Social Networks* (New York: Peter Lang, 2008), 3.

9. Exotic Cancer, *Shit Men Say in Strip Clubs*, 2nd ed. (Melbourne: Exotic Cancer, 2021).

10. House of CT, *Sex Worker's Opera*, 2018, https://www.compagnietheater.nl/programma/sex-workers-opera.

11. *Herald Sun*, "Melbourne International Comedy Festival Comedian Q&A: Bella Green, *Bella Green Is Charging for It*," March 19, 2019, https://www.heraldsun.com.au/entertainment/comedy-festival/qanda/melbourne-international-comedy-festival-comedian-qa-bella-green-bella-green-is-charging-for-it/news-story/f24bce1cea3c95e4d9ca13c05cafaad6.

12. Ryan Elizabeth Cole, Elena Jeffreys, and Janelle Fawkes, "The Best Parties Happen under the Bus: The Impact of Lesbian Institutions on Queer Sex Workers in Australia," in *Queer Sex Work*, ed. Mary Laing, Katy Pilcher, and Nicola Smith (London: Routledge, 2015), 219–31.

13. Margaret Henderson, "Pornography in the Service of Lesbians: The Case of *Wicked Women* and *Slit* Magazines," *Australasian Journal of Popular Culture* 2, no. 2 (2013): 159–82.

14. Elena Jeffreys, "Contemporary Sex Worker Cultural Practice in Australia: Sex Workers' Use of Sex Industry Skills in Public Protest and Performance," *Journal of Australian Studies* 30, no. 89 (2006): 114.

15. Elena Jeffreys and Janelle Fawkes, "Staging Decriminalisation: Sex Worker Performance and HIV," in *Viral Dramaturgies: HIV and AIDS in Performance in the Twenty-First Century*, ed. Alyson Campbell and Dirk Gindt (Cham: Palgrave Macmillan, 2018), 69–70.

16. Laura Mulvey, "Visual Pleasure and Narrative Cinema," *Screen* 16, no. 3 (1975): 11.

17. John Berger, *Ways of Seeing* (London: Penguin, 1973), 47.

18. Rachel Shteir, *Striptease: The Untold History of the Girlie Show* (Oxford: Oxford University Press, 2004), 8.

19. Katherine Liepe-Levinson, *Strip Show: Performances of Gender and Desire* (New York: Routledge, 2002), 16.

20. Catherine M. Roach, *Stripping, Sex, and Popular Culture* (Oxford: Berg, 2007), 35.

21. Jacqueline Frances, *Striptastic! A Celebration of Dope-Ass Cunts Who Like Money* (New York: Jacqueline Frances, 2017), 11.

22 Bella Green, *Bella Green Is Charging for It*, Melbourne International Comedy Festival, 2019. Script provided to author.

23. Charles Purcell, "The Funny Thing about Stripping," *Sydney Morning Herald*, September 18, 2018. Factiva.

24. Eva Pendleton, "Love for Sale: Queering Heterosexuality," in *Whores and Other Feminists*, ed. Jill Nagle (New York: Routledge, 1997), 79.

25. Purcell, "Here's the Funny Thing about Stripping."

26. Hilary Caldwell, "Women Who Buy Sex in Australia: From Social Representations to Lived Experiences" (PhD diss., University of New South Wales, 2018).

27. Exotic Cancer, Instagram, @exotic.cancer, 2018.

28. Emma A. Jane, *Misogyny Online: A Short (and Brutish) History* (Los Angeles: Sage, 2016).

29. Elisabeth Eaves, *Bare: The Naked Truth about Stripping* (New York: Seal Press, 2002), 74.

30. Ibid., 22.

31. Arlie Russell Hochschild, "Smile Wars," *Mother Jones* 8, no. 5 (December 1983): 38.

32. Green, *Bella Green Is Charging for It*.

33. Frank, *G-Strings and Sympathy*, 209.

34. Vicky Funari, "Naked, Naughty, Nasty: Peep Show Reflections," in *Whores and Other Feminists*, ed. Jill Nagle (New York: Routledge, 1997), 22.

35. Burana, *Strip City*, 78.

36. Glitta Supernova, "Let's Get METAphysical," Giant Dwarf Theatre, Sydney, 2016. Script provided to author.

37. Ibid.

38. Frankie Valentine, "Seen and Heard Cabaret," Bondi Feast Festival, 2018. Script provided to author.

39. Frances, *Striptastic!*, 60.

40. Queenie Bon Bon, "Welcome to the Mystic Hole," Melbourne Fringe Festival, 2018. Script provided to author.

41. Ibid.

42. Bonnie Jean Penn, "Preventing Violence against Performers in Adult Entertainment Venues: A Rapid Review of Interventions" (BSW thesis, University of New South Wales, 2018), 58.

43. Melinda Chateauvert, *Sex Workers Unite: A History of the Movement from Stonewall to SlutWalk* (Boston: Beacon, 2014).

44. Bianca Fileborn and Rachel Loney-Howes, eds., *#MeToo and the Politics of Social Change* (Cham: Springer, 2019).

45. Elena Jeffreys and Audry Autonomy, "Speech at Melbourne SlutWalk, State Library Victoria," May 28, 2011.

46. Green, *Bella Green Is Charging for It*.

47. Erika Langley, *The Lusty Lady: Photography and Texts* (Zurich: Scalo, 1997), 7, 148.

48. Molly Smith and Juno Mac, *Revolting Prostitutes: The Fight for Sex Workers' Rights* (London: Verso, 2018), 3.

49. Siobhan Brooks, *Unequal Desires: Race and Erotic Capital in the Stripping Industry* (Albany: State University of New York Press, 2010), 4.

50. Aura Bogado, "SlutWalk: A Stroll through White Supremacy," in *Gender, Sex, and Politics: In the Streets and between the Sheets in the 21st Century*, ed. Shira Tarrant (New York: Routledge, 2015), 33–37.

51. Rachel Anspach, "After 5 Months, the #NYCStripperStrike Is Poised to Go Nationwide," Jezebel, March 19, 2018, https://jezebel.com/after-5-months-the-nyc stripperstrike-is-poised-to-go-1823835024.

52. Ariel Hernandez, "Poles and Politics: Stripper and Activist Gizelle Marie's Fight for Sex Workers' Dignity," *The Press*, November 27, 2018, https://sashamaslov.com/Poles-and-Politics; Jonathan Turton, "Inside New York's Stripper Strike," *Dazed*, March 1, 2018, https://www.dazeddigital.com/life-culture/article/39234/1/gizelle-marie-the-woman-leading-new-yorks-stripper-strike; Amber Ferguson, "NYC Strippers Strike: Dancers Say Nearly Naked 'Bottle Girls' Are Grabbing Their Cash, Cite Racism," *Washington Post*, November 3, 2017, https://www

.washingtonpost.com/news/morning-mix/wp/2017/11/03/n-y-c-strippers-strike-dancers-say-instagram-star-bottle-girls-are-grabbing-the-cash-cite-racism.

53. Vicky Funari and Julia Query, dirs., *Live Nude Girls Unite!* (Constant Communication and Others, 2000).

54. Jason Kandel, "Strippers Win $13 Million Settlement in Wage Dispute," NBC Bay Area, November 14, 2012, https://www.nbclosangeles.com/news/local/strippers-win-13-million-settlement-wages-dispute/1942335.

55. Sascha Cohen, "Strippers Are Turning to Old-School Union Tactics to Fight for Fair Wages," HuffPost, June 13, 2019, https://www.huffpost.com/entry/strippers-union-fair-wages_n_5cf97c7ae4b06af8b505a2f2.

56. Simo Soo (featuring Racerage and Heartattracks), "Clown Cars," digital track, November 2018, https://simosoo.bandcamp.com/track/clown-cars-feat-racerage-heartattracks.

57. Summer Eldemire, "*Hustlers*: Real-Life Strippers Review Jennifer Lopez's Pole-Dancing Performance," *The Daily Beast*, September 16, 2019, https://www.thedailybeast.com/hustlers-real-life-strippers-review-jennifer-lopezs-pole-dancing-performance.

58. Jacq the Stripper (@jacqthestripper), Instagram post, September 13, 2019.

59. Frances, *Striptastic!*, 72.

ON CLICHÉ, CAMP, AND 10 QUEER TEMPORALITY

DISCUSSING SHOWGIRLS

KARA KEELING AND MEAGHAN MORRIS

Meaghan Morris (MM): My film studies foundation in the late 1970s was a double life led as an adjunct teacher of semiotics and avant-garde cinema on the one hand and as a film reviewer for Australian newspapers on the other. In the former role, I sweated through dense works of theory with students whose radical exigence exceeded mine. In the latter capacity, I saw every mainstream film release, mostly with a popular audience hooting and munching around me. I liked both jobs, but they formed a gap in my experience of criticism. Scribbling notes in the midst of real audiences on those multiplex nights made me skeptical of film readings that base critiques of social subjectivity on the forms of their own scholarly substance. They miss the wild variability of what happens when people, alone and in crowds, watch films.

So I was blown back in my armchair by Kara Keeling's *The Witch's Flight: The Cinematic, the Black Femme, and the Image of Common Sense* (2007). Bringing queer theory together with postcolonial and Africana studies on the terrain of the cinematic arts, here was a book asking how cinema articulates our innermost dreams and desires with our social and cultural lives. What happens when as viewers we bring with us both individuality and the commonsense modes of perception that link us to communities? What does it take for a momentary perception of a new possibility to change habitual ways of thinking? Within the experience of oppressed and exploited people ("colonial temporality" in

Frantz Fanon's terms), how may the impossible possibility of liberation be apprehended? With these questions, *The Witch's Flight* engaged with the powers of cliché, sometimes mobilizing powers for which my multiplex nights had given me great respect. Positing resistance to the new as a practical problem that all filmmakers deal with, it asked how commercial as well as experimental films address this problem in different ways, sometimes giving us an intimation of how other ways of living might feel. Deepening this line of thought in an engagement with Afrofuturism, technology, and new media in her book *Queer Times, Black Futures* (2019), Kara draws on Karl Marx to call intimations that come to us through acts of speculative imagination "poetry from the future."

Focusing on Kara's critical perspectives in these books, we wrote this chapter as a discussion of questions around *Showgirls* that we developed in correspondence.

T-Shirt Wisdom and Queer Temporality

MM: Early in *Showgirls*, the choreographer James Smith (Glenn Plummer) tries to break through Nomi's defenses by challenging the "wisdom" of her clichés: "'Life sucks,' 'Shit happens'—where do you get this stuff, off of T-shirts?" When James later trades his artistic aspirations for marriage and a job in a grocery store, he wryly echoes her: "Shit happens, you know? Life sucks. I'm a student of T-shirts." What do you make of the role of T-shirt wisdom in *Showgirls*, given the brutality of the "living image" economy this film makes us see? Is it possible for clichés to bring us poetry from the future rather than or as well as a communal wisdom from the past? *Showgirls* might be negative poetry, or even bad poetry, but it certainly shifted something.

This raises the broader issue of temporality, both in the reception of *Showgirls* and in your book *Queer Times, Black Futures*. You suggest there that queer temporality is "a dimension of time that produces risk," and you work through the doubleness of our understanding of "speculation" as both financial and queer imaginative.[1] *Showgirls* seems to mark this doubleness in some ways. In the Stardust Casino world, the entertainment director Zack Carey (Kyle MacLachlan) lives speculation in what you call the "Shell" mode of investing in the future in order to maximize profits; "We do what we do in Vegas—gamble!" he says when his diva Cristal Connors (Gina Gershon) has to be replaced. James decides to abandon risk along with his dreams of creativity, while Molly Abrams (Gina Rivera) takes a risk on romance and is brutally traumatized by gang rape. Nomi Malone (Elizabeth Berkley) lives imaginative risk to the full and stays with it as she heads to Los Angeles at the end of the film. Cristal once lived risk in the spirit of Nomi but became, like Zack, an enforcer of the corporate speculative system and is rewarded with a "real nice" financial settlement.

Reading your account, I wonder whether this emphasis on risk takes us past the interesting discussion of time in Susan Sontag's "Notes on 'Camp'" (1964). For Sontag, "the failure of a work of art may make us indignant. Time can change that. Time liberates the work of art from moral relevance."[2] Clearly this bears on the changing reception of *Showgirls*, but I tend to think that the speculative risks taken in that film may in fact be revealing their "moral relevance" more obviously today than they did twenty years ago. I'm wondering too whether you see a technological dimension to this escalation of relevance. Perhaps because of something to do with what you call "the irrational cut" in relation to digital modes of seeing, acting, and organizing (which were spreading to wider publics in the 1990s when *Showgirls* came out in the United States). Could there be a sense in which Nomi's character as played by Berkley is queer, not just camp, because she's the principle of "irrational cut" incarnate? That's what people mean by terms like "frantic" and "too much," starting from when she whips out her knife in the car at the beginning of the film and uses it not just to make the lecherous driver back off (rational) but to forcefully stab his radio to change the station to music she likes (irrational in its gestural excess).

***

Kara Keeling (KK): The idea of the "irrational cut" is one I developed in *Queer Times, Black Futures*. Drawing first on Gilles Deleuze's arguments about it in his books on cinema, I argued that an "irrational cut" establishes a relation of incommensurability between disparate things. It does not seek to make those things commensurate or equal. I argued further that "irrational cuts" proliferate in the digital regime of the image.[3] Moreover, in later chapters, I pointed out (via a reading of Beth Coleman's essay "Race as Technology" and James A. Snead's essays "On Repetition in Black Culture" and "Repetition as a Figure of Black Culture") that, in Black culture in particular, irrational cuts are built into the logic of Black culture, thereby providing a kind of insurance against efforts to disrupt or destroy the ongoing transformations through which the culture coheres.[4] In this regard, it is a way to embrace the risks to the culture posed by time and make them work for the continuity of the culture itself. Improvisation and rhythm are key practices here.

Although I hadn't thought of it in the way your question is prompting me to do, in the context of a discussion about *Showgirls*, I believe this way of thinking about risk, irrational cuts, and how those enable incommensuration as a relation could be quite interesting. Thinking along these lines might lead us to embrace the purported failures of *Showgirls* as precisely those things that enable us to pick it back up today as a film that is worth (another) scholarly reconsideration. It also might provide a way to think about the character Nomi not only as camp (though certainly the ways of thinking about her as "camp" are helpful) but also as a kind of figure, as you say, of the irrational. Perhaps not so much of the "irrational cut" as I described it in *Queer Times, Black Futures*, but more as a character who figures the cut of the irrational, or the work of the irrational within an aesthetic and commercial economy characterized by the coherence of genre and narrative and the manner in which commonsense understandings of class, gender, and race solidify such coherence. As you mentioned, one of the primary criticisms of Elizabeth Berkley's performance as Nomi has been about her overacting or the ways in which she is "frantic" and "too much."

If we frame her performance in precisely the terms you suggest, as "gestural excess," then we are in a position to read those excesses as that which cannot be contained or confined by the expectations around how gender, race, and class performances undergird (or undergirded at the time of the film's release) expectations about the coherence of genre and narrative. We might argue, then, that Berkley's performance was deemed a "failure" when the film was released because it could not easily be read within the accepted parameters through which a performance is deemed to have been "successful." It did not enter into the conventional circuits of value—whether value is understood in artistic terms, having to do with the quality of a signification, or in economic terms of exchange.

I learned a lot from Akira Mizuta Lippit's brief essay about *Showgirls* in *Film Quarterly* (2003) in which he argues that *Showgirls* basically explodes Leonard Maltin's rating system: Maltin rated the film as "a BOMB" (a rating that is special within the rating system because it is outside of it).[5] Lippit suggests that *Showgirls* undoes the rating system because it is a "failed film"—a film failed by the ability of the mechanisms of evaluation that have been unable to account for the extent to which it explodes those very systems. I think the key term here, then, is indeed *excess,* which we might associate with the irrational cut and its relationship to incommensuration.

I've gone on a bit here because I do find this line of analysis of the film compelling insofar as it invites a consideration of clichés and "T-shirt wisdom" (as you put it). In my understanding of it (which has gained a lot from my reading of you, Meaghan, on the cliché as well), clichés are a way to facilitate commensuration and signification (sometimes via what you call "communal wisdom from the past") even in the face of some sort of trouble in the image, something the image harbors but does not necessarily readily reveal.[6] I am not sure I can be as precise as I'd like to be here—in my thinking about it (in *The Witch's Flight,* for example), the cliché (or "the image of common sense" more broadly) also harbors pasts that have yet to become perceptible.[7] Clichés therefore do a lot of work to insist that the present and the past are coextensive and to ward off present perceptions that challenge the security of the present order of things. They work to mitigate the risk inherent in time. T-shirt wisdom does this as well. In *Showgirls,* the character James invokes clichés when Nomi is tempted to settle rather than take risks to succeed and when he is resigned to letting his dreams for his future recede. Berkley's risky performance exploded the clichés that governed performances of class, gender, and sexuality at the time. The result was that the performance itself could be read only as "bad" or "a failure."

Regarding the film itself and the discursive economies in which it circulates, it may be the case that this collection of essays about *Showgirls* is one of the ways that theorists and critics are helping to reveal how what appeared in the film as cliché when the film was released might appear to us today as generative of insights that eluded many audiences of its time, and how what was deemed to be "a failure" might actually help us to untangle the clichés that keep normative class, gender, and sexuality performances in place.

Genre Queer

MM: So how would you describe the genre of *Showgirls*? There is no consensus about this. It has variously been called erotic drama, camp, "hyperbolic" (by Paul Verhoeven), socially realistic (by Jacques Rivette), and a new take on the "ingenue vs. aging diva" backstage musical tradition of *42nd Street* (1933) and *All about Eve* (1950).[8] In the promotional phase, the film's writer, Joe Eszterhas, called *Showgirls* "a *rock'n'roll* musical," which seems a bit wishful in spite of the inclusion of songs by David Bowie and Dave Stewart. Then, two years later, after it bombed, he called the film's music "eminently forgettable."[9] *Showgirls* is certainly all about the blur between dancing and sexual performance, with a focus in the film on technologies of staging with music in different settings. Following your work in *Queer Times, Black Futures* on the imaginative force of music in relation to technologies, could thinking about sound in *Showgirls* provide another perspective on the film's genre trouble?

***

KK: You know, I just had an opportunity to watch Lorene Scafaria's *Hustlers* (2019), and I was struck by how the beginning of that film showcases the physical talent of the women performing in the strip club. I think everyone can agree that Jennifer Lopez is amazing in that film. Some of the conversation about her performance had to do with her athletic ability, the fact that she is so incredibly fit (at her age!), and reflections on the skill it takes to do performances of that kind—pole dancing, for example. Even though Jennifer Lopez had a musical career before her acting one and although the film itself purports to portray a kind of fantasy "inspired by a true story," no one seemed to locate *Hustlers* within a discourse of genre trouble. This might be because, unlike

Showgirls, Hustlers does not maintain a focus on the performances in the club throughout the course of the film, and the music is usually easily recognized as diegetic. Moreover, the gazes in the film are often feminine or at least seen from a female character's perspective—Jennifer Lopez's first performance in the club is seen mostly from Constance Wu's perspective, for example.

Showgirls is different—the dance performances of the showgirls are portrayed throughout the film. They become part of the narrative. It sometimes is unclear whether the music is diegetic. The gazes, though they may be queer or marked as being animated by a woman's desire for another woman, cannot easily be read as "feminine." Regarding the film's use of sound, in some sequences, such as the pool sex sequence, for example, *Showgirls* seems to me to be working on the level of the soundtrack to heighten the sensation of excess we talked about earlier. So it is not just Nomi's frantic gestures in that sequence—Berkley's acting—that seem irrational, but the way they work in combination with the music to heighten those gestures to the point where they seem ridiculous—over the top. Is this sequence uncomfortable for most viewers to watch? Is it funny? Is it sexy and/or erotic? Something in the film breaks for me as a viewer during this sequence, and I associate the use of sound in it as a key element why. The film disintegrates into pure audiovisual spectacle—a kind of music video that fails in its generic goal of selling the music or the album it was produced to promote. Though the aim of this NC-17 "music video" segment of the film, if you will, is not to sell music, the sequence does reveal the commercial function of sex in *Showgirls* and in Nomi's narrative.

So, to me, the question of identifying the film's genre is less interesting than noting those moments in the film when we can sense what you called "genre trouble" because it seems to me that those are the points at which normative performances of gender and sexuality disintegrate into spectacle (that cannot be easily celebrated as simply athletic performance), and one might wonder what one just experienced. Such wondering—or even just spectatorial bafflement—can be very generative when it enables some sort of critical work with or against the film.

Camp Affect

MM: Much is made of Susan Sontag's distinction between "pure Camp"—naive, unintentional, "a seriousness that fails"—and "camping" as a self-aware production of camp that means to be funny.[10] In *It Doesn't Suck*, Adam Nayman discusses applying this to *Showgirls*, suggesting that it comes down to Elizabeth Berkley's performance as Nomi.[11] He senses, though, that it's hard to identify her "failure." The filmmakers insisted that Berkley was directed to act as she did and that the film is a serious portrayal of the abuse of dancers in Las Vegas. Certainly the rape of Molly and what follows seems to confirm that. Perhaps a better angle is Sontag's claim that camp is "generous," "a *tender* feeling" nourishing "itself on the love that has gone into certain objects and personal styles."[12]

I'm wondering if these two features, innocence and generosity, could be a basis for discussing the aesthetic/performance differences between Gina Gershon and Berkley, giving a defensible basis for asking (as you did once when we were having a preliminary chat), "Why is Gina Gershon so hot?" After all, this was also Gershon's first big movie break too, but it did her no harm at all—on the contrary. I'm not satisfied with "she's a better actress." Given what happened to Berkley, the way she was mocked and her talent reviled to the point where no more big roles in cinema came her way, if we accept that she was directed by Verhoeven to act in the way she did, we have no way of knowing what her full potential as an actor might have been. Perhaps one clue is that in our private conversation you called Gershon "campy," which might take us back to Sontag's base distinction between pure and self-aware camp. Gershon said recently that three days into filming *Showgirls* she saw the aspiration to seriousness failing and "decided to make a character that the drag queens would want to perform."[13] Hers is surely a knowing camp performance. What do you think of it?

***

KK: Thank you for asking this question. Ever since I saw the Wachowskis's *Bound* (1996), I have loved to talk about Gina Gershon! I wonder how much Berkley's previous television role in *Saved by the Bell* has to do with the difficulty audiences at the time had in receiving her performance in *Showgirls*. Audiences had expectations of Berkley, but none really of Gershon, and Berkley's performance probably shattered those expectations.

The question of camp in *Showgirls* has been a central aspect of the discourse about the film, both in scholarship and among fans. Answering the question of whether *Showgirls* is "pure camp" or "camping" often is a proxy for adjudicating whether the joke is on the film or on us (the audience). If it is "pure camp," the joke is on the film because it is naive about just how bad it is. If it is "camping," the joke is on the audience, who can only evaluate it straight. The sequence in which Nomi meets Cristal Connors (Gina Gershon's character) is instructive here: after her first performance in the film (through which we are introduced to her character), Cristal calls for Molly, the costume designer and Nomi's only friend, to come to her dressing room. Molly brings Nomi with her, saying, "We can say you are my sister." The decor in Cristal's dressing room is remarkable. Promotional pictures of Cristal are on the wall—the bright red of the roses Cristal received for her performance and the red of the large hairpiece in one of the posters on the wall are the same red as Nomi's dress. The first meeting of Nomi and Cristal is filmed in a reflection in the big mirror surrounded by round lights on the wall of the dressing room while another mirror keeps Molly's work on Cristal's costume in view. Cristal is naked from the waist up, her hands covering her bare breasts, looking at herself in the mirror. Nomi is off to the side, but we see her in reflection in the mirror too while she watches Cristal's reflection. Watching Cristal, Nomi pulls her red dress up slightly with both hands.

What is going on here?!

If we can think about camp as an interaction between a text and an audience, then perhaps the economy of gazes in this scene and the circuits of desire those gazes activate hold a key to answering your questions. Cristal is aware of and seems in control of her own gaze, both at herself and at Nomi, while Nomi's gaze, like her character, is more searching. Nomi is striving and desiring. Cristal is desired and desirable. Meanwhile, Molly simply facilitates the transactions between the two other women. And the audience's gaze is directed toward all of these characters at once.

Race and Repetitive Form

MM: Speaking of Molly, how do you see race or, more specifically, "Blackness" and "Whiteness" playing out in this film? Chon Noriega notes in the *Film Quarterly* Round Table that James and Molly, Nomi's friends and the two significant Black characters, have a "Good Samaritan" function and subservient roles.[14] But you've observed that they are also city residents, unlike the entertainment blow-ins to Las Vegas. How do you see Nomi's "self-making" determination in this explicitly raced and gendered economic and social landscape?

I am asking this because I wonder whether *Queer Times, Black Futures* gives us a way to think beyond that "Good Samaritan" function of Molly and James without denying it, since Molly in particular does play a moral anchor role. In his interview with Adam Nayman, Verhoeven defends himself about the treatment of Black characters in the film by saying that the whole atmosphere of Vegas as well as Nomi's behavior damages Molly, and "there's something there about the United States."[15] Making the case for the film as "carefully thought-out" criticism, he points to the scene in which the White goddess, Cristal, is ascending to heaven, Jesus-like, onstage while the mean Black dancer Annie (Ungela Brockman) is writhing on the stage in agony with a broken knee after marbles are thrown by her meaner enemy in the chorus line, Julie (Melissa Williams). (Verhoeven, in the interview, says she "breaks her hip," but that happens later to Cristal.)

Then we have the unsettling way in which the legacy of slavery in the United States hovers in the background of the film, figuratively (as in the White goddess ascent scene) but also as a generalized reference point for the showgirls' labor conditions, and the situation of Nomi in particular. She is twice treated explicitly as a "slave" by Cristal: first, when at the Cheetah's her way of offering Zack a Nomi lap dance is to say, "I'll buy her for you" (which she does, if only for the duration of the dance); second, in the biker and S/M costume number, their final performance together, Cristal leads Nomi offstage on a leash, saying, "Come on, slave girl." Nomi then explodes and pushes Cristal down the stairs. Nomi's unfree status is underscored later by Zack's threatening behavior to Nomi when he reveals he knows about her past as a prostitute. It has a definite "forced labor" overtone: the way he grabs her by the throat with "You're going to be a big star!" is not how Nomi has imagined the freedom to follow her dream. At this level of everyday labor conditions, both Molly and James seem to have more freedom than Nomi:

Molly works hard but enjoys her skills as a seamstress, taking classes at college as she goes, and James walks away from his job as a parking valet when his boss annoys him in front of Nomi. This may be realistic at the narrative level, and yet it is unsettling how the sign, as it were, of enslavement has migrated toward the focal White character, Nomi. So how do you see Nomi in relation to the racial rhetoric of the film?

***

KK: This is a complicated question, and it is hard to know where to begin. I probably could write an entire essay on just this topic! If I were to do that, maybe I would begin (at least in the first draft and subject to revision based on additional research) with the suggestion that the Black characters in *Showgirls* are perhaps best analyzed in terms of the film's mise-en-scène—that is, I would begin by considering how the Black characters function as part of the look and feel of the film itself. They work to authenticate the film's setting in Las Vegas, where African Americans and other people of color are a significant demographic. As you know, Black folks are among the people who live and work in Vegas, whether in the service industry on the Strip or in other jobs elsewhere in the city, away from the tourist economy driven by the casinos and massive hotels. As mise-en-scène, they authenticate the film's depiction of the racial composition of the full-time residents of Las Vegas and therefore also of the workers who support the tourist and entertainment industries in that city. Starting with the role of Black characters in the film's mise-en-scène could be helpful, I think, because doing so might keep us attentive to the work they are doing in and for the film beyond its narrative and enable us to have a conversation about race in *Showgirls* that moves us away from the terms of "representation" and "authenticity" (even if, as I said, they serve an "authenticating" function as part of the mise-en-scène). We can talk instead about the ways their presence in the film asks us to think seriously about how important the construction and maintenance of the categories "Blackness" and "Whiteness" are for the story the film tells about Nomi's attempts at self-making.

In this regard, Nomi's intimacy with characters we recognize as Black alerts us to her vexed relationship to Whiteness and its privileges. By the end of the film, we realize that Nomi's access to "the American dream"—the idea that hard work, grit, and determination are all one needs to find financial and other forms of success in the United States—has already been denied her because of the circumstances of her birth: her father killed her mother and then himself, she ran away from a foster home and has multiple arrests on her record, she has worked as a prostitute, etc. So, even though in the film's narrative Nomi finds the ultimate success in her industry and we see her image on a billboard as she rides out of town, she has to leave Vegas rather than stay and enjoy that success. In this regard, she is not unlike James, who ultimately reconciles himself to inhabiting, perhaps even embracing, the clichés that constrain his character (as part of the film's mise-en-scène, that is). He is stuck in Vegas.

And Nomi is not unlike Molly, the other significant Black character in the film, who is stuck in Vegas at the end of the film too. She is in a hospital bed. The rape and brutality directed at Molly and the revelations about Nomi's past reinforce the boundaries of each character's gender and class position. They are like borders the characters do not have the requisite papers to cross. Molly is brutalized, traumatized, and immobilized at the end of the film, and Nomi is back where she began (though this time with a chance to do something differently). Neither escapes the roles into which they have been conscripted by circumstance and social hierarchies.

We can imagine that the violence Molly endures has a corollary in Nomi's mind to the violence Nomi's mother endured at the hands of her father. That Verhoeven subjects viewers to Molly's rape and battery while leaving off-screen the violence that shaped Nomi's character says to me that Molly is the character on whom rests the entire racial and gendered logic of the economy depicted in the film. Molly provides the invisible labor of costuming the showgirls and the caring labor required for Nomi to launch her adventures in Vegas. Molly also has a moral compass that seems to be intact. These "supportive" and "Good Samaritan" qualities (to invoke Noriega's critique) are indeed, as you said, moral anchors, subservient to the narrative about Nomi's adventures in Las Vegas in the middle of her enigmatic wanderings back and forth across the American West.

Yet Nomi also is intimately associated with the two main Black characters, especially with Molly, who calls Nomi her sister at one point. This association is not only a narrative one. She also is associated with the Black characters by way of the places in which she is depicted (for example, she lives with Molly when she first arrives in Las Vegas). While both Nomi and Molly move in different spaces, ultimately Nomi is the only character whose trajectory is out of Las Vegas (even Cristal is immobilized in the hospital at the end of the film, albeit with a "'real nice' financial settlement," as you said earlier). Nomi's successes in Vegas and her escape at the end of the film cannot be divorced from her affiliation with and embrace of the Black characters, and her proximity to those characters on the social hierarchy because of the places she inhabits throughout the film, and the way the details we come to know about her past resonate with the narrative trajectory of the film's recognizably Black characters. We learn those details about Nomi's past at the end of the film. They are what explain Nomi's ultimate inability to ascend the rungs of Las Vegas's social and economic ladders.

At the end of the film, Molly's suffering is palpable even though her nurse assures Nomi that Molly will be alright. The scene depicting Molly's assault is horrifying. It is graphic and hard to watch. Because the assault happens to Molly, the film's moral anchor, the film's portrayal of it illuminates the bankruptcy of the racial, class, and gender economies of interest to the film. In and out of love for Molly, Nomi "kicks the shit" out of the man who assaulted Molly, but the viewer does not witness the assault on the White man's body after the first kick. Verhoeven's inability or unwillingness to depict the injuries Nomi inflicts on Andrew Carver (William Shockley) leaves the integrity of the image of White male supremacy and its associated violences intact even as the film ends with depictions of expressions of love and/or admiration between women.

***

MM: Thank you, Kara. That way of approaching these difficult issues by *beginning* with mise-en-scène and "the look and feel of the film itself," rather than with a checklist of ideal positions and attributes in representation to be gridded across the film, is not only clarifying (certainly for me) but opens up another space to consider what has been and may continue to be "vexed" in our viewing of *Showgirls*. In the wake of #MeToo, we are beginning to see readings of the film that once again validate its claims to be what Hugh Montgomery recently called "a straight-shooting portrait of the rancid, unchecked misogyny within the entertainment industry and beyond."[16] I find that hard to deny, but then the complexities of race relations in how this portrait is composed (or how this scenario unfolds) tend to be conceded but then bracketed once the "brutal disruptiveness" of the graphic rape of Molly is seen as "the film's most necessary moment," as Montgomery puts it. In the film we also see how little Molly's life is valued by the men running the industry that depends on her invisible labor ("She can have a dress shop," shrugs Zack) and how little James feels able to define his own life. But what we don't see, as you point out, is any harm to "the image of White male supremacy and its associated violences" following from all this. Action film fan that I am, I had not even noticed that! "Why not?" is a question that will now vex me further.

KARA KEELING is Professor of Cinema and Media Studies and of American Studies and Ethnicity at the University of Southern California. She is author of *The Witch's Flight: The Cinematic, the Black Femme, and the Image of Common Sense* and *Queer Times, Black Futures*. She is editor (with Josh Kun) of *Sound Clash: Listening to American Studies*.

MEAGHAN MORRIS is Professor of Gender and Cultural Studies at the University of Sydney. She is author of *The Pirate's Fiancée: Feminism, Reading, Postmodernism*; *Too Soon Too Late: History in Popular Culture* (IUP, 1998); and *Identity Anecdotes: Translation and Media Culture*.

References

Bonnaud, Frédéric. "The Captive Lover—An Interview with Jacques Rivette." Translated by Kent Jones. *Senses of Cinema* 79 (2001). First published in French, 1998. http://sensesofcinema.com/2001/jacques-rivette/rivette-2/.

Burgos, Ryan. "Showgirls (1995) Behind the Scenes Interviews: Joe Eszterhas." YouTube, 2:08, April 15, 2018. https://youtu.be/v2g4Dngr9-U.

Coleman, Beth. "Race as Technology." *Camera Obscura: Feminism, Culture, and Media Studies* 24, no. 1 (70) (2009): 177–207.

Juzwiak, Rich. "Gina Gershon Didn't Like Scripts She Was Receiving, So She Wrote Her Own One-Woman Show." *Jezebel*, May 30, 2018. https://themuse.jezebel.com/gina-gershon-didnt-like-scripts-she-was-receiving-so-s-1826427212.

Keeling, Kara. *Queer Times, Black Futures*. New York: New York University Press, 2019.
———. *The Witch's Flight: The Cinematic, the Black Femme, and the Image of Common Sense*. Durham, NC: Duke University Press, 2007.
Lippit, Akira Mizuta. "Half-Star: Showgirls & Sexbombs." *Film Quarterly* 56, no. 3 (2003): 33–34.
McHale, Jeffrey, dir. *You Don't Nomi*. XYZ Films, Grade Five Films, 2019.
Montgomery, Hugh. "How *Showgirls* Exposed the Rot of Our Misogynistic Culture." BBC Culture, July 15, 2020. https://www.bbc.com/culture/article/20200714-how-showgirls-told-the-truth-about-americas-foul-misogyny.
Morris, Meaghan. "Transnational Glamour, National Allure: Community, Change and Cliché in Baz Luhrmann's *Australia*." In *Storytelling: Critical and Creative Approaches*, edited by Jan Shaw, Philippa Kelly, and L. E. Semler, 83–113. London: Palgrave Macmillan, 2013.
Nayman, Adam. *It Doesn't Suck: Showgirls*. 2nd ed. Toronto: ECW, 2018.
Noriega, Chon. "A Whisper of Satire." *Film Quarterly* 56, no. 3 (2003): 36–38.
Scafaria, Lorene, dir. *Hustlers*. Annapurna Pictures, 2019.
Snead, James A. "On Repetition in Black Culture." In *Racist Traces and Other Writing: European Pedigrees/African Contagions*, edited by Kara Keeling, Colin MacCabe, and Cornel West, 11–33. London: Palgrave Macmillan, 2003.
Sontag, Susan. "Notes on 'Camp.'" In *Against Interpretation and Other Essays*, 275–92. New York: Delta, 1966.
Wachowski, Lana, and Lilly Wachowski, dirs. *Bound*. Dino de Laurentiis Company and Spelling Group, 1996.
Waxman, Sharon. "Sleazy Writer." *Washington Post*, October 25, 1997. https://www.washingtonpost.com/archive/lifestyle/1997/10/25/sleazy-writer/7b99825a-9214-4cb3-ae2c-d80cbb243fa8.
Wood, Jennifer. "'Showgirls': Paul Verhoeven on the Greatest Stripper Movie Ever Made." *Rolling Stone*, September 22, 2015. https://www.rollingstone.com/culture/culture-news/showgirls-paul-verhoeven-on-the-greatest-stripper-movie-ever-made-54740.

Notes

1. Kara Keeling, *Queer Times, Black Futures* (New York: New York University Press, 2019), 19.

2. Susan Sontag, "Notes on 'Camp,'" in *Against Interpretation and Other Essays* (New York, Delta, 1966), 285.

3. Keeling, *Queer Times*, 114–16.

4. Ibid., 159–63. See Beth Coleman, "Race as Technology," *Camera Obscura: Feminism, Culture, and Media Studies* 24, no. 1 (70) (2009): 177–207; and James A. Snead, "On Repetition in Black Culture," in *Racist Traces and Other Writing: European Pedigrees/African Contagions*, ed. Kara Keeling, Colin MacCabe, and Cornel West (London: Palgrave Macmillan, 2003), 11–33.

5. Akira Mizuta Lippit, "Half-Star: Showgirls & Sexbombs," *Film Quarterly* 56, no. 3 (2003): 33–34.

6. See Meaghan Morris, "Transnational Glamour, National Allure: Community, Change and Cliché in Baz Luhrmann's *Australia*," in *Storytelling: Critical and Creative Approaches*, ed. Jan Shaw, Philippa Kelly, and L. E. Semler (London: Palgrave Macmillan, 2013), 83–113.

7. Kara Keeling, *The Witch's Flight: The Cinematic, the Black Femme, and the Image of Common Sense* (Durham, NC: Duke University Press, 2007), 11–26.

8. See Jeffrey McHale's documentary, *You Don't Nomi* (XYZ Films, Grade Five Films, 2019), and Adam Nayman, *It Doesn't Suck: Showgirls*, 2nd ed. (Toronto: ECW, 2018). See also Jennifer Wood, "'Showgirls': Paul Verhoeven on the Greatest Stripper Movie Ever Made," *Rolling Stone*, September 22, 2015, https://www.rollingstone.com/culture/culture-news/showgirls-paul-verhoeven-on-the-greatest-stripper-movie-ever-made-54740; and Frédéric Bonnaud, "The Captive Lover—An Interview with Jacques Rivette," trans. Kent Jones, *Senses of Cinema* 79 (2001), first published in French, 1998, http://sensesofcinema.com/2001/jacques-rivette/rivette-2/.

9. See Ryan Burgos, "*Showgirls* (1995) Behind the Scenes Interviews: Joe Eszterhas," YouTube, 2:08, April 15, 2018,https://youtu.be/v2g4Dngr9-U; and Sharon Waxman, "Sleazy Writer," *Washington Post*, October 25, 1997, https://www.washingtonpost.com/archive/lifestyle/1997/10/25/sleazy-writer/7b99825a-9214-4cb3-ae2c-d80cbb243fa8.

10. Sontag, "Notes on 'Camp,'" 282–83.

11. Nayman, *It Doesn't Suck*, 92.

12. Sontag, "Notes on 'Camp,'" 292.

13. Rich Juzwiak, "Gina Gershon Didn't Like Scripts She Was Receiving, So She Wrote Her Own One-Woman Show," *Jezebel*, May 30, 2018, https://themuse.jezebel.com/gina-gershon-didnt-like-scripts-she-was-receiving-so-s-1826427212.

14. Chon Noriega, "A Whisper of Satire," *Film Quarterly* 56, no. 3 (Spring 2003): 37.

15. Nayman, *It Doesn't Suck*, 135–36.

16. Hugh Montgomery, "How Showgirls Exposed the Rot of Our Misogynistic Culture," BBC Culture, July 15, 2020, https://www.bbc.com/culture/article/20200714-how-showgirls-told-the-truth-about-americas-foul-misogyny.

PART III
ARCHIVE

LOOSE SLOTS 11

FIGURING THE STRIP IN SHOWGIRLS

MELISSA HARDIE

"Occupation Du Jour"

The Las Vegas Strip, rimmed by massive casinos and punctuated by the dead space between them, observes a particular syntax. At the one end, family-style casinos like Circus Circus mingle with old-style show-oriented ventures such as the Riviera; at the other, new casinos like the MGM Grand, Excalibur, and Luxor offer ersatz entertainment environments. At the older end of the Strip, the most prominent signs promise "loose slots" and advertise precise returns on their slot machines. "Loose slots" are supposed to give the gambler more than they put in; with a transumptive sleight of hand that mimics the deception of the advertisement, they felicitously misrepresent the slot in which money is inserted as the one that returns the winnings. The ubiquitous "loose slots" signs militate against the project of differentiation, which presumably invests the gaudy displays of the casinos. In the seminal essays that located Las Vegas as the master trope of postmodern appropriation, Robert Venturi, Denise Scott Brown, and Steven Izenour made a similar point, finding in the proliferation of different styles a postmodernism that evades structural or generic descriptive power, subtended by the agency of commerce itself: "It is hard to think of each flamboyant casino as anything but unique, and this is as it should be, because good advertising technique requires the differentiation of the product."[1] It is an irony, then, that precisely the advertisement of what drives differentiation—profit—undercuts its attainability, and it is at this point of irony, the loose slot, that I wish to situate the cinema flop *Showgirls*.[2]

Aligning his film against the reinvention of a "family-oriented" Vegas over the past two decades, Paul Verhoeven's *Showgirls* allegorizes the investments signaled by those signs: the relationship between striptease and profit as it constructs the aesthetics and ethics of the Strip.[3] Highly plot driven, and offering gestural and unrealistic models of characterizations, *Showgirls* punctuates its account of Nomi Malone's Las Vegas sojourn with a series of striptease performances, as if the picaresque adventures of its leading character were best adumbrated by the revelations of dance, strip, and sex that constitute her time on the Strip. Verhoeven's picaresque circles from the journey to Las Vegas to the journey to Hollywood: the film opens with Nomi hitching to Las Vegas and closes with her picking up precisely the same ride, this time to Los Angeles. *Showgirls* is located in the interstitial detour of a road movie, or a road movie on detour; the show delays her journey as the Strip calibrates the highway. The road detours to the Strip, that few miles of casinos on Route 91 that define the gambling and other action of Las Vegas, "the example par excellence" of the "commercial strip."[4]

The Strip marks exchange as randomly good or bad "luck," but in fact the odds are always stacked. As one character reminds us, the action in Vegas is really summarized as slot action, and all the grandeur of the casinos and their spectacle are a trivial adjunct to the careful calculation of margins on the slot machines. The drama of the dancing and stripping action becomes something less than a ruse to attract gamblers: an anachronism whose function is ultimately to tie aesthetics and sexuality in the film's tropological schemes. Like its precursor, *All about Eve*, which anatomizes routes of success within the theater, *Showgirls*' actions are demonstrably tied to its own irrelevance: in *All about Eve*, the world of Hollywood lurks not merely as the competitive successor to the theatrical domain in which the film finds its own aesthetics; it is a film about theater that formally announces the irrelevance of live theater.

Showgirls similarly plays on the margins of Hollywood, the gamble of the success, or in its case the flop: it too is a "loose slot." The creation of the family entertainment casinos has tied the profit of Vegas to the normalizing discourses of family, producing an unlikely alliance of these two against the historically vitiated enterprise of striptease, an alliance implicit in the reviews of the film and its genre. In his vicious review of the film, John Patterson writes, "The artfulness and ingenuity that should have been poured into the making of this film were all diverted into the promotional campaign instead. The marketing is the message, now. Keep your money, people."[5] It is similarly ironic that the failure of the blockbuster is inversely read: usually popularity is the index of the mainstream vulgar in this account of cinema. Despite this labor of differentiation—film as casino—*Showgirls* has been read as only the harbinger, or the epitome, of a slew of films that are interested in Las Vegas as iconic location, or striptease as iconic feminine performance, or both. Joe Queenan's article on the striptease film refers to *Showgirls* as one of "a whole bevy of films of this genre . . . slated for release in the weeks and months to come."[6] Dominic Griffin similarly argues that "this year's occupation du jour is of course stripping—er, exotic dancing. . . . An occupation that was once deemed seedy and slutty has been instantaneously elevated to class status."[7]

Both articles, and particularly Queenan's, locate the "genre" of striptease film as nostalgic, and so as participants in an out-of-date discourse of feminine spectacle the reviewers then curiously invoke their evaluations of *Showgirls,* as though their position as reader is ineluctably mapped by the films themselves. And this perhaps is the historical shift they mark: instead of the films being "deemed seedy and slutty," reviewers find themselves "deemed" spectatorial participants, open to the same assignations. Of course, one of the aims of both articles is to ensure the restabilization of stripping as "seedy and slutty" by claiming that this is precisely the effect and intent of the films they survey. And in most accounts of *Showgirls*, the "seedy and slutty" becomes a test of both the film and its actresses, paradoxically because they are "seedy and slutty" and yet not sufficiently "seedy and slutty." Confusing film with subject ("bevy") reminds us of the paradoxically aestheticized domain of the female figure as subject and text; the constant reminder of the negative reviews of *Showgirls* is that it fails to arouse, that "even heterosexual male movie goers will tire" of the display of breasts.[8] Indifference is coded in the technological realization of the project; Verhoeven notes that "70 percent of *Showgirls* was shot with Steadicam . . . [which] helped me get that loose feeling I wanted."[9] Technological indifference imposes an aesthetics of the "loose" return, and although Verhoeven notes that "you never see the camera moving without being motivated by an actor," motivation is disarticulated from interest.[10] The aesthetic distance of the reviewer (and thus the review) is similarly assured by the erotic indifference of the erotically implicated spectator, who is implicated exactly at this point by such a self-nomination. In this discourse, the reviewer identifies willingly with the male spectator variously situated throughout *Showgirls* as the audience of striptease and the erotic exchange of lap dancing. The commercial failure of *Showgirls* has been subsequently hailed as an arbitration of the sheer badness of the film. Economic failure, in the face of a rhetoric of economic persuasion, becomes the sign of turpitude throughout the film's reviews; in his analysis of the effect of O. J. Simpson's not guilty verdict, Dominick Dunne ties O. J. and *Showgirls* as an instance of this rhetoric of turpitude, situating Simpson as the invisible appreciative audience of the film: "One night he was able to get out and see a film, without being seen. The film he picked was *Showgirls*."[11]

In his interview with Verhoeven, the film's director, Jeffrey Landos asks, "Is a movie about lap dancing *art*?" and the box office failure of the movie might suggest that once the profitable business of the sex industry lays claims to status as an aesthetic text, then its failure is its best reading as such.[12] The film equivocates over such a distinction, as it pits the energetic "natural" style of its main dancer against the work of a trained dancer (James), whose pedigree (Alvin Ailey and Twyla Tharp) lets him distinguish talent but whose erotic investment in "pussy" forbids him from ever authentically arbitrating artistry and eroticism. The film scripts its own economic failure as well in differentiating striptease and gambling precisely on the grounds of profit. As Zack, the entertainment director, reminds us, the profits of Vegas are generated only by the margins built into the "slot action"; striptease is only a marginal activity within the commercial transactions of the Strip. Both these experts, male, can diagnose the failure, artistic and economic, of striptease, and their position of expertise in the film is reproduced in the "expertise" of the male reviewers of *Showgirls,* who diagnose similar artistic and commercial failure. James's artistic expertise is destabilized by the vicissitudes of sex and romance—the Strip—as he loses job after job, until he finds a wife who can provide an income as well; Zack's erotic investments in the dancers are the pure professional expertise in what becomes the rhetorical antithesis of strip in the film: the return of slots that are tight, not loose. Their critique of the film then serves the useful service of extracting them from the very nostalgic discourse of striptease they reproduce in their articles and reviews, promising an alliance with the margins of profit built into the slot machine against the recidivist offer of the "loose slot" striptease, which programmatically promises more than it can ever deliver.

The promise of more than can be delivered ties striptease's basic premise (the tease) to the rhetoric of the casino that marked it as "unique" (in Venturi, Scott Brown, and Izenour's terms); if the radicalism of their claim for Las Vegas architecture was that it was premised on the contention that "learning from the existing landscape is a way of being revolutionary for an architect," then we might simply say that these reviewers don't want to learn, or don't want "to question how we look at things."[13] And it is perhaps this alliance between (post)modernity and history, the improbable founding gesture of architectural postmodernism, that is the repressed of the reviews, for it suggests instead that a film like *Showgirls* can deliver more than it promises.

Nomi Malone's route through the casinos and clubs of Vegas puns on the strip as both location and act; the detour of Las Vegas becomes another horizon of action. The Strip is the site of exchange, and the film opens with a typical gesture of ambivalence about those exchanges. Nomi's first encounter leads to her being robbed of her goods; her second, to a relationship of feminine mutual support as she meets Molly, who takes her in and supports her during her adventures as a dancer.

Moments of contemplation, few in the film, are sited through reference to the gigantic lights and signs of Vegas: Nomi, perched on the roof of the casino, contemplates the action below. Moments of exchange other than theatrical are situated in parking lots and driveways; she literally runs into Molly in a parking lot, fights with James in the parking bay of the Stardust Casino, lives with Molly in a trailer, and dances with James in his curious alleyway studio. Nomi, Molly, and James are endlessly sited through the parking lot and driveway, spaces that define their interaction and link their positions as workers in Vegas. Venturi, Scott Brown, and Izenour's *Learning from Las Vegas* was originally preceded by an essay called "A Significance for A&P Parking Lots, or Learning from Las Vegas": "The space that divides high-speed highway and low, sparse buildings produces no enclosure and little direction. . . . To move through this landscape is to move over vast expansive texture:

the megatexture of the commercial landscape. . . . But it is the highway signs, though their sculptural forms or pictorial silhouettes, their particular positions in space, their inflected shapes, and their graphic meanings, that identify and unify the megatexture. . . . The sign is more important than the architecture."[14]

If the spectacle of the Strip is the site for the musical sequences, dance routines, and striptease shows of *Showgirls*, then the unenclosed spaces of the parking lots and negative space between the casinos is the site of interlocution, illuminated by highway signs that may "unify the megatexture" but, precisely, only spotlight the plot action of the text. This characterization of negative space in Vegas reminds us of the colonial tropes that accompany the reception of the text within a discourse of directorial identity: "When he left his native Holland a decade ago to emigrate to L.A., who'd have guessed he'd reign over Tinseltown as his fellow countryman, Peter Stuyvesant, once ruled over New Amsterdam?"[15] One of the reasons, presumably, for the ferocious reviews of *Showgirls*, despite gestures to questions of taste and sexual rectitude, is precisely its depiction of Las Vegas as an allegorical location for the fortunes of America, an allegory that travesties the bizarre hybrid allegories of the family casinos.[16] Verhoeven's use of space is antithetical, for instance, to that proposed by George Stevens's 1970 *The Only Game in Town*, which was filmed in Paris and so shot entirely indoors, eliding the scenery of Vegas entirely.[17] If George Stevens's 1956 *Giant* suggested the trope of gigantic Texas to read the fortuitous fortunes of the West, the natural domain for the diverse lives of its players, *The Only Game in Town* suggests the endless recursion of its plots as the same—dancing, sex, drinking, and gambling are all the "only game"; the only plot is that of the loser. Verhoeven's film instead situates other plots outside, illuminated by but not subject to the rule of the casino.

The film's economic and artistic experts, James and Zack, locate their erotic investment in striptease at the expense of art and economy, and both are situated, like the reviewers, as the voyeuristic partners in a lap dance that draws together the schemes of the film. In a crucial scene, they are both participants in a lap dance, paid for by Zack's girlfriend, Cristal, who is the lead dancer in a revue called *Goddess*. Four people participate in this dance: Nomi, the lead character, dances; Cristal, who has already indicated her interest (rivalrous, professional, sexual) in Nomi, pays and watches; Zack is "lap danced"; and James observes from the entrance to the "private" room reserved for such exchanges. The scene, according to Verhoeven, "is rather complex."[18] "Ostensibly, Cristal is humiliating Nomi and demonstrating her power over Nomi by 'renting' her against her will—literally imposing a form of slavery on her. . . . Although Cristal bought the lap dance for Zack, it is obvious that he is really just a substitute for Cristal herself. Cristal is seduced and riveted by Nomi's sexuality. . . . [In] the end, she might be the seductress and controller of both of them."[19]

Verhoeven locates a rivalry between Zack and Cristal over the body of Nomi and situates Zack as the token of exchange between the two women. In doing so, he subscribes to two familiar accounts of lesbian sexuality. On the one hand, there is a rivalry between men and women over femmes, which can be located as a variation of lesbian desire as the "masculinity complex": Cristal is interposed as the female imposter of the masculine client. On the other, he sees staged a reversal of the theory of the homosocial that finds women exchanging men as tokens of their affective and erotic investments in each other, a kind of Eve Sedgwick *sans la lettre* that marries radical lesbian feminism's "lesbian continuum" to what Teresa de Lauretis describes as "the sweeping of lesbian sexuality and desire under the rug of sisterhood, female friendship, and the now popular theme of the mother-daughter bond, [which] has become canonical in feminist criticism to the point where it vitiates the analytical efforts of even those critics . . . who are wise to it."[20]

Verhoeven's account of the scene omits mentions of the body of James, as he peers through a beaded curtain at the triangle within, and his presence complicates the triangulation that all of these readings easily script as the lap dance. James is African American, and his body stands as the occluded "captive body," a physical manifestation made absent perhaps by the logic of slavery, which Verhoeven imputes to this transaction and which is precisely not "literal," as he claims.[21]

James is not located in the secluded or marginal space of the private dance but on its margins: a "double displacement" in Gayatri Spivak's terms, which has "resonance" within the complex displacements of the strip and its own "loose slots." When Molly, a woman of color, is raped in the hotel room of her erstwhile idol Andrew Carver, the logic of subjection of the captive body is played out within the virtual public spaces of the casinos and their sprawling architectural forms. The film scripts Nomi's competitive emergence in the world of mainstream casino performance as one with major losses attached, most particularly the sexual abuse of Molly late in the film, which engages Nomi in a plot of revenge that requires a final strip scene, in which she athletically kickboxes the major perpetrator of the assault. Real violence, rather than the performance of striptease, converts Nomi from a life on the Strip as she resumes her wandering, this time to Los Angeles, whose horizon has already been tropologically signaled in the film through its references to another set of intertexts; *Showgirls* traces its own intertextual debts through parodic points of contact and suture. Its topoi of cinematic reference release the possibility of another reading of the film in terms of its own "loose slots," which are sited on the figurative Strip as the empty lots of transitory contact—the driveway, the parking lot, the trailer park—and that are tropologically reproduced in the film's double attention to the minute exposures of striptease performance and the minute revelation of referential contact. Like the contrary logic of the "loose slot," they promise to return to what is invested in the text. It is perhaps an inevitable irony of the process of figuring striptease that precisely when a panoramic spectacle of body is offered, attention is focused on minute and discrete portions of that body. In the case of Verhoeven's *Showgirls*, small though significant portions of the female body figure its own narrative and figurative progressions.

"Minor Accents": Two Settings

A model of desire based on the premise of identification finds its parodic counterpart in *Showgirls* in the fascination with fingernails the film discovers. Nomi and Cristal's much delayed sexual rendezvous, which closes the Las Vegas action of the film in the form of a prolonged, close-up kiss, is bartered through the text as Cristal repeatedly admires Nomi's nails and asks her to do her nails for her. Nomi's elaborately decorated nails are the antithesis of the blunt fingernails that haunt lesbian feminism: long, sharp, and gaudily painted, they promise erotic peril. Nothing could be further removed from the mawkish "fingernail scene" in Rose Troche's 1994 *Go Fish*, a scene that uses the paring of fingernails to stand in place of lesbian sexual pleasure, as if the demands of "realism" in an account of sexual action is comic per se. These fingernails are tied to the hands of sexual attraction without sexual service, and they figure the asymmetry of the dynamic between the two women, leaving for Cristal the "stone" role of sexual continence and performance as the reverse of her professional ascendancy.

The oscillation of desire between the two women is staged in a dressing room, a private room, and finally publicly performed in Spago, a transplanted LA restaurant found at the center of the Forum, the shopping center adjacent to Caesars Palace casino (and only exitable through the casino). Here, the two women dine, flouting the counsel they have received to eat only brown rice and vegetables, and swapping stories of eating dog food. This location, neither casino nor parking lot, marks the ambivalence with which the text will deal with the physical intimacy of these women, as dietary restrictions function to segment the narrative of its progress in the course of the film.[22] Burgers, fries, and snack foods are eaten with much relish in the film and are often lingered on in close-up. *Showgirls'* unlikely thematization of good nutrition recalls the attention paid to smoking in Verhoeven and Eszterhas's previous film, *Basic Instinct*: as that film's ambiguous heroine is requested to refrain from smoking in the backstage interrogation room, she ripostes, "What are you going to do? Charge me with smoking?" Smoking operates here as the trope of contemporary segregation, and attention paid to dietary exigencies ties this film to the earlier's parody of the inefficiency of such practices of hygienic separation. Living up to her claim, "I have nothing to hide," Catherine Tramell famously parts her legs in this scene to reveal her untrammeled "magna cum laude pussy," an interpolation that raises the stakes on the possibility of segregation. This scene effects what is threatened throughout *Showgirls*: the accidental display of a "smiling snatch" during the course of a performance of Cristal's show, *Goddess*, much mooted in the backstage dressing space of the chorines and thematized in various instances through the ripping and tearing apart of seams on outfits.

True to *Showgirls'* origin as a modernized *All about Eve*, Verhoeven situates the crucial transactions between dancers backstage, mimicking the backstage location of the initiating contacts between Margo Channing and Eve Harrington, her emulator, in the earlier film.[23] Like Eve, Nomi is first introduced to Cristal in a dressing room, following a successful performance. In *All about Eve*, tropes of ascendance and competition are spatially orchestrated around Margo Channing's stairway and, in particular, the stairway climbed by her guests as she greets them in her apartment. The stairway reappears in *Showgirls,* as it becomes the much-mooted instrument of career destruction, and, indeed, Nomi does push Cristal down the stairs. Stairway and dressing room are marked as pedagogical in the film; Cristal instructs and torments Nomi not only in the lap dancing back room but in her dressing room, and the test of that pedagogical instruction takes place on the staircase.

Nomi wants to be, like Cristal, a performer in one of the glamorous casinos; after the lap dance, Cristal organizes an audition for her. The audition takes place in the darkened theater, and it involves the evaluation of both the dancers' skill and their bodies. Nomi maintains her composure through the audition, until her nipples are criticized as "the wrong sort" and she is told to use ice to maintain their erection. Verhoeven modeled the *Goddess* show on his reading of Anthony Summer's biography of Marilyn Monroe, and this scene borrows from Summer's account of Monroe's professional wiles: "Marilyn had some trouble with nature when she tried another old trick. She told Travilla that Jean Harlow, one of her idols, deliberately made her nipples prominent by rubbing them with ice before going into a scene. 'Mine,' Marilyn complained, 'won't get hard. They're the wrong sort.' The problem was solved by artifice—a little round button inserted in the brassiere at the relevant places."[24]

Nipples are one of the points of precise bodily attention in *Showgirls,* an interest satirized by *Film Threat*'s reviewer, who titles his review "All about Cleavage" and argues, "Indeed, with their two settings, dormant and erect, it could be argued that Berkley's nipples are capable of expressing a greater range of emotion than their owner."[25]

Intertextual Monroe figures the articulation of the staircase and the stage itself; she was, after all, one of those who made their way up the iconic staircase of *All about Eve*. The "two settings" mark the transition from back to front as a binary opposition, locating the nipple, dormant or erect, as the bodily signifier of that transition. The text articulates location through the articulation of intertextuality, true to that concept's reliance on a metaphorics of spatial invasion: the conceptual logic of "Goddess" can be found not in the show of the same name but in its rehearsal *as* rehearsal. If Nomi, like Monroe, has (is) the "wrong sort," their failure to articulate through the body these spatial shifts is a failure of the logic of the binary opposition based on a logic of segregation or separability, or *determinate* difference.[26]

The dressing room is marked as a space of segregation, back to front stage, professional versus amateur. Such segregations, according to Venturi, Scott Brown, and Izenour, were the formal liability of modernism, entailing the application of "minor accents": "The diminutive signs in most Modernist buildings contain only the most necessary messages, like LADIES, minor accents begrudgingly applied."[27] If the logic of my reading interposes an account of occluded difference to differentiate it from the reading of desire as identification, which de Lauretis critiques as the aporia of theories of spectatorship and lesbian desire, then a rereading of the spaces of the Strip allows another interpretation of the text's ability to figure (if not think) a profitable practice of feminine sexuality.[28]

The importance of "urinary segregation," the ostensible "minor accent," was not lost on Jacques Lacan, whose diagram describes "the image of twin doors symbolizing, through the solitary confinement offered Western Man for the satisfaction of his natural needs away from home, the imperative . . . by which his public life is subjected to the laws of urinary segregation."[29] For Lee Edelman, Lacan's analysis crucially invokes the phallus, because "the men's room . . . enshrines the phallus as the token not only of difference, but also of difference as *determinate,*" to compensate for an anxiety over the men's room as "the site of loosening of sphincter control, evoking . . . an older eroticism, undifferentiated by gender, because anterior to the genital tyranny that raises the phallus to its privileged position."[30] If the back room of the strip club satisfies "his natural needs away from home," the back room of the casino, like the ancillary or ancillary sign, the "minor accent," is a ladies' room, populated by women and gay men. All the male dancers are gay except one, who, like the phallus, marks a discourse of determinate difference without a satisfactory arbitration of that difference: his erotic identity remains irrelevant in the narrative of this segregated space. Lacan, among other things, wants the phallus to mark difference *à la lettre*, "to the letter," precisely, and yet in this text the phallus remains an imprecise unwitnessed signifier whose ambit presence is blunt compared to the precise and yet indeterminate referentiality of the nipple, the fingernail, and the snatch.[31] This failure to separate has been read as a sign of the relationship between postmodernism and queer: "Postmodernism's lubricious heterogeneity, its celebration of artificiality and commodification, and its association with a camp aesthetic lend it a sodomite cast."[32]

The "sodomite cast" of *Goddess* mixes with *Showgirls'* desiring women as a heterogenous ensemble at odds with the reading of the film offered by the reviewers quoted above, though not with some male reviewers in the gay press: "Lance Leopard" in *Capital Q* describes the film as a "nifty little piece of trash" and compares it at length with *Valley of the Dolls*.[33] In *Out* magazine, Bruce Steele opens his review with "How Can You Not Love *Showgirls*?" and compares the film to *Valley of the Dolls* and *Mommie Dearest*, commenting, "Screenwriter Joe Eszterhas (*Basic Instinct*) evokes *All About Eve*, but All About Tits is more like it. Short of pornography, sexism has never been so baldfaced, or so silly."[34] Both readers subscribe to a reading of the text as bad, imposing another form of aesthetic segregation, one that can only open the question of the relationship between this text, a camp reader, and a lesbian camp aesthetic.

The shooting script of *Showgirls* included a visit to the Liberace Museum in Las Vegas, a visit dropped in the final film as if the campy association of Liberace was too close for comfort. Excluding the Liberace Museum from a film whose mise-en-scène crucially implicates regimes of ostentatious aesthetics reminds us of the repressive logic at the heart of aesthetic regimes per se. What kind of aesthetic determination is at stake, then, in the classification of the film itself through the discourse of taste, the location par excellence of an aesthetic of segregation? An uncanny effect of both reviews is that they follow the logic of intertextual suture at work in the text but do so by supplying their own intertexts, deregulating the rules of association built into the film to offer the indeterminate difference of a camp canon of feminine rivalry and desire. Identification is exponential rather than reductive. The logic of segregation implicated by discourses of taste is asymmetrically located within a discursive model of exponential identification, textually rehearsed.

If the association of gay men and women, particularly perverse women, is a kind of quarantine familiar in our culture, its work backstage in *Showgirls* is to impose the indeterminate, though not indifferent, logic of this liminal space on the segregated space of the backroom lap dance. Perhaps that is what the reviewers of the film find so uncomfortable or erotically indifferent. The segregations of the lap dance, the epitomizing topos of segregated bad taste, foster subjects whose different desires are exponential, and asymmetrical, like the camp profits of gay men and lesbians. Is the *figuratively ungainly*, the "loose slot," the unlikely topos for an indeterminate difference (after Edelman) whose precision is local rather than blunt, one that can transumptively transform the logic of desiring identification?

MELISSA HARDIE is Associate Professor of English at the University of Sydney. Her recent work appears in *Australian Humanities Review, Textual Practice, Film Quarterly,* and *Angelaki*. Her most recent book chapter (with Amy Villarejo) is on the 1978 Briggs Initiative and the television drama *Family,* in *Television Studies in Queer Times*. She is editor of the Oxford University Press series Approaches to the Novel.

References

De Lauretis, Teresa. *The Practice of Love: Lesbian Sexuality and Perverse Desire*. Bloomington: Indiana University Press, 1994.

Dunne, Dominick. "O. J.'s Life Sentence." *Vanity Fair* 424 (December 1995): 84–89.

Edelman, Lee. *Homographesis: Essays in Gay Literary and Cultural Theory*. New York: Routledge, 1994.

Griffin, Dominic. "The Naked Truth." *Film Threat* 26 (February 1996): 46–48.

Grosz, Elizabeth. *Jacques Lacan: A Feminist Introduction*. London: Routledge, 1990.

Hardie, Melissa Jane. "'I Embrace the Difference': Elizabeth Taylor and the Closet." In *Sexy Bodies: The Strange Carnalities of Feminism,* edited by Elizabeth Grosz and Elspeth Probyn, 155–71. London: Routledge, 1995.

Lacan, Jacques. "The Agency of the Letter in the Unconscious." In *Écrits: A Selection,* translated by Alan Sheridan, 146–76. London: Tavistock, 1977.

Lamos, Colleen. "The Postmodern Lesbian Position: On Our Backs." In *The Lesbian Postmodern,* edited by Laura Doan, 85–103. New York: Columbia University Press, 1994.

Lance Leopard. "Imitation of Life." *Capital Q* 160 (October 20, 1995): 9.

Landos, Jeffrey. "Playing with Fire." *Movieline* 7, no. 2 (October 1995): 87.

Maltin, Leonard, ed. *TV Movies and Video Guide*. New York: Signet, 1991.

Mankiewicz, Joseph L., dir. *All about Eve*. 20th Century Fox, 1950.

Patterson, John. "*Showgirls*: All about Cleavage." *Film Threat* 26 (February 1996): 52–53.

Queenan, Joe. "Pasty-Faced." *Movieline* 7, no. 2 (October 1995): 56–60, 87.

Spillers, Hortense. "Mama's Baby, Papa's Maybe: An American Grammar Book." *Diacritics* 17 (Summer 1987): 65–81.

Steele, Bruce. "Review of *Showgirls*." *Out* (February 1996): 48.

Stevens, George, dir. *The Only Game in Town*. 20th Century Fox, 1970.

Summers, Anthony. *Goddess: The Secret Lives of Marilyn Monroe*. London: Guild, 1985.
Troche, Rose, dir. *Go Fish*. The Samuel Goldwyn Company, 1994.
Venturi, Robert, Denise Scott Brown, and Steven Izenour. *Learning from Las Vegas: The Forgotten Symbolism of Architectural Form*. Cambridge, MA: MIT Press, 1993.
Verhoeven, Paul, dir. *Basic Instinct*. TriStar Pictures, 1992.
———. *Portrait of a Film: Showgirls*. New York: Newmarket, 1995.
———. *Showgirls*. Carolco Pictures, Chargeurs, United Artists, 1995.

Notes

1. Robert Venturi, Denise Scott Brown, and Steven Izenour, *Learning from Las Vegas: The Forgotten Symbolism of Architectural Form* (Cambridge, MA: MIT Press, 1993), 34.

2. As this essay will argue at length, context is everything. My reading of *Showgirls* and of the Las Vegas Strip is itself a souvenir of my own Las Vegas sojourn in December 1994 with Kate Lilley, to whom I dedicate this essay, and in whose company my repeat excursions to see the film were so pleasurable. The advertisement for "Bronte Gourmet Tongues" that precedes most commercial films shown on the cinema strip of Sydney at present stands, as Venturi, Scott Brown, and Izenour suggest of the casinos, as an indispensable intertext for this viewer, unique as an exemplification of the "differentiation of product." Thanks also to Liz Wilson for her help in locating material for this essay.

3. Paul Verhoeven, *Portrait of a Film: Showgirls* (New York: Newmarket, 1995), 9.

4. Venturi et al., *Learning from Las Vegas*, 3.

5. John Patterson, "*Showgirls*: All about Cleavage," *Film Threat* 26 (February 1996): 53.

6. Joe Queenan, "Pasty-Faced," *Movieline* 7, no. 2 (October 1995): 87.

7. Dominic Griffin, "The Naked Truth," *Film Threat* 26 (February 1996): 47.

8. Patterson, "*Showgirls*," 53.

9. Verhoeven, *Portrait of a Film*, 13.

10. Ibid.

11. Dominick Dunne, "O. J.'s Life Sentence," *Vanity Fair* 424 (December 1995): 86.

12. Jeffrey Landos, "Playing with Fire," *Movieline* 7, no. 2 (October 1995): 59.

13. Venturi et al., *Learning from Las Vegas*, 3.

14. Ibid., 13.

15. Landos, "Playing with Fire," 57.

16. My analysis of "foreign matter" in *Showgirls* was elucidated by Efi Hatzimanolis's observations, for which I thank her. Popular newish casinos feature Treasure

Island, "Polynesia," New Orleans steamboat, Imperial Egypt, and Oz themes, for example.

17. Leonard Maltin, ed., *TV Movies and Video Guide* (New York: Signet, 1991), 850.

18. Verhoeven, *Portrait of a Film*, 17.

19. Ibid.

20. Teresa de Lauretis, *The Practice of Love: Lesbian Sexuality and Perverse Desire* (Bloomington: Indiana University Press, 1994), 116.

21. For Hortense Spillers, in this logic, 1) the captive body becomes the source of an irresistible, destructive sensuality; 2) at the same time—in stunning contradiction—the captive body reduces to a thing, becoming *being for* the captor; 3) in this absence *from* a subject position, the captured sexualities provide a physical and biological expression of "otherness"; 4) as a category of "otherness," the captive body translates into a potential for pornotroping and embodies sheer physical powerlessness that slides into a more general "powerlessness," resonating through various centers of human and social meaning. Hortense Spillers, "Mama's Baby, Papa's Maybe: An American Grammar Book," *Diacritics* 17 (Summer 1987): 67.

22. On the segmented structure of diet as a narrative of aestheticized desire, see my "'I Embrace the Difference': Elizabeth Taylor and the Closet," in *Sexy Bodies: The Strange Carnalities of Feminism*, ed. Elizabeth Grosz and Elspeth Probyn (London: Routledge, 1995), 155–71.

23. Verhoeven suggests this relationship is fortuitous: "We [Verhoeven and Eszterhas] later realized that there were elements from Joe Mankiewicz's brilliant 1950 film, *All About Eve*, in our story." Verhoeven, *Portrait of a Film*, 12.

24. Anthony Summers, *Goddess: The Secret Lives of Marilyn Monroe* (London: Guild, 1985), 53.

25. Patterson, "*Showgirls*," 53.

26. Lee Edelman, *Homographesis: Essays in Gay Literary and Cultural Theory* (New York: Routledge, 1994), 160.

27. Venturi et al., *Learning from Las Vegas*, 7.

28. The failure de Lauretis notes of theories of lesbian desire and spectatorship to account for the distinction *between* identification and desire (de Lauretis, *The Practice of Love*, 116, et passim) can be mapped onto their own problematics; under the auspices of the heuristic of textual enunciative capacities, these readings tend to impose the labor of interpretation obscurely on the texts themselves rather than their reading, in short, to supply a readerly practice of identification (of text and subject position) in place of the pleasurable practice of desiring spectatorship (the complexity of reading as the labor of desire). Tropes of identification are not simple enunciations

of an identificatory desiring subject, but, as I will attempt to show in *Showgirls*, offer a surplus of non-identificatory desire.

29. Jacques Lacan, "The Agency of the Letter in the Unconscious," in *Écrits: A Selection*, trans. Alan Sheridan (London: Tavistock, 1977), 151.

30. Edelman, *Homographesis*, 161.

31. See, for example, Elizabeth Grosz, *Jacques Lacan: A Feminist Introduction* (London: Routledge, 1990), 94–95, on the literalness of the signifier as a material object.

32. Colleen Lamos, "The Postmodern Lesbian Position: On Our Backs," in *The Lesbian Postmodern*, ed. Laura Doan (New York: Columbia University Press, 1994), 85.

33. Lance Leopard, "Imitation of Life," *Capital Q* 160 (October 20, 1995): 9.

34. Bruce Steele, "Review of *Showgirls*," *Out* (February 1996): 48.

12 ROUND TABLE

SHOWGIRLS, FILM QUARTERLY *56, NO. 3 (SPRING 2003): 32–46*

Showgirls is funny, stupid, dirty, and filled with cinematic clichés; in other words, perfect. Even better, the writer and director, no matter what they say today, don't appear to be in on the joke. I saw the film opening night in Baltimore with an audience that took it seriously. "That's what Vegas is really like," I heard a woman whisper to her husband without a trace of irony as she exited the theater. *Showgirls* will hold up; it will be great trash forever.

—John Waters

***

As recently as December 26, 2002, Elvis Mitchell in the *New York Times* evoked Paul Verhoeven's *Showgirls* (1995) as he sought to convey the true horror of the movie he was reviewing, which he described as "a picture that is mostly a desert of strangeness, a movie so bad that it quickly enters the pantheon of wreckage that includes *Battleship Earth* and *Showgirls*."[1] Yet earlier that same year, a *Film Quarterly* (*FQ*) editorial board meeting had been at first entertained by a chance mention of *Showgirls*, and then galvanized by the discussion that ensued. It turns out that there is a significant number of secret and not-so-secret devotees of the film—although their admiration takes different forms. And apparently—if unexpectedly—*Showgirls* has served to stimulate scholarly thought around what the film is, how to describe it, and issues of camp, satire, class, gender, the fallen woman, the showgirl musicals, trash cinema, sexploitation films, hedonistic criticism, and reading and teaching the film.

It was at that board meeting that we decided to present another *FQ* Round Table (the first one, on *Thelma and Louise*, appeared in *FQ* 45.2 [Winter, 1991–1992]). Seven distinguished scholars—Noël Burch, Akira Mizuta Lippit, Chon Noriega, Ara Osterweil, Eric Schaefer, Jeffrey Sconce, and Linda Williams—have contributed to this discussion. It would seem that *Showgirls* might stand a chance of entering a different pantheon than Mitchell's . . . .

Ann Martin, Editor

Half-star: *Showgirls* and Sexbombs

AKIRA MIZUTA LIPPIT

In the 2002 edition of his *Movie and Video Guide*, Leonard Maltin rates Paul Verhoeven's *Showgirls* a "BOMB."[2] Even after seven years to reconsider his opinion, Maltin describes *Showgirls* as a "stupefyingly awful movie—whose creators swear to have made it with serious intentions." Maltin, who is characterized in *Movie and Video Guide* as "one of the country's most respected film historians," explains his rating system, which ranges "from ★★★★, for the very best, to ★½, for the very worst. There is no ★ rating; instead, for those bottom-of-the-barrel movies, we use the citation BOMB." All capitals. (Among other things, BOMB is also almost an acronym of "bottom-of-the-barrel.") Why can't a film receive a single star, and what exactly is the status of a ½? Why can't the *very* very best films receive ★★★★½, like an A+ in school?

Showgirls fails to register on Maltin's star-rating system, which ends or begins, depending on one's point of view, with ★½. In Maltin's world, a BOMB is not only the worst possible film, it also has the effect of destroying the system itself. No longer a figure, trope, or acronym, Maltin's BOMB operates literally, as an assault on the—or rather, Maltin's—*star system*. Tracing the origins of the idiom "bomb" to the *Oxford English Dictionary* (*OED*), one finds the reversible function of the word, which means—specifically with regard to entertainment—both a success and a failure. A virtual palindrome, "bomb" can be used to describe either a success or a failure, or even perhaps a simultaneous success and failure. (The term is also used, according to the *OED*, as "a pregnant expression for the atomic or hydrogen bomb, . . . regarded as unique because of its utterly destructive effects.") In these senses of the term, *Showgirls* may be a BOMB for more than one reason: it may have bombed, at the box office and/or critically, while also bombing the very ratings systems that were never equipped to handle its effects. Or its utter failure, bomb, could be understood as the very basis of its success, the other meaning of bomb.

Maltin's entry, which is relatively long for a "bottom-of-the-barrel" movie, goes on to describe *Showgirls* as "part soft-core porn, part hokey backstage drama, full of howlingly hilarious dialogue." ("Hokey," *OED*: "Characterized by hokum; sentimental, melodramatic, artificial.") A hybrid, monstrous film that spreads across the genres of soft porn and melodrama. Here, a simple ★½ rating might be an accurate description if not evaluation of the movie. Maltin makes no mention of its dance numbers, choreography, and music; and he never considers the musical or other antecedents such as *Flashdance* (1983, ★★½), *Staying Alive* (1983, ★★), and *Footloose* (1984, ★★½). Nor comedy, for that matter, despite the "howlingly hilarious dialogue."

Is *Showgirls* part soft-core porn? If soft-core is exemplified by a general sexual ambiance (strip clubs, Vegas stage shows), partial nudity (topless dancing), sexual practices (lap dances, interracial sex, lesbian sex, sex in swimming pools), and sexual violence (rape), then *Showgirls* qualifies as such. It is titillating without inducing the full force of arousal. At least in part. But does the other part of *Showgirls*, the hokey half, affect the pornographic aspect of the movie? (There are hokey pornos, but in those cases, the porn is itself hokey.) Can a movie be part soft-core and part melodrama, without altering the chemistry of either genre? What does a soft-core melodrama look and feel like?

Periodically, producers and studios have sought to elevate pornography, or sexually explicit films, into a form of film art, usually by raising some of the production values (a developed narrative, character psychology, foreign accents, elaborate camerawork, and other forms of cultural depth). The objective is to mainstream pornography and increase ticket sales, or at least to assuage viewers' anxieties by disguising porn as something else. Among the notable efforts: the *Emmanuelle* films (none included in Maltin), *Café Flesh* (1982, not included), *Last Tango in Paris* (1973, ★★★½), *In the Realm of the Senses* (1976, ★★½), etc. The results are usually an unsatisfying blend of pornography and drama: *pornodrama*. Most have bombed with porn fans, as well as with fans of serious drama. In each of the mentioned examples, one senses the dissimulation of pornography, itself a form of censorship. *Showgirls*, however, can be thought of as both porn and not-porn, a type of impure half-porno that never blends with its other half. As art historian Jean-Claude Lebensztejn has noted, in the languages of mayonnaise and photography, certain mixtures can be thought of as emulsions, suspended mixtures that never really mix properly or thoroughly. Like the expression "bomb," which can indicate both failure and success, or the movie *Showgirls*. Pornographic mayonnaise.

Perhaps the way to understand *Showgirls* is as a form of obscenity, rather than pornography. And maybe the obscene nature of the film emerges precisely from the grotesque hybrid of pornography and hokum. The illicit mixture that never properly blends may be at the root of this "stupefyingly awful" picture. (How could a film that is stupefyingly anything, even awful, be a BOMB, unless Maltin means this in the positive sense of the expression: "This film is the BOMB"?) A fair description of *Showgirls* is "obscene": to the senses, to taste, to modesty (it *shows* too much show, is *monstrous,* "howlingly"). But how does one rate an obscenity? What are the standards for a rigorous criticism of the obscene? Should greater obscenity receive more or fewer ★s?

The protagonist of *Showgirls,* Nomi Malone (played by ingenue Elizabeth Berkley) has served as one of the focal points of the film's critical devastation. She can't act, she overacts, she explodes in every scene, ruining the film with an eruption of affect far in excess of the protocols of so-called good acting in cinema. (Of her expressive force, Maltin says, "Berkley sets the tone for her performance in an early scene in which she expresses fury by vigorously spewing ketchup over her French fries.") Berkley is a bomb, explosive and destructive, within and without the diegesis. But she also has a secret name, or cryptonym, a word-name that exposes, as it were, another facet of her performance. Nomi is Polly, Pollyanna, Pollyannish. When her Vegas choreographer snarlingly refers to her as "Polly," Nomi shoots back, "Why did you call me that?" "Because you're a Pollyanna." She achieves happiness through self-delusion, remains blindly optimistic and pathologically naive. Nomi believes she can succeed as a Vegas showgirl; extradiegetically, Berkley believes she can succeed as an actor. Inside-out: polymorphous, polyester, Pollyanna. By the film's end, the audience learns that Nomi's real name is Polly Ann. She really is Polly Ann, which is also to say she isn't yet anything, but believes she will some day be everything. A polymorph with many shapes past and future; a naive if not innocent child; perverse but not really a pervert. Half everything.

One can identify two ways to read the homonyms in Polly's invented (synthetic) name: "No me," the absence of a self, or "Know me," discover a true(r) self. To no or to know, a prohibition (or negation) and an imperative. Or, better yet, to no and to know. Nomi is Polly, (but also) a polynym. Everything in *Showgirls* can be said to consist in multiples, contradictions, and antinomies; for every claim one can make about the film, there is always another option or possibility. The film is too sexual, even sexist, but not sexy enough (a distinction underscored in another genre-bender, *This Is Spinal Tap*); it's bad ("stupefyingly awful"), bad (naughty), and bad (good, as in "bad motherf★cker"); it's "howlingly hilarious" (dialogue), but lacking in irony (its "creators swear to have made it with serious intentions"); and of indeterminate genre: "part soft-core porn, part hokey backstage drama." In this sense, perhaps Maltin is speaking precisely when he describes *Showgirls* as a BOMB. A description rather than a judgment. An obscene, monstrous bomb that fails and succeeds at the same time, defying a consistent standard of judgment, since about this film, every claim and its opposite can be made. (The same can be said for much of Verhoeven's oeuvre, which is marked by inexorable ambiguities. Is he or isn't he serious, sincere? Is he good or bad, in all the senses of those terms? Is he or isn't he gay, or, is he straight?) Perhaps the film is less a failure than a failed film; which is to say, a film failed by the institution and industry of film criticism, which never took into account the full extent of *Showgirls'* monstrosity, its rigorous (or at least consistent) obscenity. A more nuanced entry in Maltin's guide might have registered *Showgirls* as a ★★★★½ BOMB, which would have included every possible rating at the same time.

***

Embarrassing *Showgirls*

NOËL BURCH

Showgirls is certainly among the three films directed in America by Paul Verhoeven which are most worthy of respect. *Total Recall* and *Basic Instinct* were also—along with *Showgirls*—written by Joe Eszterhas, which is probably not coincidental. *Showgirls* is especially remarkable for the way in which it associates gender and sexual issues with the class contradictions so often glossed over in Hollywood films. This is in fact an authentic "fallen woman film" in the grand Hollywood tradition: a working-class woman's sinful past catches up with her just as she has gained access to the world of wealth. Those 1930s melodramas were theaters of forbidden pleasure *and* social injustice; they were about how it is women who must always pay under patriarchy.

Verhoeven and Eszterhas have contrived to celebrate the perfectly genuine attractions (not solely for the male eye, I would suggest) of the sexy Las Vegas revues—and more intimate ceremonies such as lap dancing—only to gradually undermine these representations with an exposure of the ferocious exploitation upon which they are founded. Critics I have read invariably emphasize the film's "vulgarity," perceived as consubstantial with that of the world it depicts. Yet the story of Nomi Malone, a dancer of undeniable talent (whose fate eerily foreshadows that of the extraordinary Elizabeth Berkley, whose career was nipped in the bud by a suspiciously violent critical reaction), is for me that of a working-class woman who rises from gutter to glory and finally rejoins her class when a succession of ugly episodes is capped by the rape of her best friend by an idolized pop star.

It is Nomi herself who demonstrates the principle of "every man for himself" which presides over this world and over American society as a whole when she pushes the current star down the dressing room stairs so that she can take her place. She is acclaimed by the well-heeled audience of a fashionable nightspot, but this success is then doubly ironized by the star's unexpected gratitude—at last she can quit the rat race, she tells Nomi from her hospital bed—and by their boss's contempt when he ferrets out Nomi's shady past. His new star spits in his face, pretends to accede to the rapist's desire for her only to punish him with karate kicks (in a perversely erotic scene redolent of the rape-revenge movies), and goes back on the road, switchblade at the ready. A kind of happy ending: life in the gutter is a rat race too, but somehow cleaner.... It is also worth noting that the only solidarities possible for Nomi in this world of showbiz are with members of her own class: two African Americans, and also, in one unexpectedly moving scene, the manager of the sleazy strip joint where she began her Las Vegas career who, though she had brutally walked out on him, comes to pay tribute to her talent and congratulate her on her success.

The film was trashed by critics on both sides of the Atlantic, in the U.S. for reasons that have been clearly perceived by a web surfer on IMDb:

> Like all of director Verhoeven's American films, *Showgirls* is an over-the-top vision of American culture and ideals. The loud chorus of negative response to the film when it opened shows just how defensive Americans can be. Every film critic in the land seemed to suddenly develop a "If-you-don't-like-it-here-then-go-live-in-Russia" attitude, typically reserved for members of the NRA.

And he goes on to add that Verhoeven has often relied on "melodramatic, 'soap-opera' qualities as a style and a method of satire."

This universal critical condemnation often takes for its pretext the vulgarity of mass culture which *Showgirls* lavishly deploys and with which it has lazily been identified, in both form and content—even though, for the conscious spectator whom the authors are addressing, the film is criticizing the "gendernomics" of that same mass culture. No feminist, or male feminist sympathizer, to whom I have shown the film has failed to see that here Verhoeven is *not* playing the ambiguous game between the sneering contempt for mass culture and the complacent exploitation of its codes which characterizes both of the films written for him by Edward Neumeier: *RoboCop* and the revolting *Starship Troopers*. In France, at least, the celebration of these last-mentioned films as Verhoeven's finest is intimately linked to the way they continually nudge middle-class adult spectators over the heads, as it were, of the juvenile target audience. *Showgirls*, on the contrary, takes mass culture seriously, as a site of both fascination and struggle. And it takes despised melodrama seriously too, as indeed an excellent vehicle for social criticism.

The French response to this film has been highly significant of a certain backlash strategy, as in this comment from *Télécable Satellite Hebdo* (December 22–28, 2001): "Verhoeven delights in this plunge into bad taste. . . . His [directorial] talent redeems a stupid screenplay signed by Joe Eszterhas, who specializes in heretical, falsely provocative subjects." A film about the exploitation of female, proletarian bodies is tarred with the brush of the abjection it denounces, in order precisely not to have to come to grips with that form of exploitation. Typically enough for France, although this magazine is aimed at a mass audience, the values of cinephilia prevail, with the tribute to Verhoeven's auteurist mastery compensating for the lowly category of value (one star) to which the pundits have consigned this film.

Of course, gender consciousness is not a very widely shared quality among the critics of France, male or female. But neither is it as universal as we might believe in countries where feminism has had more success. In *Sight and Sound*, one British critic (Linda S. Williams) faulted the film for not being sexy enough! Which all goes to illustrate a broader truth: the polysemic nature of Hollywood movie discourse, from D. W. Griffith to the present day.

***

A Whisper of Satire

CHON NORIEGA

Paul Verhoeven's *Showgirls* is something of a novelty . . . .
There is not a whisper of satire in this movie.
—Anthony Lane, *The New Yorker*

Near the end of *The Questor Tapes* (1974), the last in a series of androids that have served as guardian angels for the human race is fatally shot by an agent of the state. The assailant, who thought he shot a human, notes that there is no blood, whereupon the scientist who has befriended the android cradles him, shouting, "What do you mean? There is blood everywhere."

It is one of the most chilling moments in made-for-television movie history, because we do not see the blood, but we know it is there all the same. If we were to reconsider *Showgirls* through the filter of *The Questor Tapes,* film critic Anthony Lane is the assailant, director Paul Verhoeven is the android, and I-the-academic am the sympathetic scientist. Satire is the blood that we do not see, the effect Lane cannot hear, but it is everywhere in the film's tale of a troubled woman coming to Las Vegas in search of stardom.

One reason why we do not see the satire in *Showgirls* is that the film lacks the usual coordinates and signposts for a critique of human vice and folly provided by sarcasm, irony, and caustic wit. Such overt satire is safe because we "know" what is implied between the scare quotes and to whom it applies. Because this is not the case with *Showgirls*, critics often took the film as equivalent to or of a piece with its subject matter. According to Lane, if not most reviewers, *Showgirls* "has the distinction of being the first movie about Las Vegas that is actually more vulgar than Las Vegas."[3] In this view, the film exemplifies rather than exposes human vice and folly.

The production team embraced this ambiguity and the attendant controversy in an effort to exploit the film's NC-17 rating.[4] In fact, screenwriter Joe Eszterhas and Paul Verhoeven played the press like an old vaudeville team. Eszterhas took the high road, cloaking the film in the aura of post-civil rights rhetoric—perversely inflected with his own sense of *ressentiment*—in an open letter in *Variety*: "Society will never change if we stick our heads in the sand and pretend that abuses to women, blacks, Jews and gay people aren't happening every day."[5] Verhoeven took the low road—"I love to look at naked girls"—but he continued his ongoing investigation of authoritarianism, albeit here within the capitalist logic of the state rather than with the state itself. Both men did extensive research in a "private dancing" session with a nude stripper at the Palomino Club in Las Vegas.[6]

While we do not see the blood of satire, its signs run throughout the film. The first one is a destination marker 342 miles east of Las Vegas, a city whose Spanish-language name translates as "the fertile plains," surely ironic for a desert resort. But by the 1990s, Las Vegas had become America's fastest growing city and was launching an advertising and public relations campaign to redefine its gambling-based fecundity around the image of the family-as-consumer. *Showgirls* registers the effects of this shift, but allegorizes them within a pornographic mode that inverts them: in the class-based distinction between the Cheetah's club (strippers) and Stardust (showgirls), the former presented as a "family" of outcasts and the latter as a "classier" corporate ladder to be climbed; and, in the racial segmentation of labor (blacks provide the key service and servant roles). Contextually, then, Las Vegas represents the new frontier for family settlement, its racial problems now internal and labor-based.

The second sign is the name of the protagonist, Nomi Malone (Elizabeth Berkley), who is hitchhiking to Las Vegas to become a dancer. While everyone around her there reduces their identity to "whore," understood in terms of labor-as-commodity, Nomi insists on the ethical and aesthetic gradations from whore to lap dancer to stripper to showgirl. But the film lets us know that she is wrong. At the end, as she is leaving Las Vegas and her life as a showgirl, Nomi (no me/know me) is asked if she won anything. Her answer is simple: "Me." (Beneath this allegorical tale is an insider's joke: Nomi is also the name of Joe Eszterhas's wife.)

What makes *Showgirls* unique as a satire is the way in which Verhoeven collapses the Lumière and Méliès traditions. The film has the strange sense of being an *actualité* for Elizabeth Berkley's performance. This performance consistently stands out from the narrative proper: we are aware of watching a former television child actor do her own dance, lap dance, and striptease numbers. But we are also aware of watching her act. Lane is right in this respect: "She can't act, but the sight of her *trying* to act, doing the sorts of things that acting is rumored to consist of, struck me as a far nobler struggle than the boring old I-know-I-can-make-it endeavors of her fictional character."[7]

We end up with a rupturing of cinema's sign system: character without characterization, method acting without interiorized motivation, and the blurring of realist and histrionic acting styles. The effect is disturbing when put into relationship with the film's baroque visual style (vivid colors, a symbol-laden environment), not to mention the subject matter. Most reviewers noted the "absence of both drama and eroticism," the "lack of characterization and narrative tension," and the film's dubious achievement of making "extensive nudity exquisitely boring."[8] Viewers do not get to have it both ways, the narrative justifying the erotics. Instead, they get neither; hence, the critical heteronormative rage as blood drained from erections . . . .

The film exposes the grounds for its satire when the show producers briefly consider replacing Cristal Connors (the star of the show, *Goddess*, played by Gina Gershon) with Janet Jackson or Paula Abdul. This reference to actual entertainers is downright perverse, pulling the viewer out of the diegetic frame for the first and only time. When the show producers announce that Jackson and Abdul have been passed over in favor of Nomi, they do so at a press conference, as if the casting of a Las Vegas show were a newsworthy event. As with Verhoeven's sci-fi films, the satire derives from receiving such exaggeration-cum-exposition through the filter of a television camera.

Even so, the scene strains credibility. Madonna, perhaps, but Jackson or Abdul? Their discursive presence serves another function. In the film, all the black characters occupy subservient roles: seamstress, bouncer, bellhop, bodyguard, attendant. The two main black characters—Nomi's roommate Molly Abrams (Gina Ravera) and Nomi's erstwhile love interest and a would-be modern dance choreographer James Smith (Glenn Plummer)—represent Hollywood's usual non-white Good Samaritans. Their misfortunes—Molly is raped and her nose broken, James gets his girlfriend pregnant and becomes a grocer's bag boy—frame Nomi's redemption and escape. Jackson and Abdul upset the film, imposing an extradiegetic signified that renders the narrative fictional by comparison. Here is the Hollywood corollary to "suicide by cop": reflexivity via blackness.

And herein is the "moral" of the film: the subservient character will redeem "us" from ourselves, then leave or be left behind—a morality that conjures up the "you're my best friend" ending of *Driving Miss Daisy* (1989). While Eszterhas is liberal in his characterization of the oppressed—"women, blacks, Jews and gay people"—the film itself is more precise in its object: a white heterosexual woman. In the film, her redemption comes from blacks and lesbians. But while the underlying moral may be the same as in *Driving Miss Daisy, Showgirls* rejects Hollywood sentimentalism in favor of a perverse satire that offers nudity and banality in equal measures. Its satire comes by way of camp rather than sarcasm, while its identification is anchored in female-to-female gazes and Nomi's uncanny mimesis of Cristal's mannerisms (and not just her dance moves). Not surprisingly, the film's own redemption came from drag queens, who began hosting "Showgirls" parties and who inspired the return of the film in midnight screenings. Even so, the adoration and imitation of hyperperformative white female stars tend to obscure the racial foundation for such objects of desire. Thus, the moral itself does not become manifest; or does so only fleetingly.

The last two signs in the film announce the past and the future: "Nomi Malone Is Goddess" (billboard) and "Los Angeles 280" (highway sign). Marriage is implied: Nomi is heading back to Joe Eszterhas. For Elizabeth Berkley, it is another story. Her debut paid just $100,000, a mere five percent of Verhoeven's *reduced* directing fee. Soon after the film, Berkley was dropped by her agent and she has only recently reemerged on the silver screen. In the end, the brutality that the screenwriter and director claimed as their topic became an "allegory of cinema," wherein the celebrity of the production team crushed the rank-and-file actress who did what she was paid to do.[9] Sincerity is the sacrificial lamb of satire. In *Showgirls,* her blood is everywhere.

***

A Fan's Notes on Camp, or How to Stop Worrying and Learn to Love *Showgirls*

ARA OSTERWEIL

It is a much-celebrated phenomenon that cult audiences form interpretative communities around degraded texts. The existence of the cult film, or midnight movie, fascinates theorists from an abstract, sociological point of view. Generally, in these cases, the devotional practices of the audience make the film interesting by belatedly bringing the degraded object to life. The text itself, however, becomes quite unimportant.

The notion that "bad" films somehow increase their shelf life by affirming a marginalized community is very attractive. As critics, we are forever delighted when spectators demonstrate agency by reading against the grain; as historians, we are tickled by the idea that the most peripheral piece of rubbish can be reborn with the passage of time as an important artifact.

Unfortunately, there is a tendency to abandon the text entirely. It becomes a startling vacuum, an unfathomable gap around which the most extraordinary rituals develop. The desire of cult audiences to embrace the worst possible text, and resignify it, functions as a kind of Midas touch. In seeking out the texts with the most pronounced negative cachet, the cult audience strives to transform the worst piece of trash into gold. However, critical discourse can only partially accommodate this kind of alchemy. Some movies are such disasters that even the bad-object-seeking cult audience fails to justify their appeal.

In an era where the appreciation of pornography, bad television sitcoms, and the weepiest of mid-century melodramas has become the sign of hipness among cinephiles, Paul Verhoeven's *Showgirls* may be the last guilty pleasure this side of postmodernism. In the undergraduate course on Trash Cinema that I taught in the summer of 2001 at the University of California, Berkeley, even my most devoted "trashaholic" students found it utterly loathsome that *Showgirls* was on the syllabus.

When one's reputation on campus is made by championing "bad" films in an academic environment, as mine has (for better or worse), there seems little danger that it can be destabilized by liking something outside the norms of good taste. But this assumption is pure fallacy. All semester, *Showgirls* hovered on my screening list as the film that could make or break my perceived expertise in matters of bad taste. If I failed to make Stardust-worshipping converts of my students by the end of the term, my entire project of redeeming "cinema detritus" from the trash heap of culture was threatened with collapse. (At this point I feel obliged to state, perhaps unnecessarily, that I do not think that *Showgirls* is an excellent movie, or even a good one. Aside from my intrinsic ambivalence about the film, however, I believe it is worth watching, and I am prepared to defend it as a misunderstood camp extravaganza.)

Surprisingly, *Showgirls* is extraordinarily complex, and much more difficult to analyze than any of the other "trash" films that I have presumed to be its kinsmen. One aspect that never fails to perplex a virgin audience is its tone: it appears to connote a type of mainstream directness and sincerity. The film's relatively large budget and seemingly high production values, as well as its then A-list director and writer team, suggest that it intends to satisfy its audience not as a conspicuous piece of trash, but as a scintillating, if disposable, blockbuster. One of the many ejaculations I had to contend with when teaching the film was the accusation that Verhoeven didn't intend it to be read as a radical piece of trash filmmaking or as a masterful, ironic parody. As unintentional debauchery, *Showgirls* somehow didn't "deserve" the subversive status I was attempting to bestow upon it. If we were laughing at *Showgirls*—and dear God, were we laughing—then it appeared that we were laughing at it, not with it, and this distinction made all the difference in the world.

Rather than discarding the question of intention for its ultimate indecipherability and naivete, it is important to acknowledge how utterly central this question has been to historical formulations of camp. By disregarding *Showgirls* because of its perceived lack of ironic intent, my students were dialectically reversing Susan Sontag's dictum that the best or "purest" kind of camp was naive rather than deliberate. Although she claims that the "essential element" in naive or pure camp is "a seriousness that fails," my students had seized upon Verhoeven's failed seriousness as the very factor which eliminated the film from any valid camp appreciation.[10] Had Verhoeven been *trying* to create a text saturated in chintzy artifice, histrionic affectation, and absurd sexual display, then it would have been the most brilliant piece of camp they had seen. Without this trace of distanciation, *Showgirls* was doomed, and so, it seemed, was I.

Showgirls proposes to incite the extremities of emotional and physical affect, but delivers a series of empty cues. Although its dramatic and narrative conventions participate in the melodramatic tradition, the film ultimately fails to move its audience to pathos or sympathy. Certainly our heroine suffers, and is compelled to make decisions of dubious morality in order to overcome hostile external circumstances that are at least partially determined by her class and gender. But aside from a modicum of sympathy evoked by Nomi's underappreciated African American seamstress buddy, the characters in *Showgirls* are so uniformly idiotic and their plights so ridiculous that we cannot help but laugh, with Oscar Wilde at Little Nell's death, at their downfall.

Showgirls also boasts of being an intensely erotic, soft-core exploration of the Vegas nightclub scene, in which tits, ass, and even a bit of beaver are lavishly displayed. Yet its presentation of the bodily spectacle is so grotesque that, despite its long-sought-after NC-17 rating, the film seemed to fail to turn its audience on. If the success of both melodramas and soft-core porn can be measured in relation to how many tissues spectators consume in order to rid themselves of unseemly bodily fluids, then *Showgirls*—in failing to necessitate this kind of clean-up—appears to fall short of its "straightforward" objective.

There is, however, another way of looking at this intensely problematic film. Although I am not as invested in questions of intent as my students are, there are a few key moments in the film that stand out as the markers of good camp. Putting aside some of Sontag's more dated and disturbing claims, it can be agreed that one of the integral hallmarks of camp is the love of artifice that the camp text evinces, the "relish for the exaggeration of sexual characteristics and personality mannerisms."[11] *Showgirls* delivers this kind of self-conscious flamboyance at a breakneck pace. Set in Las Vegas, the privileged site of American excess, it manages to exceed even the most liberal standards of taste and credibility. Unfortunately, there is not space enough here to rhapsodize over the scene where Nomi and her archrival Cristal reveal to each other their love of Doggie Chow, nor where any one of Nomi's seizures on the dance floor is referred to as her possession of real talent. Nor is there time to discuss the placement of the ejaculating dolphins in the swimming pool, or the way that Nomi's eyes are consistently made up to resemble the glass peepers on a trophy deer head.

Whether or not it is intended as a piece of camp wit (though I think that the infamous "Versayce" sequence cements the fact that it is, indeed, deliberate), the film's outrageous sense of humor certainly demands at least a few tissues to wipe away the tears of guilty pleasure that it inspires. I must admit that the first time I watched it, I was too mortified to laugh. Of course, in those stone-faced days of pious Antonioni cinephilia, I had not yet learned to delight in the joys of bad cinema. I thought that I was too sophisticated a film student to enjoy such a farce.

One of the true challenges of appreciating a film like *Showgirls* is that as a piece of camp, it is decidedly middlebrow. It is much easier to appreciate a "bad" camp film like Jack Smith's *Flaming Creatures*, intended for an already marginalized audience of underground artists and homosexuals, than it is to excavate a bit of parodic truth from a lesbian fantasy marketed to a mainstream, compulsively heterosexual audience. If every blockbuster teen horror film, sitcom, and advertising campaign threatens to steal the signs of "being-as-playing-a-role" from the community of outcasts who first exalted it, then the political significance of camp begins to recede. The anxiety *Showgirls* created, and continues to create, among leftist intellectuals stems from the fear that camp, like everything else remotely subversive, is in danger of being co-opted by "the Man." For me, the desire to steal camp back, wherever it may be located, has become a kind of categorical imperative, a yearning to redeem that which seems irredeemable.

***

(As my final aside: on a questionnaire that I created for the film theory course that I taught in fall 2001, one of my former students from the Trash seminar wrote that her new favorite films were Kenneth Anger's *Kustom Kar Kommandoes* [*sic*] and *Showgirls*. So I suppose my reputation as the missionary of bad taste lives on, for better or worse.)

***

Showgirls and Sex Acts

LINDA WILLIAMS

"Tasteless," "vulgar," "exploitative," "tawdry"—these are the terms that were most frequently used to condemn *Showgirls* upon its release. Yet I loved every tawdry minute of it. Could it be that I just have bad taste? One common way of defending oneself against such a charge is to argue that what others see as bad taste is actually the prescient recognition of a cult classic, in the grand tradition of J. Hoberman's "bad movies"—movies that are so bad that they are good, failures so dire that they succeed. Such movies are usually low budget and made by outsiders; the problem with *Showgirls,* however, is that it is a very big-budget production made by quintessential insiders that is simply not that "bad," and certainly not all that alien to the Hollywood mainstream. It really won't do, then, to defend my bad taste by celebrating this film as radically "other."

Rather, I want to argue that *Showgirls* is part of an important and long-standing tradition of enduringly trashy—though never really "bad"—American movies whose tawdriness resides in the vulgar status of its primary subject: the showgirl herself. She is a figure American culture has both celebrated and despised as the quintessential commodification of womanhood. Her roots go back to vaudeville, Tiller girls, Ziegfeld girls, and early sound movie musicals immortalized by Busby Berkeley. Paul Verhoeven and Joe Eszterhas enthusiastically sought to update this figure in a post-Code, post-feminist, and post-Stonewall era in which it is permissible to foreground (and of course to exploit) the new forms of vulgar sexual display made possible by such cultural innovations as the lap dance. The vulgarity of this update is perfectly in keeping with the vulgarity of the tradition it updates, only American critics seemed too puritanical to embrace it.

Consider Anthony Lane's derogatory quip that *Showgirls* turns its title from a noun into an imperative. The filmmakers, he writes,

> have a story to tell, even a moral to expound, but their deepest wish is to get the girls to show. When Tony, who runs the dances at the Stardust, auditions a line of hopefuls, picks three, says "Show me your tits," and hands one of them a helpful cluster of ice cubes, he is acting on behalf of the entire film.[12]

Lane means to condemn this injunction to show tits. But what else have the movies or stage shows in this tradition ever done but "show" the anatomy of "girls"? The fact that these tits are now acknowledged to be surgically enhanced and made erect by ice cubes is the film's way of modernizing the tradition that once focused more exclusively on legs (or gams). Is it possible that what Lane and all the other critics so horrified by the bad taste of this film were really reacting to was its contemporary updating of a showgirl tradition that makes no bones about both the prurient appeal and the artificial constructedness of what it shows?

If we look again at the Depression-era Busby Berkeley showgirl musicals, we find that their "shows" were always about prurient displays of bleached-blonde (chemically altered) "dames" and the ambivalent moral status of a girl who earns her living by showing her body through questionable forms of dance. In *Showgirls,* that dance consists of lifting a bare-breasted (erect-nippled) woman out of an exploding papier-mâché volcano, a sadomasochistic black leather dance of lesbian eroticism consisting of a few provocative tribadic thrusts, and several variations of a lap dance.

In the Berkeley films, no less than in *Showgirls,* the girl dancers navigate the shoals of "dance" performances that ever since the can can have been uneasily perched between "legitimate" art and illegitimate prostitution. What is simultaneously fun and low-down about *Showgirls* is that it takes on this theme as its primary subject without insisting, as every Hollywood film made during the reign of the Production Code had to insist, that the showgirl who deserves to emerge as the star must also be sexually innocent. The jaded gold digger who knew the score would serve as the foil for the wide-eyed ingenue who didn't, but whose innocence would bring her success.

Showgirls offers the 1990s update of this American showgirl tradition: it abandons sexual morality for a more substantial female solidarity. The ambitious ingenue, Nomi, is revealed at the end to have previously been a hooker; her first job in Vegas is in a strip joint with a private room for lap dances; her career takes off first when she gives a lap dance to Zack, the entertainment director of the Stardust, and later when she sleeps with him. Though Nomi tries hard to walk the fine line between prostituting herself and pursuing the art of dance, everyone, including the reigning star, Cristal, who can't wait to get her hands on Nomi's breasts, insists that there is no distinction. Endlessly bantering about the relative merits of their breasts and nails (not to mention the unspoken competition between their equally inflated lips), Cristal and Nomi are richly ironic twists of old stereotypes: the reigning bitch (and butch) queen, the ruthless ingenue who will stop at nothing to succeed.

If the moral fine line that makes the ingenue deserve her stardom still functions, it is no longer in her quality as Ruby Keeler trouper, nor in her sexual innocence. Rather, in yet another twist on the genre, it is in grafting the tradition of female rape-revenge violence onto the showgirl tradition. When Nomi learns that the one person she will admit to loving, Molly, her African American roommate, has been brutally raped and beaten by a preening rock star, she dances out her revenge in the form of brutal karate kicks into his face and then walks out on everything. Nomi loses stardom, but gains herself. This happy ending, mixing violent revenge on the men who treat women like whores with ostentatious female solidarity, is no less a fantasy than the enshrinement of Ruby Keeler as star at the end of *42nd Street*. But the changes are worth noting: lesbian sex replaces heterosexual sex as the forbidden act whose sublimation creates the whole gaudy show. Lesbian sex and female solidarity give a new lease on life to the otherwise familiar titillations of the genre.

As in the earlier showgirl musicals, a principle of sexual sublimation motivates the musical numbers. It is never quite clear what the girls themselves actually desire—men or each other—since their dancing bodies are so much the source of the film's polymorphously perverse pleasures. Indeed, what is most striking about this film is that all sexual clinching tends toward dance, just as all dance tends toward sex. I submit that it may be this very blurring of the line between dance and sex that finally set off so many of the critics who hated this film.

We are informed more than once that Nomi's dancing is all heat and "pelvic thrust" rather than "true" dance. The assistant choreographer of *Goddess*, the opulent Stardust floor show in which Nomi briefly stars, tells us, nevertheless, that "she's got it . . . they don't teach it in any class." The film dances literally and metaphorically around the nature of this "it": the line between fucking and dancing is blurred at every turn. Whenever Nomi dances she seems to be having sex, and whenever she has sex she seems to be dancing; there is no pure sexual desire and there is no pure dance anywhere in *Showgirls*. Perhaps the critics' hatred of the film was due to the absence of any "pure" erotic scene that is not tinged with power or stylized as dance. Consider *Variety*'s complaint that the film "just flaunts sex without eroticizing it."[13] Could this mean that to him the film lacks a properly torrid sex scene that is "just" sex and not dance, expectations of which were aroused by the film's much-touted NC-17 rating?

It is not fair to judge *Showgirls* by the standards of a *Last Tango in Paris* or a *Henry and June*. But it may very well be that the portentious European art house sex of these films is the only kind of sex American critics can accept, while the vulgar, tawdry, showy Las Vegas sex that reworks the more authentically American tradition of the gold digger seems just too tasteless for the American critical establishment to stomach. More than one review excoriates Eszterhas for enjoying the titillation of lesbian sex, when it is precisely the bad-taste glorying in the bitchy role-playing of that titillation that seems to me to be the great fun of the movie. It is very easy to condemn movies that attempt to have trashy fun with sex. But I predict that *Showgirls* will reemerge one day, like Nomi and Cristal from their papier-mâché volcano, in triumphant glory to gain the praise that it deserves.

***

Showgirls and the Limits of Sexploitation

ERIC SCHAEFER

Some movies are genre killers. Whether it is due to their excess, overreach, or ineptitude, they have the capacity to terminate an entire class of motion pictures. Peter Bogdanovich's *At Long Last Love* (1975) was the pillow that smothered the moribund musical, and Michael Cimino's *Heaven's Gate* (1980) finished off the Western more effectively than any showdown at high noon. There was nowhere else to go with the disaster picture after Los Angeles was destroyed (in Sensurround!) by *Earthquake* (1974). It's certainly true that musicals, Westerns, and disaster flicks have been made since, but the critical and/or box office failure of these genre killers, or the way in which they exceeded generic limits, represented a symbolic end to genres that had once flourished. The release of *Showgirls* in 1995 did the same thing for sexploitation movies. Paul Verhoeven and Joe Eszterhas's high-budget exercise in low culture was the last gasp of a once thriving form already mortally wounded by the disappearance of its traditional venues, the proliferation of hardcore, and Hollywood's usurpation of its once formidable sexual spectacle. With every emphatic thrust of her hips, Elizabeth Berkley helped drive the nails deeper into sexploitation's coffin.

Surprisingly few people made a connection between *Showgirls* and sexploitation when it was released. Perhaps because critics and viewers were blindsided by its $40-million budget, *Showgirls* could simply not be thought of in terms of sexploitation, a historically low-rent form. However, having been immersed in sexploitation films for the past several years, I can say with the utmost confidence that *Showgirls* qualifies as the ultimate sexploitation film. Verhoeven and Eszterhas took a modest form, put it on a regimen of coke and steroids, and ballooned it to a point where it is impossible to imagine its bombast and excess ever being superseded.

Almost every one of *Showgirls'* characters, plot turns, and generic elements can be located in sexploitation films from the 1960s. *Showgirls'* Nomi is a woman "on the run," escaping from a troublesome past. This is a classic narrative element in sexploitation—at work in, for instance, *Bad Girls Go to Hell* (1965), *Julie Is No Angel* (1967), *Run Swinger Run!* (1967), and *Prowl Girls* (1968). Most often the narrative takes this woman to the big city, where she becomes involved in some aspect of the sex trade or in a series of sexually exploitative relationships.

With its constant references to whoredom, *Showgirls* hammers home an equation between the seedy world of exotic dancing and that of "legitimate" entertainment—in this instance, high-end Vegas floorshows. This less-than-surprising revelation is similar to the exposés of various sexually oriented businesses in sexploitation, whether it's the dirty pictures racket in *Nudes, Inc.* (1964), stag movies in *Cool It, Baby* (1967), shady modeling agencies in *Rent-A-Girl* (1965), or prostitution in *P.P.S.* (*Prostitutes' Protective Society*, 1966). *Showgirls* also includes the revenge finale that punctuates many of the sexploitation films, with Nomi "kicking the shit" out of superstar Andrew Carver in retaliation for the brutal rape of her friend Molly.

As with many sexploitation films, *Showgirls* gives a sexual twist to familiar classics or genres. Pulling together elements of backstage tales such as *42nd Street* (1933) and *All about Eve* (1950), the plot revolves around Nomi's effort to rise from strip club to glittering Vegas stage show. All of the familiar clichés are trotted out—the slow grind to the top, the casting couch (or swimming pool in this case), the backstabbing, and the grandstanding. Borrowing from, or sending up, familiar genres was a common strategy in sexploitation. (*Showgirls* has a more than passing similarity to *Starlet!* [1969] and *Beyond the Valley of the Dolls* [1970].) Not only was generic pilfering a shortcut to a serviceable narrative, but it could also play into common sexual fantasies or fetishes (jungle sex, vampire sex, prison sex). EVI [Entertainment Ventures, Inc.] was particularly adept at this strategy, with films such as *Space Thing* (1968), *Trader Hornee* (1970), and *The Erotic Adventures of Zorro* (1972). These formulations continued into the hard-core arena and hang on today, even if contemporary nods to mainstream titles and genres are usually in name only.

Along with these conventions, *Showgirls* has affinities with sexploitation in dialogue, plot, and spectacle. The dialogue is awkward: lines vacillate between banal observations, vapid pop-cult catchphrases, and overblown pontification. *Showgirls* even contains a straight-faced variation on the line, "The show must go on"—words not uttered in a movie without tongue planted firmly in cheek since the 1940s. The plot is thin at best, and motivations are cloudy or nonexistent. Upon its initial release, most critics commented on the film's illogic and the characters' lack of motivation.

In sexploitation films we expect everything to take a back seat to the display of nudity and the mobilization of sexual situations. And that is exactly the case in *Showgirls*. Berkley seems to spend half the movie either falling out of skimpy outfits or buck naked. The other supporting actresses and background extras contribute by baring most, if not all. As with sexploitation, scenes of sexual intimacy are often sublimated into sexy dances. We are treated to pole dances and lap dances, as well as simulated swimming pool sex and the requisite lesbian flirtation. All these moments are carefully spaced throughout the film to provide an even distribution of sexual spectacle.

On a variety of levels, sexploitation films were always about excess. They were about excessive desire that needed to be fulfilled. They were about excessive display—the skin, the sexual situations. They were often about fetishism that blossomed into obsession: Findlay's "Kiss" series is the archetypal example. And they were about excessive bodies; think Russ Meyer's pneumatic women, or sexploitation stars such as Marsha Jordan, Dyanne Thorne, and Chesty Morgan.

What makes *Showgirls* the end of sexploitation is that Verhoeven and Eszterhas wallow in excess in a way comparable to the later Meyer films, but without the varnish of self-parody. Everything comes off as overblown and preposterous. A few examples: Marty, the gay stage manager, hollering "Thrust it! Thrust it!" as Nomi arches her hips off the floor during rehearsal. The flimsy transformation of Al "gimme a blowjob" Torres, the sleazy manager of the Cheetah's strip club, and comedienne Henrietta Bazoom into Nomi's surrogate parents when they suddenly appear to praise her dancing in the big show. The "social relevance," in the form of repeated and crass swipes at entertainment and commerce. The stage numbers that are outrageous in their conception and execution: an explosive "creation" scene set amidst spewing volcanoes; a motorcycle rally conducted in patent-leather S/M garb. And Verhoeven's direction is excessively obvious. After being raped by Andrew Carver and his goons, Molly flies out among the elegant partygoers like a piece of trash tossed out a car window. She's been used up and thrown away. Get it?

From the opening shot as she flounces out to the highway to hitchhike to Vegas, everything associated with Nomi is overly intense. As the camera moves over the dancing crowd at the Crave Club, she is revealed at the center of the throng, moving as spastically as a rag doll in a hurricane. Even though most viewers will most likely be reminded of Elaine's clueless "dancing" in *Seinfeld*, a friend of wannabe choreographer James enthuses, "She can dance, can't she?" Nomi literally throws herself into everything, whether it's eating fries, performing a lap dance, walking off a stage, having sex, or pouting. Her lunatic frenzy is evidently supposed to signal passion, but her reactions to everyday events and perceived slights mark her as a candidate for Thorazine rather than the lead in a show. Berkley's much-maligned performance is nothing if not consistent in its glassy-eyed aggression.

What made sexploitation films of the 1960s and 1970s so interesting, and what continues to attract new audiences to them on video and DVD, is their excess and the many ways in which it is manifested. This same excess is at work in *Showgirls*, but the fact that it is so superabundant stretches the form to its breaking point. As a result, most viewers reject that excess and consider the film a ludicrous failure, although some have embraced it, most often through amusing, and at times insightful, camp readings.

Hollywood drained out whatever life was left in sexploitation during the 1980s with teen comedies such as *Porky's* (1981), arch art films like *Crimes of Passion* (1984), and politically correct explorations of alternative lifestyles such as *Desert Hearts* (1985). The remnants were relegated to the dusty, direct-to-video rental shelves. *Showgirls* revived sexploitation long enough for one last, extravagant blowout. But like the inveterate partier who leaves his deathbed for a final fling only to have it kill him, the film's overindulgence ends with a flatline for sexploitation as a genre.

Sexploitation is dead. Long live *Showgirls*!

***

I Have Grown Weary of Your Tiresome Cinema

JEFFREY SCONCE

Text of Bliss: the text that imposes a state of loss, the text that discomforts (perhaps to the point of boredom), unsettles the reader's historical, cultural, psychological assumptions, the consistency of his tastes, values, memories, brings to a crisis his relation with language.

—Roland Barthes, *The Pleasure of the Text*

There's a thin line between stupid and clever.

—David St. Hubbins, *This Is Spinal Tap*

Before embarking on his now canonical dissection of Balzac's "Sarrasine," Roland Barthes asked the rather pragmatic question: "How many readings?" In other words, how many times should a critic read and reread a repressed and repressive "readerly" text before it blossoms into the perverse plurality of the "writerly"? Barthes remained cagey in his answer. In the case of *Showgirls,* however, I can answer with precision: four. It takes four screenings of the film to transform it from one of Hollywood's most notorious flops to absolute transcendence, four screenings to cross the line from stupid to clever.

Having seen *Showgirls* five times now, I'd like to devote this brief essay to considering how Verhoeven's film has changed for me from screening to screening. Unfortunately, like most self-indulgent discussions of cinematic "guilty pleasures," mine will also resort to the confessional mode. *Showgirls* compels one to do so. It forces viewers to discuss their own personal history with the film in the same manner that one wants to share one's experience of the ancient Pyramids or work through witnessing a horrific car crash. Unlike these other arresting moments in life, however, *Showgirls'* peculiar mix of stately beauty and raw carnage only emerges in full after several viewings.

Anticipation:

Before seeing any film, we most likely have certain expectations that will inform our eventual viewing. In the case of my own experience with *Showgirls,* the film opened while I was teaching at a remote campus in Wisconsin. For weeks I had been reading the hype surrounding the film and its NC-17 rating and, being an admirer of Verhoeven's earlier work, I greatly anticipated the movie opening at my local multiplex. As things turned out, however, the theaters in the Oshkosh–Green Bay corridor were owned by a conservative family that announced it would not book such filth (in the interests of community standards). Too lazy to make the drive to Wisconsin's Sodom and Gomorrahs of Madison or Milwaukee, I missed *Showgirls* in its initial release, which of course only added to its mystique. Snow-blind and a sulking victim of rube censorship, I looked to the promise of raunchy exotic dancers catfighting in the desert utopia of Vegas as a means of almost mythic deliverance.

Screening One:

I first saw the film a year later, after moving to California and scheduling it for a course I was teaching on exploitation cinema at the University of Southern California. I thought it would be a perfect addition to a class that considered such cult and exploitation favorites as *The Rocky Horror Picture Show, Glen or Glenda,* and *Bad Girls Go to Hell.* My initial response, like that of my students, was one of amazed stupefaction. How could any film made in the era of corporate Hollywood's foolproof blandification process be this crass, this appalling, this flagrant, flamboyant, and over-the-top? *Showgirls* immediately became my film of choice for teaching the pleasures of the "bad film." Students who had previously fallen asleep during the older generation's camp masterpiece, *Plan 9 from Outer Space,* hooted and hollered throughout *Showgirls,* several of them telling me the next week that they had rented the film again for screening parties in their dorms, fraternities, and (yes) sororities. This may alarm some, given the film's rather notorious sexual politics. It shouldn't. Woe to the instructor who plans to use *Showgirls* to initiate tiresome discussions of sexism in the cinema. Your students are way ahead of you. They understand, even without a lecture, that this is a film not about sex, but the performativity of gender.

Screening Two:

If you see *Showgirls* just once, it will linger simply as an exercise in bad excess. Preparing for my second viewing, I was anticipating the standout moments I remembered from the year before: the French fry scene;

the ice cube scene; the swimming pool scene. In between the laughs, however, I gradually began to appreciate how well made the film is in terms of style and technique: the mise-en-scène, editing, and camerawork are flawless. Verhoeven manages to make a visually stunning film about Las Vegas with little use of the city's photogenic architecture and no obligatory scenes of high-stakes gambling. Instead, he relies on an adrenalized haze of spangled sleaze and hypererotic histrionics. And then it hits you: this "extra-sexy" NC-17 film isn't about sex at all—it's about *all* things crass, vulgar, and cheap in America. In this very European take on the United States of Crap, everything is surface and sleaze, from the shrill Nomi to Cristal's Diamond-Doll Texas shtick, from the desolate desert alleyways behind the casinos to the cheesy volcano choreography onstage. The Vegas of *Showgirls* is the America imagined by so many Europeans—fast, cheap, artificial, transient—a world where stupid people have moronic dreams of fame and are willing to cripple their competitors to achieve them. Leaving the theater after screening two, one begins to wonder: is the film bad or just highly, highly stylized? And how would I be able to tell the difference?

Screening Three:

At the third screening, Verhoeven's genius is unmistakable. One feels a sense of shame for not having understood the film in the first place. You emerge convinced that Verhoeven is the Douglas Sirk of contemporary Hollywood. He has taken Eszterhas's mediocre, even laughable script, and through strategies of irony and intensification, created a masterwork of Brechtian distanciation. By this screening, then, both viewer and film are released from the burdens of realism, character, and plausibility—free to engage in pure stylistic play. Suddenly, the film's reliance on stock plots, ridiculous characters, and traumatic art direction makes more sense. It's not bad filmmaking—it's a brilliant savaging of the vapidity of Hollywood's typical narrative machinery. Deeper now into this maze of style and absurdity, one begins to play the game of who in the film "gets it" and who does not. Verhoeven gets it, of course, while Eszterhas sadly, really seems to *believe* in his parable of Horatio Alger in pasties. Gina Gershon and Kyle MacLachlan get it. Poor Elizabeth Berkley does not. There is no empirical evidence to back any of these claims, but we are now entering a land of critical pleasure where textual "evidence" no longer matters; indeed, it's a hindrance. At this point I'm making my own movie in my head.

Screening Four:

When Barthes wrote "Myth Today," he believed a painstaking application of semiotics to capitalist culture would demystify the workings of bourgeois ideology.[14] By the time he gets to *S/Z,* Barthes is still interested in exploring and exploding bourgeois clichés, platitudes, and doxa, but crucially, he no longer feels the need to justify his critical excursions as a path to political enlightenment.[15] The Barthes of *S/Z* and *The Pleasure of the Text* is interested in only one thing: the pleasures to be had when a really smart person visits his or her critical prowess with extreme violence on otherwise unremarkable and even moronic texts.[16] This is where we arrive after the fourth (and possibly all subsequent) screenings of *Showgirls.* Is the film bad? Good? Racist? Sexist? Brechtian? Radical? Reactionary? Who cares to answer such unknowable and ultimately unimportant questions? It is enough that *Showgirls* exists to indulge our intoxication with its sublime catastrophes.

And now the epiphany! Media criticism must learn to give up the charade of pompous legitimization through appeals to social or political utility. It must reembrace the hedonistic pleasures of criticism as a worthy enterprise in and of itself. The world must be made safe again for the aesthete, the world-weary dandy. How many times have we suffered the bromide, "Those who can't do, teach," and its equally dimwitted cousin, "Those who can't create, critique"? I believe film educators need to expose this fiction for the evil lie that it is! We must teach our students to be smarter than the texts they consume. We must teach them that there is ultimately more power in becoming a smirking connoisseur of Hollywood's mass crap than in landing a sweet gig as the second-unit director of photography for *Highlander—The Series*. *Showgirls* can help us do this. It leads the way by giving us, in the spirit of Jean Baudrillard, the more vulgar than vulgar, the more obscene than obscene. In the process, it liberates the critic from his or her role as cultural custodian and reacquaints us with the long-lost Edenic text of bliss. No longer must we apologize for our cultivation, our wit, our condescension. Textual libertines of the new century, unite! You have nothing to lose but your boredom.

References

Barthes, Roland. "Myth Today." In *Mythologies*. Translated by Annette Lavers, 109–65. London: Cape, 1972.

———. *The Pleasure of the Text*. Translated by Richard Miller. New York: Hill and Wang, 1975.

———. *S/Z*. Translated by Richard Miller. New York: Noonday/Farrar, Strauss and Giroux, 1974.

Dowd, Maureen. "Liberties; The Rise of the Fallen." *New York Times*, September 21, 1995. https://www.nytimes.com/1995/09/21/opinion/liberties-the-rise-of-the-fallen.html.

Gelmis, Joseph. "The Joys of Sex on the Screen." *Newsday*, September 20, 1995.

James, David. *Allegories of Cinema: American Film in the Sixties*. Princeton, NJ: Princeton University Press, 1989.

Lane, Anthony. "Starkness Visible." *New Yorker*, October 9, 1995.

Maltin, Leonard. *Leonard Maltin's Movie and Video Guide 2002*. New York: Signet, 2002.

Maslin, Janet. "$40 Million Worth of Voyeurism." *New York Times*, September 22, 1995, C1.

McCarthy, Todd. "Showgirls." *Variety*, September 22, 1995.

———. "'Showgirls' Takes It Sleazy." *Variety*, September 25–October 1, 1995.

Mitchell, Elvis. "Film Review; How Many Actors Does It Take to Make a Log Talk?" *New York Times*, December 26, 2002. https://www.nytimes.com/2002/12/26/movies/film-review-how-many-actors-does-it-take-to-make-a-log-talk.html.

Sandler, Kevin S. "The Naked Truth: *Showgirls* and the Fate of the X/NC-17 Rating." *Cinema Journal* 40, no. 3 (2001): 69–93.

Sontag, Susan. "Notes on 'Camp.'" In *Against Interpretation and Other Essays*, 275–92. New York: Delta, 1966.

Turan, Kenneth. "The Naked Truth about 'Showgirls.'" *Los Angeles Times*, September 22, 1995. https://www.latimes.com/archives/la-xpm-1995-09-22-ca-48657-story.html.

Notes

The text of this chapter first appeared in Akira Mizuta Lippit et al., "Round Table: *Showgirls*," *Film Quarterly* 56, no. 3 (Spring 2003): 32–46, https://doi.org/10.1525/fq.2003.56.3.32. Reprinted with permission from University of California Press, http://www.ucpress.edu/journals. Slight edits have been made to this document to achieve consistency with the house style, and authors' bio-notes from 2003 have been removed but are available in the source material. As befits an archival document, the substance and original spellings remain unchanged.

1. Elvis Mitchell, "Film Review; How Many Actors Does It Take to Make a Log Talk?" *New York Times*, December 26, 2002, E5, https://www.nytimes.com/2002/12/26/movies/film-review-how-many-actors-does-it-take-to-make-a-log-talk.html.

2. Leonard Maltin, *Leonard Maltin's Movie and Video Guide 2002* (New York: Signet, 2002).

3. Anthony Lane, "Starkness Visible," *New Yorker*, October 9, 1995, 95.

4. See Kevin S. Sandler, "The Naked Truth: *Showgirls* and the Fate of the X/NC-17 Rating," *Cinema Journal* 40, no. 3 (2001): 69–93.

5. Quoted in Maureen Dowd, "Liberties; The Rise of the Fallen," *New York Times*, September 21, 1995, A23, https://www.nytimes.com/1995/09/21/opinion/liberties-the-rise-of-the-fallen.html.

6. Ibid.; Joseph Gelmis, "The Joys of Sex on the Screen," *Newsday*, September 20, 1995, Part II, B03.

7. Lane, "Starkness Visible," 96.

8. Janet Maslin, "$40 Million Worth of Voyeurism," *New York Times*, September 22, 1995, C1; Todd McCarthy, "'Showgirls' Takes It Sleazy," *Variety*, September 25–October 1, 1995, 91; Kenneth Turan, "The Naked Truth about 'Showgirls,'" *Los Angeles Times*, September 22, 1995, F1.10, https://www.latimes.com/archives/la-xpm-1995-09-22-ca-48657-story.html.

9. See David James, *Allegories of Cinema: American Film in the Sixties* (Princeton, NJ: Princeton University Press, 1989), especially chapter 1.

10. Susan Sontag, "Notes on 'Camp,'" in *Against Interpretation and Other Essays* (New York: Delta, 1966), 282–83.

11. Ibid., 279.

12. Lane, "Starkness Visible."

13. Todd McCarthy, "Showgirls," *Variety*, September 22, 1995.

14. Roland Barthes, "Myth Today," in *Mythologies*, trans. Annette Lavers (London: Cape, 1972), 109–65.

15. Roland Barthes, *S/Z*, trans. Richard Miller (New York: Noonday/Farrar, Strauss and Giroux, 1974).

16. Roland Barthes, *The Pleasure of the Text*, trans. Richard Miller (New York: Hill and Wang, 1975).

INDEX

For Indiana University Press

Lesley Bolton, Project Manager/Editor
Brian Carroll, Rights Manager
Allison Chaplin, Acquisitions Editor
Sophia Hebert, Assistant Acquisitions Editor
Samantha Heffner, Marketing and Publicity Manager
Brenna Hosman, Production Coordinator
Katie Huggins, Production Manager
Dan Pyle, Online Publishing Manager
Jennifer L. Witzke, Senior Artist and Book Designer